68-70 Red Lion Street
London WC1R 4NY
libraryholborn@bpp.com
020 7430 7099

341 B

(L)

OXFORD POLITICAL THEORY

Series Editors: Will Kymlicka, David Miller, and Alan Ryan

JUSTICE, LEGITIMACY, AND SELF-DETERMINATION

BPP

035 D0279968

OXFORD POLITICAL THEORY

Oxford Political Theory presents the best new work in contemporary political theory. It is intended to be broad in scope, including original contributions to political philosophy, and also work in applied political theory. The series contains works of outstanding quality with no restriction as to approach or subject matter.

OTHER TITLES IN THIS SERIES

Levelling the Playing Field
Andrew Mason

Multicultural Citizenship
Will Kymlicka

Real Freedom for All
Philippe Van Parijs

Reflective Democracy
Robert E. Goodin

Justice as Impartiality
Brian Barry

Democratic Autonomy
Henry S. Richardson

The Liberal Archipelago
Chandran Kukathas

On Nationality
David Miller

Republicanism
Phillip Pettit

Creating Citizens
Eamonn Callan

The Politics of Presence
Anne Phillips

Deliberative Democracy and Beyond
John S. Dryzek

The Civic Minimum
Stuart White

JUSTICE, LEGITIMACY, AND SELF-DETERMINATION

MORAL FOUNDATIONS FOR INTERNATIONAL LAW

ALLEN BUCHANAN

68-70 Red Lion Street
London WC1R 4NY
libraryholborn@bpp.com
020 7430 7099

OXFORD
UNIVERSITY PRESS

OXFORD

UNIVERSITY PRESS

Great Clarendon Street, Oxford OX2 6DP

Oxford University Press is a department of the University of Oxford.
It furthers the University's objective of excellence in research, scholarship,
and education by publishing worldwide in

Oxford New York

Auckland Bangkok Buenos Aires Cape Town Chennai
Dar es Salaam Delhi Hong Kong Istanbul Karachi Kolkata
Kuala Lumpur Madrid Melbourne Mexico City Mumbai Nairobi
São Paulo Shanghai Taipei Tokyo Toronto

Oxford is a registered trade mark of Oxford University Press
in the UK and in certain other countries

Published in the United States
by Oxford University Press Inc., New York

© Allen Buchanan 2004

The moral rights of the author have been asserted
Database right Oxford University Press (maker)

First published 2004

First published in paperback 2007

All rights reserved. No part of this publication may be reproduced,
stored in a retrieval system, or transmitted, in any form or by any means,
without the prior permission in writing of Oxford University Press,
or as expressly permitted by law, or under terms agreed with the appropriate
reprographics rights organization. Enquiries concerning reproduction
outside the scope of the above should be sent to the Rights Department,
Oxford University Press, at the address above

You must not circulate this book in any other binding or cover
and you must impose this same condition on any acquirer

British Library Cataloguing in Publication Data
Data available

Library of Congress Cataloging in Publication Data
Data available

Typeset by SPI Publisher Services, Pondicherry, India
Printed in Great Britain
on acid-free paper by
Biddles Ltd, King's Lynn, Norfolk

ISBN 978-0-19-829535-8 (Hbk.)   978-0-19-929798-6 (Pbk.)

1 3 5 7 9 10 8 6 4 2

PREFACE TO THE PAPERBACK EDITION

The aim of this book, which is set out more fully in the Synopsis, is to develop the outlines of a coherent, systematic vision of an international legal order that takes the protection of human rights seriously, while anchoring that vision in moral reasoning that is informed both by a due appreciation of the limitations of existing institutions and a willingness to consider possibilities for institutional reform. Much has occurred in world politics and in the literatures of international political philosophy and international law since the hardcover edition was published less than three years ago. Given what has occurred, the book is even more relevant now.

There are perhaps even greater opportunities today for employing the resources of international law in the service of human rights than ever before, because of the development of new international legal institutions, such as the International Criminal Court, and because of the growing ability of human rights NGOs to contribute to the enforcement of treaty-based human rights commitments in domestic courts. In addition, the European Union increasingly serves as a real-world example and as a stimulus for theorizing the possibilities of a supra-national rule of law with human rights at its core. The idea that sovereignty is conditional on the protection of human rights seems to be becoming more prominent in international legal discourse. At the same time, however, there are worsening human rights crises—in Iraq, Darfur, and Congo in particular—and a growing fear that 'the international community', in spite of its avowed commitment to the rule of law and the protection of human rights, is once again standing by, doing little more than issuing high-sounding condemnations of the carnage. Just as disturbingly, the Bush Administration's willingness to disregard core elements of the rule of law, including *habeas corpus*, and to violate international legal prohibitions on torture, when taken along with the unspeakable atrocities of sectarian violence in Iraq, cast serious doubts on how deep the so-called international culture of human rights really is. Under these conditions, a well-reasoned account of the main features of an international legal order committed to human rights is all the more urgently needed."

A distinctive feature of the book is its holistic, systematic approach. It provides a principled account of how an international legal order that takes human rights seriously should respond to issues concerning military intervention, secession, and claims to self-determination short of secession. The possibility that Iraq may fragment violently along ethno-religious lines, perhaps leading to wider conflicts and even more massive human rights violations across the Middle East, makes the issues of intervention, self-determination, and secession especially timely, demonstrates their interdependence, and thereby confirms my insistence that they must be dealt with in a unified, systematic way. Furthermore, in a world in which 'state-failure' in the case of multi-ethnic and/or religiously-divided states is, if anything, likely to become more common, the tensions between protecting human rights and recognizing conflicting claims to self-determination become more pronounced and the needed for a coherent, unified, principled approach becomes all the more palpable.

Developments in the scholarly literature since the publication of the hardcover edition also confirm the book's continuing relevance. The issues of legitimacy that are the focus of the third Part of the book are increasingly at the forefront of scholarship in international legal theory and in the new, exciting interdisciplinary literature in which international relations theorists, political philosophers, and international lawyers are participating.

The Bush administration's decision to invade Iraq without Security Council authorization and more generally its apparent disregard for at least some aspects of international law have helped to stimulate a vigorous debate about the commitment to the rule of international law. Some American international lawyers have argued that commitment to the rule of international law is purely contingent and instrumental—that it is perfectly appropriate for states that are powerful enough to do so with impunity to comply with international law only so far as it is in their interest to do so. Some of those who hold this purely instrumental view of the value of international law have also claimed that anything more than such a contingent, instrumental commitment is incompatible with constitutional democracy at the domestic level. My book is also a contribution to this debate, which is still very much developing. I argue that the same values that ground the commitment to domestic democracy require a moral commitment to the enterprise of international law, a commitment that cannot be reduced to pursuit of 'the national interest'.

ACKNOWLEDGMENTS

In the long process of writing this book I have incurred many debts. I have learned a great deal relevant to this project from my former graduate students, Avery Kolers, Kristen Hessler, Cindy Holder, Stefan Sciaraffa, and Kit (Christopher) Wellman, all of whom provided excellent comments on drafts of this book. My Arizona colleague Tom Christiano has taught me much about democratic theory and Political Philosophy generally; I hope this is evident in the chapters that follow. I also thank David Miller and Will Kymlicka, co-editors of the series in which the present volume appears, and Margaret Moore, who provided insightful comments on the typescript.

I especially want to thank Kit Wellman for stimulating me to think harder about the nature of political legitimacy and for organizing a workshop in which he and the following scholars generously commented on a draft of the typescript: Andrew Altman, Andrew I. Cohen, William Edmundson, Peter Lindsay, Larry May, George Rainbolt, Andrew Valls, and Clark Wolf. The comments I received from the participants in this workshop were invaluable. They helped me focus the typescript on and the most important points I wish to make, enabling me to correct a number of errors to eliminate several unclarities. I am extremely grateful to Kit for taking the initiative to devise this generous gift to me and to all the participants for their constructive and gracious comments. Special thanks are due to Larry May, whose expertise in international law and philosophical acumen enabled him to make several key suggestions for improving the typescript, and to Andy Altman whose remarks resulted in a clearer and more direct presentation of my central argument concerning the nature of political legitimacy. Those who are interested in the moral foundations of international law should look forward with keen anticipation to May's forthcoming book on international criminal law.

My thinking on international legal reform and on humanitarian intervention has benefited from stimulating conversations with Jeff Holzgrefe, Bob Keohane, and Jane Stromseth. Holgrefe also provided probing comments on a draft of the typescript.

I also wish to thank Richard T. DeGeorge for inviting me to participate in a lecture series on international justice at the University of Kansas. DeGeorge and the students of his graduate seminar provided me with many useful comments on an early draft of this volume.

David Luban read through a draft of the entire book and gave me the benefit of many constructive criticisms. As a result, every chapter was improved.

I hope my debt to David Golove is apparent from the frequent references to his thinking in footnotes scattered throughout the book. My work with him on an earlier co-authored paper on the Philosophy of International Law encouraged me to go further and deeper.

To Hurst Hannum and Fernando Teson I owe perhaps the greatest debt of all. In responding to my 1991 book on secession, Teson encouraged me to draw the implications of my view for the question of intervention. Doing so eventually led me beyond the confines of thinking about secession as a two-party conflict to a systematic consideration of the moral foundations of international law. I hope that my book will complement Teson's work. He is in fact a leading exponent of the general approach taken in this volume, having argued passionately for many years that the international legal system should above all serve to protect human rights, not the interests of states.

Hurst Hannum is a model of sensitive, informed, and critical thinking about international law. With characteristic generosity he made me feel like a valuable contributor to the issues he had thought long and hard about at a time when I was just becoming aware of them. His combination of theoretical insight and dedicated human rights activism exemplifies the best in the community of international lawyers.

I am also grateful for the kind and constructive criticism I have received from other prominent members of the community of international legal scholars as well, when I presented papers that explored issues addressed in this book at a number of law schools. Instead of regarding me as an interloper, they have shown remarkable patience with my ignorance of their areas of expertise and done much to help me ameliorate it.

I have benefited from the warm encouragement of Christopher Maloney of the University of Arizona. I cannot imagine a more supportive department head. Sandy Arneson provided constant support and exceptional research and editing expertise.

I also wish to acknowledge several institutional debts. I thank the Udall Center for Public Policy at the University of Arizona for awarding me a fellowship to work on the issue of indigenous peoples' rights. The Earhart Foundation generously sponsored research leaves, for the writing of this volume and my earlier book on secession as well. The National Humanities Center, where I had the honor of being awarded the John Medlin, Jr. Senior Fellowship for 2001–2, provided the ideal environment for working through the entire manuscript and adding significant new material on humanitarian intervention. I am grateful to the Center's Director, Bob Connor, to the Fellows Program Director, Kent Milliken, and to the entire staff of the Center who made my stay there so enjoyable and productive.

This volume draws on previously published articles and book chapters. Some material from Chapter 1 comes from "The Philosophy of International Law," co-authored with David Golove. This chapter also draws on the argument of "The Internal Legitimacy of Humanitarian Intervention," which appeared in *The Journal of Political Philosophy*. Chapter 3 contains material from "Justice, Legitimacy, and Human Rights," which appeared in *The Idea of Political Liberalism*, edited by Victoria Davion and Clark Wolf. Chapter 5 draws on my article "Political Liberalism and Democracy," which appeared in *Ethics*. Chapter 6 includes material from "Recognitional Legitimacy and the State System," in *Philosophy and Public Affairs*. Chapter 8 utilizes material from "What's So Special About Nations?" in *Rethinking Nationalism*, edited by Jocelyne Couture, Michel Seymour, and Kai Nielsen. Chapter 11 is based in part on "From Nuremburg to Kosovo: The Morality of Illegal Legal Reform," which appeared in *Ethics*, and on "Reforming the International Law of Humanitarian Intervention," in *Humanitarian Intervention: Ethics, Law and Policy*, edited by Jeffrey Holzgrefe and Robert O. Keohane.

The foregoing articles and book chapters were written over a period of over a decade, during which time my views changed considerably. Consequently the material from them that appears in this book is considerably modified and integrated with new material.

CONTENTS

SYNOPSIS   1

1. INTRODUCTION: THE IDEA OF A MORAL THEORY OF INTERNATIONAL LAW   14

PART ONE   JUSTICE

2. THE COMMITMENT TO JUSTICE   73

3. HUMAN RIGHTS   118

4. DISTRIBUTIVE JUSTICE   191

PART TWO   LEGITIMACY

5. POLITICAL LEGITIMACY   233

6. RECOGNITIONAL LEGITIMACY   261

7. THE LEGITIMACY OF THE INTERNATIONAL LEGAL SYSTEM   289

PART THREE   SELF-DETERMINATION

8. SELF-DETERMINATION AND SECESSION   331

9. INTRASTATE AUTONOMY   401

PART FOUR   REFORM

10. PRINCIPLED PROPOSALS FOR REFORM   427

11. THE MORALITY OF INTERNATIONAL LEGAL REFORM   440

Bibliography   475

Index   489

Synopsis

This book is an attempt to develop moral foundations for international law. The existing international legal system, like any domestic legal system, can and ought to be evaluated from the standpoint of moral principles, including, preeminently, principles of justice. Legal institutions and for that matter all institutions that deeply affect the life prospects of human individuals must be designed to function in conformity with principles of justice, because principles of justice specify the most basic moral rights and obligations that persons have. It does not follow, of course, that the same moral principles will be valid for international and domestic legal systems. And even when the same principles do apply, different institutions may be needed to realize them, depending upon whether they are applied domestically or internationally.

Initially my aim in writing this volume was to supplement and strengthen my earlier work on secession, in particular by making explicit and justifying my tacit assumption that the state's claim to territory ultimately depends upon its protection of human rights. But eventually it became clear to me that the topic of secession could not be effectively addressed in isolation. A more inclusive moral theory of international law was required.

Beginning with the problem of secession and working back toward more foundational issues has advantages. It is valuable to devote as much space as I do to issues of secession for two reasons. First, at present state-breaking is a prominent feature of the international landscape and is likely to continue to be so for some time. Second, working out a principled view on secession requires coming to grips with the right of self-determination, the recognition of which is surely one of the most important and perilous developments in international law in the last half-century. Third, working out a theory of the right to secede requires the theorist to take a stand on a number of core issues, including those of political legitimacy and intervention. Nevertheless, I am sure that approaching the larger topic of the moral theory of international law via this route has its costs.

From time to time in this book I refer to "the international legal order" or "the international legal system." Sometimes I refer to the whole international legal system as an institution, meaning that it is a super-institution including many institutions within it. So let me clarify here at the outset what I mean: An institution is a kind of organization, usually persisting over some considerable period of time, that contains roles, functions, procedures, and processes, as well as structures of authority.

Institutions also embody, and sometimes formally proclaim, principles. More specifically, a description of the institution of international law will include a list of its legal principles. But international law taken as a whole also consists of institutions in a more tangible sense. For example, the existing international legal order includes the United Nations, with its many constitutive institutions, including the Security Council, the General Assembly, the World Health Organization, various bureaucracies, committees, and commissions, and so on.

For the most part in this book I will focus on evaluating some of the most important principles of the existing international legal order and proposing new principles or modifications of existing ones that are more consonant with the demands of justice. But I will also attend to the implications of the simple fact that principles must be embodied in appropriate institutions. In some cases I will make fairly concrete suggestions for institutional reform, not just in the sense of incorporating new principles into old processes and structures, but also in the sense of changing some of the processes and structures themselves. My enterprise, then, is to articulate a set of moral principles that should guide the design and reform of international law as an institution in the broad sense that includes not only principles but also roles, processes, and structures.

Some will be skeptical of such a project. Unfortunately, it is still common for theorists of international relations to dismiss the very idea of moral reasoning about international institutions, assuming that the contest for dominance leaves little room for morality. Yet even those who eschew moral argumentation about international law often unwittingly take a moral position on it. Because they avoid moral argumentation, their moral judgments are unsupported. But they are moral judgments nonetheless.

For instance, many international relations theorists as well as international lawyers and diplomats say that whether a state grants recognition or withholds recognition from a new political entity created by secession is purely a political matter. This is false if it implies that a state's behavior in recognizing another entity as a state or refusing to do so is not subject to moral evaluation. Recognition is not morally neutral even though it is true that under current international law states have the right to grant or withhold recognition as they see fit.

The choice to recognize or not recognize has moral implications and can be made rightly or wrongly. To recognize an entity as a state is to acknowledge that it has an international legal right of territorial integrity and this in turn lends strong presumptive support to its territorial claims and thereby presumes the illegitimacy of claims on its territory that others may make. For the same reason, simply continuing the current practice of recognizing the legitimacy of existing states is not a morally neutral activity. Recognizing an entity as a legitimate state empowers certain persons, those who constitute its government, to wield coercive power over others, for better or worse.

To participate without protest in a practice of recognition that empowers governments that engage in systematic violations of human rights is to be an accomplice to injustice. Once we take seriously the moral implications of granting or withholding recognition, we must examine the arguments for and against rival proposals for what the practice of recognition should be like, and this examination inevitably requires an attempt to develop a moral theory that integrates prescriptions for a just practice of recognition with a principled approach to other important issues that arise in an international legal system. To know what criteria an entity must satisfy to warrant recognition as a legitimate state, we must know what values the international legal order should serve and what role the practice of recognition is to play in serving them. This requires a moral theory of international law.

In contrast to international relations theorists, many of whom think that the ubiquity of competition for power leaves little or no room for morality, international lawyers tend to be uncomfortable with moral thinking about international law for another reason: They fear that it will detract from a scientific study of the law. This fear is unfounded. The moral evaluation of existing international law and the articulation of proposals for reforming it need not involve the confusion between law and morality that legal positivists vigorously condemn.

My project is to evaluate certain fundamental aspects of the existing international legal order and, on the basis of the same moral principles that inform this evaluation, propose legal norms and practices which, if implemented with reasonable care, would make the system more just. My concern, then, is with what the law should be. For example, I evaluate several alternative conceptions of what an international legal right to secede should be like.

In the past few years there have been several valuable attempts at moral theorizing about various issues in international law, including global distributive justice, secession, immigration, and humanitarian intervention. But these issues have been addressed separately, each in isolation from the others. In the chapters that follow I take a holistic approach, criticizing existing international law and arguing for proposals to reform it in a more systematic fashion, offering a normative framework that links issues too often dealt with in isolation from one another. I make the case for an integrated approach to secession, the recognition of new states, international support for limited self-government for minorities within states, coercive diplomacy, and armed intervention.

More specifically, I argue that a principled, human rights-based approach to the problem of secession would reduce the need for armed humanitarian intervention by providing constructive alternatives to secession and the massive violations of human rights that almost always accompany it. In addition, my analysis makes it clear that without a morally defensible, consistent international legal framework for responding to secessionist conflicts, states run the risk of intervening unjustly when secessions occur.

The architecture of my approach is simple and is conveyed by the title of this book. Part One develops the case for grounding the international legal system in principles of justice, understood primarily as principles that ascribe basic and relatively uncontroversial rights to all persons as such. There I argue that the moral foundation for the international legal order is the (limited) obligation to help ensure that all persons have access to institutions that protect these basic human rights. Part Two constructs an account of legitimacy according to which political entities are legitimate only if they achieve a reasonable approximation of minimal standards of justice, again understood as the protection of basic human rights. This account of legitimacy is then adapted so as to encompass both the legitimacy of individual states within the international legal system and the legitimacy of the international legal system itself. Part Three uses the justice-based conception of a legitimate state presented in Part Two to construct a position on how the international legal order should respond to the problems of self-determination and secession, arguing that international law should recognize a unilateral right to secede—as distinct from a negotiated or constitutional right—only as a remedy of last resort against grave injustices.

These three parts, on Justice, Legitimacy, and Self-Determination, comprise the theoretical core of the volume. Part Four, Reform, includes two chapters. The first summarizes the central argument of the book and the main proposals for reform that I derive from it, and then explores some of the changes in legal doctrine and institutional structures regarding intervention that would be needed to realize them. The second chapter examines the feasibility and morality of alternative paths for getting from where we are to where we should be, focusing on the problem of how to reform the international law of intervention.

So, in addition to being more holistic, this volume differs in another respect from other works that include the moral evaluation of international legal principles and practices. I not only propose what I believe would be moral improvements in the system, but also explore some of the moral issues of the enterprise of reform. Unless proposals for reform can be implemented in morally acceptable ways, they are worse than useless.

The moral theory of international law I begin to develop in this volume is in many respects quite radical. It represents a fundamental challenge not only to some central features of the existing legal order, but also to the dominant ways in which theorists conceive of international law and international relations. I offer a sustained, principled argument for rejecting the almost' universally accepted assumption that the international legal order not only is but ought to be a society of equal sovereign states, governed by laws grounded in the consent of states. I also argue systematically against the dogma that the proper goal for the international legal system is peace among states, not justice.

First, I argue for abandoning the traditional international legal principle of effectivity, according to which an entity is a state, entitled to all the powers, rights, privileges, and immunities ascribed to states in international law, if it has a stable population and controls a determinate territory. I develop a normativized conception of what it is to be a legitimate state, arguing that unless an entity meets certain minimal standards of justice, it ought not to be regarded as a primary member of international society. So I deny that some existing entities that are now accorded the title of state deserve the attributes of sovereignty. Moreover, I argue that the decision whether to recognize a new entity as a legitimate state should not be a matter of discretion. I advance a proposal for a justice-based practice of recognition, supported by enforceable international legal principles that require states to recognize new entities that meet the appropriate minimal standards of justice and that would forbid them to recognize entities that do not meet those standards. This proposal clearly represents a serious erosion of sovereignty—a diminution of the powers traditionally accorded to states under international law.

I reject the unreflective, or at least poorly argued, assumption that all states should wield equal political power in the making, application, and enforcement of international law. I argue that it is a mistake to think that the principle of democracy and the commitment to the fundamental equality of individual persons that grounds it imply that all states, regardless of how just or unjust they are and independently of the size of their populations, ought to have an equal say in the creation, application, and enforcement of international law. I also argue that although "state majoritarianism"—equal political power for all states in the making and application of international law—has some attractions as a device for restraining more powerful states, there may be other safeguards that are less costly to the cause of moral progress in international law.

As to the idea that international law is and ought to be created by the consent of states, I show that the state-consent model is neither an accurate description of the way international law comes into being nor an ideal worth aspiring to. The key point is that so long as many states do not represent the interests or preferences of all their citizens, the consent of state leaders does not carry anything like the moral weight of the informed, voluntary consent of individual persons.

Third, I reject the unitary state paradigm that still dominates thinking about international law and international relations. I argue that in most cases the impulse to secede from an existing state betrays a fundamental lack of political imagination—that paradoxically secession is the most conservative of political acts. The secessionist tends to assume that his problems are due to the state in which he finds himself and that the solution is to get his own state. The anti-secessionist tends to be equally unimaginative, seeing in every demand for autonomy a threat to the state's existence. The imaginations of both the secessionist and the anti-secessionist are cramped by the narrow horizons of the statist paradigm.

What the usual rhetoric of both parties overlooks is that sovereignty can be "unbundled" in many ways—that the only choices are not "stay in this state as it is" or "get your own state." Once we take seriously the indefinitely large range of possible regimes of political differentiation within what we now regard as state borders—the rich menu of intrastate autonomy arrangements—we liberate ourselves from the confining assumption that we must choose between honoring aspirations for self-determination and order. What is novel and perhaps even radical about my discussion of various intrastate autonomy regimes as ways of coping with or avoiding secessionist conflicts is that I propose a role for international legal institutions in efforts to support and in some cases even to mandate intrastate autonomy regimes. This too represents a significant curtailment of the traditional powers of sovereignty.

A final distinctive feature of my view is that I argue that critical engagement with the system of international law—the effort to create and support a just system of international legal institutions—is not simply permissible, but morally obligatory. On this view, participation in an international legal order is not simply a matter of discretion; it is a requirement that derives from a rather fundamental moral obligation, the (limited) obligation to help ensure that all persons have access to institutions that protect their most basic human rights.

In the last chapter I argue that progress toward a more just international legal system will probably require changes in the international law of humanitarian intervention, and that this in turn may require abandonment of the assumption that the UN-based law of humanitarian intervention is sacrosanct, along with the development of a less inclusive, treaty-based, law-governed regime for intervention consisting of the most democratic, rights-respecting states.

By arguing that the state's posture toward international law should be shaped by a commitment to protecting the basic human rights of all persons, I am plainly rejecting the dominant view in international relations, namely, that state policy should or at least may exclusively pursue "national interest." According to the conception of justice I lay out in Part One, the state is not merely an instrument for advancing the interests of its own citizens; it is also a resource for helping to ensure that all persons have access to institutions that protect their basic human rights. This is not to deny that state leaders are obligated to accord priority to the interests of their own citizens, of course, but it is to insist that this priority is not without limits.

The national interest view is pervasive among diplomats and state leaders and also endorsed by many international relations scholars. Legal absolutism, the view that it is virtually never morally justifiable to violate the more basic norms of international law for the sake of morality, seems to be pervasive among international legal theorists. (Sometimes this view is misleadingly called 'legal positivism', but the more common usage of the latter term is to denote a thesis about the nature of law, namely, that whether a norm is a law does not depend upon its satisfying any moral criteria.)

This book is a sustained critique of both the national interest and legal absolutist positions. Regarding the thesis that states should or may exclusively pursue the national interest in all their foreign relations, I proceed as follows. First, I argue that if there are any human rights, then there is a heavy burden of argument to be borne by those who endorse the national interest thesis. Next, I articulate and show to be unsound what I take to be the two most promising attempts to provide the needed justification: the Fiduciary Realist Argument, according to which it follows from the nature of the state and the character of international relations that state leaders should act exclusively in the national interest, and the Instrumental Argument, which holds that the risks of states attempting to promote moral values directly in their foreign policies are so great that it is better for humanity if each pursues only the national interest.

I argue that Legal Absolutism rests either on: (1) the empirically unsubstantiated prediction that unless compliance with the basic norms of existing international law is perfect, the whole system of international order will unravel in a rapid descent into violent chaos, or upon (2) an unsupported and unsupportable assumption that those who violate basic norms of international law for the sake of morality are guilty of moral hubris, a willingness to impose their own "subjective values" on others. In brief, I show how respect for the rule of law in international relations, far from precluding illegality for the sake of legal reform, may even make it obligatory under certain exceptional circumstances.

Because the national interest and legal absolutist positions are pervasive and uncritically endorsed, they warrant the title of dogmas. So, quite apart from the other distinctive features of my approach sketched above, the fact that I reject both of these positions makes this book radical (if not heretical).

Yet from one perspective my position is not radical. All of my proposals for reform, like my rejection of the dominant understanding of what the international legal system should be and my critique of the national interest view, are grounded in the idea of basic human rights. In Part One I show that if one takes basic human rights seriously there is no alternative to a justice-based approach to the international legal system. The rest of the book is an attempt to work out the implications of a justice-based approach.

Although my enterprise is theoretical and to that extent inevitably abstract in some respects, its relevance is eminently practical. As I write this Synopsis the United States is waging a "war against terrorism" in response to the attack on the Pentagon and the World Trade Center on September 11, 2001. One especially problematic aspect of this "war" is the policy of sending American troops to aid other states in suppressing insurgent groups that the states in question have labeled as terrorists. American troops have been posted to the Philippines, Yemen, and Georgia. President Putin of Russia has affirmed his willingness to cooperate in the war against terrorism, undoubtedly in part because he believes that if he does so the United States will be more likely to continue to accept the Russian claim that Chechen secessionists are simply terrorists.

By branding the Chechens as terrorists, the Russian government hopes to divert attention from both the question of whether their attempt to secede is justified and from the grave breaches of the humanitarian law of war committed by Russian troops in Chechnya. (The Russian failure to discriminate between combatants and noncombatants has been so severe that it might be said that for the Russian army a "smart bomb" is any explosive projectile that lands somewhere in Chechnya.) Furthermore, it is also highly likely that the training given by the U.S. military to Georgian troops will not be put to use primarily to combat Chechen terrorists, but to suppress secession in Abkhazia.

The post-September 11th U.S. policy of global military involvement poses strategic and moral risks that should be familiar to even the most casual student of U.S. policy during the Cold War. For the sake of combating communism, the United States became enmeshed in internal conflicts in many states, in some cases supporting colonial regimes against national liberation movements, and frequently supporting regimes that engaged in large-scale violations of human rights.

The danger that similar wrongs will be committed in the global military dimension of the war against terrorism is greatly exacerbated by the fact that the United States, like the international community as whole, has failed to develop a coherent, principled framework for responding to—or, better yet, preventing—secessionist conflicts. Lacking such a framework, the United States and its allies in the war against terrorism are likely to fail to discriminate between insurgent groups that have legitimate grievances and those that do not.

The sad fact is that when self-determination conflicts are allowed to degenerate into violent secessions, both the secessionists and the state in its efforts to suppress them usually engage in terrorism. Given that the Kosovo Liberation Army engaged in terrorism against Serbs in Kosovo in the months preceding the NATO intervention, one wonders what the attitude of the United States toward that secessionist group would have been if the attacks on the Pentagon and World Trade Center had occurred in early 1999 rather than in September of 2001.

The current danger is that the United States will too readily accept the label "terrorists" as the essential or exclusive characterization of what are primarily secessionist groups, and in some cases groups that are justified in seceding. In the absence of a coherent normative framework for evaluating secessionist claims, the United States may support an oppressive state's attempt to ignore a minority group's legitimate grievances.

When a group that has suffered sufficient injustices to warrant secession resorts to terrorism, difficult questions arise as to whether or in what way to support their efforts to achieve independence. But unless we are in possession of a coherent, morally defensible framework for evaluating the conflicting claims that states and secessionists advance, we cannot hope to grapple with this problem in a morally responsible way.

Instead of blindly accepting the state's labeling of secessionists as terrorists, we should invoke a distinction in just war theory. We should first ask whether the secessionists are justified in attempting to achieve independence without the consent of the state and hence in using force against the state's attempt to block independence (the analog of the just war question: Is it morally justifiable to go to war in these circumstances?). Then we should try to determine whether either or both parties to the conflict are limiting their efforts to acceptable means for employing force (the analog of the just war question: Are the means of waging war just?).

In contrast, if we indulge the tendency to assume that all who use unconventional weapons and tactics to attack states are terrorists (and "only terrorists"), we will be likely to overlook both the question of whether the secessionists are justified in seeking independence and the fact that the state is using terrorism to suppress them.

The moral risks of waging a war against terrorism are great in a world in which there are many groups that have legitimate grievances against their states, especially if we lack a normative framework for evaluating and responding to claims to self-determination. Without a defensible account of state legitimacy, we cannot hope to have an adequate normative framework for addressing self-determination claims since these can call into question the legitimacy of the state's own claims to territory. A defensible account of legitimacy in turn must rest upon a conception of justice, since the only thing that can justify the powers the state claims is its success in providing the fundamentals of justice within its borders. Thus we see that a morally responsible strategy in the war against terrorism must be grounded ultimately in a moral theory of international law.

There is another urgent practical reason for trying to develop a moral theory of international law at this time. The Bush administration's "war on terrorism" has recently been expanded (some might say, stretched) to encompass the permissibility of preventive war. What is disturbing about this development is not that in doing so the administration is rejecting an important element of existing international law concerning the use of force—the absolute prohibition on preventive force. That restriction, as I and Robert Keohane have argued elsewhere, may need to be relaxed somewhat due to changes in the circumstances that made it compelling in the past.[1] Instead, it is the fact that the administration is apparently willing to destroy this constituent of the edifice of international law without taking on the responsibility of helping to forge a new, more satisfactory legal structure for the preventive use of force.

Even if President Bush had secured unambiguous Security Council support for a preventive war against Iraq if the latter failed to dismantle its weapons of mass destruction, this should not count as discharging this responsibility for legal reconstruction after destruction. Proper safeguards for the authorization of preventive war would surely include more than the success of the world's one superpower in persuading the Security Council to conform to its wishes, especially when persuasion is accompanied by the threat that if authorization is not secured, it will act anyway and thereby demonstrate the irrelevance and impotence of the UN.

The willingness of the United States to violate the international legal prohibition against preventive war is all the more portentous, given its earlier violation of international law on the use of force in leading the NATO intervention in Kosovo. That action, which was neither a case of self-defense by NATO nor sanctioned by the Security Council, was perceived by many to be a serious blow, not only to the UN but to the enterprise of international law itself.

I shall argue that whether or not the Kosovo intervention and the abandonment of the prohibition on preventive war presage the end of international law or only the obsolescence of some of its current institutional embodiments in the UN will depend upon whether the United States and its allies are willing and able to create better international legal institutions to replace those they are damaging. The crucial point is that the only alternatives are not continued support

---

[1] Allen Buchanan and Robert O. Keohane, "The Preventive Use of Force: A Cosmopolitan Institutional Perspective" (unpublished paper).

for the whole existing structure of international law, on the one hand, or a kind of refined vigilantism orchestrated by the world's one superpower that is insufficiently faithful to the ideal of the rule of law, on the other.

Bypassing the UN Charter-based law on the use of force, even if this seriously damages the UN, need not mean the destruction of international law, if it is accompanied by the development of more adequate institutions and procedures for authorizing the preventive use of force. However, new institutions and procedures—if they are not to be ad hoc and morally indefensible—must be grounded in a more comprehensive moral theory of international law that situates the law concerning the use of force within a larger legal framework.

CHAPTER 1

———

Introduction: The Idea of a Moral
Theory of International Law

This chapter (1) explains why a moral theory of international law is needed, (2) refutes several prominent views that purport to rule out the possibility of such a theory, (3) sets out the criteria that the needed theory should satisfy, (4) previews the main outlines of the theory developed in the remainder of the book, and (5) explains and supports the thesis that institutional moral reasoning is needed to develop such a theory.

I. *The Need for a Theory*

A new world order?

Despite optimistic predictions of a new world order to follow the end of the Cold War, recent attempts to bring the rule of law to international relations have produced disappointing results. Consider the inconsistent and drifting response of the international community to the dissolution of Yugoslavia, or the half-hearted, abortive intervention to rebuild a shattered civil order in Somalia, or the world's paralysis (or indifference) in the face of genocide in Rwanda, or the absence of a genuinely global, multilateral response to global terrorism. The conclusion frequently drawn from these experiences is that there is a failure of commitment among those states that have the resources to further the rule of law. Thus the title of a probing analysis of the violent dissolution of Yugoslavia: *Triumph of the Lack of Will.*[1]

---

[1] James Gow, *Triumph of the Lack of Will: International Diplomacy and the Yugoslav War* (Hurst, London, 1997).

Principles and practice

This diagnosis is correct but incomplete. Lack of sound principles contributes to failure of will. The problem is not simply that the existing corpus of international legal norms is inadequate to the task of coping with secession crises, ethnic conflicts, failed states, and global terrorism. Even worse, at present there is no coherent set of normative principles—no moral theory of the rule of law in international relations—capable of providing guidance for improving international law to make it more responsive to these problems.

The deficiency is not a lack of *legal* principles. Not just opposing factions, but the same parties invoke a number of principles, some of them apparently quite inconsistent with one another. During the Yugoslav crisis, the United States and other Western powers sometimes appealed to the hoary principle of the territorial integrity of existing states, sometimes to the stirring but vague principle of self-determination (that perennial threat to the territorial integrity of states), sometimes to the principle of *uti possidetis* (according to which boundaries are to remain fixed unless changed by mutual consent), and sometimes to the principle of democracy (which on some interpretations implies self-determination for minority groups, but on others overrides it). But so too did those massive violators of human rights, Milošović and Tudjman.

Responses to the break-up of the Soviet Union revealed the same confusion about principles. Americans felt indignant when Gorbachev said it was inconsistent for them to revere Lincoln for preserving the Union and condemn him for resisting the dissolution of the Soviet Union. Yet few could explain precisely why his analogy was mistaken.

When I say that moral theorizing about international law is needed, I do not mean something grandiose. I mean that there is a need for self-conscious, systematic moral reasoning, the attempt to produce an interrelated, mutually supporting set of prescriptive principles that will provide substantial guidance for at least most of the more important issues with which international law must deal or which it could profitably address. I remain agnostic about how comprehensive the best version of such a theory will turn out to be. For those who are uncomfortable with the term 'moral theory' I suggest as a humbler alternative 'systematic moral view.'

A coherent, defensible moral theory (or systematic moral view) of international law would not of course be sufficient for achieving better responses to crises of self-determination, ethnic conflict, state failure, and global terrorism. Yet it may well prove necessary. When political will is not firmly anchored in consistent moral principles it is all the more vulnerable to failure. Unless they are reasonably interpreted and embedded in the structure of a moral philosophy of law, principles of self-determination, state sovereignty, democracy, and *uti possidetis* become opportunistic tools for rationalizing failure to act or for wrongful action, rhetorical veils to mask the unrestrained pursuit of narrow self-interest or the lack of will to follow through on basic moral commitments.

Confusion about principles is not simply a failure of the masses or of political leaders to understand the rules that comprise the existing international legal order. Those rules themselves are in some central instances defective. Canonical (one might almost say liturgical) pronouncements of the most fundamental international legal rules suffer not only from ambiguity but also from apparent inconsistency. For example, as I have already suggested, the UN Resolutions and international human rights treaties that herald "the right of self-determination of all peoples freely to determine their social, economic, and political status"—including the right to choose full independence—at the same time affirm the right of states to maintain their territories intact.[2]

Of course the content of legal rules is not determined simply by the wording of a text, but ultimately by legal practice, and it is true that in practice the right of self-determination of peoples has been interpreted rather narrowly in international law, as a right of colonized peoples to independence from colonial rule. Nevertheless, it would be naive to assume that coherence of legal rules can be achieved by practice, unless practice is guided by coherent theory. So far, international practice—at least in matters of self-determination and humanitarian intervention—has been neither conceptually coherent nor morally defensible.

---

[2] See, for example, United Nations General Assembly (1960), 'Declaration on the Granting of Independence to Colonial Countries and Peoples' [Internet, http://www.unhchr.ch/html/menu3/b/c_coloni.htm].

II. *Curious Neglect*

Fixation on the domestic case

Contemporary political philosophers tend to neglect international relations. This is true even in what may be the most developed area of contemporary political philosophy, the theory of distributive justice. Despite the dramatic increase in theorizing about distributive justice since the appearance of Rawls's great book in 1971, work on *international* distributive justice is comparatively undeveloped.[3] Rawls himself has at last turned to the extension of his theory to the international sphere, but the results are both incomplete and disappointing.[4] (As I shall argue in Chapter 3, Rawls's theoretical framework for developing principles for the international legal system gives short shrift to international distributive justice. And as I have argued elsewhere, it also makes it impossible even to raise the most pressing issues concerning the justification of secession.[5])

Contemporary philosophers of law usually have even less to say about international law than contemporary political philosophers have to say about international relations. In fact, the major contemporary figures in this field largely have proceeded as if there were no international legal system to theorize about.

There are some quite recent notable exceptions to this general neglect. Fernando Teson offers the broad outlines of a Kantian moral theory of international law that takes human rights seriously and issues a bold challenge to unthinking deference to state sovereignty. But Teson's view is incomplete in several respects, and includes a rather robust natural law understanding of the nature of international law that many international legal scholars and philosophers of law find problematic.[6]

---

[3] John Rawls, *A Theory of Justice* (The Belknap Press of Harvard University Press, Cambridge, MA, 1979).

[4] John Rawls, *The Law of Peoples* (Harvard University Press, Cambridge, MA, 1999).

[5] Allen Buchanan, 'Rawls's Law of Peoples: Rules for a Vanished Westphalian World', *Ethics* 110/4 (2000), 697–721.

[6] Teson appears to assume a rather strong version of Ronald Dworkin's quite controversial view that in hard cases the law is determined by the best moral theory consistent with the bulk of settled law. It is not clear to me that Teson restricts this view to hard cases or that he takes seriously enough the qualification "consistent

In contemporary political philosophy there are several important discussions of some aspects of international distributive justice.[7] However, much of this work suffers from a lack of an *institutional* focus. Even when the importance of institutions for securing international distributive justice is acknowledged, little is said about what distinctive role, if any, international law should play.

In contrast, there has been a rich outpouring of work in the positive (that is, purely explanatory, as opposed to normative) liberal theory of international relations, including valuable explorations of the role of international law in the overall system of international institutions.[8] But little has been done to connect positive theory with moral theory.

A moral theory of international law must build upon or at least be consistent with the best available positive theories of international institutions, but must go beyond them, providing a coherent, defensible, organized set of prescriptive principles that apply not just to the conduct of individuals who occupy positions of authority in institutions, but also to the institutions themselves. Thus the moral philosophy of international law must include *institutional* moral reasoning: some of its most important principles must be formulated and justified in light of the assumption that they will be embodied in institutions. The meaning of this last assertion, and its

with the bulk of settled law." Fernando Teson, *A Philosophy of International Law* (Westview, Boulder, CO, 1998).

[7] See e.g. Darrel Moellendorf, 'Constructing the Law of Peoples', *Pacific Philosophical Quarterly* 772 (1996), 132–54; Liam Murphy, 'Institutions and the Demands of Justice', *Philosophy and Public Affairs* 274 (1998), 251–91; Thomas Pogge, *Realizing Rawls* (Cornell University Press, Ithaca, NY, 1989); Pogge, 'An Egalitarian Law of Peoples', *Philosophy and Public Affairs* 23 (1994), 195–224; Henry Shue, *Basic Rights: Subsistence, Affluence, and U.S. Foreign Policy*, 2nd edn. (Princeton University Press, Princeton, 1996); Charles Beitz, *Political Theory and International Relations* (Princeton University Press, Princeton, 1979), 125–76; and Beitz, 'Rawls's Law of Peoples', *Ethics* 110/4 (2000), 669–98.

[8] See Thomas Risse, Stephen Ropp, and Kathryn Sikkink (eds.), *The Power of Human Rights: International Norms and Domestic Change* (Cambridge University Press, New York, 1999); Andrew Moravcsik, 'Taking Preferences Seriously: A Liberal Theory of International Politics', *International Organization* 51 (1997), 513–54; Anne-Marie Slaughter, 'International Law and International Relations Theory: A Dual Agenda', *American Journal of International Law* 87 (1993), 205–39; Slaughter, 'International Law in a World of Liberal States', *European Journal of International Law* 6 (1995), 503–38; Slaughter, 'The Liberal Agenda for Peace: International Relations Theory and the Future of the United Nations', *Transnational and Contemporary Problems* 4 (1995), 377–420.

implications for moral theorizing about international law, will become clearer as this volume proceeds.

There is also a thoughtful and burgeoning contemporary literature on the morality of self-determination, secession, and group rights—all topics that are central to the moral theory of international law.[9] However, with few exceptions these works fail to draw clear institutional implications from the principles they enunciate or, when they do, they focus only on domestic institutions. To cite one prominent example, Will Kymlicka has developed a systematic and provocative account of self-determination for indigenous groups and minority nations within states, but has concentrated on the implications of this view for domestic policies rather than for international institutional reform.[10]

---

[9] Avashai Margalit and Joseph Raz, 'National Self-Determination', *Journal of Philosophy* 87 (1990), 439–61; Daniel Philpott, 'In Defense of Self-Determination', *Ethics* 105/2 (1995), 352–85; Lehning (ed.), *Theories of Secession* (Routledge, New York, 1998); Yael Tamir, *Liberal Nationalism* (Princeton University Press, Princeton, 1993); Christopher Wellman, 'A Defense of Secession and Political Self-Determination', *Philosophy and Public Affairs* 24 (1995), 357–72; David Copp, 'Do Nations Have the Right of Self-Determination?', in Stanley French (ed.), *Philosophers Look at Canadian Confederation* (Canadian Philosophical Association, Montreal, 1979); Harry Beran, *The Consent Theory of Obligation* (Croom Helm, New York, 1987); Beran, 'A Liberal Theory of Secession', *Political Studies* 32 (1984), 21–31; Lea Brilmayer, 'Secession and Self-Determination: A Territorialist Interpretation', *Yale Journal of International Law* 16 (1991), 177–202; Allen Buchanan, *Secession: The Morality of Political Divorce from Fort Sumter to Lithuania and Quebec* (Westview Press, Boulder, CO, 1991); Buchanan, 'Theories of Secession', *Philosophy and Public Affairs* 261 (1997), 31–61; Buchanan, 'Federalism, Secession, and the Morality of Inclusion', *Arizona Law Review* 37/1 (1995), 53–63; Jocelyne Couture, Kai Nielsen, and Michel Seymour (eds.), *Rethinking Nationalism* (University of Calgary Press, Calgary, 1998); Hurst Hannum, *Autonomy, Sovereignty, and Self-Determination: The Accommodation of Conflicting Rights* (University of Pennsylvania Press, Philadelphia, 1996); Hannum, 'Rethinking Self-Determination', *Virginia Journal of International Law* 34 (1993), 1–69; Chandran Kukathas, 'Are there any Cultural Rights?', *Political Theory* 20 (1992), 105–40; Will Kymlicka (ed.), *The Rights of Minority Cultures* (Oxford University Press, New York, 1995); Robert McKim and Jefferson McMahan (eds.), *The Morality of Nationalism* (Oxford University Press, New York, 1997); Margaret Moore, (ed.), *National Self-Determination and Secession* (Oxford University Press, New York, 1998); and Wayne Norman, 'The Ethics of Secession as the Regulation of Secessionist Politics', in Margaret Moore (ed.), *National Self-Determination and Secession* (Oxford University Press, New York, 1998).

[10] Will Kymlicka, *Liberalism, Community, and Culture* (Oxford University Press, New York, 1989) and *Multicultural Citizenship* (Oxford University Press, New York, 1995).

Explaining the neglect

The relatively undeveloped state of contemporary philosophy of international law may be due to several factors. First, it is only one instance of a more general failing in contemporary moral and political philosophy: a near total absence of institutional moral theorizing. Too often it is assumed that the process of justifying moral principles that are intended to be institutionalized need not take into account the effects of attempting to institutionalize them, or even whether they can be implemented effectively given existing institutional constraints.[11]

Second, Realism has dominated the positive (that is, descriptive-explanatory) study of international relations, and according to Realism moral theorizing about international relations and hence about international law is futile. In the past two decades Realism has been vigorously—and to my mind successfully—challenged. Yet Realism's scornful attitude toward the possibility of a moral theory of international law persists, especially among political philosophers and philosophers of law who are unfamiliar with the work of its most astute critics.

Third, many take a dismissive view of international law, viewing it as at best a pale shadow of what we ordinarily think of as a legal system. Thus it has been said that international law is to law as professional wrestling is to wrestling—the implication being that international law is largely pomp and posturing, with outcomes that are more or less scripted by dominant states. The most extreme form of this dismissive view—Legal Nihilism—denies that what is called international law is really law at all. Fourth, at least until quite recently, legal positivism has been the dominant jurisprudential view in international law, and the positivists' rejection of natural law views of international law has often been overgeneralized to a hostility toward any moral reflection on international law.

However, it is a mistake to assume that if legal positivism is correct, then moral theorizing about international law is misguided. By 'legal positivism' I mean the view that whether a rule is a law

---

[11] For an example of this mistake, see Chris Naticchia, 'Recognition and Legitimacy: A Reply to Buchanan', *Philosophy and Public Affairs* 28/3 (1999), 242–57.

does not depend upon whether it meets moral criteria. Naturalism (the natural law view) may be defined as the denial of the positivist thesis. To determine what the law is, the positivist looks to legal texts, patterns of state behavior, and legal practice; the naturalist looks not only to these but also to moral reasoning (or, in traditional terms, to the principles of natural reason or natural law).

Because positivism is a view about what the law is, not about what it should be, it is entirely neutral as to whether moral reasoning can determine how the law ought to be. It is true that some who have attempted to engage in moral theorizing about how international law ought to be have adopted naturalism as a view about which rules are international law (Teson is one example). However, legal positivists have sometimes failed to distinguish between cases where theorists have appealed to moral reasoning to determine whether a particular rule is international law (naturalism) and cases where they have appealed to moral reasoning to determine how international law should be.

When a theorist develops a natural law view of what the law is and in the same work theorizes about how the law ought to be without making it clear at every juncture which enterprise he is engaged in, this confusion is perhaps understandable. Nevertheless, legal positivists make a fundamental mistake when they move from arguments against naturalism (as a position on what the law is) to the conclusion that moral theories of international law ought to be rejected.

One of the main points I hope to establish in this book is that it is possible to develop a coherent, defensible, systematic, and practically useful view about how the international legal system ought to be, without embracing a naturalist view of what international law is. I will neither assume nor argue that moral reasoning is needed to determine whether something is a rule of international law (while not denying that in some cases, especially where human rights are concerned, moral reasoning does in fact, under current institutions and processes of international law, play a role in specifying the content of legal rules). Nor will I attempt to refute naturalism.

What I say about how international law ought to be will of course make certain assumptions about what currently is international law, but these assumptions will be relatively uncontroversial and largely neutral as to the positivist/naturalist debate. Moreover, I will attempt to resist the temptation to which some naturalists succumb and which positivists rightly criticize: letting my beliefs about what the law should be distort my judgment about what it is.

III. *Institutional Moral Reasoning*

The necessity of taking institutions seriously

Even those few theorists who suggest that their views on secession or self-determination or humanitarian intervention might be incorporated into international law tend to assume that the moral reasoning they use to support their favored principles need not take the prospects for institutionalization into account. The difficulty is not simply that they fail to consider whether or how their proposals could be incorporated in the existing international legal system, though this is bad enough.[12] Quite apart from failing to address the question of whether it is feasible to get from where we are to where they think we should go, these theorists proceed as if the justification of moral principles for institutions is wholly independent of the question of what the consequences of institutionalizing these principles would be. A central contention of this book is that such a view of the relationship between moral principles for institutions and their justification is dead wrong.

Principles that may be plausible for an isolated case often prove inadequate or even counter-productive if institutionalized to govern a practice that covers many cases. An example from outside the international sphere may help to make this fundamental point clearer. It may not be difficult to describe a particular hypothetical case in which a physician would be morally justified in actively terminating the life of a hopelessly ill, incompetent patient whose quality of life is extremely poor. And one may be able to formulate the conditions C, D, and E, that make this case one in which active termination of life is morally justified.

But it is quite a different matter to show that it would be morally justifiable for physicians to apply the rule: "Whenever conditions C, D, and E obtain, they may actively terminate life." Whether it

---

[12] Donald Horowitz notes the prevalence of this error in the philosophical literature on secession. Donald Horowitz, 'Self-Determination: Politics, Philosophy, and Law', in Ian Shapiro and Will Kymlicka (eds.), *Ethnicity and Group Rights, Nomos* XXXIX (New York University Press, New York, 1997).

would be a moral improvement or a moral disaster for physicians to act on the rule the philosopher abstracts from a particular favored case will depend upon a number of factors that are conspicuously absent from the description of that particular case. For instance, one must take into account the overall character of the institutions within which physicians work and in particular whether reimbursement schemes or other features of the institutional framework create incentives that generate an unacceptable risk that physicians would exercise this authority wrongly. The more general problem is this: even if it is possible by calm reflection on a hypothetical case to formulate conditions under which a certain action would be morally justified, the real world agents who are supposed to follow a rule that is abstracted from the hypothetical case may not reliably identify those conditions and perform the action only when they obtain.

The simple but neglected point is that one cannot go from a moral argument for the soundness of a particular course of action in a single (usually highly idealized) type of case to a general principle that is suitable for institutionalization. Institutions matter, and if moral principles are to provide guidance for institutional reform, they must take institutions seriously.

More specifically, when rules are institutionalized, this typically involves their application by persons occupying certain roles. A principle that might be appropriate for an individual to act on in a particular case may be inappropriate as a principle to be applied to many cases by a person occupying an institutional role. To the extent that proposed principles are to be implemented through the actions of persons in institutional roles, the moral justification of principles must take into account institutional structures, and especially the incentives to which those in institutional roles will be subject.

Secession as an institutional concept

Most of the recent work on the morality of secession illustrates a deeper sense in which moral reasoning can fail to be sufficiently institutional. That literature typically focuses on the nature of the right to secede, understood as a moral claim-right—that is, as including both the moral permissibility of seceding and a correlative moral obligation on the part of others not to interfere with the secession. Thus, to say that the Chechens have the right to secede from Russia is to state not only that they are morally justified in asserting their independence from Russia (in the sense that it is morally permissible for them to do so) but also that others (including the government and people of Russia) are morally prohibited from interfering with their assertion of independence.

However, this way of understanding the right to secede is incomplete unless the nature of the notion of independence is made clear. Does "The Chechens have the (claim-)right to independence" merely mean that they have the right to repudiate Russian authority over Chechnya and establish *some form of control* of their own over that territory? This is certainly *not* how the Chechen secessionists, or secessionists in general, understand the assertion of a right to secede: by 'independence' they mean *statehood*, which is a particularly robust form of territorial control defined by international law. To put the same point somewhat differently: secessionists typically assert that they have the right to their own legitimate state, and a legitimate state is an institutionally defined entity, an entity defined as having certain rights, powers, and immunity under international law.

So, if we understand their assertion as they do, to say that the Chechens have a right to secede—in the claim-right sense of 'right'—is at the very least to say that (1) they are morally justified in attempting to establish Chechnya as a legitimate *state* and that (2) others are morally prohibited from interfering with this attempt to create this new legitimate *state*. Both (1) and (2) are institutional statements, because they both employ the concept of a state, which is an institutional concept—not just in the sense that states are institutions—but because to be a legitimate state is to be an institutionally defined entity, an entity that has a certain status according to the institutions of international law. For example, under international law, legitimate states have certain rights (such as the right of territorial integrity and the right of immunity for their diplomats, as well as the right to enter into treaties with other states), and they also have certain responsibilities (such as responsibilities for the safety of diplomats and other foreign nationals within their territory).

To summarize: Secession is not simply the formation of a new political association among individuals who repudiate the existing state's authority over them. It is a taking of territory that is claimed by an existing state, accompanied by the assertion that those doing the taking have a right to attempt to exercise over that territory the kind of control that only legitimate states have. Thus the acceptance by the international community of a group's assertion that they have a right to secede has two implications regarding *institutional status*: first, that the group is entitled to attempt to form a new state and that others are obligated not to interfere with this endeavor; second, that the state against whom the secessionist claim is made does not have a right to that territory, that its sovereignty is to that extent diminished.

So a moral theory of the right to secede must articulate the conditions under which a group is justified in asserting the right to try to set up a legitimate state of their own in a portion of the territory now claimed by an existing state. Showing that a group has the right to political association of some sort, or the right to repudiate the authority of the state over the members of the group, is not sufficient to establish that the group has the right to secede because this does not address either the state's conflicting claim to the territory or the secessionists' claim to be entitled to set up an independent legitimate state. Thus secession is also an institutional concept in the sense that to evaluate assertions of the moral right to secede we must take a principled stand on what sorts of conditions an entity ought to satisfy in order to count as a legitimate state and the conditions under which existing states have a valid claim to all of their territory, and this in turn will depend upon what role legitimate states are to play in a morally defensible international legal system.

Justifying rights statements

It is important to realize that statements about the moral right to secede, like other statements about moral rights, are best seen, not as moral primitives or axioms, but as conclusory statements (though they do in turn serve as premises for further, more specific statements about what individuals should or may do and how institutions ought to be structured). In other words, it is always legitimate to ask for a justification for a statement that there is such and such a right. The most cogent way to support a rights statement is to identify an interest that is especially important from a moral point of view and then argue that all things considered this interest is deserving of the special protections that the ascription of a right confers. In particular, if you have a right to something (in the claim-right sense, that is, including a correlative obligation on others), then the mere fact that greater overall utility might be gained by denying you what is yours as a matter of right is not itself sufficient for doing so.

This is *not* to say that rights are absolute constraints that invariably "trump" all other considerations. Rather, the point is that the existence of a right makes a difference as to which considerations are sufficient reasons for a course of action. Thus the fact that some action would increase overall well-being may often be a sufficient reason in favor of it; but in cases in which the action would violate a right, the fact that the action would increase overall well-being is not a sufficient reason for doing it. This is perfectly compatible, of course, with acknowledging that it may be justifiable to infringe a right under certain extraordinary circumstances, as when respecting the right would be almost certain to produce an enormous amount of suffering for many innocent people. To assume that one cannot hold that there are human rights without regarding them as carrying absolute, exceptionless obligations that always "trump" every other consideration is to indulge in caricature.

Now it might be thought that by moral reasoning we can determine whether the Chechens have the moral right to secede without raising the question of what would be a morally justifiable international legal rule regarding secession—that we can first settle the issue of whether the Chechens have the moral right to secede and then consider whether the principle according to which Chechen secession is morally justified would be appropriate for incorporation into international law. This, however, is a mistake. Recall that the assertion that the Chechens have the right to secede implies at the very least that they have the right to attempt to form a new legitimate state in a part of the territory of an existing state and that others ought not to interfere with this attempt.

Notice that if one produces a moral argument to show that the Chechens have the right to secede understood in this way because their situation satisfies conditions C, D, and E, then one is committed to holding that any group that satisfies those conditions also has this right, and hence that states ought to refrain from interfering with attempts to form new states by groups that satisfy those conditions. But whether states should refrain from interfering with groups that attempt to form new states when those conditions C, D, and E are satisfied will depend, among other things, upon how states acting in that way will affect the international legal system and its effectiveness in helping to protect human rights and secure peace.

So to justify the assertion that a group that satisfies conditions C, D, and E has a moral (claim-)right to attempt to create its own legitimate state, then, one must consider what the effects on the system would be of allowing groups that satisfy those conditions to attempt to create states of their own, in particular the effects on human rights and peace. But to determine what these effects would be, one must consider the nature of the international legal system in which assertions of independence occur. In particular, one must consider whether recognizing a right for groups that satisfy those conditions to attempt to sever portions of the territory of existing states and create new states there is compatible with states fulfilling the roles in the system that they ought to fulfill. To answer that question, one must have a moral theory of the international legal system. For all these reasons, one cannot first determine a pure, noninstitutional moral right to secede, and then, as a separate task, determine whether institutionalizing it makes sense.

To avoid misunderstanding, let me stress that I am *not* saying that a moral theory of international law will consist *solely* of institutional reasoning. The moral theory I offer in this book is based on what I call the Natural Duty of Justice, according to which each of us—independently of which institutions we find ourselves in or the special commitments we have undertaken—has a limited moral obligation to help ensure that all persons have access to institutions that protect their basic rights. Although the Natural Duty of Justice requires us to help build just institutions, it is not an institutional principle in any interesting sense. Instead, it applies to us simply because we are persons. Moreover, the Natural Duty of Justice itself rests on a more basic principle, namely, the obligation each of us has to treat every person with equal concern and respect, which itself is not an institutional principle in any interesting sense, though of course it has implications for how institutions ought to be. So even though the view I am advancing in this volume relies heavily on institutional reasoning, I am not claiming that all moral reasoning is institutional, nor that all moral principles are institutional, nor that the moral theory of international law is exclusively institutional.

The idea of a systematic philosophy of international law

One important implication of the thesis that moral theorizing about international law must include institutional reasoning is *holism*: to determine whether a particular rule (concerning humanitarian intervention, self-determination, secession, etc.) ought to be included in international law will depend in part upon what is being assumed about the other principles that it will coexist with, how they fit together, and what the effects of their joint implementation is likely to be. It follows that those political philosophers who believe that they can offer a moral account of secession or of self-determination or of humanitarian intervention, while conveniently leaving the development of a moral philosophy of international law to others, are in error. Attempting to work on any of these topics in isolation from the others might be called Leaf-Blower Theorizing; it simply displaces problems to some location conveniently out of sight, without solving them.

This point about holism may be obvious to the point of banality; yet most who write about matters germane to the moral theory of international law usually ignore it. Since the publication of my book on secession in 1991 a large and interesting literature on the morality of secession has emerged (mainly due to the proliferation of secessionist movements, but also perhaps partly in response to my book). Yet in much of this literature proposals concerning the right to secede are offered without connecting them to proposals concerning forms of self-determination short of secession, without a consideration of the role of the practice of recognition of new states in a morally defensible international legal system, and without addressing the fundamental question of when, if ever, existing states have valid moral claims to their territory.[13]

Similarly, proposals for rules to govern humanitarian intervention are offered without any serious effort to show how they are grounded in an understanding of human rights and often without any clear view of the distinction between what justice requires and what any particular agent may legitimately do. (For example, from the fact that female genital mutilation is a human rights abuse it does not follow that anyone has the right to intervene to stop its occurrence.)

---

[13] I was guilty of the latter omission, which I rectified with the publication of Buchanan, 'Recognitional Legitimacy and the State System', *Philosophy and Public Affairs* 28 (1999), 46–78.

Even worse, much of the moral literature on self-determination, secession, and humanitarian intervention leaves it unclear as to when its conclusions are grounded in the most basic moral principles and when instead they are concessions to the constraints of feasibility and the fallibility of institutional implementation. For example, it is often said that humanitarian intervention is justified only to stop gross and large-scale violations of the most fundamental human rights, in particular the right against genocide, not to stop "lesser" human rights violations. What remains obscure is whether this constrained view on intervention is (1) grounded on a belief that a wider range of interventions is in principle morally justifiable, tempered by an appreciation of the fallibility and abuse that a less constrained rule would risk, (2) a concession to feasibility (on the assumption that states would not agree to a more permissive rule), (3) an implication of a particular theoretical tenet about the moral right of self-determination, according to which this right provides a fundamental moral barrier to intervention, or (4) a combination of all the preceding. Only a self-consciously systematic approach—an attempt to develop a moral theory of international law that distinguishes between basic moral principles and practical prescriptions responsive to the constraints of feasibility—can sort these matters out.

For all of these reasons a moral *theory* of international law is needed, both for responsible criticism of the status quo and for guiding progress toward a better state of affairs. But before embarking on this daunting theoretical project it is necessary to respond to several challenges to the whole enterprise.

IV. *The Realist Challenge*

According to Realism (at least in its more extreme forms), the nature of international relations rules out morality in that sphere. And because morality is not operative in the international sphere, a moral theory of international law is an exercise in futility.[14]

---

[14] George F. Kennan, *American Diplomacy, 1900–1951* (University of Chicago Press, Chicago, 1951); Thucydides, *Complete Writings: The Peloponnesian War*, the unabridged Crawley translation, introd. John H. Finley, Jr. (Modern Library, New York, 1951); Kenneth Waltz, *Man, the State, and War: A Theoretical Analysis* (Columbia University Press, New York, 1959); and Waltz, *Theory of International Politics* (Addison-Wesley, Reading, MA, 1979).

The traditional Realist characterizes international relations as a Hobbesian state of nature: (1) there is no global sovereign, no supreme arbiter of conflict capable of enforcing rules of peaceful cooperation; (2) there is (approximate) equality of power, such that no state can permanently dominate all the others; (3) the fundamental preference of states is to survive; (4) but (given conditions (1) and (2)) what is rational for each state to do is to strive by all means to dominate others in order to avoid being dominated (to rely on what Hobbes calls the Principle of Anticipation). In a situation in which all parties strive to dominate, without constraints on the means they employ to do so, moral principles are inapplicable.[15]

Contemporary political scientists sometimes utilize a somewhat different conception of Realism which, though grounded in the three assumptions stated above, may warrant making explicit. Thus Robert O. Keohane and Joseph S. Nye in their classic work *Power and Interdependence* (3rd edition) state that "For political realists, international politics...is a struggle for power but, unlike domestic politics, a struggle dominated by organized violence..."[16] These authors go on to emphasize that for the Realist, military competition is the dominant form of international competition, that states function as unitary actors whose dominant "issue" is military security, and that whatever cooperation exists among states is derivative on the struggle for physical security through military dominance.[17] The Realist conception of what states are like, especially of what state leaders are and should be most concerned about, precludes a

[15] For a valuable exposition and critique of the Hobbesian Realist position in international relations, see Beitz, *Political Theory and International Relations*, 15–36.

[16] Robert Keohane and Joseph Nye, *Power and Interdependence*, 3rd edn. (Addison Wesley Longman, Boston, 2001), 20.

[17] It is worth noting that Keohane and Nye's conception of Realism does not preclude morality in international relations. That would only follow if one adds the premise that military competition, war and preparation for war, which according to the Realist view is the dominant activity in international relations, leaves no significant room for morality. Since I am interested in critically evaluating Realism as a purported bar to substantial moral theorizing about international law, I will assume that the Realist as Keohane and Nye describe him is one who thinks that at most a moral theory of international law could include something like principles of *jus in bello*, constraints on the means of war (though state support for these would have to be grounded in the assumption that each state finds it in its interest to have such constraints).

meaningful role for systematic moral reasoning about international relations.

There are several variations on the Realist theme, and in some cases it is not clear exactly what is meant by the thesis that morality cannot be a significant consideration in international relations. This could mean that (1) moral 'oughts' do not apply to international relations—that there are no true or justified statements about what anyone ought (morally) to do in that sphere. Or it could mean that (2) no one in fact acts morally in international relations (nor will do so in the future). Or that (3) moral behavior in international relations is fundamentally irrational and therefore infrequent (assuming that actors in this sphere do not often act in fundamentally irrational ways).

On any of these interpretations Realism leaves no room for anything that would merit the title of a moral theory of international law. If (1) is true, then there can be no true or justified moral theory of international law, since such a theory would include 'ought'-statements. If (2) is true, then a moral theory of international law will be practically irrelevant because no one will ever attempt to implement it. If (3) is true, then a moral theory of international relations will be relevant only for fundamentally irrational actors (who, it is assumed, will constitute a minority of international actors).

The critique of Realism

As entrenched as Realism still is in certain quarters, it is vulnerable to such serious objections that it poses no insurmountable obstacle to the project of developing a moral theory of international relations. The empirical generalizations about international relations that constitute Realism are not only far from being self-evident truisms; they are in fact disconfirmed by a balanced view of the facts.

Much of the most interesting work in international relations in the past two decades shows that international relations are not in fact a Hobbesian war of each against all. There are stable patterns of peaceful cooperation, some bilateral, some multi-state, some regional, and some genuinely global. These include financial regimes, trade agreements, structures for scientific cooperation, environmental accords, and international support for human rights, economic development, labor standards, and disaster relief. And as Keohane and Nye and other critics of Realism point out, it would be dogmatic

and inattentive to the facts to assume that in all these cases cooperation is derivative on the competition for military dominance or security. The point is that issues that concern states are not so
hierarchically structured (with military security at the apex) as the
Realist assumes. Extensive cooperation occurs in a number of areas
in which military security is simply not a concern.

Survival is simply not an issue, much less the paramount issue, in
many contexts of state interaction. (Consider, for example, relations
between Britain and the United States over the past 120 years or so,
or relations among most Western European states over the last fifty
years.) Nor is it true, as the Realist insists, that all states are seriously vulnerable to being destroyed or dominated if they choose to
observe any moral constraints. Powerful states can afford to take
risks in efforts to build cooperation and they also face lesser risks of
others defecting from cooperative commitments because the costs
of betraying their trust may be very high.

Perhaps most important, contrary to the Realist, state preferences
are neither fixed nor uniform among states. The positive (that is,
explanatory as opposed to normative) liberal theory of international
relations marshals impressive evidence for the thesis that state preferences (more precisely the preferences expressed by state leaders in
foreign policy) vary, depending upon the internal character of the
state and its domestic society. Realists, in contrast, treat "the state"
as a black box actor, thereby failing to appreciate the implications of
the fact that it is state leaders who act and that they act under the
constraint of complex and conflicting domestic and transnational
political forces.

Equally important, Realists fail to see that so-called state preferences change over time as a function of the activities of various groups
within the state, particularly as these interact with and are empowered by transnational and international governmental and nongovernmental entities. And the evolving structures of international
law increasingly facilitate this transnational interaction and empowerment.[18] Finally, according to one important strand of positive
liberal theory, democratization promises to expand the sphere of

[18] Risse, Ropp, and Sikkink, *The Power of Human Rights*; Moravcsik, 'Taking
Preferences Seriously', 513–54; Slaughter, 'International Law in a World of Liberal
States', 503–38; Slaughter, 'International Law and International Relations Theory',
205–39; and Slaughter, 'The Liberal Agenda for Peace', 377–420.

peaceful cooperative interaction while at the same time more fully implementing human rights principles, because developed democracies tend not to make war on one another and because democracy provides the most reliable assurance that human rights will be respected domestically.[19]

Realism shares the same defects which even some economists have begun to recognize in psychological egoism, the thesis that all individual behavior is motivated exclusively by self-interest.[20] The chief defect of psychological egoism is that it is either a substantive but false empirical generalization, or a tautology, to which any putative counterexample to the thesis of universal egoism is accommodated by stretching what counts as self-interest to include everything ordinarily included under regard for the interests of others.

If we say that the Soviet soldier who, laden with Molotov cocktails, throws himself on a German tank, acts from self-interest because he derives so much satisfaction from the thought that he is dying for the Motherland, then we reduce the psychological egoism thesis to an empty tautology. Similarly, diehard defenders of Realism seem to be willing to stretch the notion of state preferences for survival (or for power) to the point that the Realist thesis becomes uninteresting. For example, if Canada makes a disproportionate investment in international peacekeeping compared to much more populous and wealthier states, the Realist will desperately conclude either that Canada's only motivation for doing so must be that she hopes to gain favorable world opinion and the greater influence this brings, or that self-interest, in the case of Canada, includes the satisfaction derived from knowing that one has done the right thing. In the former case one suspects that the Realist is so dogmatically committed to the state-egoism thesis that nothing whatsoever would ever count, in his eyes, as disconfirming evidence. In the latter case, the Realist has also rendered his hypothesis unfalsifiable

---

[19] Michael Doyle, 'Kant, Liberal Legacies, and Foreign Affairs, Parts 1 and 2', *Philosophy and Public Affairs* 12 (1983), 205–35, 323–53; Bruce Russett, *Grasping the Democratic Peace: Principles for a Post-Cold War World* (Princeton University Press, Princeton, 1993); and Amartya Sen, *Poverty and Famines: An Essay on Entitlement and Deprivation* (Oxford University Press, New York, 1981).

[20] Jane Mansbridge (ed.), *Beyond Self-Interest* (University of Chicago Press, Chicago, 1990).

and hence uninteresting by obliterating the distinction between self-interest and other-regarding interest, assuming in effect that all interests *of* a self are interests exclusively *in* the self. Furthermore, the Realist fails to appreciate that there can be mixed motives and that it is often extremely difficult to determine whether self-interest or regard for others is the dominant motivation, if there is one.

Moreover, the fact that an agent derives satisfaction from helping others does nothing whatsoever to show that he was motivated by the expectation of such satisfaction. If an agent acts from moral commitments, then to the extent that these commitments are integrated into his character, we would expect him to derive satisfaction from doing what he believes he ought to do. And if this is so, then it is a fallacy to infer egoistic motivation from the fact that the agent derives satisfaction from having acted in a certain way.

In fact, Realism is even less plausible than psychological egoism, granted the positive liberal theorists' insight that state preferences are the outcome of diverse domestic and transnational forces. Given the multiplicity of forces that contribute to state preferences, it would be remarkable if they possessed the unity that psychological egoists attribute to the preferences of individuals.

We can now summarize the main conclusion of our critical discussion of Realism. Realism either implausibly denies the existence of significant peaceful international cooperation or assumes without justification that, because the struggle for military dominance is paramount, the extent and nature of cooperation does not and never will provide adequate space for genuinely moral behavior and hence for a moral theory of international law. Once the Realist spell is broken by revealing the unsubstantiated character of its constitutive empirical generalizations, the path is clear for developing a moral theory of international law, as an element of a broader moral theory of international relations.

A disclaimer is in order. I do not pretend to have provided a refutation of Realism. Nor do I wish to endorse without serious qualification any particular version of the positive liberal theory of international relations. Instead I have only tried to outline the main objections to Realism in sufficient detail to show that it does not rule out moral theorizing about international law *ex ante*. Furthermore, this sketch of a refutation of Realism's conclusion that moral theorizing about international law is a doomed endeavor does not require wholesale endorsement of the positive liberal theory of international relations. After all, serious criticisms of Realism were advanced prior to the development of a systematic positive liberal view.[21]

The core of positive liberal theory does, however, provide a more systematic exposition of the flaws of Realism, while supplying materials for a constructive alternative vision of international relations. Even if positive liberal theory should require serious revision or even rejection, the plausibility of its core theses counters the Realist claim that there is no point to moral theorizing about international law. At the very least, positive liberal theory helps to open up a provisional space for the enterprise of moral theory, establishing that we cannot dismiss it before attempting it.

Realism Proper and Fiduciary Realism

So far I have been criticizing what might be called Realism Proper, which is a purely positive as opposed to a normative view—an explanatory or descriptive account of the nature of international relations, not an account of how they ought to be. But the most prominent proponents of the positive theory usually draw normative implications from Realism Proper, even while denying the applicability of moral principles to international relations. It is useful, therefore, to distinguish between Realism Proper and Fiduciary Realism. Realism Proper, as I have already noted, is the view that international relations are a Hobbesian state of nature, along with the meta-ethical implication that morality is generally inapplicable in that area of human affairs. Fiduciary Realism adds a single normative claim to Realism Proper: State officials, if they are responsible, will recognize the Hobbesian character of international relations, and therefore will act only so as to maximize the survival prospects of their states, without regard for moral constraints.

Fiduciary Realists are not moral nihilists or moral skeptics. They believe that state officials have moral obligations to their fellow citizens. Indeed, with regard to the moral obligations they do recognize, Fiduciary Realists are moral absolutists. But they also believe

---

[21] Beitz, *Political Theory and International Relations*, 4–66.

that fulfilling these obligations requires rejecting any moral con-straints on their behavior toward other states. They advocate disre-garding all other moral principles for the sake of fulfilling one overriding obligation: to serve the interests of their own states no matter what, even when this means showing no moral restraint in their dealings with other states.

Hans Morgenthau adds an interesting twist on the Fiduciary Realist position. In his view state leaders ought to concentrate on furthering their own states' interests chiefly because any attempt on their part to act in the interests of humanity at large is likely to result in large-scale human disasters, due to a deadly combination of fallibility, ideological bias, and hubris.[22]

However, this version of Realism, properly understood, does not rule out a significant role for moral reasoning regarding interna-tional law; it is best viewed as a precaution against overambitious blueprints for improving the international system. The proper response to its kernel of truth is to examine proposals for reform critically from the standpoint of feasiblity, and to recognize the importance of the distinction between ideal and nonideal theory, as well as that between short-term and longer-term goals within non-ideal theory. I discuss these matters in some detail below, so for now I will focus on the more familiar forms of Realism.[23]

The Realist Proper denies that morality applies to international relations at all, while the Fiduciary Realist holds that international relations are so inhospitable to moral behavior that it would be irre-sponsible for a state official to observe moral constraints in dealing with other states. The two types of Realist have in common the rejection of any significant space within which a moral theory of international relations or international law can operate.

The objections to Realism Proper undercut Fiduciary Realism. If international relations is not a Hobbesian war of each state against

---

[22] Hans J. Morgenthau, *Politics among Nations: The Struggle for Power and Peace*, 6th edn., rev. Kenneth W. Thompson (Alfred A. Knopf, New York, 1985), 267–74, 574–5.

[23] For a more detailed criticism of Morgenthau's twist on the Realist view, see Buchanan, 'Beyond the National Interest', in Martha Nussbaum and Chad Flanders (eds.), *Global Inequalities*, a special issue of *Philosophical Topics* Vol. 30, Number 2, 2002.

all, then state officials can sometimes observe moral constraints without acting irresponsibly toward their own people. Fiduciary Realism is also subject to an objection of its own. Its picture of morality is gravely truncated: Even though state officials have a fiduciary obligation to their countrymen, it cannot be an absolute one.

When a person becomes an agent of some other individual or of a collectivity, she does not thereby wipe the moral slate clean. For example, a mother has fiduciary responsibilities toward her child, but this does not justify her forcibly taking a kidney from another child to save her child's life. The most basic general obligations—including those that are the correlatives of human rights—are not swamped by any fiduciary obligation that a state official could have. One cannot contract out of one's basic moral obligations.

A more sophisticated proponent of Fiduciary Realism might reply that even though the state official's fiduciary obligation is not literally absolute, she ought to treat it as if it were (just as a Rule Utilitarian argues that even though the Principle of Utility is the ultimate moral principle, agents occupying certain roles should proceed as if the secondary rules they are following were basic). The difficulty with this reply is that it is plausible only if the nature of international relations is such that the only way a state official can meet his genuine, though in fact limited, obligation to his countrymen is by treating that obligation as if it were absolute.

In other words, the Fiduciary Realist would have to argue that unless the state official treats her fiduciary obligation as if it were absolute, she will impose unacceptable risks on her fellow citizens' most fundamental interests. But to make a case for this latter claim, the Fiduciary Realist would have to fall back upon Realism Proper's characterization of international relations as a Hobbesian state of nature, and that characterization, we have seen, is dubious.

The weakness of Fiduciary Realism undermines what is probably the dominant popular view that impedes reform in the international legal system, the view that the national interest should be or at least may be the exclusive concern of the leaders of any state and its citizens. Chapter 2 presents a frontal assault on the national interest view. The rest of the book is devoted to drawing out the implications for international legal reform of rejecting the national interest view.

V. *The Moral Minimalist Challenge*

There is a position that is at least superficially similar to Realism and which, while not denying the possibility of a moral theory of international relations, implies that any such theory must be of such limited scope as to preclude anything that could be called a moral theory of international law. According to what I shall call the Moral Minimalist, an essential and distinguishing feature of international law is that it is a system of rules for the interaction of entities, namely states, that do not share ends.[24] The implication is supposed to be that the lack of shared ends severely limits the possible moral content of international law and hence the scope of moral theorizing about international law.

There are four serious difficulties with Moral Minimalism—if it is thought to preclude significant moral theorizing about international law. First, in one unproblematic sense at least most of the societies that make up the international community do share some ends: in particular, peace and the creation and maintenance of a stable, predictable framework of interaction, given the interdependence of modern societies. It may even be said that for a substantial portion of the members of the international community justice is a shared end (though frequently not an overriding one) and that there is evidence of an expanding consensus on some of the substance of justice, in particular, in resolutions, treaties, and monitoring mechanisms that give increasingly determinate content to at least the most basic human rights.

So at the very least the Moral Minimalist must show that in spite of agreement on these sorts of ends, there are more substantive ends that the international community not only does not share but also will not come to share in the future, and that this precludes anything worthy of the title of a moral theory of international law. However, the Moral Minimalist's notion of what counts as a shared end (or what counts as a sufficiently substantive end) is so obscure that it is hard to tell whether the alleged absence of shared ends in the international domain really does undercut or trivialize the enterprise of moral theorizing about international law.

[24] Terry Nardin, *Law, Morality, and the Relations of States* (Princeton University Press, Princeton, 1983).

The second difficulty with Moral Minimalism is that it rests on an open-ended, sweeping empirical generalization to the effect that societies will never be able to achieve sufficient agreement on substantive ends or on a core conception of justice in the future to make a significantly contentful moral theory of international law possible. This empirical generalization is not backed by solid evidence, especially if it is understood in a temporally unbounded way. On the contrary, the slow but perceptible movement toward a global culture of human rights—the expanding consensus on the content of the most basic human rights—suggests the falsity of the pessimistic prediction that members of the international community are and will always remain moral strangers to one another.

In fact there are already some impressive instances of international convergence on fairly specific normative principles. Only in the past decade a large number of states have adopted remarkably similar principles for the protection of human subjects of scientific research. Just as impressive, an international effort has recently been undertaken to iron out the remaining inconsistencies between human subjects ethics codes in different countries.[25] Prior to this convergence and the commitment to bringing it to completion, one might have thought that cultural differences would have made agreement on principles for the treatment of human subjects of scientific experimentation impossible. (Attention to the facts is a good antidote to a priori assumptions about the depth of moral disagreement across cultures, but one that few theoretical political philosophers and ethical theorists ever ingest.)

Moreover, there is good reason to believe that such consensus as has already occurred is not a fluke and that it may increase, because the institutions of international law, as well as a variety of other less formal private and public institutions, already include functioning mechanisms for building consensus. For example, the processes by which human rights compliance is monitored, including the workings of the International Human Rights Commission in responding to complaints about violations, do not leave our understanding of the content of human rights unchanged. Instead, these processes

[25] Baruch Brody, *The Ethics of Biomedical Research: An International Perspective* (Oxford University Press, New York, 1998).

contribute to the formation of more determinate shared beliefs about what the various human rights are.[26]

Third, the Moral Minimalist puts the cart before the horse. Whether or not a consensus on substantive ends (or upon a core conception of justice) is possible in the international community may depend in part on how international law evolves and whether a moral theory of international law can be articulated in such a way that its central principles gain widespread support. It is true that international society currently lacks the institutional resources for bringing about the degree of agreement on substantive ends or on a core conception of justice that some (though certainly not all) domestic societies enjoy. The possibility that this may change cannot be ruled out a priori.

Fourth and finally, there is an obvious difficulty in the Moral Minimalist's assertion that what distinguishes international law from domestic law is that the latter consists of a framework of rules for those who share ends while the former does not. After all, it is a truism about a liberal domestic society that its public order does *not* rest on shared ends. So to make a case that there is negligible scope for moral theorizing about international law the Moral Minimalist must either reject the broad distinction she tries to draw between the nature of international law and the nature of domestic law and accept the radical conclusion that there is no room for a substantive moral theory of domestic law in liberal societies, or spell out exactly why it is that the lack of shared substantive ends rules out any significant scope for moral theorizing in international law, but not for domestic liberal legal systems.

Rawls's later thought, as developed in *Political Liberalism* and in *The Law of Peoples*, might be thought to provide an answer to the latter question. His view explains how there can be a consensus on principles of justice in a liberal society that is not based on shared ends and it also shows why those principles cannot simply be transferred to the international sphere. But Rawls's view, while acknowledging that principles for the international order are in a sense minimal when compared to those appropriate for a liberal society, does *not* support the Moral Minimalist's claim that there is no place for significant moral theorizing about international law.

[26] Kristen Hessler, 'A Theory of Interpretation for Human Rights', Ph.D. dissertation (University of Arizona, 2001).

According to Rawls, although the members of liberal societies do not share substantive ends, they do share what might be called a core conception of justice, the idea of a society as a cooperative venture among free and equal persons, while the international order contains societies that do not share this core conception. The shared core conception of justice supplies a foundation for a morally robust system of law in a liberal domestic society; its absence implies that the moral content of international law must be minimal *when compared with the former*.

According to Rawls's more moderate moral minimalism, the fact that people in nonliberal societies do not share the core conception of society as a cooperative venture among free and equal persons implies that they can reasonably reject substantive principles that legitimately can be included in a liberal domestic legal system. Similarly, the legal systems of nonliberal societies can justifiably include substantive moral principles that it would be illegitimate to impose on the members of a liberal society—principles that liberals could reasonably reject, given their shared core conception of justice. Therefore, the lack of a globally shared core conception of justice implies that the moral content of international law, which is to bind all societies liberal and nonliberal, must be acceptable from the standpoint of the conceptions of social order of both liberal societies and nonliberal ones, so far as the latter qualify as what Rawls calls "decent societies." The principles that satisfy this criterion, according to Rawls, include only a rather lean *subset* of what liberals usually take to be human rights. Thus when compared to the full list of liberal human rights, they may be called minimal.

However, contrary to the more extreme view I have labeled 'Moral Minimalism', Rawlsian minimalism holds that there can be sufficient consensus on certain human rights to function as an important component of a moral framework for international law. Thus Rawls's minimalism with regard to moral principles for the international legal system does *not* preclude moral theorizing about international law. Indeed Rawls's book on the principles of international law is an instance of such theorizing.

So Rawls's view can explain the sense in which liberal societies are subject to principles of justice that are not based on shared ends and can do so in such a way as to make it clear that principles of justice for the domestic order cannot simply be extended to the international order. Yet the theory that accomplishes this refutes rather than supports the Moral Minimalist's claim that there is no room for significant moral theorizing about international law.

In Chapter 3, in discussing the role of human rights in a moral theory of international law, I will raise what I believe is a fatal objection to Rawls's conception of a legitimate international legal order and to the particular understanding of tolerance as respect for persons' reasons upon which it is based. If that objection succeeds, then the fact (if it is a fact) that there is greater disagreement on conceptions of justice globally than there is within societies does not preclude the validity of a more morally robust theory of international law than Rawls's, one that includes a richer set of human rights. For now I will only emphasize that Rawls's variety of moral minimalism does not imply that there is no conception of justice that can command sufficiently wide assent to serve as the basis for a moral theory of international law. Indeed Rawls's central point is that even though the principles of a liberal domestic legal order cannot be exported wholesale to the international order, there is a core list of rights—which Rawls refers to not as basic human rights, but as human rights properly speaking—that are applicable internationally.

Rawls assumes that there not only is not, but will not come to be, an international consensus on a richer set of human rights. His version of minimalism, therefore, is an assertion about the content of the ideal moral theory of international law, not a nonideal theory concession to what is currently feasible in international law.

Like the more extreme Moral Minimalist view, Rawls's position on the limited content of ideal theory for international law is based on an empirical assertion about the extent of moral disagreement across boundaries. Furthermore, it is a sweeping empirical assertion that is not qualified by any limitation on how long it is assumed to remain true. Yet Rawls offers no evidence to support this sweeping, temporally unbounded empirical assertion.

Rawls seems to overlook the fact that there is an expanding global culture of human rights that exhibits a broad consensus on the idea that justice requires respect for the inherent dignity of all persons, that this notion of dignity includes the idea that all persons are equal, so far as the importance of their basic interests are concerned, and that among the latter is an interest in freedom. My point is *not* that the notion of freedom and equality expressed in the international human rights language of inherent dignity is identical to that found in liberal societies or that it will ever come to be, but rather that at present there is no reason to assume that it cannot provide the foundation for the eventual development of a moral theory of international law whose content is more robust than Rawls assumes.

One cannot assume, of course, that the existing institutional resources of international law are sufficient for achieving a morally defensible determinate content for international legal norms concerning human rights, nor for producing a system of rules that is as a whole coherent and powerful enough to address all the issues. Moral theorizing has its own contribution to make, by articulating basic principles and providing a rationale for developing the institutional resources needed to give them determinate content and implement them effectively. In the end the best way to determine the scope of a moral theory of international law is to engage in the process of constructing a theory and then see whether or not it provides practical guidance for improving the system.

Degrees of minimalism

It is important to understand that minimalism regarding the moral theory of international law comes in degrees and that there may be more scope for moral theorizing in some dimensions of international morality than in others. The only type of minimalism that poses a threat to the enterprise of moral theorizing about international law, what I have called Moral Minimalism, is at the extreme point of the continuum of minimalisms in three respects: (1) It denies that any significant global consensus on basic moral principles or values exists, (2) dogmatically assumes that no such consensus will emerge, and (3) holds (1) and (2) to be true of the bearing of morality on international law in general, failing to consider the possibility that the prospects for consensus may be greater in some areas of morality than in others.

I have already noted that Rawls's view in *The Law of Peoples* is a different, more moderate sort of minimalism, one which, unlike Moral Minimalism, does not preclude significant scope for moral theorizing about international law, but which does limit it by virtue of a rather constricted view of human rights. In Chapter 6 I will argue for a quite different kind of position that might be called minimalist, distinct from both Moral Minimalism and from Rawls's minimalism regarding human rights. There I advance a proposal for creating a normativized practice of state recognition, for making international recognition of a new entity a legitimate state conditional upon its satisfaction of certain standards of justice that I describe as minimal, even though they include a richer set of human rights than Rawls's.

My position is also minimalist in another sense: I hold that generally speaking the nonideal moral theory of international law, at least for the foreseeable future, should only regard what I have called *basic* human rights as providing the main content for the notion that the system of international law should be justice based. My conception of the role of human rights differs from Rawls's in two respects: my list of basic human rights, as the focus of nonideal theory, is richer—that is, more demanding—than Rawls's; and unlike Rawls I leave open the possibility that the best ideal theory may include a list of human rights that is more ambitious still.

Although it is framed in terms of basic human rights, there is one sense in which my proposal for a morally defensible practice of recognition is not minimalist. I argue that this minimum or threshold of justice that ought to be required for recognition should not be viewed as forever fixed, but should be raised in the future when conditions permit us to demand more by way of the protecting what I describe in Chapter 3 as the most basic shared human interests. Rawls, in contrast, believes that his leaner list of human rights is not a concession to what is now justifiable or feasible, but rather is a fixed feature of the ideal moral theory of international law.

There is still another sense in which my own view might be described as minimalist: In Chapter 4 I present a more nuanced view, a kind of *partial* and *moderate* minimalism. There I argue that for the present there is likely to be less international convergence on substantive, comprehensive principles of distributive justice than on the most basic civil and political human rights and that this has important implications for a nonideal moral theory of international law for the time being. Thus my version of minimalism reflects the conviction that nonideal theorizing should be sensitive both to the diachronic dimension of moral agreement or disagreement—the fact that the scope of agreement may change over time—and to the possibility that the prospects for agreement may be greater in some areas of morality than in others. Despite these complications regarding the notion of minimalism, the analysis of this section supports the conclusion that only the more extreme form of minimalism, Moral Minimalism (as including (1), (2), and (3) above) would preclude meaningful moral theorizing about international law and that at present we have no good reason to accept that pessimistic view of the possibility of moral convergence.

One of my aims in distinguishing the various minimalisms regarding international law is to clarify the difference between my own view and that of others such as Rawls or Nardin (whom I take to be an exponent of the more extreme minimalist view). Another is to make it clear that *one can engage in moral theorizing about international law while recognizing that there are limits on the enterprise.*

This is a significant point, because it rebuts a common criticism voiced by those who reject any attempt to advance a moral theory of international law—the complaint that it is a mistake to export to the international sphere the same moral principles that are applicable in the domestic context. The upshot of my discussion of the variety of moral minimalisms is that the moral theorist of international law can acknowledge that the scope of moral principles in international law may be limited in significant ways—and that they are not principles of domestic morality writ large—without abandoning his project.

In this regard I agree with what I take to be Rawls's main point in *The Law of Peoples*: The moral theory of international law must recognize that principles that are appropriate for a liberal domestic legal system cannot simply be transferred to the international legal order. Rawls's great contribution in *The Law of Peoples* is to show that one *can* theorize about the moral foundations of international law without making that mistake.

VI. *Legal Nihilism*

Challenging the assumption that there is an international legal system

Both Realism Proper and Fiduciary Realism are to be distinguished from Legal Nihilism. The Legal Nihilist contends that there is no subject matter for a moral theory of international law, because there is no such thing as international *law*. There are two ways the Legal Nihilist view can be understood: as a claim about the features a system of rules must have if it is to be a legal system, paired with the assertion that what we call international law lacks some of these features; or as a claim that a system of rules is not a legal system unless its rules effectively determine the behavior of those to whom the rules are directed, along with the observation that states are not effectively bound by what we call international law.[27]

In support of the first view, the Legal Nihilist notes that the so-called international legal system is not a legal system because it lacks (1) an enforcement mechanism for its rules, (2) courts with universal and compulsory jurisdiction, and (3) what Hart calls a rule of recognition, a criterion for determining what is law in the system.[28] In addition, some who deny the existence of international law do so on the grounds that the very concept of state sovereignty is incompatible with the idea of a law that binds states: to be sovereign is to be the ultimate maker of law, and hence not subject to any law.

The charge that what is called international law is not really law raises fundamental questions about the nature of law that cannot be addressed adequately in this volume. I will only sketch the main outlines of a rebuttal of the Legal Nihilist challenge to the enterprise of developing a moral theory of international law. I make no pretensions to having settled the complex question "What is Law?" My aim is only to show that the Legal Nihilist challenge does not undercut the enterprise of moral theorizing about international law.

Unduly restrictive assumptions about law

First, one cannot assume that a system that lacks a supreme enforcer is not a legal system. Legal historians have observed that there have been systems that lacked a supreme enforcer (and indeed any regular public enforcement mechanism at all) but which are worthy of being called legal systems. For example, in medieval Iceland and early medieval England enforcement of public rules was achieved exclusively or chiefly by private agents, subsequent to judgments made by a public authority.[29]

---

[27] I thank David Golove for this distinction.

[28] H. L. A. Hart, *The Concept of Law* (Clarendon Press, Oxford, 1961), ch. 13.

[29] Jesse Byock, *Viking Age Iceland* (Penguin Books, New York, 2001). This book contains an excellent bibliography, including works on Medieval Icelandic Law.

Furthermore, even in the case of some of the most highly developed, modern legal systems, especially constitutional systems in which there is a systematic division of authority to create checks and balances, there may be no single, ultimate legally constituted power capable of conclusively resolving all disputes that might arise regarding the proper division of constitutional authority or the interpretation of the law.[30] On the contrary, the very point of such a system of checks and balances is to ensure that there is no truly supreme, unchallengeable legally constituted power. Moreover, systems of customary law typically lack any such ultimate enforcement mechanism, and international law still has a very substantial customary component. Second, some of the most interesting work in legal theory in recent decades demonstrates that even in highly developed legal systems there are effective mechanisms for compliance other than enforcement (i.e., other than coercion).[31] In sum, to deny international law the title of law because it lacks a Hobbesian enforcement agent is to assume a now discredited Austinian conception of law and to ignore the realities of systems that certainly deserve the title of legal system.[32]

Legal Nihilism is on equally shaky ground in its insistence that the lack of a supreme global legislature and of courts of compulsory universal jurisdiction entails that there is no such thing as international law. To assume that a legal system must have a supreme legislature is again to overlook the existence and importance of customary law, not just in the international sphere, but in many domestic legal systems as well. In addition, the assumption that there must be a supreme legislature may reflect the same hyper-rationalist bias that underlies the dogma that there must be a power capable of settling every dispute that might arise. It is a tautology that unless there is a supreme lawmaker, there is the possibility of a conflict of laws for which there is no authoritative resolution. But why assume that a legal system cannot exist unless the *possibility* of conflict is ruled out?

---

[30] Christopher Morris, *An Essay on the Modern State* (Cambridge University Press, New York, 1998).

[31] Anthony Kronman, 'Contract Law and the State of Nature', *Journal of Law, Economics, and Organization* 1 (1985), 5–32.

[32] According to the Austinian conception, law is a set of commands backed by force.

Nor is it obvious that what we call international law is not law because there is no "rule of recognition" in Hart's sense of that phrase in the international legal system. First of all, Hart held only that a rule of recognition (along with a set of primary rules) is sufficient for the existence of a legal system, not that it is necessary.

Second, and more important, one might argue that the international legal system does include a rule of recognition in Hart's sense, namely, the authoritative statement of the sources of international law contained in Article 38 of the treaty that created the International Court of Justice.[33] This document cites three sources of international law: custom, treaty, and general principles of law, as well as two sources relevant to the "determination" of law (meaning, presumably, the determination of the specific content of particular rules), the opinions of international tribunals and the writings of well-respected "publicists" (commentators on and theorists of international law). One could argue that this statement of the sources of international law is neither significantly more complex nor more indeterminate than the rules of recognition that could be formulated for any developed, modern domestic legal system.

Even if such an authoritative statement of the sources of international law cannot provide an unequivocal answer to all questions about the existence of legal norms in the international system, it is far from evident that whatever rules of recognition could be formulated for domestic legal systems would be clearly superior in this regard. And what I said earlier about the assumed requirement of a

---

[33] "1. The Court, whose function is to decide in accordance with international law such disputes as are submitted to it, shall apply:

   a. international conventions, whether general or particular, establishing rules expressly recognized by the contesting states;
   b. international custom, as evidence of a general practice accepted as law;
   c. the general principles of law recognized by civilized nations;
   d. subject to the provision of Article 59, judicial decisions and the teachings of the most highly qualified publicists for the various nations, as subsidiary means for the determination of rules of law.

2. This provision shall not prejudice the power of the Court to decide a case *ex aequo et bonno*, if the parties agree thereto." United Nations (1945), 'Statute of the International Court of Justice', repr. in Barry E. Carter and Phillip Trimble (eds.), *International Law: Selected Documents* (Little, Brown & Company, Boston, 1995), 29–43, article 38.

supreme enforcer and a supreme legislature applies here as well: It is a hyper-rationalist bias to assume that a legal system cannot exist unless it contains a rule that is capable of answering the question "Is this norm a law?" in every possible case.

My purpose here, however, is not to provide a thoroughly convincing argument for the claim that international law does contain a rule of recognition that is sufficiently like the rules of recognition in domestic legal systems to support the assertion that there is such a thing as international law. My critique of Legal Nihilism does not depend upon that. For as I shall argue presently, there is both the need and the scope for a moral theory of what we call international law, even if it is not law properly speaking or is only a "primitive" system of law.

A primitive legal system?

Some legal theorists, including Hart, have suggested that what we call international law is at best a primitive legal system because it consists entirely of primary rules (roughly, rules that specify certain behavior as permitted or obligatory or prohibited, rather than rules for determining the validity of rules or for changing rules). But whether or not the international system contains a rule of recognition in Hart's sense, it is implausible to characterize it as consisting only of primary rules and therefore as primitive. Even international customary law (which one might assume is the most primitive part of the system) is much more complicated than the notion of primary rules suggests.

There is a complex, highly normativized conception of what counts as customary international law, including not only the requirement of *opinio juris* (that to count as custom state behavior in conformity with a norm must be thought to be legally required or legally permissible), but also the idea of peremptory norms (*jus cogens*), which have a status similar to that of constitutional law in determining the validity of other norms.[34] The international legal system also includes norms governing the interpretation and validity of treaties (in part codified in the Vienna Convention on

---

[34] This point is due to David Golove.

Treaties).[35] Once these complexities are appreciated, the assertion that international law is a primitive legal system or a proto-legal system looks rather dubious or must be sufficiently qualified to render it innocuous from the standpoint of the enterprise of providing a moral theory for the system. Moreover, even a primitive legal system (perhaps especially a primitive legal system) requires a moral theory for its evaluation and improvement.

Misunderstanding sovereignty

The final ground for Legal Nihilism also ought to be rejected. As Hart among others persuasively argued, to say that there is no international law because the sovereignty of states precludes their being bound by law is to fail to understand that the powers, rights, liberties, and immunities that constitute sovereignty are defined by international law. To be sovereign is to be a member of a system of entities defined by and subject to international law.[36]

The powers of sovereignty as defined by international law have changed and presumably will continue to change in the future. Before the mid-sixteenth century or perhaps somewhat later, state sovereignty was much more limited (e.g., by religious authority) than it was after that time. After 1948 (with the Universal Declaration of Human Rights) or at least after 1976 (when the two major Covenants on Human Rights went into effect), those powers were again limited, by the obligation to respect human rights and the prohibition against aggressive war.[37]

My aim is not to provide a conclusive refutation of the various Legal Nihilist assertions about what features a system of rules must have to be a legal system or to make a conclusive determination of which of those features what we call the international legal system includes. As I have already hinted, to engage wholeheartedly in this

---

[35] United Nations (1969), 'Vienna Convention on the Law of Treaties,' repr. in Carter and Trimble, *International Law: Selected Documents*, 55–80.

[36] Hart, *The Concept of Law*, ch. 13.

[37] United Nations (1948), 'Universal Declaration of Human Rights', repr. in Carter and Trimble, *International Law: Selected Documents*, 381–6; United Nations (1966), 'International Covenant on Civil and Political Rights', repr. in *International Law: Selected Documents*, 387–403; and United Nations (1966), 'International Covenant on Economic, Social and Cultural Rights', repr. in *International Law: Selected Documents*, 410–18.

analytic debate would be to concede too much to the Legal Nihilist. For even if it were true that what we call the international legal system is not a legal system strictly speaking, this would not preclude the sort of moral theorizing to which this book is devoted.

What we call international law is sufficiently law-like to raise virtually all of the important issues that a moral theory of law should address. In particular, this system requires morally defensible principles because it claims supremacy in its domain and includes provisions for the use of force to compel compliance with its rules. Whether we award it the title of a legal system or do so only with serious qualifications is of little consequence.

Effectiveness and law

The other variant of Legal Nihilism—the position that what we call international law is not sufficiently effective in determining the behavior of international actors to qualify as law—faces a dilemma. If the idea is that a system of norms must achieve something close to full compliance to count as law, then many systems we routinely call legal will fail the test, since they have areas of serious noncompliance (think, for example, of the Italian tax code, or laws in several U.S. states prohibiting fornication and adultery). And thus the putative contrast between international and domestic law crumbles. Moreover, the idea that a legal system may be either more or less effective in binding those in its domain makes perfectly good sense. On the other hand, once it is admitted that full compliance (or anything approaching it) is not a reasonable requirement for a system to count as a legal system, it is very difficult to determine just how effective it must be; and it would be an exaggeration to say that international law has no significant effect.

Finally, the notion of effectiveness is itself ambiguous. In particular, we should not assume that compliance with rules is the only dimension of effectiveness relevant to the question of whether something is law. Human rights law has important effects even on oppressive governments that routinely violate it. The very fact that there are human rights covenants signed by the great majority of states exerts pressure on oppressive states to deny that they are violating human rights when they do so, equips forces within and outside the oppressive states with powerful mechanisms for exerting pressure on them, influences the character of normative discourse, provides the basis for economic and cultural boycotts, and may lead a ruthless regime to place a human rights dissident under house arrest rather than executing her.[38]

Equally important, there are many areas of international law in which compliance is quite impressive (for example, with regard to treaties governing the exploitation of outer space and the Antarctic, international postal and communications regulations, etc.). And even though there are areas of international law (such as the prohibition of torture) where norms are not effective in the sense of achieving a high degree of compliance, this may change over time, as the force of transnational public opinion becomes more effectively mobilized and as better mechanisms for monitoring compliance and attaching costs to noncompliance evolve.

Before concluding this discussion of Legal Nihilism, it may be useful to articulate that view's relationship to Realism. I have argued that if it is understood as an analytic claim about the features a system of rules must have to count as law or about the connection between law and effectiveness, the Legal Nihilist position poses no serious bar to moral theorizing about international law, because the system is sufficiently *law-like* to require a moral foundation. Further, even if the Legal Nihilist provided a more convincing case than he has that there is no international law properly speaking, this would not rule out the possibility that an international legal system (strictly speaking) is emerging. (The claim that international law is 'primitive' is less damaging if development is not precluded.) If the Legal Nihilist is to make a convincing case that what we call international law is not law *and* will not evolve into law, he must rely on more than analytic claims about what constitutes law.

Realism, if true, would supply the needed explanation of why this allegedly primitive system must remain so. The idea would be that because international relations is a Hobbesian state of nature, with all states being confronted with what game theorists would call a massive assurance problem, states will never allow the emergence of a system that would have the features (including an enforcement

---

[38] Risse, Ropp, and Sikkink, *The Power of Human Rights*; and Jonathan Power, *Like Water on Stone: The Story of Amnesty International* (Northeastern University Press, Boston, 2001).

mechanism and courts of compulsory jurisdiction, etc.) that would genuinely bind them. But if Realism is no longer assumed to be true, the Legal Nihilist position becomes much less interesting even if true. For nothing in the Legal Nihilist position itself precludes the possibility that what we now call international law can become law in the strict sense.

VII. *The Moral Legitimacy of the State System*

Inevitable conservatism?

One last challenge to the very enterprise of moral theorizing about the international legal system is worth considering. International law, as it exists and has existed, consists primarily of rules for the interaction of states. So a moral theory of international law must assume the existence of states. Otherwise, the enterprise of theorizing succumbs to what might be called the Vanishing Subject Matter Problem. But states are institutionally defined within the international legal system as having unique rights and privileges vis-à-vis other actors. To that extent moral theorizing about international law seems to assume the moral legitimacy of the state system and to endorse the ascendancy of states. By doing so, moral theorizing about international law helps to perpetuate the capacity of states to commit great evils and to impede moral progress. (It is states, after all, that engage in wars, the most destructive of human conflicts, and who are the most frequent and egregious violators of the most basic human rights.) In addition, some would argue that the control over resources that international law accords to states as an element of sovereignty is the single greatest impediment to eradicating the most grievous distributive injustice in our world—the vast disparity of wealth between the "developed" and the "underdeveloped" countries.

We seem to be faced with a dilemma. Unless a moral theory of international law takes the ascendancy of states as a given, it is vulnerable to the Vanishing Subject Matter Problem and in addition to the charge that its proposals are not feasible because they ignore the fact that what becomes international law must be acceptable to states. But if a moral theory of international law takes the ascendancy of states as a given it cannot be sufficiently critical of the existing state system to be useful as a guide for evaluating and reforming the statist quo. In its most extreme form the second horn of the dilemma can be stated as follows: Given that international law is state-centered, the enterprise of developing a moral theory of international law is morally defensible only on the assumption that the state system is legitimate. But the defects of the system are so great that the legitimacy of the system is very much in doubt. So the enterprise of developing a moral theory of international law is not morally defensible.

Furthermore, perhaps the moral ideal should be a rights-protecting world state, a system of genuine global governance, not an improved multi-state system. Beginning the task of theorizing with statist assumptions creates a bias against this alternative.

This objection raises a warning flag that any moral theory of international law ignores at its peril. But it does not show that the enterprise is doomed. A moral theory of international law need not be unduly conservative, so long as it takes the state-centered character of the existing system as only *provisionally* given—as a starting point for theorizing for the time being—and subject to critical re-evaluation.

A moral theory of international law should provide an account not only of the proper scope and limits of state sovereignty and of which entities ought to be regarded as legitimate states, but also of the conditions under which the international legal system itself is morally justifiable. Exploring the issue of system legitimacy may turn out to be quite subversive. One cannot assume in advance that such an investigation will uncritically affirm the legitimacy of the existing system or even of any system very like it. So conceiving of the theoretical enterprise in this way—on the assumption that what we have to work with initially is a state-centered system—is not inherently conservative. It allows for the possibility that neither existing states nor the state system itself are morally legitimate.

Whether a moral theory of international law will condemn or support a state-centered system cannot be known in advance. Suppose, for example, that the best moral theory turns out to support the following conclusions. (1) Current international law is too restrictive regarding the right to secede. A more morally defensible international legal system would support secession in a wider range of situations than is now the case. In particular, international law should confer legitimacy on and support for groups for whom secession is a remedy of last resort against persistent patterns of large-scale violations of basic human rights. (2) International law should be modified so as to include rules supporting autonomy regimes within states (i.e., self-government short of full independence) for certain groups and in some cases should impose on the international community clear obligations to monitor and enforce such autonomy arrangements. Suppose also that the best moral theory of international law turns out to conclude that: (3) For the system to be morally legitimate it would have to be much more democratic than it currently is.

A moral theory of international law having these three features would pose a very serious challenge to the statist quo. Yet such a theory might nevertheless begin by taking seriously—though provisionally—the state-centered character of the existing system. It so happens that the theory developed in this volume includes features (1), (2), and (3). It is hardly conservative, yet it takes the existence of states and their primacy in the system as provisionally given.

The possibility of transcending the statist paradigm

A distinction Rawls made in *A Theory of Justice* in 1971 between ideal and nonideal theory is relevant here. Ideal theory sets the ultimate moral targets, articulating the principles that a just society or a just international order would satisfy, on the assumption that there will be full compliance with these principles. Nonideal theory provides principled guidance for how to cope with the problems of noncompliance and how we are to move closer toward full compliance with the principles of ideal theory.

Whether or not the most comprehensive and defensible ideal moral theory of international law will include a uniquely primary role for states is a complex question—and one that probably cannot be answered until we have much more developed examples of moral theories of international law than we now possess. Nevertheless, it could be argued that even the best ideal moral theory will include a prominent place for something like states, though with considerably reduced powers in certain dimensions of sovereignty.

First, as Kant emphasized, a plurality of territorially based units each having considerable powers of self-government is probably preferable to the risk of inescapable tyranny that a world government would pose.[39] Second, a world government might be intolerably inefficient. Third, persistent pluralism with regard to conceptions of public order and justice speak in favor of a plurality of political units, within which different values can find effective expression; and primary jurisdiction over a territory is the most reliable way to protect pluralism. Fourth, some (including most famously Rousseau) argue that there are limits to the scale of the political units in which democracy can flourish and that a democratic global state is not possible. For all of these reasons, and perhaps others as well, the division of the world's area into something resembling states may be morally defensible if not wholly attractive, quite apart from the fact that for the foreseeable future we are likely to be stuck with a system in which states are the most prominent constituents.

I do not regard these four arguments for something like a multi-state system as conclusive. At most they open up the possibility that the best ideal theory may have a prominent place for something like states. I prefer to remain agnostic about whether the ultimate ideal is a world-state. In any event, shortly I will explain why the controversy between those whose ideal is a state-centered system and those who advocate a world-state is rather misguided.

Unbundling sovereignty: a subversive strategy

At a number of crucial junctures in this volume I make a case for "unbundling" the set of powers, claim-rights, liberties, and immunities that have traditionally been thought to define sovereignty. In Chapter 6 I argue for a kind of staged, conditional, and provisional practice of recognition, according to which in some cases an entity claiming statehood status would not be granted all the attributes of sovereignty at once, but would be accorded them in steps, contingent on satisfying certain normative standards, including, preeminently, a credible effort to protect the basic human rights of all its citizens, especially minorities. Thus, for example, the question at

---

[39] Immanuel Kant, *Perpetual Peace*, trans. and ed. Lewis White Beck (Bobbs-Merril Educational Publishing, Indianapolis, 1957).

present should not be: "Should Kosovo be recognized as a sovereign state," but rather, "Which attributes of sovereignty should be accorded to Kosovo and when?"

In Chapter 9 I advance the view that the international legal order should encourage various forms of intrastate autonomy for certain minority groups as an alternative to secession. This too involves unbundling sovereignty, according significant powers of self-government to groups within the state, short of "full" independence.

Both of these unbundling strategies, if widely implemented, would do a great deal to break the mesmeric hold of the unitary, all-or-nothing sovereignty paradigm. To that extent they are deeply subversive of the existing state-centered system. So even though my attempt at moral theorizing starts with the existence and dominance of states, it is not conservative.

Once we take the idea of unbundling sovereignty seriously we must consider the possibility that the contrast between a "state-centered" and a "world-state" system will become blurry. The more political differentiation there comes to be within states (the more pervasive sovereignty-eroding, intrastate autonomy arrangements become) and the stronger international legal structures become, the more difficult it will be to draw a sharp contrast between a state-centered and a world-state system. This is another reason to believe that beginning the task of moral theorizing with the provisional assumption that states are major actors and subjects of international law does not bias the outcome against radical change.

The existing international legal system as obstacle to and resource for progress

The system as it exists is deeply defective. Yet it would be naive to think that the question for those who care about justice is a simple choice between working within the system to improve it or rejecting it utterly as morally tainted. The international legal system is a fact of our lives for the foreseeable future and it includes both daunting obstacles to progress and powerful resources for improvement. It would certainly be far-fetched to say that because it is so defective, it is morally impermissible to engage with it, to utilize its resources to make it better, even when this might mean changing it so considerably that eventually we speak of it in the past tense and refer to its successor.

Consider, for example, the work of international human rights activists. No one is likely to be more aware of the deficiencies of states and of the state system than these dedicated, sometimes heroic individuals. Nevertheless, they do from time to time achieve victories that, together with other forces, contribute to improvements in the system, chiefly through the erosion of state sovereignty. It would be very implausible to say that activists who strive to protect human rights act wrongly because the system within which they work is defective.

Nor is evidence of progress in the system lacking. Little more than fifty years ago few informed persons would have predicted that international law would place substantial limitations on the state's right to treat its own citizens as it sees fit. Given the short time span of these developments, as well as their radical departure from the statist paradigm of traditional international law that has dominated since the mid-seventeenth century and reached its apogee in the nineteenth, it is not unreasonable to work within the system for further improvements.

Louis Henkin aptly conveys the surprising capacity of a state-centered system to initiate changes that eventually result in serious constraints on state sovereignty in the following insightful comment on the UN Charter:

The United Nations Charter, a vehicle of radical political-legal change in several respects, did not claim authority for the new human rights commitment it projected other than the present consent of States.... In fact, to help justify the radical penetration of the State monolith [in the name of protecting human rights], the Charter in effect justifies human rights as a State value by linking it to peace [among states] and security.[40]

Henkin goes on to observe that although the UN Charter became a vehicle for radical change, including change that greatly eroded state sovereignty, the states that agreed to it did not at that time accept the idea that they had a legal obligation to refrain from violating the

[40] Louis Henkin, 'International Law: Politics, Values and Functions', *Collected Courses of the Hague Academy of International Law, 1989* (Martinus Nijhoff Publishers, Boston, 1990), iv. 214–15.

rights of their own citizens, much less an obligation or even a right to intervene to protect the human rights of citizens of other states.[41]

Some who despair of working for progress within the existing system may do so because they confuse international law with some of its most prominent current institutional embodiments. In particular, the United Nations is thought by many, especially in the United States, to be corrupt, ineffectual, hypocritical, and wasteful of resources.

In addition, some would argue that the very constitution of the UN, as articulated in its Charter, makes it both inadequate and incapable of significant reform. For example, the same veto right of permanent members of the Security Council that is often used to block effective responses to massive human rights violations in internal conflicts also makes reform of the Charter very unlikely, because amending the Charter requires the consent of all the permanent members.

Here I will only preview a point to be elaborated in the final chapter of this book: The UN is not identical to international law. Whether the UN can be reformed and whether international law is redeemable are two different questions. In Chapter 11 I suggest that reforming the international law of humanitarian intervention may require developing institutions of intervention that lie outside the UN structure—and violate UN-based law.

VIII. *The Nature and Scope of a Moral Theory of International Law*

Content

So far I have argued that the enterprise of moral theorizing about international law makes sense. Now I want to achieve some preliminary clarity on what a moral theory of international law should be like.

The fundamental content of a moral theory of international law, as ideal theory, would consist of the following elements: (1) An account of the most important moral goals of the institution of international law, (2) an articulation of the most weighty moral reasons for supporting the institution of international law as a means for achieving those goals, (3) a specification of the conditions under which the international legal system would be morally legitimate,

[41] Ibid.

at least in the sense of there being an adequate moral justification for individuals and groups to participate in the system's processes of creating, applying, and enforcing rules, and (4) a statement of and justification for the most fundamental substantive norms of the system, including principles specifying the scope and limits of human rights, minority rights, and rights of self-determination and secession, principles governing the use of force on the part of states, insurgent groups, and international organizations (just war, humanitarian intervention, etc.), principles specifying criteria for recognition of entities as members of the system, and principles regulating just trade and other economic relations, the distribution of global resources, environmental protection, and international financial regimes. The needed justification of these principles would consist chiefly in showing how their implementation would further the most important moral goals of the system and would do so in morally acceptable ways.

To convey just how contentious moral theorizing about international law is, I will merely note that there is still disagreement as to the first item—the nature of the goals that the institution of international law is to help achieve. Until very recently the dominant and rarely challenged view has been that the only legitimate goal of the system is peace—or, more accurately, peace among states (which is, we have learned in recent years, compatible with horrific violence within states). On this view, justice is only a legitimate aim to the extent that pursuing it promotes peace.

A more ambitious moral theory of international law, and one I shall argue is more cogent, takes the chief moral goals of the international legal system to be peace (not just among, but also within states) and justice.[42] In the next chapter I argue that justice should be a primary goal of the international system, and that making it so need not show a lack of appreciation for the importance of peace among states.

A proper 'Realism': setting moral targets under the constraint of moral accessibility

The task of ideal theory is to set the most important and most distant moral targets for a better future, the ultimate standards for

[42] David Luban, 'Just War and Human Rights', *Philosophy and Public Affairs* 9 (1980), 160–81.

evaluating current international law. Nonideal theory's task is to guide our efforts to approach those ultimate targets, both by setting intermediate moral targets, as way-stations on the path toward the ultimate standards laid down by ideal theory, and by helping us to determine which means and processes for achieving them are morally permissible. Nonideal theory must steer a course between a futile utopianism that is oblivious to the limitations of current international law and the formidable obstacles to moral progress erected by vested interests and naked power, on the one hand, and a craven capitulation to existing injustices that offers no direction for significant reform, on the other.

Here a distinction between *feasibility, accessibility*, and *moral accessibility* is useful. An ideal moral theory is feasible if and only if the effective implementation of its principles is compatible with human psychology, human capacities generally, the laws of nature, and the natural resources available to human beings. Obviously, a theory that fails to meet the requirement of feasibility is of no practical import. But feasibility, though necessary, is not sufficient for a good theory. A theory should also be accessible.

A theory is accessible if it is not only feasible, but if in addition there is a practicable route from where we are now to at least a reasonable approximation of the state of affairs that satisfies its principles. In other words, if an ideal theory is to be useful to us, the ideal it specifies must be accessible to us—those to whom the theory is directed. Not all theories that are feasible are accessible to us. Even though some human beings, in some circumstances, might be able to realize the principles of a particular theory, contingencies of our history or culture or the inertia of our severely defective social institutions might bar us from doing so.

Even accessibility is not enough; ideal theorizing should also satisfy the constraint of *moral* accessibility. Other things being equal, a theory should not only specify an ideal state of affairs that can be reached from where we are (though perhaps only after a laborious and extended process of change), but also the transition from where we are to the ideal state of affairs should be achievable without unacceptable moral costs.[43]

---

[43] In earlier papers I used the term 'moral accessibility' in another sense, to refer to what I now call 'moral congruence'.

The requirement of moral accessibility signals that nonideal theory should make a case that the corresponding ideal theory's principles can be satisfied or at least seriously approximated through a process that begins with the institutions and culture we now have and that does not involve unacceptable moral wrongdoing in the process of transition. Whether the moral costs of transition are acceptable will depend in part upon how defective the current state of affairs is and upon the probability that efforts to reach the ultimate moral targets set by ideal theory will in fact succeed, without substituting other, comparable evils.

Other things being equal, greater costs are acceptable if needed to escape great evils. Yet surely there are limits to what we may do to bring about morally desirable ends. Part of a nonideal theory's task is to provide an account of when the moral costs of transition are unacceptable.[44]

The morality of transition

For those who are committed to the rule of law in international relations, the morality of transition raises particularly perplexing issues. For example, in Chapter 11 I will explore the morality of acts that are directed toward the moral improvement of the international legal system, but which are themselves violations of existing international law. This is no academic exercise. Some of the most significant improvements in the international legal system, including the emergence of prohibitions against slavery, genocide, aggressive war, and nonconsensual experimentation on human subjects, appear to have resulted in part from state actions that were almost certainly illegal under international law at the time they were performed. Prominent examples include the British Navy's attacks on the transatlantic slave trade in the nineteenth century, some aspects of the "Victor's Justice" at Nuremburg, and possibly the NATO intervention in Kosovo in 1999.

Other desiderata for a moral theory of international law

Both in order to construct a moral theory of international law and to engage in the comparative evaluation of rival theories, it is necessary

---

[44] I owe the distinction between feasibility and accessibility to Joshua Cohen. It is not clear to me whether his notion of accessibility includes what I have called moral accessibility, that is, accessibility without moral costs.

to be clear about what such a theory should do. Some of the desiderata for a moral theory of international law are obvious and require little comment. A theory should have broad scope, providing guidance on the full range of important moral issues pertaining to the international legal system. It should also feature a relatively small number of powerful principles capable of generating substantive conclusions about how international law can be improved and which targets of improvement are to be given priority. I have argued in detail elsewhere that a moral theory of international law should satisfy several additional requirements: moral progressivity, moral congruence and (what I shall paradoxically call) "progressive conservatism".[45]

A theory satisfies the requirement of moral progressivity if the successful implementation of its principles would constitute on balance a significant moral improvement over the status quo. A theory possesses the virtue of moral congruence to the extent that the principles it proposes can be supported from a wide range of moral perspectives, secular and religious. In the next chapter I will argue that what might be called the most basic human rights meet this condition. They are, to use Rawls's phrase, the focus of an overlapping moral consensus of considerable breadth—though in my view the breadth of this consensus is likely to be somewhat wider than Rawls supposes.

By 'progressive conservatism' I mean that the theory should build upon, or at least not squarely contradict, the more morally acceptable principles of the existing international legal system. The most obvious reason for this requirement is that satisfying it will generally contribute to the accessibility of the theory's proposals, assuming that the most powerful participants in the existing system are not likely to support radical and rapid change. But there is another reason: Where possible the theorist should build upon the moral strengths of the existing system, because it would be irresponsible to advocate, unnecessarily, a disregard for whatever progress has already been achieved in the system. Taken together, these theoretical desiderata imply that the theoretical task includes not only criticism of the existing system, but also conservation of its morally progressive elements and construction of new principles where they are needed for progress.

[45] Buchanan, 'Theories of Secession', 31–61.

How ideal is ideal theory?

As I have already noted, the distinction between ideal and nonideal theory is familiar and frequently invoked. However, it is rare to find theorists who provide an explicit account of what exactly is included in ideal theory and what is not.[46] In fact, much theorizing, not only about international law, but also about domestic political institutions as well, is often unclear as to whether ideal or nonideal principles are being proposed.

In an outstanding work on the justification of claims to territory, Avery Kolers makes an observation that underlines the importance of handling the ideal/nonideal distinction carefully. Kolers observes that the plausibility of a moral principle may depend upon the assumption that certain injustices are present in the system of institutions to which it is to be applied.[47] For example, in Chapter 7 of the present volume, in an examination of the conditions for the international legal system itself being morally legitimate, we will encounter the view, endorsed by international legal theorist Benedict Kingsbury, that the principle of the formal equality of all states plays a beneficial role in reducing the risk of predation of stronger states on weaker ones. According to this principle all states—no matter how large or small, weak or powerful—are equal so far as the elements of sovereignty are concerned.

Kolers's point would be that the risk of predation, and hence the plausibility of the principle of the formal equality of states as a means of reducing that risk, may depend upon the assumption that the system contains certain injustices—in particular distributive injustices that result in inequalities of power among states that make predation a serious risk. In a world in which these distributive injustices were eliminated, the principle of the formal equality of states would not be plausible (unless some other reason in favor of it besides the need to prevent predation could be produced). For example, in such a world it might be more just for states with larger populations to have more say in the making of international law, on

[46] Liam Murphy, *Moral Demands in Nonideal Theory* (Oxford University Press, New York, 2000).

[47] Avery Kolers, 'A Theory of Territory', Ph.D. dissertation (University of Arizona, 2000).

the grounds that this would be a more genuinely democratic system. (Why should Lichtenstein have as many votes as India?)

Kingsbury might agree that this is so, replying that he is concerned only with nonideal theory—that he is proposing the principle of the formal equality of states as an element of nonideal theory. But the question then arises: What are the ultimate moral targets, the principles of ideal theory?

The attempt to answer this question forces the theorist to state and defend the most basic principles and values of his theory. In the case at hand, one would have to explain just why it is wrong for stronger states to have more of a say in international law than weak ones, and ultimately this would require articulating the most basic principles of one's ideal theory. On one type of ideal theory, what is ultimately wrong with such an asymmetry of power is that it is injurious to the collectivities that states represent. According to a quite different type of ideal theory, what is wrong is that the asymmetry of power inevitably leads to domination that violates the human rights of individuals who are citizens of weaker states. In the next chapter, I opt for the latter sort of view. With important qualifications, I argue that the most basic principles of an ideal theory of international law are individual human rights principles.

Kolers's observation raises a troubling methodological issue. If the system for which we are providing a moral theory is pervaded by serious injustices, the theorist must be careful to determine whether any particular principle he advocates is defensible only upon the assumption that certain injustices exist (in which case it is to be relegated to nonideal theory) or whether it is a principle whose satisfaction partly constitutes what full justice requires. Failure to make this distinction may result in mistakenly thinking that principles that are only valid for the time being—so long as certain remediable injustices exist—are the ultimate moral targets at which we ought to aim. So, which principles we find plausible as nonideal principles will depend upon what we are assuming about what is likely to change and what is not. Yet whether a particular injustice will persist may depend upon the complex interplay of many factors, and for the foreseeable future our state of knowledge (or rather ignorance) does not allow us to make accurate predictions about whether they will persist. For this reason, ideal theorizing is inescapably speculative—and highly risky—when it goes beyond specifying the most basic principles.

My own view, as I have already suggested, is that for the foreseeable future the principles of ideal theory should be chiefly if not exclusively those that specify the basic human rights of individuals. Following Thomas Scanlon, I understand human rights principles as stating or implying a constraint on institutions: that certain interests are so important for human flourishing that the most basic institutions should be designed so as to protect them.[48]

The point is that although human rights principles set constraints on institutions, they are not themselves institutional principles in the sense of rules that specify the substantive institutional arrangements. Which particular institutional arrangements will satisfy the constraints laid down by these ideal theory principles may vary depending upon a number of contingencies of time, place, and culture.[49]

At present we know little about the range of institutional arrangements that would, under various circumstances, satisfy the constraints laid down by human rights principles (though we do know that some institutional arrangements do not satisfy them, including those that exist today in many states around the world). But if this is so, then it appears that ideal theory at present must be lean. It will consist largely if not exclusively of principles stating what the human rights are, along with justifications for these statements.

I will argue later that there may be one notable exception: We now know enough about human beings and institutions to be fairly confident that what might be called minimal constitutional democracy is generally the most reliable political institutional arrangement for protecting basic human rights. This is not to say, of course, that ideal theory should include the assertion that one specific version of democracy or one kind of constitution is required for all situations.

Apart from the requirement of minimal constitutional democracy, we are presently not in a position to specify with any confidence the substantive institutional arrangements that any system of

---

[48] Thomas Scanlon, 'Human Rights as a Neutral Concern', in Peter Brown and Douglas MacLean (eds.), *Human Rights and U.S. Foreign Policy* (Lexington Books, Lexington, MA, 1979).

[49] Cindy Holder, 'Group Rights and Special Obligations: Towards an Ethics of Group Membership', Ph.D. dissertation (University of Arizona, 2001); and Hessler, 'A Theory of Interpretation for Human Rights'.

international law would have to satisfy in order to achieve full compliance with these most basic principles of ideal theory. Indeed, as I noted earlier, it is not even clear whether a plausible ideal theory will include substantive institutional principles that recognize the existence of what we now call states, much less principles that make states the primary subjects and creators of international law. A proposed ideal theory that goes beyond the basic constraints that human rights principles and the requirement of minimal constitutional democracy provide to include more specific institutional arrangements can only be viewed as a prediction based on information about the workings of institutions that we do not now possess.

Accordingly, my suggestion is that for the time being we should eschew speculation about what constitutes a *comprehensive* set of ideal substantive institutional principles (as distinct from human rights principles understood as constraints on the range of acceptable institutional arrangements) and concentrate on nonideal theory. Because we know so little about the full range of institutional arrangements that would satisfy the principles of ideal theory, we should focus on ascertaining which principles, if implemented, would produce moral improvements in the particular system that now exists. For the most part, those principles will be directed toward promoting better compliance with human rights principles.

This strategy seems reasonable. It provisionally restricts ideal theory to the most basic moral principles, avoiding irresponsibly speculative predictions about ideal institutional design. At the same time, by focusing on (nonideal) principles to remedy the injustices present in the international legal system we actually have, it acknowledges the dominant role of states in that system, and thereby avoids the Vanishing Subject Matter Problem.

The main point of this rather complex methodological discussion can now be summarized briefly. An *ideal* moral theory of international law would include two types of principles: (1) the most basic principles of justice that ought to be satisfied by any system that could be called an international legal order and (2) a set of more concrete principles that specify the institutional arrangements common to all systems of international law that satisfy the constraints laid down by the most basic principles of justice. The content of *nonideal* theory will then vary according to which actual or possible system of international law is being addressed; appropriate substantive institutional principles for dealing with noncompliance with principles of types (1) and (2) will differ, depending upon the particular defects and institutional resources of the system in question. However, because our present knowledge of the full range of institutional possibilities is so meager, there is little to say about the substantive institutional principles that any system of international law would have to satisfy in order to comply fully with (1), the most basic principles of ideal theory. Perhaps all we can say at present is that these institutions must be minimally democratic and that government must be constitutional. Consequently, our efforts should be directed, for the time being, to articulating and defending (1), the most basic principles of ideal theory, and to working out plausible nonideal substantive institutional principles suitable for coping with the defects of the *existing* international legal system.

It will become clear as we proceed that what moral theorizing there has been about international law is often ambiguous about whether the substantive institutional principles it proposes are supposed to be part of ideal theory or nonideal theory. I will try to avoid this confusion in the chapters to follow, though I doubt I will fully succeed.

IX. *An Overview of a Proto-theory*

Limitations of scope

What I offer in this volume falls far short of a comprehensive moral theory of international law. The first and most important limitation is that my focus is entirely on international public law.[50] What I have to say later, especially with regard to international distributive

---

[50] Carter and Trimble speak of the distinction between public and private international law in the past tense, acknowledging that it is becoming harder to draw due to the fact that "the norms of traditional public international law also purport to regulate or affect private conduct." "Public international law primarily governed the activities of governments in relation to other governments. Private international law dealt with the activities of individuals, corporations, and other private entities when they crossed national [i.e., state] borders. A large body of private international law consisted of choice-of-law rules (determining which state's domestic law would apply to transactions between nationals of two states, such as an international sales contract, or to controversies that had some significant connection with more than one state)." Barry Carter and Phillip Trimble, *International Law* (Little, Brown & Company, Boston, 1995), 1–2.

justice, has implications for private law, but for the most part I do not draw them. Second, I do not pretend to provide a principled account of all areas of international public law. Instead, my focus is on what I believe to be the conceptual heart of a moral theory of international law: the relationship between justice, legitimacy, and self-determination. Whether I am correct in assuming that these concepts are primary can only be determined by evaluating the theory that I produce by proceeding on this assumption.

'Proto-theory' might be more accurate, given that I will not in this work attempt to extend my view of the relationship between justice, legitimacy, and self-determination to several important areas of the moral theory of international public law. These lacunae include, but are not limited to: the moral foundations of international criminal law, the rules for how war is to be conducted (*jus in bello*), and the morality (or otherwise) of including the right to restrict immigration among the elements of state sovereignty. In Chapter 4 I will draw some connections between what I have to say about distributive justice and immigration issues. There I will suggest that for the time being liberalized immigration policies may be one of the most important means of moving toward distributive justice. But I will provide nothing like a moral theory of immigration.[51] Moreover, for reasons that will become clear in Chapter 4 (Distributive Justice), I will offer only the broadest principles for responding to urgent issues concerning the distribution of global resources and the protection of the environment.

The theoretical core

In its barest essentials, the conceptual structure of my approach to the moral theory of international law can be stated in the form of four basic theses. (1) Justice ought to be a primary goal of the international legal system, where the main content of justice is supplied by a conception of basic human rights. (2) Legitimacy, both for states (understood as enduring institutional structures) and governments (understood as collections of agents occupying key institutional

---

[51] For what promises to be an extremely valuable contribution to this subject, see Joseph Carens, *Migration, Membership, and Morality: The Ethics of Immigration in Contemporary Liberal Democracy* (forthcoming).

roles) requires a credible effort to satisfy at least a minimal thresh-old standard of protection of basic human rights by means that respect those same rights. (3) Rights of self-determination are con-strained by the claims of legitimacy, and hence ultimately by justice. The right to secede, understood as the unilateral right or noncon-sensual entitlement to seek independent statehood by groups presently within the jurisdiction of a state, is a remedial right only, a right that a group comes to have by virtue of persistent and seri-ous violations of the human rights of its members, or of rights con-ferred on them by intrastate autonomy agreements, or by virtue of violations of the rights of legitimate states (as when one state unjustly annexes another). Hence there is no right to secede from a legitimate state with a legitimate government, unless secession is by mutual agreement or constitutional provision. (4) Groups can have legitimate interests in various forms of self-determination short of secession without having a right to secede, and the international legal order ought to provide active support for a wide range of intrastate self-determination arrangements, both because failure to do so greatly increases the risk that human rights will be violated and for other reasons, including efficiency and the enhancement of participation in democratic governance.

In the chapters to follow I: (1) argue that each of us has a general though limited moral obligation to help ensure that all persons have access to just institutions, (2) develop a substantive account of the core of justice anchored in a conception of basic human rights, (3) use this account of justice to frame a principled view of legitimacy, and then (4) advance a theory of secession and of other, less extreme forms of self-determination that gives proper weight to the claims of legiti-mate states and governments, while serving the primary goal of pro-tecting basic human rights and acknowledging the legitimate claims of groups within the state to forms of self-government.

I also begin the task of integrating the theories of self-determination and legitimacy with an account of the morality of intervention. I use the case of armed humanitarian intervention to explore the problem alluded to earlier: the morality of illegal acts directed toward moral improvement of the system of international law.

PART ONE

Justice

CHAPTER 2

The Commitment to Justice

I. *Introduction*

The strategy

In Chapter 1 I showed why a moral theory of international law is needed, criticized various views that purport to rule out a significant role for moral theorizing about international law, explained what a moral theory of international law should do, set out criteria for the comparative evaluation of rival theories, and argued that beginning with the assumption that the existing international legal order gives a prominent role to states need not result in overly conservative conclusions. This chapter begins the task of laying the foundations for a justice-based theory of international law.

The moral theory of international law whose main elements I develop in subsequent chapters is justice based in two senses: (1) justice, understood chiefly as respect for basic human rights, serves as the fundamental vantage point from which to evaluate the existing international legal system and to formulate proposals for improving it; and (2) a recognition of the moral obligation to help ensure that all persons have access to institutions of justice—understood as institutions that protect their basic human rights—supplies the chief moral reason for trying to develop an international legal system guided by the ideal of justice. In the next chapter, I begin to flesh out the understanding of basic human rights that is the core of the justice-based approach.

In the present chapter I argue that justice should be a primary moral goal of the international legal system. This is a normative statement about the value that *should* shape the construction of the international legal system, *not* a description of the purpose for which the system was created, and *not* a claim about the main function of the system as it now exists or has existed in the past. In making the case that justice should be a primary goal, I first rebut the charge that peace is the only proper goal for the international legal system and argue that the pursuit of justice in and through international law need not be inimical to peace.

Second, I argue that justice is not only a permissible goal for the international legal system—something we are permitted to pursue—but a morally obligatory one. In other words, I argue that the enterprise of trying to construct a just international legal system is morally required. To accomplish this step in the overall argument, I explain and support what I call the Natural Duty of Justice, the principle that each person has a limited moral obligation to help ensure that all persons have access to institutions, including legal institutions, that protect their basic human rights.

Third, I show that taking seriously the idea that justice is a primary, morally obligatory goal of the international legal system requires a particular conception of the state. On this conception, the state is to serve in part as an instrument of justice; it should not be conceived as a discretionary association whose sole function is to serve the mutual benefit of its members. In rejecting the conception of the state as a discretionary association for mutual benefit, I am directly attacking the dominant international relations view that states should support international law only so far as it serves their "national interests." I aim to make it clear that acknowledging that there are human rights is incompatible with the widely held view that foreign policy should be or may be determined solely by the national interest.

II. *Justice as a Primary Moral Goal of International Law*

The role of goals in institutional moral reasoning

Chapter 1 stressed that the moral theory of international law relies substantially on institutional moral reasoning. To understand how institutional reasoning works it is essential to appreciate a simple point: Moral reasoning about how to design new institutions or about the evaluation and improvement of existing institutions requires that we identify the goals the institutions are to serve.

Institutions are human creations that ought to serve human purposes, and they can be made more effective in serving those purposes by changes that human beings can make.

Although institutions usually are not created deliberately, once we undertake to evaluate them morally we come to regard them as if they were artifacts designed to achieve certain goals. To the extent that moral reasoning about institutions is guided by the goals the institutions in question are to serve, institutional reasoning may be called teleological. For example, we evaluate institutions of criminal justice in part by seeing how well they achieve the goal of deterrence.

But to say that a goal of the criminal justice system is deterrence is hardly informative unless we know what sort of behavior we are trying to deter. At least for broadly liberal theories, the goal of protecting individual rights plays a primary role in determining what sort of behavior to try to deter. So emphasizing that institutional reasoning must be teleological in the sense of being concerned with goals is not incompatible with taking rights seriously.

There is a second, quite different way in which regard for individual rights qualifies the assertion that a goal of the criminal justice system is deterrence: Pursuit of the goal of deterrence must be constrained by respect for individual rights. For example, we should not punish an innocent person (thus violating his rights) in order to deter others from violating rights.

Moral reasoning about institutions that takes rights seriously is therefore anti-consequentialist in the sense that it regards the protection of rights as placing constraints on efforts to maximize the achievement of even the most worthy goals. But as we have just seen in the case of moral reasoning about the institution of criminal justice, institutional moral reasoning is nonetheless teleological in the sense of being goal guided, even when the goal is specified in terms of rights and rights serve as constraints on how we pursue the goal. So the statement that institutional moral reasoning is teleological does *not* imply that it is consequentialist in the sense of defining as right whatever maximizes some goal that is specified independently of what is right. Institutional moral reasoning is both teleological and non-consequentialist.

The moral assessment of an existing or proposed institution requires evaluating the rules that partly constitute the institution. These rules prescribe patterns of behavior to be followed by many individuals as they interact over time. To determine whether the institution is in fact promoting the achievement of its goals, it is therefore necessary to consider both the cumulative effects of large numbers of people acting on a particular rule and the interactions of the cumulative effects of compliance with the other rules the institution includes.

For this reason moral reasoning about institutions requires attention to incentives. Certain combinations of rules, each of which may seem appropriate when considered in isolation, may create incentives that thwart institutional goals. At a minimum, rules should not be self-defeating in this way. Rules that provide incentives that are not only consistent with, but actually promote, behavior that contributes to the attainment of institutional goals are preferable to those that do not, other things being equal.

Peace or Justice?

In Chapter 1 I noted that it is a symptom of the undeveloped state of the moral theory of international law that there is disagreement on what the primary goal of the international legal system ought to be. In fact, there is surprisingly little serious discussion of what the goal ought to be, though many writers are confident in asserting or assuming what the goal is. More precisely, many who reflect on the nature of international law, including Daniel Webster, who served as U.S. Secretary of State prior to the Civil War, do not distinguish clearly between statements about what the goal of international law (as it now exists) is and what it ought to be. Webster defines international law as "those principles...which have obtained currency among civilized states and which have for their object the mitigation of the miseries of war."[1]

There are two things to note about this quotation. First, as already suggested, there is no indication of a distinction between what the goal of international law (as it currently exists) is and what the goal ought to be. Second, what Webster takes to be the goal of the system is not peace but the mitigation of the miseries of war, where war is conceived quite narrowly as armed conflict *between states.*

---

[1] John Moore, *A Digest of International Law* (8 vols.) (U.S. Government Printing Office, Washington, DC, 1906), viii. 11.

This belief that the goal of international law is primarily to restrain the damage done by wars between states rather than to prevent war reflects an important fact about the character of international law at the time Webster was writing, namely, that states were conceived of as having the right to go to war for any reason of "state interest" (including territorial aggrandizement). At least since 1945, however, international law does not recognize any such broad right on the part of states. Aggressive war is legally prohibited (though of course there can be disagreement as to what counts as to aggression).

The difference between Daniel Webster's very narrow conception of the goal of international law (the mitigation of the miseries of war between states) and the more ambitious conceptions of the goal that are now current (peace, or peace and justice) shows that it is a mistake to assume that there is no sensible question to be asked about what the moral goal of the system should be, as opposed to what the goal of the system is. The international legal system has changed since Webster's time (in part by restricting states' rights to make war, but also by recognizing legal subjects other than states) and there is reason to believe it is capable of further change.

So even if it were now accurate to say that the goal of the international legal system is peace, not justice, we should still have to determine what the *proper* goal is—what goal (or goals) the system ought to promote. To repeat: By a moral goal of the international system I mean a goal the system ought to promote, not one it does promote or has up to the present been designed to promote.

For most of the twentieth century peace was generally thought to be the only proper goal of international law. This goal is even more limited than it might at first appear, because, as with Webster, what was meant by peace was peace among states.

As we have come to learn in the past two decades, peace among states is compatible with unspeakable violence within states— systematic torture perpetrated by governments against their own citizens, pervasive violence against women, ethnic cleansing of minorities, even genocide. Very recently international law has begun to try to address intrastate violence, but its halting steps, as I noted in Chapter 1, betray deep confusion over principles.

Only with the growing penetration of human rights discourse into international law over the past fifty years has justice come to be considered a proper goal of the system. Even so, the language of some of the most prominent international and regional documents on human rights could be read as presenting justice as being valuable chiefly as a means toward peace, not as a basic goal in its own right.[2] So the assumption upon which my approach to the moral theory of international law proceeds—that justice should be a primary goal of the system—is far from trivial.

It must be defended, and defending it requires a response to two objections. The first is that peace must be a goal of the system but that the goals of peace and justice are in conflict. The second is that the goal of justice is unrealistic, given the nature of the international system.

It is true that justice sometimes requires breaking the peace among states, as in the Second World War when the Allies fought to stop fascist aggression with all its massive violations of human rights. But this does not show that an institution that values peace cannot also have justice as a primary moral goal. Virtually all institutions have more than one goal, and these goals can come into conflict. To recur to an earlier example, the criminal justice system's moral goals include both punishment of the guilty (either for deterrence or retribution or both) and procedures designed to reduce the risk of convicting the innocent; yet conscientious adherence to the requirements of procedural justice can result in guilty parties going free, as when illegally obtained evidence is thrown out of court. No one would take the fact that the goals of deterrence and procedural justice can conflict as a reason for abandoning the pursuit of procedural justice.

To say that procedural justice is a goal of the criminal justice system might at first sound odd, given that we often think of procedural justice, or the rights that comprise it, as being a constraint on the pursuit of goals rather than a goal. However, that is compatible with saying that procedural justice is a goal in the sense intended here: It is an ideal state of affairs, a moral target that we aim at, and which we can strive to continue to approach more closely, even if it is not possible ever to achieve it fully or perfectly. Not only procedural

---

[2] See e.g., Conference for Security and Co-operation in Europe, 'Document of the Copenhagen Meeting of the Conference on the Human Dimension of the Conference for Security and Co-operation in Europe', *International Legal Materials* 29 (1990), 1306.

justice, but justice in all its forms can serve as goals for institutional evaluation and design in this sense.

Furthermore, it is wrong to assume that justice and peace are somehow *essentially* in conflict. On the contrary, justice largely subsumes peace. Justice requires the prohibition of wars of aggression (understood as morally unjustifiable attacks as opposed to justified wars of self-defense or of humanitarian intervention) because wars of aggression inherently violate human rights. To that extent the pursuit of justice is the pursuit of peace.

And once we look beyond the goal of peace among states to peace that includes relations within states as well, it is clear that protecting some of the most important human rights *is* securing peace. To take only the more obvious examples, security of the person and respect for the right not to be tortured partly constitute peace. A country in which the government routinely tortures or kills dissidents, or in which minorities are violently persecuted, is not a peaceful place. More generally, human rights are secure only under conditions of peace.

Recent liberal theorists of human rights, reviving a thesis advanced by Kant over 200 years ago in his essay "Perpetual Peace," stress another compatibility between peace and justice. According to the Democratic Peace Hypothesis, developed democracies tend not go to war with one another. A more controversial thesis, but one which enjoys considerable empirical support, might be called the Democratic Internal Peace Hypothesis: developed democracies—those which facilitate political participation by all, including minorities, and which effectively constrain majority rule by entrenched human rights—as a general rule are not plagued by large-scale internal violence (government terror or ethnic violence). If either of these theses is correct, even as a broad generalization, and if democracy is a requirement of justice, then again it is mistaken to assume that peace and justice are inherently incompatible goals.

Nevertheless, it would be obtuse to deny that conflicts between the pursuit of justice and the pursuit of peace can occur. Indeed we should expect that they will occur, at least during the transition from our very unjust world to a more just one. For instance, in order to achieve the goal of democracy, whether democracy is viewed as a requirement of justice itself or merely as instrumentally valuable for protecting human rights, it may be necessary to use military force to oust a junta that has overthrown a democratic government. Similarly, serious attempts to hold China to the observance of human rights norms might result in devastating armed conflict.

To put this last point in perspective, it is important to reemphasize that the fact that the pursuits of peace and justice can conflict does not show that they cannot both be appropriate goals of an institution, anymore than the fact there can be conflicts between punishing the guilty and procedural justice shows that the latter are inconsistent goals for a criminal justice system. What examples of conflicts between pursuing peace and pursuing justice show is not that justice cannot be a primary goal of a system that takes the value of peace seriously, but only that clashes between these goals can be expected to occur during the transition toward justice. This hardly detracts from the plausibility of the assertion that justice is a chief moral goal of international law. After all, there may be almost no cases in which the pursuit of a moral good consisting of the attainment of more than one goal, or of a moral ideal composed of more than one value, is immune to this sort of conflict.

The most obvious reply to the inconsistency objection, properly understood as a point about the potential for conflict during the transition from very unjust to more just conditions, is that in general fidelity to justice promotes peace better than an absolute commitment to avoiding conflict in every instance. This familiar defense of adherence to the requirements of justice is greatly strengthened when combined with a sophisticated account of what the commitment to justice as a primary goal of the international legal system amounts to.

In Part Two I will argue for a justice-based, principled way of determining when new political entities ought to be recognized as having the rights of independent, legitimate states. That discussion will make it clear that adherence to a rule for state recognition that promotes justice need not pose an unacceptable threat to peace, but can instead promote it. The more general point is that taking justice to be a primary moral goal of international law does not commit one to a fanatical moral absolutism that takes all too literally the dictum: "Let there be justice, though the world perish."

In other words, a sincere commitment to justice as a primary goal of the system does not require allowing considerations of justice to trump all other moral considerations in every instance. For one thing, not all injustices are equally serious. In some cases it may be morally permissible to tolerate a relatively minor injustice or forgo a reform that would further improve a situation that is already commendable from the standpoint of justice, in order to reap some significant gain, not just with respect to some other moral value, but also in efficiency. My view is only that the core of justice, protection of basic human rights, should be a primary goal of the international legal system. This is compatible with the realization that justice is not all that matters.

The position I am advocating also looks less extreme once we distinguish clearly between the goal of an institution and the institutional rules that are designed to serve that goal. Making a particular exception in an extreme case to a rule that generally promotes a goal is fully compatible with a sincere commitment to the goal.

Finally, it is worth noting that the assumption that peace and justice are not compatible goals achieves what little credibility it enjoys by reducing peace to peace among states. But if what we should be fundamentally concerned about is preventing violations of human rights, then there is no reason to give an absolute priority to peace among states. Conflict between states sometimes may be an acceptable price to pay to prevent massive violence within a state. A moral philosophy of international law that takes basic human rights as fundamental—rather than the sovereignty of states—thereby reduces the tension between justice and peace by supporting peace within states through observance of human rights norms.

A different, more serious objection is not that justice and peace are incompatible, but that justice is not a realistic goal, given the nature of international relations. However, this claim is just a special application to justice of the more general Realist assertion that there is no room for morality in international relations.

In Chapter 1 I argued that the empirical generalizations about international relations that constitute the core of Realism are sufficiently weak to make the project of developing a moral theory of international law worthwhile. My reflections in the present chapter on the ways in which justice subsumes peace casts further doubt on the assumption that we must choose between peace and justice as goals for the system.

An understanding of the evolution of domestic legal systems makes the assumption that peace is not a feasible moral goal for international law still more problematic. In the case of domestic legal systems, there is evidence of progress toward justice over the centuries, especially with regard to increasingly effective due process protections and the transition from systems of civil and criminal liability in which strict liability was ubiquitous to systems in which liability largely depends upon voluntariness, intent, and whether the actor exercised due care.

In fact it can be argued that the early systems of liability that gave short shrift to these determinants of responsibility were more directed toward peace than justice. Yet even if this is true, the point is that these primitive legal systems had the capacity to change, and that as they made progress in securing peace, it became more reasonable to assert that justice also should be a moral goal of the system, and to expect more justice. So even if it is true of a legal system that in its early development peace is to a large extent the only feasible goal, this can change.

Just as Locke argued against Hobbes that we can reasonably expect the domestic legal system to do more than merely keep the peace—that the protection of individual rights should be required as well—so we can reasonably expect international legal institutions to do more than secure peace among states. At least from the standpoint of a broadly liberal political philosophy, this is not a controversial assumption. From Locke onward, liberal political philosophers have provided a strong case for not settling, in the domestic case, for political institutions that only achieve peace; they have insisted on justice as well.

This is not to say that it is reasonable to expect perfect justice or to expect great progress toward justice to occur soon, whether in a domestic or an international legal system. Nor is it to imply that the existing international legal system is as well suited or will ever be as well suited for the pursuit of justice as the more developed domestic systems. Making justice a primary goal of the international legal system implies none of these immoderate expectations.

The point, rather, is that those who reject justice as a feasible goal for the international legal system bear a heavy burden of argument. They must show why it is unreasonable to expect from international institutions even an approximation of what we expect from domestic political institutions. Given the weakness of the empirical core of Realism, this burden of argument has not been borne.

Justice as a morally imperative primary goal

So far I have argued that it is reasonable to make justice a primary moral goal of the international legal system—that a proper appreciation of the value of peace does not preclude us from attempting to make the international legal order an instrument for and an embodiment of justice. Now I want to advance a stronger claim: doing so is morally obligatory.

There are two arguments for this stronger claim, corresponding to two fundamentally different conceptions of the nature of justice. The first conception founds obligations of justice in our *cooperative interactions with others*; the second bases them directly in the *nature of persons*, regardless of whether we interact with them or not. In the end I will suggest that the latter approach is more promising, because of certain difficulties with the interactionist approach. But since interactionist views of global justice perhaps comprise the most developed approach to global distributive justice currently available, I will consider them in some detail as well.

The global basic structure argument

The first, interactionist argument relies on the premise that there is a global basic structure—a worldwide cooperative scheme consisting of a complex pattern of institutions, including the international legal system, whose workings have profound, pervasive, and lifelong effects on individuals and groups. The global basic structure contains many elements, among which are a widely recognized system of private property rights (including intellectual property rights), the law of the sea, financial and monetary regimes, basic trade regimes, and the systematic patterns of interaction among states under various aspects of public international law. The second premise is that because the workings of the global basic structure have such profound and enduring effects on individuals and groups—and because these effects are for the most part neither chosen nor consented to by those affected—the global basic structure is subject to assessment from the standpoint of justice. The intuitive idea behind the second premise is that justice includes the fairness of distributions of benefits and burdens, at least so far as these are both subject to human control and not chosen or consented to by the individuals or groups who receive them.

The third premise is that if an institution is subject to assessment from the standpoint of justice then justice ought to be a goal of the institution, at least when the institution has important effects on basic human interests.[3] If we grant one further premise, that when justice ought to be a goal of an institution, it ought to be a *primary* dimension of the moral assessment of that institution, we get the desired conclusion that justice ought to be a primary goal of the international legal system. Given the central role of justice in the moral assessment of basic social institutions, this last premise also seems unproblematic.

This first argument for the conclusion that justice is a morally obligatory goal of international law focuses on the global basic structure as a set of institutions, or a super-institution, within which individuals and groups in different states interact cooperatively. It is this interaction, which takes the form of participation in the global basic structure, that makes the justice of the basic structure a matter of moral concern for all of us, regardless of which state we happen to live in. The argument itself does not state that we can have obligations of justice *only* toward those with whom we interact cooperatively or, more specifically, with those with whom we are included within the institutional framework of cooperation, but those who rely exclusively on it apparently think that the fact of cooperative interaction is morally crucial.

This argument concerning the global basic structure parallels one offered by Rawls regarding the domestic basic structure. In *A Theory of Justice*, which focuses on domestic institutions, Rawls rightly emphasized that the basic structure of the cooperative scheme of a particular state has profound and enduring, nonconsensual and unchosen effects on the prospects of individuals and groups interacting within it, and that this makes the domestic basic structure a subject of judgments of justice. But if the domestic basic structure is a subject of justice, and the institutions that comprise it can be made more just, then justice must be included among the institutional goals because, as Rawls says, justice is the first virtue of

---

[3] This qualification is important. There are some institutions that are subject to evaluation from the standpoint of justice for which justice might not be a goal. This is true of the institution of baseball, for example. This point is due to David Luban.

social institutions. In other words, when the concept of justice applies to basic institutions—those which profoundly affect persons' most fundamental human interests—justice is a morally imperative institutional goal, so long as those institutions have not yet achieved justice, but have the potential to be made more just. Substituting 'global basic structure' for '(domestic) basic structure' in Rawls's argument appears to make no difference to the soundness of the argument.

As I have already suggested, a distinction can be drawn between theories of distributive justice that ground obligations in the fact of interaction and those that do not. According to the interactionist view, relations of justice only obtain among those who are engaged in cooperation with one another. The global basic structure argument stated above provides those who subscribe to the interactionist conception of justice with a way of arguing that justice ought to be a primary goal of the international legal system.

Thomas Pogge offers a special version of the interactionist approach, one that relies on the general moral obligation not to harm other persons.[4] According to Pogge, we ought to work to make the global basic structure more just because by participating in an unjust global basic structure we inflict harms on persons. Assuming that the international legal system is an important element of the global basic structure, it follows that we ought to make justice a goal of international law. And assuming that justice is fundamental to the assessment of institutions that affect the basic interests of persons encompassed by them, we ought to make justice a primary goal of international law.

Pogge's insight is invaluable. He reminds us that the global basic structure is a human creation and that by simply accepting it as a fact of life we are supporting massive injustices.

The Natural Duty of Justice argument

The second argument for the conclusion that justice is a morally obligatory goal of the international legal system does not rely on an interactionist conception of justice. It does not assume that

---

[4] Thomas Pogge, *Realizing Rawls* (Cornell University Press, Ithaca, NY, 1989), and Pogge, 'An Egalitarian Law of Peoples'.

obligations of justice obtain only among those who interact cooperatively and it therefore does not need to assume that there is a global basic structure within which individuals around the globe interact.

Instead, this second type of argument relies on the premise that there is a Natural Duty of Justice: that even if there were no global basic structure of cooperation or any form of interaction whatsoever among individuals across borders, we would still have a limited obligation to help create structures that provide all persons with access to just institutions. (The modifier 'Natural' signals that this obligation attaches to us as persons, independently of any promises we make, undertakings we happen to engage in, or institutions in which we are implicated). If we add to the assertion that there is such a Natural Duty of Justice the premise that international law can play an important role in ensuring that all persons have access to just institutions, we get the conclusion that justice is a morally obligatory goal of international law.

The Natural Duty of Justice is the limited moral obligation to contribute to ensuring that all persons have access to just institutions, where this means primarily institutions that protect basic human rights. The Natural Duty of Justice assumes that securing justice for all persons requires institutions, but this is not an unreasonable assumption.

However, the Natural Duty does not assume an exclusively institutional view about justice of the sort that Liam Murphy has effectively criticized.[5] This is the view, which Murphy attributes to Rawls, that the most basic principles of justice apply only to institutions or to persons in their institutional roles.[6] According to this hyper-institutionalist conception of justice, there are no basic principles of justice that apply directly to the actions of individuals as such. All principles of justice that apply to individual actions are derived from principles of justice that apply directly to institutions.

Murphy is right to reject the hyper-institutionalist thesis. There are principles of justice that apply directly to individuals. Included among them are the Natural Duty of Justice itself which, though not a principle specifying how institutions are to be if they are to be just, directs individuals to contribute to the development of just

---

[5] Murphy, 'Institutions and the Demands of Justice'.   [6] Ibid.

institutions where this is needed to ensure that all persons have access to institutions that protect their basic human rights. Another example of a basic principle of justice that applies directly to individuals is the principle that each person ought to be treated with respect—which is in fact the more basic moral principle upon which the Natural Duty of Justice is grounded.

It would be absurd to say that in every instance what it is to treat another person with respect is or even ought to be determined by institutional principles. Whether or not the hyper-institutionalist view is rightly attributed to Rawls, as Murphy assumes, it ought to be rejected.

As I have just suggested, the Natural Duty of Justice is not a rock-bottom, basic moral principle, though it is close to it. It rests on three premises, one factual, the other two moral. The factual premise is that ensuring that all persons are treated justly requires just institutions (including legal institutions). The first moral premise is that all persons are entitled to equal respect and concern—or, as Kant would say, that each is to be treated as an end. The second moral premise is that treating persons with equal concern and respect requires helping to ensure that they are treated justly, where this primarily means helping to make sure that their basic human rights are not violated (not merely refraining from violating them ourselves). Call the first moral premise the Moral Equality Principle (or the Equal Moral Consideration or Equal Regard Principle).

Together the factual and moral premises imply that each of us has a limited moral obligation to help to ensure that all persons have access to institutions that protect their basic rights. I call this latter principle the Natural Duty of Justice, but want to emphasize that it is more robust in its demands on us than the principle Rawls uses this label to denote. Rawls's principle only requires that one support *just* institutions that (already) *apply to one*.

Taking the Moral Equality Principle seriously commits us to the Natural Duty of Justice, because a proper understanding of the Moral Equality Principle implies that to show proper regard for persons we must help ensure that their basic rights are protected. And this in turn requires us to embrace a cosmopolitan view of international law, rejecting both the idea that states are moral persons and the position that states are merely institutional resources for their own peoples. As Brian Barry puts it: "At the heart of moral

cosmopolitanism is the idea that human beings are in some fundamental sense equal."[7]

The Natural Duty of Justice as I understand it says that equal
consideration for persons requires helping to ensure that they have
access to institutions that protect their basic human rights. This will
sometimes require creating new institutions and will often require
reforming existing institutions.

The factual premise is unproblematic. No one could reasonably
doubt that just institutions, including legal institutions, play a necessary role in ensuring that persons are treated justly in the domestic
sphere. Similarly, for reasons that will become clearer as we explore
the idea of a global basic structure in Chapter 4 on distributive
justice and the legitimacy of the international legal system in
Chapter 7, just international institutions, including legal institutions,
are also necessary. International institutions, including international
legal regimes designed to protect human rights, already make a significant contribution to ensuring that persons are treated justly. In
some cases these contributions would not and probably could not be
achieved in any other way.

In my judgment, the Moral Equality Principle itself is fundamental to any conception of morality worth seriously thinking
about. Notice that it not only requires that in some basic sense we
treat all persons equally (which is compatible with treating them all
badly), but also that we treat them well, that we show a high regard
for their basic interests, an equally high regard.

Because I have no intention of systematically engaging those who
are skeptical about morality altogether or about the fundamental
moral equality of persons in this work, I will make no effort to
argue for the Moral Equality Principle. However, I will provide
what I believe are sufficient considerations in support of the second
moral premise, the assertion that a proper respect for persons and
concern for their well-being require helping to ensure that their
basic human rights are protected (and hence that they have access to
just institutions, on the reasonable assumption that just institutions
are required if people are to be treated justly).

---

[7] Brian Barry, 'International Society from a Cosmopolitan Perspective', in
David Maple and Terry Nardin (eds.), *International Society: Diverse Ethical
Perspectives* (Princeton University Press, Princeton, 1998), 146.

Consider first the implausibility, if not the outright incoherence, of acknowledging the Moral Equality Principle, that we ought to accord all persons equal concern and respect, while at the same time denying that we are obligated to bear any significant costs to help ensure that their basic human rights are protected. This combination of views would be plausible only if a proper equal respect and concern for persons required only that we do not ourselves violate their human rights, leaving us entirely free to refrain from helping to prevent others from violating those rights, even when we could do so without significant cost to ourselves.

Suppose, for example, that I do nothing to violate your human rights, stating that I do so out of equal concern and respect for you, out of a proper recognition of the fact that you are a person. But suppose also that someone else is intent on violating your most basic human rights and I can help prevent you from being treated unjustly, without incurring serious costs to myself—all I need do is to help support a police and court system that will prevent you from being murdered by people who hate you because of the color of your skin or from being persecuted because of your religious beliefs. If I refuse to make such efforts to prevent you from having your most basic human rights violated, can I reasonably expect you or anyone else to believe me when I say that I respect all persons and am concerned about their well-being?

Only a laughably anemic conception of what it is to recognize the moral importance of persons—an absurdly attenuated view about what it is to respect persons and to be concerned about their well-being—would count my merely refraining from violating other persons' rights as sufficient. Of course it is another matter as to whether or under what conditions I ought to undergo *sacrifices* to help ensure that other persons' basic human rights are protected. But the Natural Duty does not generally require sacrifices.

Notice this feature of the foregoing hypothetical example: Nothing was said about my relationship to you. The intuition that I ought to do something to help ensure that your basic human rights are protected did not depend upon any assumption that you and I are interacting cooperatively, much less that we are citizens of the same state. It depended only on a proper recognition of what I owe you as a person. The fact that there is something obvious I can do to help ensure that your basic rights are protected may depend upon your being within the jurisdiction of law enforcement institutions that I can work to improve, but that is not what drives the intuition.

The fundamental point can be put in another way, by making more explicit the connection between equal concern and respect for persons, human rights, and basic human interests. One of the most important ways we show equal concern and respect for persons is by acknowledging that there are human rights. Assertions of human rights signal that certain basic human interests are of such profound moral importance that they merit extraordinarily strong protections. If, for example, there is a human right against religious discrimination, the implication is that the interest in being free to practice one's religion without fear of oppression or penalty is so important that even the good of society as a whole is generally not sufficient reason to justify discrimination. In other words, human rights principles specify fundamental moral constraints on actions, policies, and institutional arrangements; they are not merely assertions of desirable or worthy goals.

But surely if these interests are so extraordinarily important that the corresponding rights should not be violated even when violating them would promote overall social utility, then recognizing their importance requires not only refraining from violating the corresponding rights, but also being willing to bear some significant costs to ensure that these rights are not violated by others. How could it be the case that a particular interest is of such profound moral importance that we should not violate the corresponding right even to achieve a significant benefit for many people and yet also be true that we have no significant obligation to help ensure that all persons have access to institutions that protect this interest? A regard for the moral equality of persons sufficiently robust to ground the assertion that there are human rights also implies that we ought to bear significant costs to ensure that all persons' rights are protected.

The moral priority of the interests that respect for basic human rights promotes is also reflected in the fact that these rights carry obligations that are so important that they are not to be violated even for the sake of one's own happiness or even one's survival. For example, it is morally impermissible for me to kill you, even if my happiness or even my continued existence depends upon my doing so—so much is implied by the acknowledgment that you have human rights, including the right not to be unjustly killed. Those who agree that we are obligated not to violate the basic human rights of others (but deny that we are obligated to help ensure that they are not violated by others) would presumably admit this. But if the interests that ground basic human rights are of such great moral importance that they underwrite obligations that may not be breeched even when doing so would be of great personal advantage or would be necessary for one's own survival, then how could it be that a proper regard for these interests requires only that we not violate the corresponding human rights, but are not required to bear any significant costs to ensure that they are not violated by others? My conclusion, then, is that to explain the binding force of so-called negative duties not to violate basic human rights, one must assert the extraordinary moral importance of protecting certain basic interests shared by all persons, but that one cannot consistently do this without acknowledging that human rights ought to be protected, not merely that we should ourselves refrain from violating them.

This conclusion, that embracing the Moral Equality Principle requires helping to ensure that all persons do not suffer violations of their human rights, is consistent with the view, held by some moral theorists, that so-called negative duties (duties not to kill, harm, etc.) are "stricter" or weightier than so-called positive duties. However, it is one thing to say that negative duties (sometimes) have some sort of priority over positive ones, but quite another that we have no positive duties regarding persons. My point is that a proper understanding of the Moral Equality Principle implies that there are positive duties, not just negative ones.

The intuitive implausibility of simultaneously affirming that we ought not to violate persons' rights and that we have no significant obligation, not even a limited one, to do what is necessary to help ensure that their rights are not violated, can be more fully appreciated by focusing on the *ground* of our obligation not to violate persons' rights. According to what might be called the modern, secular conception of human rights, the duties (not to persecute, torture, etc.) that are entailed by human rights are not simply duties *regarding* persons (constraints on how we may act toward them); they are *owed to* persons. In other words, the ground of the obligation lies in the nature of persons. In contrast, what might be called a religious conception of human rights holds that the ground of the obligation to act toward persons in certain ways lies in the will of God, in the fact that God commands us to behave thus.

Now if the only ground for the obligations entailed by human rights were the will of God (or something else other than the nature of persons, such as the commands of the sovereign), then there would be no incoherence in simultaneously affirming that we ought not to violate persons' rights and affirming that we have no obligation to help ensure that their rights are not violated. (God might will only that individuals refrain from violating persons' rights without willing that individuals interfere with each other's violating person's rights, for all we know.) But given the modern, secular conception of human rights—and the Moral Equality Principle itself—it is hard to see how a fundamental obligation to refrain from violating persons' human rights can cohere with the absence of an obligation to bear some costs in order to help ensure that persons' rights are not violated.

To put the same point in a slightly different way: If the obligation to show respect and concern for all persons is grounded in the nature of persons, it seems arbitrary to limit the fulfillment of this obligation to refraining from violating person's rights. If I stand idly by when I could cooperate with others to provide police protection that will prevent people with your skin color from being murdered or assaulted by racists, or if I refuse to cooperate to ensure that you are not prevented from getting a basic education because you are a woman when I could do so without excessive cost to myself, I cannot plausibly say that I believe respect for persons and concern for their well-being to be a fundamental moral principle grounded in the nature of persons.

There are of course sound reasons for thinking that the Natural Duty of Justice, the duty to help ensure that all persons have access to institutions that will protect their human rights, is a limited obligation. Similarly, there are sound reasons for thinking that other so-called positive obligations, as well as many if not all so-called negative obligations, are limited in the sense of admitting exceptions. In particular, the Natural Duty of Justice is presumably most plausibly construed, as are the duties of beneficence and of rescue, as including an implicit proviso that the cost of acting on it is not "excessive." This is not to say that there is no such duty, only that it is a limited duty.

As individuals we can do little to help ensure that all persons live under institutions that protect their human rights. And if we attempt to act independently the costs to us are likely to be exorbitant. Collective action is required, and institutions are needed if collective action is to be properly coordinated and, just as important, if the costs of contribution are to be appropriately limited and fairly distributed among individuals and groups. That is why conscientiously acting on the Natural Duty of Justice means supporting institutional efforts to secure justice for all.[8]

At present and for the foreseeable future this requires, among other things, efforts to direct the existing resources of the international legal system toward the goal of justice. So, if the Natural Duty of Justice is a genuine moral requirement, as I have argued that it is, then justice is a morally obligatory goal of international law, not a merely optional one.

The interactionist argument and the Natural Duty of Justice both support the conclusion that justice is a primary, obligatory goal of international law. In that sense, I need not choose between them to

---

[8] Here I will only acknowledge, but not try to answer, a difficult and fundamental question: How is the extent of one's obligation affected by the failure of others to join one in acting collectively to try to ensure that all persons have access to institutions that protect their basic rights? I would venture this much, however: The failure of others to cooperate for the sake of justice does not *void* one's own obligations (unless that failure either increases the costs of one's acting on the obligation to the point where they are excessive, or renders one's efforts futile). In addition, I am inclined to say that when others default on their fair share of the burden of discharging the obligation, the extent of one's own obligation generally does not greatly exceed what it would be under a fair allocation of responsibilities in an appropriate collective effort. See Murphy, *Moral Demands in Nonideal Theory*, 75. However, I am also inclined to say that there may be exceptions to this generalization, when two conditions are satisfied: (1) one's fair share in an appropriate collective scheme involves very low costs to oneself (because the total costs would be distributed among many people), and (2) acting alone one could prevent a great injustice at a cost that exceeds what one's fair share would be in the collective scheme, but which is still in some intuitive sense clearly not "excessive"— roughly, does not involve a serious setback to one's more important interests. Of course, this line of thought falters if there is no way to determine what is an "excessive" cost except by saying that it is one that exceeds what one's fair share would be in an appropriate collective scheme.

I am inclined to say that an excessive burden cannot be reduced to an unfair one, that there is a notion of excessive costs that is not simply costs beyond what the costs of one's fair share would be. In other words, it seems to me that even with respect to a collective enterprise that achieves a perfectly fair distribution of costs among all, we can still ask whether the cost that each is bearing is excessive—that there are limits to what we owe others, and that therefore considerations of fairness among the contributors are not the only limits on our obligations. However, I know of no way of giving a principled account of what counts as excessive costs (apart from considerations of fair distribution of responsibility), even though I think there are clear cases of excessive costs and clear cases of costs that are not excessive.

launch the project of developing a moral theory of international law. There is an important difference, nevertheless. The interactionist view assumes that global cooperation already exists—and that this cooperation is already sufficiently robust to ground comprehensive principles of justice for the international legal order.

The most prominent version of the interactionist view holds that this cooperation takes place within a global basic structure of institutions and looks to international legal reform to help ensure that the global basic structure is made more just. The argument based on the Natural Duty of Justice, in contrast, implies that even if there were no global basic structure, nor any form of global cooperation, nor any system of international law, we ought to develop an international legal system to ensure that all persons have access to just institutions.

Because my main concern is to support their shared conclusion that justice ought to be a primary goal of international law, I will not discuss in detail the comparative merits of the interactionist and Natural Duty of Justice views. However, I will say that in my opinion the interactionist view has serious deficiencies. The chief difficulty with the interactionist view is this: Unless we assume the Moral Equality Principle it is hard to see how the mere fact of cooperation with others, whether within a basic structure or not, is sufficient to ground any obligation to treat them justly. But if we assume the Moral Equality Principle, then we seem to be committed as well to the Natural Duty of Justice Principle, and this means that we have obligations to others whether we interact with them or not.

In addition, Pogge's "Do No Harm" version of the interactionist view is subject to problems of its own. Pogge apparently thinks that his view is preferable to a Natural Duty of Justice view because he

Although the problem of specifying what counts as excessive costs is a serious theoretical problem and *sometimes* a practical one as well, I do not believe that the lack of a solution to it undercuts the practicality of the Natural Duty of Justice. At least for the world's most fortunate people, living in the most powerful states with the greatest resources, there is much more they can do to promote the protection of human rights before it becomes reasonable to worry that they may be bearing excessive costs. They can, to take only one example, try to influence their own states not to grant recognition, and all the privileges this entails, to governments that persist in massive violations of the most basic human rights. To take another example, I think that by spending 0.15% of GDP, the citizens of the United States are not bearing excessive cost in the provision of foreign aid. For a thoughtful exploration of the issue of how the burdens of meeting obligations ought to be distributed, see David Miller, 'Distributing Responsibilities', *Journal of Political Philosophy* 9/4 (2001), 453–71.

thinks that negative duties, or at least the duty not to harm, are more morally obvious than positive duties, including the duty to help ensure that all have access to just institutions.

However, Pogge's reliance on the negative duty not to harm is not as much of an advantage as might first appear. First, it can be argued that the assumption that negative duties are somehow stronger or clearer than positive ones is mistaken, and that the mistake rests in part on the failure to understand that fulfilling negative duties often requires positive actions. For example, the obligation to avoid convicting innocent people requires devoting substantial resources to ensuring that the police and the courts do not discriminate against racial or ethnic minorities.

Second, and more important, due to the great complexity of the global basic structure, the causal connections between one individual's participation in the global basic structure and the harm that other individuals suffer is often so indirect and indeed so speculative that the attribution of individual responsibility for harm, and hence the duty to refrain from doing harm through participation in the basic structure is correspondingly attenuated. In some cases, it will be plausible to attribute causation of harm to persons in positions of power in the global basic structure, such as leaders of the most powerful states or of global corporations or financial institutions such as the World Bank. But it will be much more difficult to argue that ordinary persons cause harm to others through their participation in the global basic structure. In addition, to the extent that the existing global basic structure is "the only game in town" it may be misleading to say that the participation of ordinary people in it is voluntary; yet it would seem that voluntariness is a necessary condition for responsibility.

This point about voluntariness has another troubling implication for Pogge's view: from the standpoint of many people interacting within it, it is inaccurate to characterize the existing global basic structure as a *cooperative* scheme, if this implies that participation is significantly voluntary or at least is assumed by the participants to be mutually beneficial. But if duties of justice apply only among participants in a cooperative scheme, then the fact that there is a global basic structure is not sufficient to ground principles of international justice.[9]

---

[9] This formulation of the point is due to David Luban.

A final difficulty with Pogge's interactionist view is worth noting. In any comprehensive cooperative scheme, no matter how just, some individuals will be harmed. For example, simply due to bad luck or to poor judgment on my part or to the fluctuations of the commodities market due to changes in the weather, I may suffer a setback to my economic interests and in that sense be harmed. Or, I may lose my job to a better-qualified person, and thereby suffer harm. But not all harms are injustices (wrongs, that is, violations of rights). Therefore, Pogge's attempt to base international distributive justice on the obligation not to cause harm is incomplete, unless an account is provided that enables us to distinguish between just and unjust harms. However, to do this one needs a theory of justice, including an account of what people are entitled to as a matter of just distribution. The question then arises: If an account of distributive justice is available, why not appeal directly to it rather than to the rather problematic notion of causing harms through participation in the global basic structure?[10]

Because of these difficulties with interactionist views, and for other reasons that will emerge in the next section, I am inclined to conclude that a moral theory of international law should rely chiefly on the Natural Duty of Justice view to explain why we ought to be committed to justice as a moral goal of the international legal system. Nevertheless, in Chapter 4 I do avail myself of one premise of the interactionist view, arguing that there is a global basic structure and that because there is it is necessary to develop international institutions to regulate its distributive effects. It is important to understand that even a view of justice that does not assume that interaction is necessary for us to have obligations of justice to others can nonetheless appreciate the moral significance of the fact that there is a global basic structure—whether it qualifies as a cooperative scheme or not—and that it has profound effects on individuals and groups. Even though we have obligations of justice toward all other persons whether we interact with them or not, doing justice toward them requires that the global basic structure, if there is one, be regulated by principles of justice, because the global basic structure has important effects on persons' well-being and freedom.

---

[10] I thank David Golove for clarifying this objection.

My main concern at this juncture is to avoid the assumption that we *only* have duties of justice toward those with whom we are interacting cooperatively. Elsewhere I have argued that this assumption is based ultimately on a view I call Justice as Self-Interested Reciprocity, according to which obligations of justice only obtain among those who are potential net contributors to social cooperation with one another.[11] Without rehearsing my objections against that conception of justice, let me simply say that its implication is that there is no such thing as human rights, whether these be negative or positive rights. Human rights are rights persons have simply by virtue of their being persons, independently of what might be called their strategic attributes, that is, whether they can be net contributors to our well-being (or can detract from it by harming us).

The crucial distinction is between (1) holding, as the proponent of Justice as Self-Interested Reciprocity does, that we *only* have obligations of justice to those who are or can be net contributors with us in a cooperative scheme and (2) holding that even if we do have some obligations of justice to persons with whom we are not interacting, the fact of interaction grounds important, and relatively uncontroversial obligations of justice. My surmise is that Pogge does not embrace (1), but rather (2). Consequently, he and I both can appeal to the fact that there is interaction within a global basic structure to ground obligations of justice that go beyond borders. My only disagreement with him is that I am not convinced that the best argumentative strategy is to appeal to a duty not to harm (through "supporting" an unjust global basic structure) rather than to rely on the Natural Duty of Justice while also appealing to the need to regulate the global basic structure for the sake of justice.

Nevertheless, I wish to emphasize that much of what I say in the remainder of this volume does *not* depend upon the argument that there is a Natural Duty of Justice. My main concern is to develop some of the main outlines of a moral theory of international law that takes justice—understood as respect for basic human rights—seriously. All that is required is the assumption that there are basic human rights; whether or not they are ultimately grounded in an interactionist view of justice or the Natural Duty of Justice is of

[11] Allen Buchanan, 'Justice as Reciprocity Versus Subject-Centered Justice', *Philosophy and Public Affairs* 19 (1990), 227–52.

secondary importance. In the next chapter I show that there are a number of justificatory routes toward the conclusion that there are basic human rights.

III. *Two Conceptions of the State and its Relations with Those beyond its Borders*

The discretionary association view of the state

I have argued that a proper appreciation of the moral equality of persons grounds a limited obligation to help ensure that all persons have access to just institutions, understood as those that protect their basic human rights. Fulfilling this obligation, as I noted earlier, requires collective action, and collective action can in turn help ensure that helping to see that all persons have access to just institutions does not entail excessive costs for individuals, and that costs are distributed fairly.

In a world in which states are still the primary subjects and actors in international law, state action will often be the most effective means for helping to ensure that all persons have access to just institutions. From this it would seem to follow that to a significant degree individuals should fulfill the Natural Duty of Justice through the agency of their governments, if they are able to do so.

At this point in the argument, however, a complication arises. Given a familiar conception of the state whose pedigree can be traced to Locke and other exponents of the venerable social contract doctrine, it is illegitimate for governments to act so as to help protect the human rights of persons other than their own citizens, unless doing so is for the benefit of the latter. On this conception of the state, there is no room for a genuine moral commitment to helping ensure that persons in other states have access to just institutions.

According to what I shall for convenience call the Lockean view, the state is nothing more than a discretionary association for the mutual advantage of its citizens.[12] The government is simply the agent of the associated individuals, an instrument to further *their*

---

[12] My discussion here is drawn from Allen Buchanan, 'The Internal Legitimacy of Humanitarian Intervention', *Journal of Political Philosophy* 7 (1999), 71–87.

interests, or, on a democratic variant of the conception, to promote the satisfaction of *their* preferences as the latter are expressed through democratic processes.

It seems likely to me that Locke subscribed to the discretionary association view, but my purpose here is not exegesis. The idea under consideration, whether it is Locke's or not, is that the state is a *discretionary* association in this sense: Although there is no moral obligation to enter into political society, it is permissible and even advisable for individuals who interact in a state of nature (that is, where there is no government) to avoid its "inconveniences"—especially those attendant on private enforcement of the moral rules—by forming a political society and authorizing a group of individuals to be the government, which is to serve only as the agent of the people.

On this view political society is discretionary, not only in the sense that there is no obligation to form a state, but also in that individuals may choose with whom they associate politically. There is no indication in this line of thought that the Natural Duty of Justice acts as a constraint on the associated individuals' pursuit of their own interest (or the satisfaction of their own preferences).

The very idea of a social contract that plays such a large role in liberal theorizing about justice suggests the discretionary association view. The state is understood as the creation of a hypothetical contract among those who are to be its citizens, and the terms of the contract they agree on are justified by showing how observing those terms serves their interests. No one else's interests are represented, so political authority is naturally defined as authority exercised for the good of the parties to the contract, the citizens of the state to be. Even in variants of the contract doctrine that view the parties as representatives of future generations, such as Rawls's, it is only insofar as future generations are presumed to be citizens of this state that their interests are considered in the making of the contract. The state is conceived as the enforcer of principles of justice, and principles of justice are thought of as specifications of the terms of cooperation among those who are bound together in one political society, rather than as specifying how persons generally are to be treated.

The discretionary association conception accommodates a distinction between state and government. The state is a relatively enduring structure of institutions, which include roles to be filled by those who comprise the government. The justifying function of the state—what justifies the interference with liberty that its enforcement of rules entails—is the well-being and freedom of its members. There is no suggestion that the government must or even may do anything, no matter how minimal, to serve the cause of justice in the world at large.

On this view what makes a government legitimate is that it acts as the faithful agent of its own citizens. So government acts legitimately only when it occupies itself exclusively with the interests of the citizens of the state of which it is the government. To do anything else—including serving as an instrument for the fulfillment of the Natural Duty of Justice—is to violate its fiduciary obligation.

According to the democratic variant of the discretionary association conception, government is not strictly constrained to act in the *interests* of its citizens. If the majority of the citizens opt for a foreign policy that includes support for the human rights of persons beyond the borders of the state even when this is not in their own best interests, then the government must carry out this policy. However, government action in support of the human rights of noncitizens is legitimate only if it is authorized by democratic decision-making. Within the confines of the discretionary association conception of the state, if the majority chooses not to support human rights abroad (except where it is in their interest or the interests of the citizenry as a whole to do so), there is nothing to criticize in their behavior, at least from the standpoint of justice. They are not obligated to show regard for the human rights of noncitizens.

The democratic variant makes the discretionary association view look less morally jarring because it allows that citizens may democratically authorize support for human rights abroad, and that where such authorization exists, the government may legitimately carry out such a policy. However, one should not be too quick to assume that purely humanitarian foreign policies (as opposed to those that support human rights instrumentally, on grounds of self-interest) are within the proper sphere of what can be authorized by democratic processes. For recall that according to the discretionary association view the state is not even in part an instrument for moral progress. It has a much more limited function: the advancement of the interests of *its* citizens. Therefore a proponent of the discretionary association view might hold that this justifying function of the state places an antecedent constraint on what sorts of decisions may be taken by majority rule. Accordingly, the proper role of government is to carry out legitimate democratic decisions—understood as those that concern the choice of means to serve the interests of the citizens—and this precludes executing policies designed to help protect human rights abroad when doing so is not in the interests of the citizens of this state.

I do not want to put undue weight on this suggestion that the discretionary association view of the state, if taken seriously and developed consistently, rules out a democratic choice to use the resources of the state to help ensure that all persons have access to just institutions. It is important to understand that even if this suggestion is mistaken, the discretionary association view even in its democratic variant is incompatible with the conclusion that we have an *obligation* to use the resources of our state to try to fulfill the Natural Duty of Justice. The democratic variant of the discretionary association view at best shows that when democratically authorized to do so governments *may* carry out policies designed to support human rights abroad even when doing so doesn't serve their own citizens' interests; it does not show that citizens are *obligated* to use the resources of the state in this way.

The discretionary association view is widely held, not just in the liberal tradition of the social contract, but among politicians and ordinary people as well. To take only one recent instance, U.S. leaders were at great pains to argue that intervention in Kosovo was in the United States' interest, whereas the most vociferous critics of the intervention denied that it was. The assumption shared by both sides to the debate was that it was appropriate for the United States to intervene only if doing so was in its interests.

The enduring popularity of the discretionary association view is no accident. It has several signal attractions, at least from the standpoint of a broadly liberal political philosophy. First, the discretionary association view puts government in its place. It makes abundantly clear who the master is, namely, the people. Thus the discretionary association view is a powerful expression of the idea of popular sovereignty with its implication that the government, being the instrument of the people, serves at their pleasure. In other words, the government has no independent moral status, no rights on its own account. Second, it expresses the equal freedom

of individuals. Individuals freely decide whether to enter into association with one another.

The idea that political society originates from the free choice of
individuals suggests that there is no such thing as the state's interest,
apart from the interests of the individuals who make up the citizenry,
in sharp contrast to views that elevate the state to a kind of super
person. Instead, the state itself is justified only because it serves
the interests of the people. Especially at a time when states were
regarded as the private property of dynastic families, this was a
revolutionary, liberating idea.

In spite of these attractions, the discretionary association view of
the state and of the proper role of government must be rejected once
we take the Natural Duty of Justice seriously. Because we have a
limited moral obligation to help ensure that all persons have access
to rights-protecting institutions, we cannot regard our state simply
as an institutional resource for pursuing our own interests. We must
also recognize that, under current conditions, effective efforts to
fulfill the Natural Duty by improving the international legal system
require state action. But if this is the case, then we must reject the
common view that all that should count is the "national interest"
when it comes to state action in the international sphere.

The important kernel of truth in the discretionary association
view can be preserved. Recognizing that we ought to use our
domestic political resources to support a system of international law
designed to ensure that all persons' rights are respected is quite
compatible with a clear recognition that government has no independent moral status and no independent legitimate interests, but is
to be regarded strictly as a fiduciary, and that the state is created for
individuals rather than vice versa.

The trick is to understand how popular sovereignty in a system
of states can be made compatible with state policy in support of a
more just international legal order. The key to seeing how this compatibility can be achieved is to realize that popular sovereignty does
not mean unlimited sovereignty. Instead, popular sovereignty
means only that the people of a state are the ultimate source of
political authority within the state and that government is chiefly to
function as their agent. The extent of the peoples' sovereignty—
including the limits placed on it by international law and the moral

limits on how it may be exercised that are imposed by the Natural Duty of Justice—are another matter.

Of course, rejecting the discretionary association model does not entail viewing the state *simply* as a resource for fulfilling the Natural Duty of Justice. Instead, the same reasons noted in Chapter 1 in favor of having a system of states as opposed to a single world-state speak in favor of constraining the use of state resources for the pursuit of global justice by recognizing that the state's resources are to be used first and foremost, though not exclusively, to serve the interests of its own citizens. And there may be a deeper reason why the citizens of a state may rightly assume that their well-being, at least up to a point of reasonable sufficiency, ought to be a priority for their state: It may turn out, as many moral theorists have argued, that any acceptable view of morality will allow a limited priority for our own interests.

In other words, the position I am advocating—that we reject the discretionary association view of the state as being incompatible with the Natural Duty of Justice—requires only what Samuel Scheffler has called a moderate cosmopolitanism about justice.[13] According to moderate cosmopolitanism, we do have moral obligations beyond our own borders, but these are seen as being compatible with giving special priority to the needs and interests of our fellow citizens. The view is cosmopolitan because it recognizes genuine moral obligations to those outside our own polity, and that for this reason the special priority given to our own polity cannot be absolute. It is moderate because it rejects the extreme cosmopolitan position that all of our particular obligations, including our obligations to our fellow citizens, are strictly derivative upon our obligations to humanity at large.

The shift from the discretionary association view to recognition of the Natural Duty of Justice understood as a moderate cosmopolitanism does not end debates about whether and how to use our state's resources to support efforts to achieve moral progress in and through international law; it only makes it possible to engage in them. For one thing, there is the extremely difficult issue of how

[13] Samuel Scheffler, 'Conceptions of Cosmopolitanism', *Utilitas* 11 (1999), 255–76.

much priority we may give to our own interests and how great the costs are that we ought to bear in helping to protect the rights of those who are not our fellow citizens.

In addition, there is what David Luban calls the problem of consent, or what might be more accurately described as the problem of democratic authorization.[14] Suppose that we agree that the discretionary association view is mistaken, that we ought to think of the state as in part a resource for global, not just local, progress toward justice, and that we therefore understand that when government officials act to promote global justice they do not necessarily violate their fiduciary obligation to their own citizens.

From this it does not follow that government officials can simply use the resources of the state to pursue global justice whenever they see fit, as if the state were their private property, which they are free to use as they choose, in fulfillment of the Natural Duty of Justice. A plausible understanding of how state resources may be used to further global justice must make a place for the fiduciary, subordinate role of government officials, and must distinguish between their moral obligations as private citizens and their role-defined obligations as public fiduciaries. To take Luban's example: Even if we suppose that a sincere and wise effort to act on the Natural Duty of Justice required citizens of the United States to authorize their government to contribute to the NATO intervention in Kosovo, two questions remain: (1) did the government in fact receive authorization to intervene, and (2) what sorts of procedures for such an authorization are morally justifiable? The gravity of the authorization problem should not be underestimated. It is one thing to say that we as citizens ought to use the resources of our state to promote global justice on some particular occasion, but whether and if so under what conditions our government is justified in acting to enable us to do what we ought morally to do is quite another.

It is beyond the scope of this volume to offer a theory of democracy that would include substantive guidance for what sorts of authorization processes would be appropriate. Nor am I concerned

---

[14] David Luban, 'Intervention and Civilization: Some Unhappy Lessons of the Kosovo War', in Pablo de Greiff and Ciaran Cronin (eds.), *Global Justice and Transnational Politics: Essays on the Moral and Political Challenges of Globalization* (MIT Press, Cambridge, MA, 2002), 79–115.

here to determine whether the existing constitutional law of any particular state erects barriers to using some of the state's resources to further global justice. Instead, my aim is to clear the way for theorizing about appropriate processes for authorization and to motivate the question of whether existing authorization processes are appropriate, given a genuine commitment to the Natural Duty of Justice. (Thus whether the U.S. Constitution, and in particular the authority it accords to individual states of the Union, is compatible with a robust commitment to using the political power of the United States to help achieve progressive change in international law, though a very interesting question, is irrelevant to the core theoretical enterprise of this book.)

IV. *The Plurality of Ways of Acting on the Natural Duty of Justice*

Considered on its own, the Natural Duty of Justice is unsatisfyingly abstract. Though it is based on a recognition of the importance of institutions for protecting human rights, it provides no guidance for how individuals should work together to utilize or create institutional resources for a more just world.

Thus individuals who take the Natural Duty of Justice seriously will be faced with complex choices as to how best to act on it. Sometimes the most effective strategy will be to work through one's own state's political processes, either to achieve greater compliance with human rights standards at home, or to influence foreign policy to make it more supportive of reform in international law. One may also honor the Natural Duty by supporting international and regional governmental organizations, or by facilitating the work of nongovernmental transnational organizations, including those that make no pretense of affecting the character of the international legal system.

My focus in this book is on the role that efforts to reform international law can play in helping to ensure that all persons have access to institutions that protect their basic human rights. In the chapters that follow I develop specific proposals for reforming the international legal system so as to make it more effective in contributing to the attainment of this goal. But I do not mean to suggest that international legal reform is the only way to act on the Natural Duty of Justice, or even the most effective way.

V. *Abandoning the National Interest Thesis*

The aim of this chapter has been twofold: first, to show why justice ought to be a primary goal of the international legal system, in order to prepare the way for a justice-based account of state legitimacy and self-determination; and second, to show that the Natural Duty of Justice provides a plausible foundation for a commitment to developing a theory and a practice of international law that is justice based. Two fundamental implications of the argument of this chapter bear emphasis: (1) A proper recognition of human rights requires a rejection of the view that the state is merely an association for the benefit of its own citizens and hence also requires the abandonment of the view that state policy may be or ought to be devoted exclusively to the pursuit of the "national interest" and (2) participation in the enterprise of constructing a just international legal order is morally obligatory, not optional.

In the next chapter, I clarify the concept of basic human rights and explain how they constitute the core of justice, thus giving greater specificity to the claim that a primary goal of the international order ought to be justice. But before proceeding to that task I want to emphasize the most radical result of this chapter: Taking human rights seriously requires abandonment of the dominant view in international relations, namely, that states ought to, or at least may, exclusively pursue the national interest in their foreign policies.

I have argued that if there are human rights, then the same equal moral regard that obligates us not to violate these rights also obligates us to help ensure that they are not violated by others and that this in turn obligates us to help create a world in which all persons have access to just institutions, institutions that protect their basic human rights. From this it follows that the national interest should not be all that matters in making decisions about foreign policy; the human rights of those beyond our borders should count for something as well. Elsewhere I have offered what I believe to be a systematic and telling critique of the national interest thesis.[15] Here I will only summarize some of its main points.

---

[15] Allen Buchanan, 'Beyond the National Interest', in Martha Nussbaum and Chad Flanders (eds.), *Global Inequalities*, a special issue of *Philosophical Topics* Vol. 30, Number 2, 2003.

As I have already emphasized, my aim in this volume is not to provide a conclusive rebuttal of the assertion that there are no human rights. Consequently, my main concern is to make it clear that those who acknowledge that there are human rights cannot consistently hold that states ought to or may exclusively pursue the national interest in their foreign policies. There appear to be three justifications for the national interest thesis (henceforth NIT) that do not rest in any explicit way on the assumption that there are no human rights. I now want to state each very briefly and show why they fail.

The first argument has already been criticized in detail in Chapter 1 under the heading of Fiduciary Realism. According to this view, because the world of international relations is a Hobbesian anarchy, the only responsible course for a state leader is to act solely in the national interest; to do otherwise is too risky. Because international relations comprise a state of nature in Hobbes's sense, a situation in which rationality requires each state to attempt to dominate all the others, there is no room for moral constraints on the state leader's fiduciary obligation.

I have already argued that this justification for NIT fails because it rests on an inaccurate characterization of the world of international relations; there is no need to repeat that argument here. To summarize: Survival is not always at stake in foreign policy decisions and acknowledging moral constraints is not always irrational. The Fiduciary Realist argument does not show that international relations are so different from the rest of human life that the most fundamental moral principles, which include those that require basic human rights to be respected, have no application or should always be subordinate to the national interest.

The instrumental justification

The second justification for NIT concedes that the national interest is not the supreme value, but contends that conditions in international relations are such that those who conduct foreign policy should act as if it is. This argument is analogous to arguments to show that overall utility is maximized, not by pursuing it directly, but by following rules other than the principle that utility is to be maximized. In other words, the Instrumental Justification for NIT concedes that in principle the pursuit of the national interest ought to be constrained by consideration for the human rights of foreigners, but also holds that under the conditions that prevail in international relations the best outcomes for everyone (or at least for most of humanity) will occur if each state aims exclusively at maximizing the national interest in foreign policy.

For the Instrumental Justification for the NIT to work, it must include a convincing explanation of why it is that respect for the human rights of all will be achieved by each state exclusively pursuing its national interest. Presumably the needed explanation would be of the invisible hand variety—the world-political analog of the theory of the ideal market.

The theory of the ideal market explains how self-interested individuals can achieve mutually beneficial outcomes—but only when a constellation of demanding conditions is present, including secure property rights, access to (perfect) information about goods and services, the absence of monopoly, zero transaction costs, and rational consumers with transitive preferences.

It is hard to imagine what the analogous conditions would be in the case of international relations, especially since states are very different from actors in a market. The needed explanation has not been produced and it is doubtful that it could be, because there are too many obvious instances in which the exclusive pursuit of the national interest results in disregard for the human rights of persons in other states. The difficulty, then, is that there is neither a theory to show why there would be a harmony of interests under certain ideal conditions, nor any reason to believe that if the theory were produced our world would sufficiently approximate its ideal conditions to make the Instrumental Justification for the NIT credible.

As I indicated in Chapter 1, Hans Morgenthau offers an interesting variation on the Instrumentalist Justification, and one that does not require an invisible hand explanation. According to Morgenthau, it is better for humanity, not just for the people of a particular state, if each state exclusively pursues its own interest, because any attempt to shape foreign policy by moral values leads to moral imperialism and ultimately to fanatical, mutually destructive conflicts among states.

Morgenthau can be seen as providing a different reason than that offered by the Hobbesian Realist for why the state ought to be regarded simply as a resource for pursuing the interests of its own citizens, as an association exclusively for their mutual benefit. In brief, he holds that this is how the state should be understood, because a more ambitious role for the state will lead to disaster for all.[16] Ironically, his defense of NIT is cosmopolitan: It is for the good of humanity that states should exclusively pursue the national interest in their foreign policies.

Morgenthau appears to assume that (1) each society has its own view of morality, that there is little or no commonality of values among societies, and that (2) once a state attempts to guide its foreign policy by morality rather than the national interest, it will forsake tolerance and attempt to enforce its views on other states regardless of costs to others and ultimately to itself.

However, Morgenthau presents no evidence to show that there are as many moralities as societies, that there is no significant commonality among different societies' moral points of view. He merely observes that the cosmopolitan, aristocratic value system that was previously shared by (Western) diplomats has disappeared with the advent of democratization, without considering the possibility that there is a growing global culture of basic human rights that represents a minimal moral consensus.

Given that a shared morality performs certain functions that all societies need (they are, after all, human societies), it would be surprising if different societies had as little in common concerning values as Morganthau assumes. Indeed we should expect some congruence of moral values across societies, given the roles that morality plays in human life by coordinating behavior and providing relatively peaceful means for resolving or avoiding the more common mutually destructive conflicts that can occur wherever human beings go about the basic tasks that all humans must perform.

As Stuart Hampshire has observed, there is a lethal tension in the view that there is a fundamental diversity in basic ethical principles across societies, because for something to count as a *basic* ethical principle it must be grounded in and responsive to human

---

[16] Morgenthau, *Politics among Nations*, 267–74, 574–5.

interests—interests that all human beings have, rather than in the parochial interests that some humans happen to have.[17] By the most basic ethical principles, Hampshire means those that, if followed, help avert the worst harms to which all human beings are vulnerable, those principles adherence to which is necessary for people being able to lead decent human lives. But if this is so, then it is hard to see how different societies, so long as they are societies of human beings, could disagree entirely in their most basic ethical principles. At the very least, strong evidence of such fundamental disagreement would have to be marshaled.

More important, Morgenthau's argument overlooks the fact that there is an apparently broadening global culture of basic human rights, evidenced not only by human rights treaties signed by states, but by the growing power of transnational organizations to exert pressure on states to comply with these treaties.[18] It is true that there is disagreement about the precise contours of even some of the least controversial human rights and much controversy about whether some rights—especially those recognizing robust economic entitlements—really are human rights. But none of this should blind one to the fact that there is considerable consensus on a minimal, core conception of human rights that includes the rights against slavery and involuntary servitude, the rights to physical security of the person, including the right not to be tortured or to be subject to arbitrary arrest and detention, the right to subsistance and the right not to be excluded from political participation on the basis of race.

Just as important, this growing consensus on basic human rights operates within an international institutional framework that places significant constraints on moral imperialism in at least two respects. First, the idea of human rights still functions within a state-centered system that values state sovereignty very highly and an international legal system that prohibits humanitarian intervention without UN Security Council authorization and also prohibits aggressive war. Second, due to the admission of newly liberated colonial peoples in the 1960s and 1970s to the UN and to the institutions of international

---

[17] Stuart Hampshire, *Innocence and Experience* (Harvard University Press, Cambridge, MA, 1989), 90.

[18] Risse, Ropp, and Sikkink, *The Power of Human Rights.*

law and politics generally and due to the growing appreciation for cultural diversity in almost all of the most developed and powerful states, it is more difficult for any state to try to impose on the world its own peculiar conception of morality.

Furthermore, Morgenthau too quickly assumes a sharp distinction between the national interest and a society's moral values. This is to proceed as if the national interest is something exogenously determined—as if a group's interest is in no way shaped by its conception of its relationship to the realization of its moral values. But if the national interest and the society's moral values are not so separable, then the attempt to avoid what Morgenthau takes to be the risks of a morally guided foreign policy by cleaving to the pursuit of national interest is doomed.

Presumably what Morgenthau had in mind when he warned against forsaking national interest for morality was the danger of states attempting to impose grand ideologies like fascism or communism, through total war if necessary. But the risk of efforts to guide foreign policy by a modern conception of human rights that accords priority to the most minimal, widely accepted human rights and recognizes the value of diversity of cultures within the constraints of that minimum is clearly much lower.

Even if one state—say the world's one superpower—were to attempt to impose its own conception of justice on the world, there is little reason to believe that it would do so at the risk of total war in an era of nuclear and other weapons of mass destruction. Even during the Cold War, U.S. "moral imperialism" operated within the constraint of a fundamental commitment to avoiding a war among the great powers. The depth of this commitment can be gauged by the fact that it led the United States to accept defeat in the Vietnam War rather than risk war with China and the U.S.S.R.

Moreover, in the current context in which the most serious violent conflicts occur within states, Morgenthau's assertion that we reduce the risk of violence by setting aside concern for human rights and pursuing only the national interest rings hollow. Today the subordination of human rights and other moral concerns to national interest often takes the form of the oppression of national minorities. The pursuit of national interest, rather than being an effective strategy for peace as Morgenthau envisioned it, has proved to be a recipe for violent internal conflict that often spills across borders.

(One might overlook this fundamental point if one wrongly believed that each state contains one nation and that therefore the pursuit of the national interest serves the interests of everyone in the state.)

Morgenthau's admonition to states to stick to the pursuit of national interest might be good advice in a world in which the major threat to human well-being is horrendously destructive competition for world domination among states driven by intolerant, totalizing ideologies, unconstrained by a global culture of human rights, by international institutions prohibiting aggressive war and upholding the sovereignty of states, or by a resolve on the part of the most powerful states to avoid global total war; but this is not to say that it is sound advice for our world. The flaw in Morgenthau's defense of NIT is that it wrongly assumes that the only alternatives are (1) the exclusive pursuit of national interest (somehow defined in a morally neutral way) and (2) unconstrained moral imperialism. So Morgenthau's argument from the risk of pursuing moral values in foreign policy does not justify NIT.

The epistemic justification

Recent statements by Condoleeza Rice suggest yet a third argument for NIT.[19] She asserts that U.S. foreign policy should be based on "the firm ground of national interest" rather than on the abstract and shifting views of the international community. Taken at face value, this is an attack on a strawman, since virtually no one advocates the United States simply doing what the majority of the international community or even the majority of its allies say it should do. Perhaps Rice instead is trying to make a point about the epistemic accessibility of alternative goals for policy: The national interest is concrete and knowable, whereas moral values—at least those that are not encompassed by U.S. national interest—are indeterminate and a matter of unresolvable controversy. Hence pursuit of the national interest is the only practicable goal for foreign policy.

Now presumably Rice would concede that at least in the case of the United States a commitment to protecting the human rights of

---

[19] Condoleeza Rice, 'Campaign 2000: Promoting the National Interest', *Foreign Affairs* 79 (Jan.–Feb., 2000), 45–62.

its own citizens is an important constituent of the national interest. If this is so, then pursuit of the national interest requires that we know what is conducive to the human rights of Americans and this in turn requires that we have some fairly clear idea of what human rights are and what respecting them requires. But if the goal of protecting our fellow citizens' human rights is sufficiently determinate to guide policy, why is a direct concern for the human rights of others an unsuitable consideration for policy?

Of course there may be complicated issues concerning what policy best promotes human rights, especially in societies with very different cultures and political systems from our own. But there is nothing in principle less determinate about the goal, simply because it is to be pursued abroad.

This is certainly true for the most basic human rights. For example, though it would be more difficult to achieve, the goal of ensuring that all people are free from slavery or have enough to eat or are not subject to arbitrary arrest and torture by the police is no more indeterminate than doing the same for Americans. No doubt there often are special difficulties in knowing how best to bring about this end in societies quite different from ours; yet it would be very implausible to hold that we so seldom have sufficient knowledge about what would improve the human rights of people abroad that we ought to banish concern for their human rights from foreign policy discourse and cleave only to the pursuit of our national interest.

There is one interpretation of 'national interest' that might be thought to lend some plausibility to the claim that it is a better goal for foreign policy because more determinate and knowable. If 'national interest' can be reduced to national survival, then there is something to be said for the view that *when national survival is at stake*, the first order of business is to act in the national interest, that is, to do what is necessary to ensure the national survival. And there may be circumstances in which we can know just which set of actions will do that. On this interpretation of Rice's remarks, her point is that sticking with basics—and what could be more basic than survival?—is a firmer basis for foreign policy than pursuing more ambitious goals.

There are several serious limitations on this variant of the Epistemic Argument for NIT. First, as the current U.S. situation shows, it will often not be possible to know what should be done to ensure the national survival (assuming, which seems dubious, that global terrorism really is a threat to America's survival—as opposed to a threat to her extraordinary dominance, high standard of living, and the exceptional sense of security her citizens have enjoyed until recently). Should the United States focus on destroying Al Qaeda? Invade Syria? Exert more pressure for a Mid-East peace settlement? Become independent of foreign oil? Provide aid for economic development in countries likely to spawn terrorists?

To take another example: consider the situation of Britain in 1940 after the fall of France. Was it so clear that the national survival of Britain required fighting on alone, as opposed to negotiating a settlement with Hitler that would have preserved Britain's independence and the Empire and bought more time to enlist American support if Hitler violated the agreement? In opting for the former course of action, was Churchill wise or was he simply morally lucky in that his bad decision did not lead to bad results? The point is that in some cases—perhaps many—it may be easier to know whether a particular policy will promote or adversely affect the human rights of persons in some other country than to know what best promotes our own survival prospects.

Second, there is one respect in which guiding foreign policy by a concern for human rights is less epistemically demanding and more determinate than subordinating policy exclusively to national interest. Working with other states and international and transnational organizations to ensure that all persons enjoy the most basic human rights is a much more *minimal* goal than maximizing the national interest. The latter presents a moving target; so long as the state and its citizens can be made better off or an additional increment of security can be gained, the task is never complete. In that sense, the national interest is *more* indeterminate.

Third, as my earlier criticism of Hobbesian Realism emphasized, it is simply not the case that national survival is always or even usually at stake in foreign policy decisions, especially for a country as powerful as the United States. And even during periods when the national survival is threatened, as perhaps it was during the Second World War, not every decision regarding foreign policy is a matter of survival. As I have already noted, critics of Realism have emphasized for well over two decades that policy choices are not so thoroughly connected and hierarchical as all that; they do not form a pyramid with all decisions being subject to the one concern of national survival at the peak. So if the Epistemic Argument for NIT reduces to the Hobbesian Realist Argument, it fails, because as we have already seen the latter is based on a false assumption: namely, that we run an unacceptable risk of national extinction if we depart from the exclusive pursuit of the national interest.

Finally, once we realize that the common situation for policy choice is not one in which survival is at issue, we can begin to see just how indeterminate and epistemically problematic the national interest is, quite apart from the fact that if it is to be maximized there is no end to what its pursuit requires. The nation in this context, of course, is a fiction. Though we commonly speak of nation-states, and pretend that pursuing the interest of a particular state is the same as pursuing the interests of a nation, almost all states contain more than one nation and all contain a plurality of cultural, political, and religious, as well as socio-economic, groups with distinct and sometimes conflicting interests.

Once we jettison the fiction of the nation-state, how exactly is the state leader or maker of foreign policy to know what the national interest is? The national interest in the multinational, multicultural state may prove to be exceedingly elusive—unless it is taken to be constituted primarily by the protection of every citizen's basic human rights. In what sense, then, is the national interest "firmer ground" than a commitment to human rights, where human rights are understood as providing a moral minimum to which all persons are entitled?

Moreover, efforts to pursue the national interest, where, as is usually the case, this is really the interest of one group that claims the state as its own, often results in the destruction of other nations or cultural or religious or ethnic groups within the state. NIT thus provides a powerful weapon for so-called nation-building, which in virtually every case is nation-breaking, the destruction or at least subordination of all national groups except the one that has captured control of the state. Given how weak the justifications for NIT are, the fact that its acceptance carries this potential for grave harm is a strike against it.

There is one more interpretation of the claim that the national interest is a more determinate, and hence more suitable goal, than any other, including the protection of human rights. On this reading the national interest is identified with the state's *power*, understood as the capacity to achieve our ends, especially by being able to get others to do what we want, whatever our ends happen to be. The difficulty with this way of trying to support NIT is twofold. First, it is not clear that the maximization of power is a determinate goal—instead it is a moving target that is never reached. So from the standpoint of epistemic accessibility it is hardly a winner. Second, taken literally the goal of maximizing power is irrational: rather than maximizing one's assets for action, a rational agent will attempt to achieve an appropriate balance of acquiring and maintaining assets for future action (investment) and making choices that reduce assets for future action (consumption). But if the goal is to optimize (not maximize) power, it seems far-fetched to say that optimizing, that is, selecting the proper trade-off between the pursuit of power and its use to achieve one's goals, is more epistemically accessible than any other goal, including the protection of basic human rights. Knowing when to use the power one has and when to seek more power, when one cannot do both simultaneously, is often not easy. It may in fact be more difficult than knowing how a particular foreign policy decision would affect basic human rights of persons in another country.

For the Epistemic Argument for NIT to work, it would not only have to do a much better job than it does of showing that the national interest is a more determinate and hence a more practical goal for policy than any other. It would also have to show that the national interest is so much more epistemically accessible as a goal for policy than any other consideration, including concern for basic human rights, that a responsible state leader would opt for pursuing the national interest, no matter what the opportunity costs— regardless of what would be lost by narrowing the scope of policy in this way. Given that excluding the protection of human rights from foreign policy represents an exceptionally high moral cost and given how indeterminate the notion of the national interest is, this claim is very dubious.

VI. *Conclusions*

In this chapter I have made the initial case for a justice-based theory of international law, arguing that justice, understood as protection for basic human rights, ought to be a primary goal of the international legal system and that treating it as such need not lead us to undervalue peace. I have argued that a proper acknowledgment of the existence of human rights requires not simply that we refrain from violating them but also that we help to ensure that they are not violated, and that this in turn requires helping to create a world in which all persons have access to institutions that protect their basic human rights. The most radical conclusion of this chapter is that the dominant view in international relations, the thesis that foreign policy should be or may be guided exclusively by the national interest, must be rejected by those who believe in human rights. Finally, I briefly stated what I take to be the three most promising attempts to justify the NIT and showed why they all fail to do so.

In the next chapter I begin to flesh out the justice-based approach to theorizing about international law by giving more determinate content to the idea of basic human rights and by rebutting several attempts to show that the notion of human rights cannot serve as a basis for constructing a moral theory of international law.

CHAPTER 3

Human Rights

The purpose of this chapter is to articulate an understanding of basic human rights that is sufficiently clear and cogent to serve as the core of a justice-based moral theory of international law. To accomplish this goal I first analyze the concept of human rights into its key elements, use this analysis to explain how assertions about human rights can be justified, and show that plausible justifications for basic human rights can be grounded in a diversity of moral and religious perspectives. Then I state and refute several objections to the claim that there are human rights or that they can play a fundamental role in a moral theory of international law. Next, I argue that the right to minimally democratic governance should be included among the rights that international law ascribes to all persons, whether it is a human right or of instrumental value in securing human rights or both. I then show that the use of coercion to protect basic human rights is compatible with a proper tolerance for the diversity of values. I conclude this chapter with a discussion of how the international legal order can cope with the ineliminable abstractness of human rights norms.

I. *Clarifying the Idea of Human Rights*

Abstract moral rights specified through institutionalized moral reasoning

The aim of this chapter is *not* to provide a fully developed normative theory of human rights. It is to show how a widely shared conception of human rights that is already partly implemented in international law, with some philosophical clarification and refinement, can provide the core of a justice-based moral theory of international law. Although a fully developed normative theory of human rights is certainly needed and not presently available, it would be a mistake to assume that moral theorizing about international law cannot proceed in its absence.[1]

As moral rights, human rights exist independently of whether they are enshrined in legal rules or not. Indeed, it is only because they have meaning and validity independent of any particular legal system that human rights norms can serve as a critical touchstone for reforming the law. Any legal system, whether domestic or international, can and should be criticized if it does not include rules and practices that provide adequate protection for human rights.

Nevertheless, it is misleading to think of our understanding of human rights and the attempt to implement them in a legal system as entirely independent. Even if the existence and basic character of human rights can be determined by moral reasoning without reference to the particular features of any legal system, institutionalized efforts to monitor and improve compliance with these rights are needed to specify their content, if they are to provide practical guidance, and these must be context specific.

In order to monitor compliance with a norm it is necessary to operationalize it—to develop concrete guidelines and procedures for determining when the norm is being complied with and when it is not. Attempts to operationalize norms force us to get clearer about their content. The process of operationalizing human rights norms is an institutional one, with increasingly broad representation from governmental, intergovernmental, and nongovernmental groups.

A striking feature of the current international legal system is that it includes increasingly sophisticated institutional resources for monitoring compliance with human rights norms and, in the process of doing so, filling out their content. These include specialized human rights conventions, such as the Convention on the Elimination of All Forms of Discrimination against Women; various agreements, such as the Helsinki Accords, that are designed to help implement human rights conventions; and standing agencies such as the International Human Rights Commission and various

---

[1] For what still may be the best philosophical treatment of the subject, see James Nickel, *Making Sense of Human Rights* (University of California Press, Berkeley and Los Angeles, 1987).

regional committees, commissions, and courts, which perform a judicial or quasi-judicial function in reviewing complaints about violations and in the process of doing so offer interpretations of key clauses of international human rights conventions.

It would be misleading to say that the institutionalized reasoning involved in clarifying the content of the norms in order to operationalize them is purely legal. Instead, it is more accurate to say that the law provides institutional structures within which the reasoning can occur, processes for determining who can participate in the reasoning, and constraints on the reasoning that occurs within these structures. To a large extent the reasoning that occurs is moral reasoning—the give and take of arguments to clarify the fundamental values expressed in abstract human rights norms and to determine how to realize those values in institutional arrangements.[2]

One of the most profound changes that has occurred in the international legal system since the 1960s is that participation in the processes that specify the content of human rights has been greatly broadened, as membership of the UN became open to all countries, including former colonies. In contrast, throughout most of the history of the international legal system, membership was limited to a handful of Western states. Perhaps even more important, the remarkable growth of transnational, nongovernmental organizations increasingly allows for meaningful participation in the process of specifying norms that is not fully controlled by states.

There are two reasons to welcome these developments. First, broader participation can be expected to reduce the risk of parochial biases in moral reasoning about which rights are truly human rights and how their content is to be understood. The specification of human rights norms that would result from a process of operationalization in which the only participants were Westerners or representatives of Western states might be quite different from one in which a broader sampling of humanity participated. Second, quite apart from the fact that broader participation is, other things being equal, more likely to capture adequately the content of norms that

---

[2] Note that this descriptive observation about how international human rights norms are in fact specified is not to be confused with the more general Natural Law view that for anything to be a law it must accord with moral principles and that hence the determination of whether something is law always requires moral reasoning.

are supposed to apply to all human beings, not just to Western Europeans, arbitrarily restricted participation impugns the legitimacy of the process of operationalization and thereby threatens to undercut the effectiveness of appeals to human rights in the international legal order as a whole.

The first benefit of broad participation is epistemic, the idea being that a system that features broad participation is more likely to result in an accurate specification of the content of human rights norms; the second concerns procedural justice and its contribution to perceived legitimacy, not the quality of the outcome of the process. Later in this chapter, when I consider the objection that human rights are an instance of Western cultural imperialism, and in Chapter 7, which examines alternative views of the requirements for the legitimacy of the system of international law, the procedural justice issue will be explored in more detail when I consider proposals to "democratize" international law.

For now I will only observe that even if it is true that the abstract formulation of human rights norms not only originated in the West but also is somehow distorted by parochial Western concerns or values, it still does not follow that human rights cannot form the core of a justice-based international legal system. Everything depends upon whether the institutionalized reasoning that specifies the content of human rights norms through the effort to operationalize them has the capacity to correct these biases.

Widening access to participation is one important resource for correction. But one should not overlook the fact that the very concept of human rights itself contains resources for correcting biases in its interpretation. Such correction has already occurred in the incorporation of human rights in domestic constitutions. For example, the framers of the U.S. Constitution operated with a conception of natural rights that was first largely restricted not just to men, but to white men. Eventually, however, the universality of the notion of natural rights proved uncontainable; these rights were extended to African-American men, then to women.

The universality of human rights

Human rights, as the name implies, are ascribed to all human beings simply by virtue of their humanity or personhood, regardless of whatever other characteristics differentiate them from one another, and regardless of where they live. Assuming that the basic humanity that grounds these rights is unchanging, human rights, as moral rights, also apply to all persons regardless of when they exist.[3]

Some find the supposedly atemporal character of (moral) human rights hard to square with the fact that our understanding of the content of these rights changes over time. There is no inconsistency here, however. From the fact that we do not come into the world equipped with a fully adequate understanding of what human beings are entitled to, it does not follow that there is no correct answer to the question of what they are entitled to.

Furthermore, as I observed in Chapter 2, although human rights principles specify constraints on how institutions should be, they do not themselves determine the particular institutional arrangements needed to satisfy those constraints. Because this is so, it is sometimes hard to tell whether our conception of what a particular human right is has changed or whether we have merely come to hold different empirical hypotheses about which sorts of institutional arrangements best satisfy its constraints. Moreover, institutionalized processes for specifying human rights norms through operationalizing them tend to obscure this distinction. It may be difficult, and in some cases arbitrary, to say precisely when a change in our conception of human rights, as opposed to our views about which sorts of institutional arrangements would best respect them, has occurred.

The generality of human rights

Human rights are the most general moral rights that can be ascribed to us and the correlative obligations they carry are the most general moral obligations we can have. For example, the assertion that the right not to be tortured is a human right entails that everyone is under an obligation not to torture any human being.

As international *legal* rights, human rights were originally conceived as being addressed to governments, and hence the correlative

---

[3] For a discussion of the possibility that radical genetic engineering might make it possible to alter human nature, see Allen Buchanan, Dan Brock, Norman Daniels, and Daniel Wikler, *From Chance to Choice: Genetics and Justice* (Cambridge University Press, Cambridge, 2000), ch. 3.

obligations were thought to be obligations of governments. There is a growing tendency, however, to view the obligations that human rights carry as entirely general, even if it is assumed that governments have the chief responsibility for ensuring that these obligations are met. It is now recognized that not only governments, but also corporations, private death squads, and other groups, as well as individuals, violate human rights. Most recently, various forms of violence against women by spouses, partners, and other family members, are recognized to be human rights violations.

Weighty obligations, owed to right-holders

Claim-rights, of which human rights are one instance, have two essential elements: a permission or liberty and a correlative obligation.[4] Something more can be said about the obligation: It is owed to whoever is said to have the right, the right-holder.[5]

In the case of human rights, as with moral rights generally, the correlative obligation is conceived as being especially weighty. Ronald Dworkin expresses this basic point by saying that the correlative obligation "trumps" appeals to what would maximize utility.[6] The idea is *not* that considerations of social good are irrelevant to determining what our rights are, *nor* that rights may never be limited out of consideration for the social good, but rather that if we have a right to something, then the mere fact that depriving us of it would maximize social good is not itself a sufficient reason for doing so. In other words, rights supply extraordinarily weighty reasons for acting or not acting in certain ways, though they are not "absolute."

For example, if there is a human right not to be discriminated against on grounds of religion, then the fact that a particular act or policy of religious discrimination would maximize social utility is not itself a sufficient reason to violate the obligation not to discriminate. From this it follows that rights are not merely worthy moral

---

[4] It can be argued that some human rights, for example the right to freedom of conscience, also include immunities.

[5] W. N. Hohfeld, *Fundamental Legal Conceptions as Applied in Judicial Reasoning*, ed. Walter Wheeler Cook (Yale University Press, New Haven, 1923), 36.

[6] Ronald Dworkin, *Taking Rights Seriously* (Harvard University Press, Cambridge, MA, 1978), 191–2.

goals. Their correlative obligations have a special priority among all the things we ought to do or that it would be good to do.

The idea that the obligation is owed to the right-holder is also essential to human rights as claim-rights; it has implications that are absent from the mere statement that something ought to be done. In particular, ascribing a claim-right to someone morally empowers that individual by making clear that the source or ground of the obligation lies in him or her. Thus if I violate your human right, thereby failing to fulfill an obligation I owe *to you* (rather than simply doing something I ought not to do), I have wronged you, and it is to you that redress, compensation, or apologies are due. Among all those who might object to my behavior or be affected by it, you, the person whom I wronged, have a special status.

Human rights discourse therefore focuses on human beings as subjects of primary moral importance, as the ground or source of especially weighty obligations. This focus on the right-holder captures the common belief, expressed in the most important human rights declarations and conventions, that to recognize human rights is to acknowledge the inherent dignity of persons.

Rights and the protection of morally important interests

Because an assertion that R is a human right implies that there is an especially weighty obligation owed to persons as such (one that cannot be overridden even by appeals to what would maximize overall utility), respecting human rights means acknowledging the necessity of extremely robust protections of interests. Sometimes the name given to the human right makes the interest in question obvious, sometimes not. For example, the right against torture more or less wears the interest to be protected on its sleeve. Human beings, as the embodied, sentient entities they are, have an interest in not being subjected to the pain, suffering, degradation, and terror that torture inherently involves. The phrase "the right not to be tortured" rather directly conveys some of the more important interests at stake.

Sometimes the identity of the interest that is said to be deserving of protection is not so obvious. Consider the right to political participation. According to some political theories, political participation is intrinsically important; persons are thought to have a basic, nonderivative interest in political participation. According to other theories, there is no morally fundamental interest in political participation per se (at least not on the part of all persons), but everyone's being able to participate in important political processes promotes other basic interests that all individuals do have, such as the interest in having a government that does not disregard their well-being.

On this second type of theory, the phrase "the right to political participation," unlike "the right not to be tortured," does not so immediately implicate the interests that are protected when the right is respected. In either case, however, the connection with the protection of morally important interests is what makes respecting rights so crucial.

On this understanding of rights, they are not moral primitives. As I noted in Chapter 2, they are interest based, and assertions of the existence of this or that right require support from arguments that appeal to the importance of certain interests and therefore the importance of protecting them. In this sense, the moral theory of international law explored in this volume is not properly characterized as "rights *based*." Indeed, any moral theory that took rights as literally basic would be of limited use because it would not advance our understanding of the nature of rights.

The institutional implications of human rights assertions

These shared basic human interests are affected by the character of the institutions within which we live, human rights impose constraints on how institutions should be. However, as I also observed in Chapter 2, human rights principles do not by themselves entail anything approaching a full specification of the institutional arrangements needed to uphold human rights.[7]

First, there may be more than one institutional scheme that will do the job, but a particular scheme may be more appropriate for a given society at a particular time, due to its history and culture. For example, if one of two ideal schemes for protecting rights in a particular society can be implemented more fully and with lower moral costs of transition, then it is preferable, other things being equal. But knowing which of the possible institutional implementations of

[7] My discussion in the following paragraph has benefited greatly from Kristen Hessler's outstanding dissertation, 'A Theory of Interpretation for Human Rights'.

human rights for a particular society would be effective while minimizing transition costs requires empirical premises about the distinctive features of the society in question, and this takes us beyond the abstract human rights norms themselves.

Second, in some cases just what the implementation of a human rights norm requires will depend upon the resources available in the society in which it is to be implemented. For example, if the right to health care is a human right, then what counts as adequate satisfaction of the requirements of this right in a very poor country may be less generous than what is appropriate in a rich one, at least as a matter of nonideal theory, prior to the effective implementation of whatever principles of international distributive justice might reduce the inequality of resources among societies.[8]

Third, which particular institutional arrangements are appropriate for implementing human rights norms will vary across societies depending upon the nature of the defects of existing institutions. The sorts of institutional arrangements that best achieve respect for human rights in one society will be different from those best for another, if the causes of human rights violations differ in the two societies. In a country that has a strong tradition of one-man rule, with the pattern of human rights violations that typically goes with this, establishing term limits for the presidency along with an independent legislature and an independent judiciary may be the most appropriate institutional reforms from the standpoint of protecting human rights. In another society, where the most serious threat to human rights is ethnic conflict, greater protection for human rights may require constitutional changes to recognize intrastate autonomy (limited self-government) for ethnic groups within the state.

Martha Nussbaum's path-breaking book *Women and Human Development* supplies many vivid examples of the role that attention to the defects of existing institutions should play in the specification or operationalization of human rights norms. She focuses on the special problems that women tend to face regarding respect for their human rights.

---

[8] Kristen Hessler and Allen Buchanan, 'Specifying the Content of the Human Right to Health Care', in Rosamond Rhodes, Margaret Battin, and Anita Silvers (eds.), *Medicine and Social Justice: Essays on the Distribution of Health Care* (Oxford University Press, New York, 2002), 84–96.

Women in much of the world lack support for fundamental functions of a human life. They are less well nourished than men, less healthy than men, more vulnerable to physical violence and sexual abuse. They are much less likely than men to be literate, and still less likely have preprofessional or technical education. Should they attempt to enter the workplace, they face greater obstacles, including intimidation from family or spouse, sex discrimination in hiring, and sexual harassment in the workplace...[9]

Because this is so, any serious attempt to operationalize and implement abstract human rights norms prohibiting discrimination or ascribing rights to education or even subsistence must take into account the special burdens of women and accordingly develop special institutional strategies to cope with them.

To summarize: Given the role of appeals to rights as signaling the need to protect certain interests, the implication of the phrase "human rights" is that there are some interests common to all persons that are of such great moral concern that the very character of our most important institutions should be such as to afford them special protection. These interests are shared by all persons because they are constitutive of a decent life; they are necessary conditions for human flourishing. It is more accurate to think of human rights norms as expressing basic moral values that place constraints on institutional arrangements rather than as prescriptions for institutional design. Which particular institutional arrangements will best implement human rights norms will depend upon a number of factors.

II. *The Justification of Assertions about the Existence of Human Rights*

Elements of an adequate justification

The preceding clarification of the nature and function of human rights discourse supplies the key to understanding how assertions about the existence of human rights as moral rights can be justified. If human rights principles signal the need for especially robust protections for the most important interests shared by all persons, with the implication that institutions should be structured so as to afford

---

[9] Martha Nussbaum, *Women and Human Development* (Cambridge University Press, Cambridge, 2000), 1.

the needed protection, and if assertions of the existence of human rights include the idea that certain behavior is owed to all persons by virtue of the sorts of beings they are, then the justification for assertions of the existence of human rights must proceed accordingly.

First, it is necessary to identify the interests to be protected and to make the case that they are of such moral significance as to warrant such extraordinary protection, including the idea that respecting the corresponding rights "trumps" appeals to what would maximize utility. Second, since the rights in question are supposed to be human rights, it must be shown that the interests that ground them are indeed shared by all persons, being conditions for a good human life. Third, it must be shown that institutional arrangements are necessary for protecting these interests and can be reasonably effective in doing so.[10] (Unless the third condition is met, it has not been shown that human rights should constrain the way institutions are.)

Basic human rights

I have emphasized that respecting human rights means acting in ways that provide exceptionally strong protections for certain interests shared by all persons. These interests are shared by all persons because they are the conditions for a decent human life. The modifier 'human' in the last phrase is important. What is a decent life for human beings depends upon what human beings are, and more importantly what they are capable of.

Put negatively, human rights are such that their violation makes it very difficult if not impossible for individuals to enjoy a decent human life. The discourse of human rights presupposes, then, that sense can be made of the idea of the conditions for a decent human life.

Notice that this is not an exorbitant demand. Human rights discourse does not require a specification of what the *best* sort of human life is. It only requires that we have a grasp of what the necessary conditions for a minimally good or decent human life are.

There may be considerable controversy as to what is *sufficient* for a decent human life and there certainly is disagreement about what is the best life for human beings (and about whether there is one state of existence that is the best for human beings). It is much less

---

[10] See Scanlon, 'Human Rights as a Neutral Concern'.

controversial to say that certain severe deprivations generally undermine the possibility for a decent life. When human rights are violated, people suffer those severe deprivations.

I shall refer throughout this volume to *basic* human rights. These are the rights whose violation poses the most serious threat to the individual's chances of living a decent human life. Put more positively, they are those rights that, if respected, protect those interests that are most crucial for a having a good human life. As I deploy the notion of basic human rights in subsequent chapters, the reasons for relying chiefly upon these most important human rights in the moral theory of international law will become clearer.

My hypothesis is that the most basic human rights—those most important for the capacity to live a decent human life—include the following: the right to life (the right not to be unjustly killed, that is, without due process of law or in violation of the moral constraints on armed conflict), the right to security of the person, which includes the right to bodily integrity, the right against torture, and the right not to be subject to arbitrary arrest, detention, or imprisonment; the right against enslavement and involuntary servitude; the right to resources for subsistence; the most fundamental rights of due process and equality before the law; the right to freedom from religious persecution and against at least the more damaging and systematic forms of religious discrimination; the right to freedom of expression; the right to association (including the right to marry and have children, but also to associate for political purposes, etc.); and the right against persecution and against at least the more damaging and systematic forms of discrimination on grounds of ethnicity, race, gender, or sexual preference.

These rights are acknowledged in the central human rights conventions of the existing system of international law. These same conventions also recognize other rights, but in many cases it would be more difficult to argue that they are necessary conditions for a good human life or at least a minimally decent life. In some extreme cases, such as the notorious right to holidays with pay, it is pretty obvious that they are not necessary for a decent human life, though they may make for a better life for many people.

Even violations of the right against religious or gender discrimination (as opposed to persecution) may frequently be compatible with living a decent human life, depending upon how severe the discrimination is. For that reason I have only included the right against persecution and against the more damaging and systematic forms of discrimination, in an attempt to make it clear that the notion of a decent human life does not mandate anything so strong as strict equality of treatment, while at the same time emphasizing that it does place significant restrictions on unequal treatment nonetheless. Though there will be borderline cases, we can and do distinguish between less damaging forms of inequality that qualify as discrimination and those that constitute persecution, and between more and less damaging forms of discrimination as well.

For the purposes to which I shall put the notion of basic human rights in this book, it may not matter much if the list above is somewhat incomplete. My main point is that protection of those rights that are most necessary for a decent human life ought to be the touchstone for moral theorizing about the international legal system. Whether I am fully accurate in my hypothesis as to which rights those are is of secondary importance. Those who disagree with my conjecture as to which human rights are basic can substitute their own list and still explore with me the enterprise of articulating the outlines of a justice-based conception of international law.

Of course each of the rights listed above is formulated in a very abstract way and this raises the question of how minimal or how demanding the notion of basic rights is. Later in this chapter I take up the issue of the abstractness of human rights norms.

The requirement of humanistic reasons

Given the foregoing understanding of what human rights are, and above all given the crucial idea that the obligations they carry are owed to persons in their own right, as independent subjects of moral consideration, only certain kinds of justifications will be appropriate. Most crucially, justifications for assertions about human rights must (at the risk of banality) be *humanistic*—they must focus on human interests, upon what contributes to human well-being and freedom.

This requirement does not rule out believing that one's religion provides a foundation for human rights. Nor does it ignore the fact that the human rights movement as a historical struggle, especially in the form of the attack on the institution of slavery, to a large extent has been religiously motivated. Rather, the point is that because human rights norms, at least in their modern form, assert that exceptionally weighty obligations are owed to human beings as such in recognition of the importance to them of their basic interests as human beings, the justification for these norms must appeal to those interests, rather than to extra-human concerns, including the will of God.

So, to accept the idea that there is such a thing as human rights is already to acknowledge a significant constraint on the sort of justification that can count in favor of saying that this or that is a human right. Suppose, for example, that someone acknowledges that there are human rights—that human beings have sufficient moral importance in their own right that certain obligations are owed to them as human beings in order to ensure that their basic interests are protected—but at the same time denies that freedom from religious persecution is a human right. If he attempts to support his denial with appeals to the will of God, without any reference to the well-being or freedom of human beings as having weight in its own right, he has not offered the right sort of justification for his attack on the claim that the right to freedom from religious persecution is a human right. A key element of the nascent global culture of human rights is the widening acceptance of this "humanistic" constraint on justifications for endorsing or rejecting assertions about human rights.

III. *A Plurality of Converging Justifications for Human Rights*

This constraint on arguments concerning human rights—that they must be framed in terms of the interests of human beings as being important in their own right—leaves open a range of possible justifications. And in fact a variety of justifications have been offered in support of assertions about human rights that satisfy the humanistic constraint on justification. Furthermore, in spite of the fact that some of these different arguments rest on incompatible ethical or political theories, they converge in support of a fairly standard list of the most important human rights, what I refer to as basic human rights.

The moral equality of persons or equal consideration argument

As I noted in the preceding chapter, the Moral Equality Principle, the assertion that all persons as such are worthy of equal regard, is so fundamental that it is difficult to know how to argue for it. Indeed it is hard to see how there would be much practical point to constructing a moral justification for the Moral Equality Principle, since it seems unlikely that anyone who doubted its truth would accept any moral premise that might be marshaled in support of it. Whether there are nonmoral arguments—arguments appealing only to a conception of rationality and certain factual premises about human beings and the circumstances they find themselves in—that can support the Moral Equality Principle is a much disputed question. Since, as I have already emphasized, this is not a treatise to refute moral skepticism, I will not attempt to justify the Moral Equality Principle, but instead indicate how it can serve as a foundation for basic human rights.

Before doing so, however, I will note an intentional ambiguity in my formulation of the Moral Equality Principle. I have stated it so abstractly as to be neutral between three different views about what it is about persons that is to receive equal consideration. On one view, it is the well-being or good of persons that is deserving of consideration (call this the welfarist interpretation). On a second view, it is the autonomy of persons that is the object of equal consideration (call this the Kantian interpretation). According to a third view, the ultimate object of equal concern is composite: Persons are to be treated in a way that reflects both concern for their well-being and respect for their autonomy (the composite interpretation). In practice—in terms of their implications for what obligations we owe to all persons and how our institutions should be—there may be little discernible difference among the three interpretations.

Although the second view seems to be most different from the first and third, it nevertheless is explicated, at least by Kant, in a way that gives a prominent role to concern for well-being. Kant says that our respect for persons as autonomous beings requires that we make their ends our own so far as this is possible, that is, that we have the well-being of others as an obligatory end. Given this, the second view does not seem to be as much of a controversially one-sided perfectionist view as might first appear. In particular, it is not so obviously vulnerable to the objection that it assumes a Euro-centric, exclusive focus on individual autonomy or that it rationalizes paternalism in the name of autonomy.

In my judgment the first view is the most persuasive, if it is construed so as to accommodate autonomy as an especially important element of well-being, both as something that is valued by people for its own sake under conditions of good information about what it is like to be autonomous (though in varying degree by different people in different circumstances) and because it is of great instrumental value for securing other ingredients of one's good. The advantage of the welfarist interpretation of the Moral Equality Principle over the composite view is this: With the concept of well-being understood as the individual's good overall, the welfarist interpretation at least in principle provides a way of understanding how conflicts between autonomy and welfare can be resolved: Even if autonomy is thought to be an especially important ingredient of most or all individuals' well-being, it is at least conceivable, and indeed probable, that in some circumstances concern for a person's overall good could justify constraints on autonomy. The composite view, however, seems to abandon any attempt at balancing autonomy against well-being, by stating both values as fundamental and coordinate, that is, as having equal weight.

Without pretending to resolve these deep theoretical matters, the proponent of the Moral Equality Argument for basic human rights can argue that regardless of which of the three views one takes, basic human rights represent the most fundamental institutional constraints by which equal consideration for persons is to be achieved. But since I think that the welfarist interpretation is correct (given an understanding of it that views autonomy as a very important ingredient of well-being), I will present the moral equality of persons argument for human rights in that form.

1. All persons as such are entitled to equal consideration.
2. Equal consideration requires appropriately protecting interests $I1, I2, I3$, etc. (the interests that are necessary for a decent human life).
3. If $I1, I2, I3$, etc. are to be appropriately protected, then all persons as such (i.e., independently of any considerations other than their personhood) are owed the obligations that are correlatives of rights R, R', R'', etc.

To begin to see how the argument might be filled out to show how equal consideration of persons provides a justification for a fairly standard and relatively uncontroversial list of human rights, we can trace the connection between several important interests that are key ingredients of human well-being and certain rights generally acknowledged to be human rights.

Consider first the right not to be tortured. As I have already observed, securing this right protects several important interests, thereby contributing significantly to individual well-being. First, and most obviously, there is the interest in avoiding pain, suffering, and terror. Second, there is the interest in avoiding the gross indignity of being a mere object, completely at the mercy of another who acknowledges no constraints on how he treats one. (Whether we consider this indignity merely as detracting from well-being or as being incompatible with recognizing the autonomy of persons understood as a value independent of well-being, it supplies an important reason for regarding the right not to be tortured as a human right.) Third, the effects of torture, both physical and psychological, are often debilitating, robbing the victim of the capacity for pursuits and enjoyments that would contribute to her well-being, including the capacity for intimacy and healthy family relations.[11] Fourth, so far as torture has a point (as opposed to being an exercise in pure sadism), being tortured or being under the threat of being tortured makes one vulnerable to betraying one's principles, one's associates, or both. Fifth, where institutions do not secure the right against being tortured, individuals may fear that they will fall victim to it and this sense of vulnerability itself reduces well-being and constrains choices. For all of these rather obvious reasons, there is a strong case for the assertion that the right not to be tortured is a basic human right.

The right to resources for subsistence can be justified as a basic human right by showing its connection with basic human interests in a similar fashion. Most obviously, when human beings are malnourished or lack shelter or potable water, they suffer, physically and psychologically. But material deprivation also limits their opportunities for achievements and enjoyments, for attaining what contributes to their well-being, even when it does not result in premature death. Even more obviously, having access to resources for

---

[11] John Conroy, *Unspeakable Acts, Ordinary People: The Dynamics of Torture* (Alfred A. Knopf, New York, 2000), 169–83.

subsistence is clearly a necessary condition for a decent life because it is necessary for any life at all.

Consider next the right against the more damaging forms of discrimination on grounds of gender. The fundamental idea is that some institutional policies and social practices that impose restrictions on the freedom and opportunities of women violate the Moral Equality Principle. We have already seen that the justifications for asserting that the right not to be tortured and the rights to subsistence and basic health care are human rights appeals to the shared interests of human beings that are protected when these rights are respected. Thus the full justification for the right against gender discrimination as a human right would first show that all human beings, regardless of gender, have certain basic interests that warrant special protection and then argue that policies or practices that fail to extend this protection to women do not meet the requirements of the Moral Equality Principle.

What makes the justification of the right against gender discrimination as a human right more complex—or at least some putative institutional specifications of the right more contestable—is that we cannot assume that every policy or practice that results in different treatment for women and men constitutes a failure to provide equal protection for the basic interests of women and hence is a violation of the requirement of equal consideration. We cannot assume that a society fails to treat women with equal moral regard simply because it supports gender roles that include some inequalities, since such "local" inequalities may be compatible with equal treatment of women and men overall. Nevertheless acknowledging a human right against gender discrimination requires that a compelling justification be given for such inequalities—and one that fundamentally appeals, not to the good of society, but to that of women.

Finally, consider the right against persecution on grounds of religion. A brief exploration of how it might be justified as a human right by appeal to the Moral Equality Principle will clarify the power of what I referred to earlier as the humanistic constraint on human rights argumentation—the requirement that justifications for and against assertions about which rights are human rights must refer ultimately to the interests of human beings.

Preventing people from practicing their religion, or subjecting them to serious penalties if they do, clearly interferes with some of the most important interests human beings have. Included are the interest in being able to express one's deepest feelings and beliefs about the human condition and the nature of reality, in being able to fulfill what one believes to be among one's most important obligations (religious duties), and the freedom to participate in one's religious community, with all the goods this makes possible. Given that religiosity broadly conceived is very widespread among humanity, and given that even those who at one time appear not to be concerned with religion at all may come to be so, the right to freedom from religious persecution and against at least the more serious and systematic forms of religious discrimination is a strong candidate for inclusion in the list of basic human rights.

Consider, however, the response a Christian religious imperialist might make to this sketch of a justification. He might say that it is precisely because he is so concerned about protecting the most basic interest of all human beings that he endorses coerced religious orthodoxy. For surely, he would insist, the interest in salvation is the most important interest that a human being can have—and outside the one true religion no salvation is possible. Notice that this justification for denying the right against religious discrimination appears to be of the right sort; it seems to satisfy the humanistic constraint because it appeals to human interests, not to the will of God as such.

Later in this chapter I will examine the right against religious persecution more closely, in a discussion of the compatibility of the use of force to protect human rights with the virtue of tolerance. There I will argue that although the humanistic constraint does rule out certain kinds of justifications for or against assertions about human rights, it is not sufficient by itself to define the proper framework for justification. In addition, I will argue, there are certain minimal standards of *justificatory responsibility*—basic requirements as to what counts as reasons for a moral view—that rule out the Christian imperialist's 'argument'. To preview that discussion: It is not enough to require that justifications for or against claims about human rights must be grounded ultimately in human interests; in addition what counts as human interests and what is said to be conducive to them must be accessible from the standpoint of practices concerning the evaluation of arguments and evidence that satisfy certain minimal requirements of human rationality and that are accessible to all persons who possess normal capacities for reasoning, whether they hold a particular religious view or not. For now I will only note that if we confine ourselves to what uncontroversially contributes to or detracts from human well-being, we must conclude that human beings have such an important interest in being free to practice their religion that the right against religious persecution is a strong candidate for inclusion in a list of basic human rights.

The argument from central human capabilities

A close relative of the moral equality justification for human rights has been advanced by Amartya Sen and Martha Nussbaum.[12] I will focus on Nussbaum's articulation of the capabilities view because in some respects it is worked out in greater detail, makes the connection to the Moral Equality Principle more explicit, and stresses the importance of examining the special burdens of women for an adequate theory of human rights.

In *Women and Human Development* Nussbaum states that

> The intuitive idea behind the [capabilities] approach is two-fold: first, that certain functions are central in human life, in the sense that their presence or absence is typically understood to be a mark of the presence or absence of human life; and second—this is what Marx found in Aristotle—that there is something that it is to do these functions in a truly human way, not a merely animal way.[13]

According to the capabilities view as Nussbaum develops it, basic constitutional principles for all states as well as the principles of international law should foster the capabilities of every person to exercise these distinctive, central human functions. Respecting what we call human rights protects and promotes persons' capabilities for truly human functioning. She lists ten "central human functional capabilities," including being able to live to the end of a human life of normal length; being able to have good health, including reproductive health; being able to move freely from place to place; being

---

[12] See Amartya Sen, 'Equality of What?', in *The Tanner Lectures on Human Values*, I (Cambridge University Press, Cambridge, 1980).

[13] Nussbaum, *Women and Human Development*, 71–2.

able to use the senses, to imagine, to think, and reason; being able to have attachments to things and people outside ourselves; being able to form a conception of the good and to engage in critical reflection about the planning of one's life; and being able to live with and toward others, to recognize and show concern for other human beings, to engage in various forms of social interaction.

In Nussbaum's theory the ultimate ground of the commitment to protecting and promoting every person's central human capabilities is what she calls the Principle of Every Person as an End, which I take to be more or less equivalent to what I have referred to as the Moral Equality Principle. According to Nussbaum, respecting human rights promotes and protects the central human functional capabilities. That is the ultimate justification for the assertion that human beings as such have certain rights.

The great virtue of the capabilities view is that it emphasizes the importance for a good human life of *activity*, of *doing*, not just of having things or being in certain states. By focusing on capabilities, Sen and Nussbaum supply crucial content for the idea of treating persons as moral equals or as ends.

It seems to me that the capabilities view can be accommodated under the general position that human rights ought to be respected because doing so promotes and protects certain fundamental *interests* that all human beings have and that are worthy of the utmost moral consideration. The capabilities view can be seen as emphasizing that to a large extent these are interests in being able to perform certain essentially human functions.

The concept of interests is helpfully broader than that of capabilities when it comes to justifying some human rights claims. For example, it is true that respecting the right not to be tortured enables people to function effectively in many ways; and this is surely part of what makes it so important. But quite apart from the fact that torture impairs functioning, human beings have a right not to be subjected to it because it causes severe pain, terror, and humiliation. Pain, terror, and humiliation are in themselves bad states to be in, quite apart from the fact that those experiencing them are likely to experience impaired functioning.

The concept of interests is broad enough to capture the fact that avoiding certain states as well as being able to perform certain functions is central to a truly human life. Consequently, I suggest that instead of viewing the capabilities view and the interest-based view of human rights as rival theories, we should see the emphasis on capabilities as an explication of what many of those fundamental interests are. To a large extent the interests that respect for human rights promotes and protects are interests in having what Nussbaum calls the central functional human capabilities. Her valuable explication of what the central functional capabilities are does a great deal to specify the fundamental interests that respect for human rights promotes and protects.

The utilitarian argument for human rights

Utilitarianism in its simplest form is a comprehensive moral-political theory that defines right acts as those that maximize overall utility, where utility is variously defined by different versions of the theory as pleasure, happiness, or the satisfaction of preferences. A utilitarian justification of human rights would proceed according to the insight that reliance on *secondary rules* is in some cases the best way to maximize overall utility. In other words, instead of attempting to ascertain in a case-by-case fashion whether torturing individuals, persecuting them for their religious views, or denying them resources for subsistence would maximize overall utility, we can be assured of producing more utility overall and in the long run by giving extraordinary weight to rules that preclude such behavior. In addition, a utilitarian could argue that institutions that instill the belief that certain forms of behavior are not only obligatory but owed to individuals as human beings does the best job of promoting utility. Thus the utilitarian seems to be able to account for the main characteristics of human rights.

There can be little doubt that if human rights were respected, much human unhappiness would be avoided, in large part because human beings would be much freer to promote their own well-being effectively. This much follows from the fact that respect for human rights provides strong protections for the most important human interests—those interests that are the most significant contributors to individual well-being comprehensively understood. To this extent, utilitarianism provides a potent prima facie justification for institutions to secure basic human rights.

However, to make a fully convincing utilitarian case for basic human rights much more is needed. Most obviously, each putative basic human right must be shown to make such an extraordinary contribution to overall utility as to justify institutional arrangements that rule out acting contrary to the right for the sake of gaining more utility. But just as importantly the utilitarian must show that affording *every* person these rights is required by utility maximization. More specifically, the utilitarian must rebut the view that utility maximization is consistent with—or perhaps even mandates—selective ascription of what are usually taken to be human rights.

For example, suppose that there are some persons who, because of the disabilities they suffer, require extraordinary outlays of resources if they are to have access to anything like the range of opportunities available to those who are not disabled, or even merely to survive. It appears that utilitarian reasoning might justify denying to such individuals the right to life (understood as including at least the right not to be killed) or the right to resources for subsistence.

Presumably there are individuals who have the characteristics necessary and sufficient for being persons, and whose lives contain a net balance of well-being over suffering, but who meet this description. (One possible example would be babies born with mild to moderate mental retardation who also have serious physical disabilities that are very expensive to treat.)

To show that her moral-political theory does indeed support human rights—a basic set of rights for all persons—the utilitarian would have to argue that the best way to promote utility is to have institutions that do not make exceptions in the case of disabled individuals or other subsets of humanity, but instead extend protection of basic interests to all persons. Whether or not this project would be successful is an interesting question. My aim, however, is not to determine whether it would be, but rather to show that utilitarianism provides at least prima facie support for institutionalizing at least the usual candidates for basic human rights, even if the utilitarian case for making these rights genuinely universal for all persons is more complicated and to that extent more problematic than is the case with the argument from equal moral consideration. At the very least, utilitarianism supports efforts to protect what are generally considered to be human rights in this sense: because the massive violations of human rights that now occur are a great source of disutility, efforts to develop institutional support for human rights would clearly be a priority for utilitarians.

To summarize: The connection between utility and the right not to be tortured, the right against religious persecution and the more harmful forms of religious discrimination, the right to liberty and physical security of the person, the right to resources for subsistence, the various rights of due process and equality before the law, and other rights that are widely thought to be basic human rights is rather straightforward. To that extent utilitarian argumentation tends to converge on the same list of rights that the equal moral concern argument supports.

Religious justifications for human rights

The movement to abolish slavery, one of the most heroic battles for basic human rights, was for many who participated in it a matter of religious obligation. All of the major religions, with the possible exception of that traditional strand of Hinduism that endorses the caste system, appear to include a commitment to the equality of persons. To that extent they are all open to interpretations of their doctrines that support human rights as the proper expression of human equality.

The fact that religious views typically converge on the same list of human rights that are justifiable by appeal to secular arguments is worth emphasizing. Too often there is a tendency to assume that so-called religious fundamentalism is the enemy of human rights while overlooking the fact that religious motivation often makes a positive contribution to the struggle for human rights.

This is not to deny that religiously motivated conflict causes massive violations of human rights. In this respect Christianity is more tainted than the other major religions, because of its ruthless, institutionalized persecution of nonbelievers and its wars of religion, including the Crusades. Nevertheless, as a broad generalization it is correct to say that today the mainstream doctrines of the major religions provide greater resources for supporting human rights than for rationalizing their violation.

It is not surprising that religious justifications for human rights, with some exceptions, tend to converge on the same list of rights as secular ones. The commitment to human equality, whether it takes the form of regarding all persons as children of God or as created in God's image, presumptively requires acting so as to protect the basic interests of persons, and it is these basic interests that shape the list of human rights.

IV. *Is Democracy a Human Right?*

Two questions about democracy

So far I have argued that from a number of ethical perspectives certain familiar civil and political rights can be regarded as basic human rights. Whether a right to democratic participation (and hence to democratic institutions in which to participate) is a human right is more controversial. A moral theory of international law must answer two questions about democracy: (1) Should international law include the requirement that individual states be governed democratically (and if so, should this requirement take the form of an international legal human right to democratic governance ascribed to individuals, and what understanding of democracy should it employ), and (2) is democracy (in some form) a requirement for the legitimacy of the international legal system itself (must the system be democratic for it to be morally justifiable to try to enforce its rules)? My concern in this chapter is with the former question. In Part Two, on legitimacy, I take up the latter.

It is probably fair to say that the majority of international legal scholars would not be willing to declare with any confidence that international law currently ascribes a right to democratic governance to all individuals as a human right.[14] However, our concern is not with what international law currently is, but with how it ought to be.

Justifying an international legal entitlement to democratic governance

There are three main arguments in favor of international law requiring the governments of states to be democratic. The first provides support for the conclusion that democratic governance is a human right properly speaking by grounding democracy in equal

---

[14] Thomas Franck, 'The Emerging Right to Democratic Governance', *American Journal of International Law* 86 (1992), 46–91 is an exception.

consideration for persons. The second, instrumental argument, contends that democracy ought to be required of governments because democratic governance is the most reliable way of ensuring that human rights properly speaking are respected. The third holds that only if governments are democratic is it appropriate to treat them as agents of their peoples and hence as legitimate.

The first argument relies on the same basic principle that I have already suggested provides the best justification for human rights generally: the Moral Equality Principle. The claim is that equal consideration (whether cashed out in terms of respect for autonomy, concern for well-being, or both) requires that all persons have the same fundamental status, as equal participants, in the most important political decisions made in their societies.[15] On this view, the right to democracy is an important element of the institutional recognition of the equality of persons, quite apart from any value that democracy might have as a reliable way of ensuring that decisions are made with optimal information or that they maximize social welfare.

The second argument holds that even if democratic governance is not a human right, it is of such great instrumental value for the protection of human rights that it ought to be required of all governments as a condition of their legitimacy under international law. The outstanding work of Amartya Sen provides support for the instrumental argument. Sen marshals impressive evidence to show that while democracies may face food shortages due to natural disasters, they do not reach the level of famines. Famines are as much a political as a natural phenomenon; political mismanagement virtually always plays a crucial role. Where governments are democratic, they are accountable, and accountability tends to prevent them from persisting in the mismanagement that is an essential contributor to the occurrence of famines.

Not only the right to resources for subsistence but also other human rights are violated when famines occur, due to the breakdown of law and order that inevitably occurs in such extreme circumstances. If Sen is correct, the instrumental case for democratic governance is strong.

[15] For what may be the best exposition of this argument for democracy, see Thomas Christiano, *The Rule of the Many* (Westview Press, Boulder, CO, 1996).

It is not difficult to see how Sen's argument regarding the role of democracy in safeguarding the right to resources for subsistence might be generalized to the protection of other human rights. In general, governments that are held accountable through democratic elections are less likely to violate the human rights of their citizens.

The "democratic peace" literature adds an interesting twist to the argument that democracy is the most reliable form of government for securing human rights. If it is true that developed democracies tend not make war on each other, then encouraging the spread and development of democracy should lessen the violation of human rights, or at least those violations that occur in wars.

The third argument for the assertion that international law should require states to be democratic takes seriously the claim of governments to represent or serve as the agents of their citizens. Especially in a system in which so-called state consent still plays such an important role in the making, application, and enforcement of law, it is vital that the international acts of state leaders actually reflect the preferences and interests of citizens. Democratic institutions are necessary if state consent is to carry much moral weight in international law.

Moral and legal rights

It might be thought that only the first argument—the argument from equal moral consideration—can support the conclusion that a right to democratic governance ought to be included in the list of human rights recognized in international law, since the second argument only shows that democracy is instrumentally valuable for human rights, not that it is a human right, and the third only asserts that democracy is a condition for the legitimacy of state consent in the international arena. This conclusion is mistaken, however, because it confuses moral with legal human rights.

The first argument concludes that the right to democratic government is a moral human right, with the implication that it ought to be recognized as a human right in international law. The second, instrumental argument can concede that democracy is not a moral human right, but nevertheless conclude that it is of such great instrumental value for securing moral human rights that a legal right to democratic government under international law should be established. Similarly, the cogency of the third argument does not depend upon an assumption that the right to democratic governance is a moral right; instead, it only makes a claim about the conditions under which the international legal system should recognize the consent of state leaders as representing the citizens of the state. Yet if the second and third arguments are sound, they provide support for including the right to democracy in the list of international *legal* human rights. In other words, if we distinguish clearly between human rights as moral rights that exist independently of whether they are incorporated in a legal system and legal rights, we can see that not all legal rights must be justified by appeals to corresponding moral rights. In some cases, the best justification for recognizing a legal right to X is not that it is the legal counterpart of a moral right to X, but rather that including X as a legal right best serves to protect some moral right Y or, in the case of the third argument, to ensure that appropriate conditions of agency or representation are satisfied.

The democratic minimum

The argument from equal consideration of persons, the instrumental argument, and the agency argument are compatible; we need not choose between them. Together they provide strong support for recognizing the right to democratic governance as a basic human right under international law. The difficulty, of course, lies in exactly how we are to understand the requirement of democratic governance.

Here the distinction developed in Chapter 1 is relevant. We must try to distinguish between what is included in the right itself and the various institutional arrangements by which it can be secured in various circumstances, in different societies. If, as seems reasonable, we rely primarily on the equal moral consideration and the instrumental and agency justifications for a right to democratic governance, then it is to those arguments that we must look for guidance as to what is the content of the right itself.

Different democratic theorists try to cash out the key notion of participation as an equal in governance in different ways. Thomas Christiano, for instance, opts for the idea of each citizen having "an equal say" in determining the most fundamental public rules. For my part, I am more confident about our ability to ascertain the range of representative institutions that most reliably achieve the accountability necessary for protecting basic human rights than I am about how to cash out the notion of having an equal say. Moreover, accountability is a necessary condition for governments serving as legitimate agents of their peoples, so to that extent evidence that supports the instrumental argument will also support the agency argument.

One difficulty is that an "equal say" cannot be understood literally as "having equal influence" over decisions, since that seems to be an unattainable ideal, given the fact that differences not only in wealth, education, "connections", and also personal attractiveness translate into inequalities in political influence, even in the most just systems. My sense is that theorists of democracy who argue that it is required by equal consideration of persons have not yet sufficiently explicated the notion of all having an "equal say" to make clear exactly which sorts of representative institutions would count as achieving equal consideration. Empirical studies of which sorts of representative institutions achieve the accountability required to ensure that human rights are protected may provide better guidance about how we are to understand the content of the right to democratic governance.

Without pretending to have provided a systematic case, I would suggest that using accountability as the key notion what counts most are the following characteristics: (1) There are representative, majoritarian institutions for making the most general and important laws, such that no competent individual is excluded from participation, (2) the highest government officials are accountable to the people by being subject to removal from office through the workings of these representative institutions, and (3) there is a modicum of institutionally secured freedom of speech, association, and assembly required for reasonably free deliberation about political decisions and for the formation and functioning of political parties.

The conception of democratic government I am operating with is that of a constitutional democracy with entrenched civil and political rights that provide constraints on majoritarian decision-making. Thus item (1) above must be qualified to reflect the fact that the constitution, including a bill of basic individual rights, is not revocable by the sort of majoritarian decision process that is suitable for

laws passed within the framework of the constitution. And item
(2) must be qualified so as to accommodate provisions for the independence of the judiciary as reflected, say, in the lifetime tenure of
members of the Supreme Court in the case of the United States.[16]

In Part Two, on legitimacy, I will argue that the minimal conception of democracy that includes these three elements (suitably qualified) should *eventually* be included in the requirements for
recognitional legitimacy for all states—that to be recognized as a
member in good standing of the system of states an entity should be
democratic in this minimal sense. There I also recommend that a
more immediate goal for reform is to require that *new* entities seeking recognition as sovereign states, including those formed by secession, should be required to satisfy the minimal democracy criterion.

Now I want to suggest that the right to democratic governance as
having this minimal content ought to be included in the list of basic
human rights in international law. If, as the instrumental argument
asserts, democratic governance is the most reliable protector of
human rights—at least in a system in which states are strong and international governance institutions are weak—then ascribing the right to
democratic governance to individuals as a human right under international law provides important institutional support for human rights.

Notice that I am not claiming that the rather abstract notion of
minimal democracy set out in items (1) through (3) above is sufficiently contentful to serve as a standard in international law. As I
emphasized earlier, to be applicable in law, such an abstract standard
must be made more concrete through complex institutional processes
that include efforts to monitor compliance, as well as by the rendering of legal opinions by courts, the discourse of international lawyers,
etc. In the final section of this chapter I offer a sketch of a proposal
for how to cope with the abstractness of human rights norms.

V. *Critiques of Human Rights*

Cultural ethical relativism

Despite the convergence of various secular and religious views on
the notion that there are human rights, there are those who either

---

[16] I thank Bill Edmundson for making clear to me the importance of these
qualifications.

deny that there are such rights or reject the assertion that they can play a fundamental role in international law. I evaluate these views in the next sections.

One of the most frequently voiced criticisms of appeals to human rights invokes the cultural 'relativity' of ethical values. There are in fact two distinct cultural ethical relativist theses, and the tendency to confuse them makes this criticism of human rights look more plausible than it is. The first, descriptive cultural ethical relativism, is the thesis that different ethical values or ethical principles are found in different cultures. The second, meta-ethical cultural ethical relativism, is the thesis that the differences in ethical values or principles found in different cultures cannot be resolved by reasoning.

Descriptive cultural ethical relativism looks rather less exciting when combined with the undeniable observation that different ethical values and principles are also found within the same culture. (Cultural groups are not monolithic in their values and principles, ethical or otherwise.) Apart from that, the descriptive thesis is deeply ambiguous. It could mean only that there are *some* ethical values or principles that are encountered in some societies but not in others. Or it could mean that for each culture there is a different set of *basic* ethical values or principles.

On neither interpretation is the truth of cultural ethical relativism incompatible with the existence of human rights. From the fact that there are disagreements among people from different cultures as to what is moral, even disagreements about basic moral values or principles, it does not follow that there are no protections of interests that are owed to human beings as such. To *assume* that disagreement means there is no right answer is to beg the question. And there is in fact much evidence that moral disagreements are resolvable by reasoning.

After all, each of us knows of cases in which moral disagreements are resolved through reasoning, including cases in which those who formerly held certain views about what is morally permissible come to recognize their error and are able to explain wherein their error consisted. Consider, for example, the case of those who grew up as racists in racist societies but later came to renounce racism. At the very least, the ethical relativist must do more than simply point to the fact of moral disagreement.

Meta-ethical cultural ethical relativism would, if true, rule out the possibility of rational agreement on a list of human rights, but only if we add the premise that the differences among cultures regarding values or principles include disagreements about which rights are human rights or whether there are any human rights. This added premise is needed because it might be the case that the rationally unresolvable ethical differences among cultures that the meta-ethical cultural ethical relativism thesis refers to do not include disagreements about human rights, or at least not about some subset of them, the basic ones.

This latter possibility is worth considering for two reasons. First, it would be very surprising if different cultures held no ethical principles at all in common; they are, after all, human cultures. Second, human rights are rather minimal moral requirements specifying what is owed to all persons; hence agreement on them leaves open a great deal of room for disagreements on other ethical matters.

The first point warrants elaboration. Why should we expect there to be considerable congruence in basic ethical principles across different cultures? As I noted in the previous chapter, morality performs certain important functions in every society—in particular it helps to coordinate behavior (for example through the practice of making and keeping promises) and provides relatively peaceful means for resolving or avoiding mutually destructive conflicts. Given that this is so, it would be remarkable if every society or culture had a wholly different system of basic ethical principles. Fundamental and irresolvable conflicts on the most basic moral principles seems unlikely and at the very least is not something one can simply assume, without the benefit of substantial evidence.

One should be suspicious, therefore, about quick inferences from the fact that there are disagreements about particular ethical *issues* among cultural groups to the conclusion that different cultural groups have different *basic ethical principles*. In some cases, what initially appear to be disagreements about fundamental ethical principles turn out to be either disagreements about derivative ethical principles or about the empirical assumptions needed to apply ethical principles. If morality performs the same basic functions in different societies due to the fact that there are some common human interests that morality serves (at the very least the interest in social coordination and the peaceful resolution of mutually destructive conflicts), then it may be possible to resolve even fairly basic ethical disagreements by reasoning that appeals to those common interests and what sorts of shared principles most effectively promote them.[17]

This is not to say that we should expect all societies to formulate the most basic ethical principles in terms of human rights. But that is not required in order to undermine the ethical relativist's assumption that there are basic and irresolvable moral disagreements across societies that preclude a role for human rights in a defensible moral theory of international law. Instead, all that is needed are two assumptions, both of which seem plausible enough.

The first is that the language of basic human rights is or can become accessible to people across a broad spectrum of societies. This assumption gains plausibility from the fact that many people from societies to which the notion of human rights may not be endemic find the discourse of human rights extremely valuable for protecting their basic interests in both domestic and international legal contexts. After all, transnational, nongovernmental human rights organizations often help people from cultures in which human rights discourse is not prominent to invoke human rights to protect their basic interests.

The second assumption is that, from an institutional standpoint, principles formulated in terms of human rights are likely to do the best job of protecting the most important interests common to persons because, by designating persons as those to whom the corresponding obligations are owed, they empower individuals by according them the standing to invoke their rights for their own protection. Protections for basic interests formulated in terms of rights therefore have the advantage of presenting obstacles to paternalism and to the harms and indignities that paternalism often entails. This is a significant advantage, given the fact that, especially in dealings with persons from different cultures than their own, those acting paternalistically often fail to identify properly and protect adequately the interests of those they are supposed to be serving. In brief, paternalism both expresses and reinforces the assumption that those whose interests are supposedly being protected are incapable of acting in their own behalf, whereas the concept of human rights is inherently anti-paternalistic. Finally, formulating protections for basic interests in the language of rights

[17] Hampshire, *Innocence and Experience*, 90.

has one more advantage: It makes more transparent the connection between equal moral regard and respecting rights by emphasizing not just that there are obligations we have in regard to all persons, but obligations that *are owed to them by virtue of their humanity.*[18]

It is also worth emphasizing that even if, contrary to what the social functions of morality would lead one to expect, different societies or cultures have different *basic* moral principles, it would not follow that these disagreements cannot be resolved by reasoning. To *assume* that it does is to confuse meta-ethical cultural ethical relativism with descriptive cultural ethical relativism—to mistake a statement about the existence of disagreement for one about the impossibility of resolving disagreement by rational means.

One final distinction is pertinent to evaluating the cultural ethical relativist challenge to human rights. There are in fact two versions of meta-ethical cultural relativism: one cognitivist, the other noncognitivist. (Noncognitivism, as a meta-ethical position, is the thesis that ethical principles or judgments cannot be justified or unjustified— that there is no such thing as ethical reasoning properly speaking; cognitivism is the denial of noncognitivism.)

The cognitivist version holds that it is possible to resolve ethical disagreements within, but not across cultures. According to the cognitivist meta-ethical cultural ethical relativist, ethical statements, to the extent that they are justifiable, make an implicit reference to a particular society or culture. What is justifiable vis-à-vis one group may not be justifiable relative to another.

The noncognitivist version of meta-ethical cultural relativism is simply a corollary of a more general noncognitivist meta-ethical view: If there is no way of rationally resolving ethical disputes in general, then there is no rational way of resolving those ethical disputes that arise between different cultures. Because this is not a treatise designed to refute those who deny that morality is a matter about which we can reason, I will not take the trouble to make a systematic case for rejecting the general noncognitivist view upon

---

[18] For a more thorough defense of the claim that the value of rights discourse is not restricted to certain forms of society, and in particular a criticism of the Marxian view that rights are valuable only for "egoistic," alienated man, see Allen Buchanan, *Marx and Justice: The Radical Critique of Liberalism* (Rowman & Allanheld, Totowa, NJ, 1982). See also Allen Buchanan, 'What's so Special about Rights?', *Social Philosophy and Policy* 12/1 (1987), 61–83.

which the noncognitivist version of meta-ethical cultural ethical relativism rests.

At any rate, the cognitivist version seems to have more adherents nowadays, especially among what might be called meta-ethical communitarian relativists, such as Alasdair MacIntyre.[19] He holds that the justification of ethical judgments does occur, but can only occur within the framework of a cultural tradition, and that the differences that exist among cultural traditions make universally valid justifications for some ethical judgments impossible.

Note the qualifier 'some' in the last sentence. Presumably MacIntyre would not hold the very implausible view that there are no ethical judgments upon which persons who have internalized the values of different cultural traditions can rationally agree. (It must be said, however, that he is none too clear about what the extent of disagreement is.) According to MacIntyre's view, which is held perhaps in less extreme form by other communitarians including Michael Sandel and Michael Walzer, moral justification is a social practice in a community defined by a tradition.

To be a threat to the enterprise of basing a moral theory of international law on a conception of human rights, meta-ethical communitarianism must establish not only that (1) the differences that exist among different cultural traditions' practices for justifying ethical judgments preclude rational agreement on basic human rights among members of different cultural groups, but also that (2) these differing traditions cannot change or are not likely to change in ways that make such rational agreement possible. The first statement appears to be false, at least for many cultural traditions. As we saw above, there is a plurality of traditions, ethical and secular, whose belief systems not only support the thesis that there are human rights but also converge to a considerable extent on which rights are human rights. At the very least, it is difficult to think of a major religious tradition that precludes the endorsement of basic human rights, even if in practice religious authorities sometimes have promoted systematic violations of them.

The second statement is if anything even less defensible. Cultural traditions are not impermeable social billiard balls that are unaffected

---

[19] Alasdair MacIntyre, *After Virtue: A Study in Moral Theory* (University of Notre Dame Press, Notre Dame, IN, 1984).

by contact with exogenous forces. What I referred to earlier as the emerging global human rights culture is in one sense a new cultural tradition, but in another it is a reflection of the fact that various cultural communities (to the extent that we can distinguish them at all) are increasingly incorporating a commitment to respect for human rights. Understood as a challenge to the possibility of a moral theory of international law founded on a conception of basic human rights, meta-ethical communitarianism is a philosopher's armchair prediction that where differences about basic human rights exist among cultural traditions they will never be reduced, regardless of the growing contact and interpenetration of cultures that we call globalization.

What MacIntyre and other cognitivist meta-ethical relativists appear not to appreciate is that modes of ethical reasoning that originate in one culture penetrate into other cultures, just as number systems and scientific discoveries do. They also fail to take up the empirical burden of argument that their position requires.

Consider one example among many. Suppose we agree that the concept of individual human rights is not endogenous to the culture of the Cree Indians of Northern Quebec. Nevertheless, in their long and heroic struggle to combat injustices inflicted on them by the Canadian Federal Government, the Government of Quebec, and settlers and developers, the Crees have come to appreciate the power of the discourse of human rights. Moreover, while they may have at first embraced the concept of human rights only as an effective though uncomfortably alien instrument, many Crees now seem to have a sincere belief in human rights, even if in some cases they also believe that the existing understanding of human rights that is expressed in domestic and international law is not fully adequate for the protection of their legitimate interests.[20]

This example is not intended to suggest that the cross-cultural flow of values is unidirectional. It can be argued that the voices of indigenous peoples have begun to influence the initially "Western" understanding of human rights, partly through the growing presence of indigenous peoples' concerns in international human rights institutional processes. For example, in the Lubicon Lake case, the

[20] Grand Council of the Crees of Quebec, *Sovereign Injustice* (The Grand Council of the Crees, Nemaska, Quebec, 1995).

International Human Rights Commission's consideration of a claim brought by another indigenous group in Canada led it to interpret Article 27 of the Optional Protocol of the Convention on International Civil and Political Rights in a novel way so as to extend the scope of the individual's right to culture to include protection of his community's claims to control over land and natural resources.[21] To assume, as MacIntyre and other meta-ethical relativists seem to, that such a change in culture-based moral beliefs and patterns of justification for ethical judgments cannot take place is to adopt an indefensible—and demeaning—view of cultures (whether Western or otherwise) as inflexible, impermeable structures, incapable of growth.

I have just suggested that meta-ethical cultural ethical relativism, at least in its communitarian form, rests on unsupported speculations not just about the existence of deep cultural disagreements about human rights, but also about their permanence. I do not wish to commit the opposite error of issuing confident but empirically unsupported predictions that the global human rights culture will triumph, yielding universal agreement on a substantive list of human rights, in the foreseeable future, or ever for that matter.

My more cautious position is that the moral theorist should take heart that there does seem to be a movement toward wider consensus that some rights are human rights and that this consensus has both been facilitated by international legal institutions and has contributed to their improvement. This encouraging development—along with the weaknesses of meta-ethical cultural ethical relativism and the irrelevance of descriptive cultural ethical relativism—is sufficient to make the project of this volume intelligible and worth pursuing.

Before turning to other criticism of human rights that might, if valid, pose obstacles to the enterprise of assigning a fundamental role to human rights in a moral theory of international law, I wish to point out one peculiarity of the meta-ethical cultural relativist view. Many who call themselves ethical relativists, including those who object to assertions about human rights, also strenuously (and with more than a whiff of self-righteousness) recommend toleration,

[21] *Lubicon Lake Band* v. *Canada*, Communication No. 167/1984 (1990), UN Doc. Supp. No. 40 (A/45/40) at 1.

condemning those who would attempt to enforce human rights globally as intolerant ethical imperialists.[22]

This all-too-common combination of views is inconsistent to the point of absurdity, whether the relativist is a cognitivist or not. If the meta-ethical cultural relativist is a cognitivist, then he must admit that it is inappropriate to expect his charge of intolerance or ethical imperialism to carry any argumentative weight with those whose own cultural tradition endorses human rights norms and accepts them as placing limits on what is to be tolerated. For example, if the so-called ethical imperialist is a member of a culture whose tradition provides resources for justifying human rights norms, then he should not in any way feel embarrassed about seeking to enforce them on those in other cultures. If, on the other hand, the charge of ethical imperialism comes from a noncognitivist meta-ethical cultural relativist, then he must admit that his plea for toleration is merely an expression of disapproval toward acts intended to enforce human rights, not a statement that can be supported with reasons. My sense is that self-styled cultural ethical relativists who accuse others of cultural imperialism believe they are doing more than merely expressing their disapproval.

Later in this chapter I will argue that descriptive cultural ethical relativism—the view that in fact there are differences in ethical values or principles among cultures—is directly relevant to the issue of intervention for the sake of human rights, even though it does not show that there are no human rights. If this is the case, then the appropriate strategy for those who are impressed with cultural differences is not to slip from descriptive cultural ethical relativism into meta-ethical cultural relativism (which makes their own conviction that ethical imperialism is wrong nothing more than an expression of taste or at best a parochial ethical view) and from there to challenging the very notion of human rights. Instead they should concentrate on developing a principled view about intervention for the sake of human rights that takes the facts of cultural differences seriously. The best way to do this is to ground limits on intervention in the same equal consideration for persons that is the

---

[22] Nussbaum points out this inconsistency on the part of many meta-ethical relativists in *Women and Human Development*, 49.

basis of human rights and which implies that intervention to protect human rights is sometimes justifiable.

Excessive individualism

Sometimes it is said that the putative human rights found in the Universal Declaration of Human Rights and the two International Covenants are excessively individualistic.[23] This charge is usually accompanied by the further assertion that this excessive individualism reflects a Western bias and that the endeavor to enforce these rights is therefore an instance of cultural imperialism. The charge of cultural ethical imperialism I probe later in this chapter in a discussion of the relationship between tolerance and the commitment to human rights. Here I concentrate on the idea that human rights, as represented in these key international documents that together form what is sometimes called the International Bill of Human Rights, focus on individual interests at the expense of the community's good or are founded on a conception of the individual as an isolated atom rather than as a being deeply embedded in community.

To anyone familiar with the history of what we now call human rights and the function that appeals to human rights have in the world today, the charge of excessive individualism must appear puzzling if not bizarre. Since the end of the religious wars of the sixteenth and seventeenth century in Europe, and with greater effectiveness today because they are supported by international legal institutions, rights to freedom of expression and association and to freedom of religion have played a valuable role in protecting *communities*. Therefore, to maintain that these core human rights are only rights for atomistic individuals requires something approaching willful stupidity. They are rights that contribute greatly to the flourishing of communities, whether they are religious, political, or "lifestyle" communities.

---

[23] United Nations (1948), 'Universal Declaration of Human Rights', repr. in Carter and Trimble, *International Law: Selected Documents*, 381–6; United Nations (1966), 'International Covenants on Civil and Political Rights', repr. in *International Law: Selected Documents*, 387–403; United Nations (1966), 'International Covenant on Economic, Social and Cultural Rights,' repr. in *International Law: Selected Documents*, 410–18; and United Nations General Assembly (1948), 'Convention on the Prevention and Punishment of the Crime of Genocide', repr. in *International Law: Selected Documents*, 419–21.

Similarly, the right against torture and the right to liberty of the person, understood as including rights of due process under the law and freedom from arbitrary arrest and seizure, are of great value to groups, since often it is because of their hostility toward groups that governments and others attack individuals. In brief, some of the most important human rights, though ascribed to individuals, are justified in part by their value in protecting communities and hence should be enthusiastically endorsed by communitarians who rail against the excessive individualism of modern societies.

To pose an obstacle to the enterprise of developing a moral theory of international law that gives a preeminent place to human rights, the complaint about excessive individualism would have to be reformulated: Human rights as exclusively individual rights—rights ascribed to individuals—are an inadequate account of justice for a justice-based moral theory of international law. Put more positively, this is the claim that the conception of justice appropriate for international law must include *group* rights, as well as individual rights.

Of course, international law already includes group rights: All the legal rights of states are group rights, as are the legal rights of corporations recognized in international commercial law. In Chapters 8 and 9 I develop an account of one important class of group rights, rights of self-government short of independent statehood. There I argue that the protection of individual human rights requires both international legal recognition of a limited right to secede and international support for intrastate autonomy arrangements that accord rights of self-determination short of full statehood to minority groups, including indigenous peoples. In that discussion I make it clear that an emphasis on individual human rights as the core of justice in no way prejudices the theory I am advancing against groups, their interests, or group rights. A theory can take individual rights as morally primary, but make plenty of room for the moral necessity of recognizing legal rights that are group rights.

Sometimes the charge of excessive individualism is elaborated as follows. The doctrine of human rights, understood as individual rights, is rooted in liberal moral theory. But (so the objection goes) liberal moral theory rests on indefensibly individualistic ontological and motivational assumptions. Therefore, human rights, understood as individual rights, cannot serve as the basis for a moral theory of international law.

This version of the excessive individualism objection can be dismissed rather quickly. It rests on a mistaken understanding of liberalism. Liberalism is individualistic in a moral or justificatory sense, not an ontological or motivational sense. According to liberalism it is only individuals ultimately that matter morally speaking and hence justifications for moral principles, actions, and policies must ultimately refer to the well-being and freedom of individuals. It follows that liberalism can accommodate group rights if their ultimate justification is that they provide protections for important interests of individuals—including their interests in their identity as members of a group.

This justificatory or moral individualism must be distinguished both from motivational and from ontological individualism. As an individualistic view about moral justification and what ultimately counts morally speaking, liberalism can freely acknowledge that individuals can be motivated by direct concern for others or for groups of which they are members; it is not committed to motivational individualism, much less to psychological egoism. Similarly, liberalism's justificatory individualism need not deny the existence of groups nor need it assert that all putative properties of groups can be reduced to properties of individuals—it can remain agnostic as to the truth or falsity of ontological individualism. Although some critics of liberalism blithely assume that justificatory, motivational, and ontological individualism must go together, none has shown why this is so.[24]

VI. *Human Rights and the Bounds of Toleration*

The allegation of moral imperialism

Earlier in this chapter we encountered the familiar charge that appeals to human rights in international law constitute moral imperialism. The term 'imperialism' implies intrusion and domination, as well as disrespect. Thus the charge is that alien ethical concepts or values are being inappropriately imposed on someone, that this

---

[24] For a more detailed discussion of the nature of liberalism, see Allen Buchanan, 'Assessing the Communitarian Critique of Liberalism', *Ethics* 99 (1989), 852–82.

imposition both facilitates domination and is itself a form of domination, and that those who impose alien values thereby fail to show proper respect for the values of others. The source of the alien ethical values or concepts is said to be European culture or "the West."

I have already addressed one variant of the ethical imperialist charge: the assertion that human rights are excessively individualistic, thus reflecting the excessive individualism of the West or of the liberal moral theory that arose in the West and is so prominent there. That allegation, I argued, is based on a failure to appreciate the communitarian value of appeals to human rights—their efficacy in protecting communities. I also noted, however, that there is a more sophisticated variant of this objection according to which it is said that human rights as individual rights are insufficient to protect certain communities, that group rights also deserve protection by international law. My initial response to the latter charge was that international law is already primarily a system of group rights (of states), but that an interesting question remains as to whether, or rather to what extent, international law should recognize group rights of various sorts for entities other than states. I postpone that issue until Part Three (Self-Determination).

A different criticism of the modern human rights movement and of any attempt to base an international legal order on the idea of human rights is the charge of intolerance. I now want to examine what I take to be the two most developed and influential views on tolerance, those of Rawls and Walzer, to see whether giving tolerance its due undercuts the possibility of a moral theory of international law grounded in what I have called basic human rights. My conclusion will be that exercising the virtue of tolerance is quite consistent with endorsing such a theory and that Rawls and Walzer both overestimate the constraints of tolerance.

Rawls's view on the relationship between tolerance and human rights

As I emphasized in Chapter 1, Rawls contends that the list of human rights is significantly shorter than that found in the International Bill of Human Rights (the Universal Declaration of Rights and the two Covenants) and shorter than what I take to be the list of basic human rights. Rawls is not merely skeptical about some of the more dubious putative economic rights, such as the "right to periodic holidays with pay." His list includes only rights against slavery, involuntary servitude, and forced occupations, a right against religious persecution (but not a more robust right to freedom of religion or even to freedom from serious forms of discrimination on grounds of religion), a right to hold personal property, a right to emigrate (but not a right of acceptance, even for political refugees), a right to resources for subsistence, and a very limited right to political participation and dissent at an appropriate level of what he calls a "consultation hierarchy," a structure of institutions that allows for representation, but only for individuals as members of socially recognized groups, and which is compatible not only with significant inequalities of political power but with legal prohibitions on the vast majority of citizens participating in the higher levels of government.[25]

Presumably Rawls also includes the right not to be tortured, though he does not say so. Nor does he mention security of the person as provided by rights of due process (freedom from arbitrary search and seizure, etc.). Most conspicuously absent from Rawls's list of human rights are the right of freedom of expression, the right to freedom of association, rights against discrimination on grounds of ethnicity, nationality, gender, or sexual orientation, and the right against various forms of religious discrimination that fall short of "persecution."

However, in describing a hypothetical nonliberal but "decent" society—one that he believes is entitled to be treated with tolerance—Rawls does stipulate that religious minorities, though barred from government office, are not subject to other forms of religious discrimination. It is not at all clear, however, that either his list of human rights or the theory he develops to support them rules out such discrimination.

Rawls's lean list of human rights appears to imply that a society that included the following features could *not* be characterized as one in which human rights violations occur: there is a permanent, hereditary caste whose members are systematically relegated to a condition of poverty (barely above subsistence) and women are systematically denied the opportunity for an education, are excluded

---

[25] Rawls, *The Law of Peoples*, 71–8.

from political participation (except by being represented in a "consultation hierarchy") and from desirable economic positions, and are not allowed to go outside the home except under highly restrictive conditions (they must wear cumbersome garments that cover virtually the whole body regardless of season; they must be accompanied by a male relative; they are not allowed into many important kinds of public places at all). Depending upon how the right against religious persecution is construed, Rawls's list might also allow a great deal of religious discrimination, so long as members of minority religions were not subject to violence or severe legal penalties. To repeat: his right against religious persecution is not as extensive as a right to freedom from religious discrimination; nor does he list a human right against discrimination on grounds of ethnicity, nationality, or race.

I pointed out in Chapter 1 that for Rawls this truncated list of human rights is not subject to expansion as the institutions of international law become more effective. It is not Rawls's concession to what is now feasible; for him it is a matter of deep principle in ideal theory. More specifically, his conception of human rights is a consequence of his views about the connection between reasonableness and toleration. He approaches the question of which rights are human rights in an unusual way, by asking: What conditions must a society meet if we (citizens of liberal societies) are to recognize it as a legitimate member of the society of peoples, entitled to noninterference in its domestic affairs?[26]

According to Rawls, a society that respects his truncated list of human rights and is nonexpansionist (does not engage in wars of aggression) meets the test. He also thinks, however, that not just liberal citizens but also those who are members of nonliberal societies that qualify as "decent" societies would have reason to agree on the same list of conditions for recognition that liberals should endorse.[27]

Where does Rawls get this lean list of human rights? He derives them from his conception of reasonableness, which includes the idea of acknowledging the burdens of judgment, in combination with his understanding of what it takes for a society to exemplify what he calls a common good conception of justice. In a recent

[26] Rawls, *The Law of Peoples*, 27, 42, 79.   [27] Ibid. 65, 68, 79.

article I have analyzed the relevant Rawlsian texts to reconstruct the following argument, which links these concepts in a coherent way.[28]

1. A society is entitled to noninterference (and to be regarded as a member in good standing of the society of peoples under international law) if and only if it is organized by reasonable principles.
2. Principles for organizing a society are reasonable if and only if they would be accepted by reasonable persons, that is, by those who (*a*) acknowledge the burdens of judgment and (*b*) are willing to propose and accept fair terms of cooperation.
3. Those who acknowledge the burdens of judgment will not attempt to impose their conception of the good on other societies that are organized by reasonable principles.
4. A society is organized on the basis of fair terms of cooperation if and only if it is organized by a common good conception of justice.
5. If a society is organized by a common good conception of justice, then it will respect (the Rawlsian) human rights.
6. Therefore, a society is entitled to noninterference (and to be recognized as a member in good standing of the society of states under international law) if and only if it is nonexpansionist (i.e., does not attempt to impose its conceptions of the good or of justice on societies organized by reasonable principles) and respects (the Rawlsian) human rights.

A significant advantage of this reconstruction is that it presents Rawls's thought as a coherent whole, integrating in a consistent manner his emphasis on the connection between reasonableness and legitimacy in *Political Liberalism* with his project of determining the bounds of tolerance in international law in *The Law of Peoples*. Without the link between reasonableness, fair terms of cooperation, a common good conception of justice, and noninterference supplied by premises 2, 4, and 5, one would be left with the impression that Rawls's list of human rights appears out of nowhere or is merely

---

[28] Allen Buchanan, 'Justice, Legitimacy, and Human Rights', in Victoria Davion and Clark Wolf (eds.), *The Idea of Political Liberalism* (Rowman & Littlefield, Lanham, MD, 2000).

Rawls's intuition about what conditions a "decent" society would satisfy.

To evaluate Rawls's argument we must examine closely his conception of reasonableness, including the idea of what it is to acknowledge the burdens of judgment and the idea of a common good conception of justice. For Rawls being reasonable requires showing proper respect for the reason of others. It is this respect for reason that is the foundation of Rawls's conception of toleration and which leads him to endorse only a truncated list of human rights.

Since showing respect for reason and thereby observing the bounds of toleration requires not imposing one's own conception of justice on those who hold different but reasonable conceptions, we need to know what counts as a reasonable conception of justice. According to Rawls, for a conception of justice to be reasonable it must include or qualify as a common good conception of justice. The key element of a common good conception of justice, according to Rawls, is that public institutions must express the principle that the good of every member of society counts. Rawls also appears to believe that a society that is organized according to a common good conception of justice will be a genuine scheme of *cooperation*, by which he apparently means that all can participate voluntarily in it on the assumption that it is an enterprise for mutual benefit. In contrast, a slave society, which he assumes can only be maintained by force, is not a genuine cooperative scheme. On this interpretation, Rawls is saying that only societies that are genuine cooperative schemes are decent and warrant toleration.

It seems to me that Rawls wavers between saying respect for his list of human rights is a necessary condition for a society being a cooperative scheme and saying that it is necessary for fair cooperation. It also seems to me that the latter idea is more promising.

There are two problems with the idea of a society being entitled to toleration if it is a genuine scheme of cooperation where this means that its members participate voluntarily rather than being held together by force. First, all societies rely on force in so far as they include the enforcement of laws and it is probable that some degree of enforcement of some laws is necessary for a society to function, at least in the case of large-scale societies. The difficulty for Rawls, then, is how to distinguish between acceptable and unacceptable levels or types of force. He provides no basis for making such a distinction. Instead he only points to slavery as what he takes to be an uncontroversial case of a society founded on force, not a genuine cooperative scheme. Second, it appears that a society may be indefensibly inegalitarian and yet may not rely excessively on force if it has powerful resources for acculturating people to accept their inferior status. That is why the fact that a society is not held together by naked force in the way in which slave systems are is not a sufficient condition for it being worthy of toleration. The fact that a society enjoys the "voluntary" support of those it treats in grossly demeaning ways may not carry much normative weight if such "voluntariness" is itself an artifact of inegalitarian institutions and practices.

Nor does the fact that every person's good counts seem sufficient to make a society worthy of toleration. Everyone's good counting is compatible with the good of some counting much less than the good of others; indeed, it is compatible with the good of some not counting much at all and with there being nothing approaching a minimally rational justification for grossly unequal treatment.

In addition, there is a fundamental ambiguity in Rawls's explication of the idea of a common good conception of justice: Does each individual's good mean his or her good as conceived according to the dominant values of the society in question or according to some independent, objective conception of human good? If the former, then the reasonableness criterion would seem to allow conceptions of justice that are very deeply and arbitrarily inegalitarian, so long as their dominant values conceive of the good of some individuals (for example, women or untouchables or blacks) as being defined primarily or exclusively in terms of how the role assigned to them contributes to the good of others or of society or on the basis of some assumption that they are different by nature from those who are accorded greater rights and benefits—for example, according to the idea that they are incapable of higher pleasures or higher forms of human existence.

My point is not that Rawls would himself regard profoundly inegalitarian societies as "decent" or that he would agree that a common good conception of justice is compatible with them. (As I have already observed, the one sketchy example of a "decent" (though non liberal) society Rawls gives—the mythical land of Kazanistan—does not appear to include such extreme inequalities, at least with regard to the treatment of religious minorities.) My point is that regardless of what Rawls thinks it implies, his standard for what counts as a decent society allows extreme inequalities and indeed extreme inequalities that are morally arbitrary and indefensible.

Rawls thinks that societies that only satisfy his truncated list of human rights exemplify a common good conception of justice. This is not surprising, given how minimal is the requirement that each individual's good is to count. Even if 'good' in "everyone's good is to count" is defined in some objective way, rather than simply as it is conceived in that society, a society can exemplify a common good conception of justice and still be severely inegalitarian and can base profound social inequalities on hereditary status or even race. Even if a society as severely racist as apartheid South Africa would be ruled out—on the grounds that it could only be maintained by unacceptable types or levels of force—it appears that Rawls's notion of a common good conception of justice, of each person's good counting, is compatible with more severe inequalities than his sketch of a hypothetical "decent" society suggests. In particular it seems compatible with systematic discrimination against religious minorities in both the private and the public sphere, which Rawls simply stipulates does not occur in Kazanistan.

My concern, however, is not whether Rawls's description of a hypothetical decent though non liberal society conforms to his conditions for a decent society. My aim is to determine whether Rawls is correct in thinking that international law should refrain from imposing standards of justice on societies that satisfy his criteria for being decent.

Why should the international community only require that a society should count each person's good (even when a society's conception of justice defines it as the good of a naturally inferior being) and not be so dependent upon the use of force for maintaining order as a slave society? Why is it intolerant to expect societies to meet a higher standard than the truncated list of rights? And why should we assume that where Rawls's truncated list of rights is satisfied, participation in social relations will be voluntary for all persons in any morally significant sense of 'voluntary'? For Rawls, the answer to these questions lies in a proper understanding of what it is to be reasonable and this in turn requires an appreciation of what he calls the burdens of judgment.

Acknowledging the burdens of judgment means giving proper weight to the fact that reasonable persons can have unresolvable disagreements even on fundamental questions, including questions of justice and concerning what he calls comprehensive conceptions of the good (which are value systems that extend beyond principles of public order to include ideals of individual flourishing). According to Rawls, such disagreements can be due to any of several factors, including the fact that "evidence...[can be] conflicting and complex, and thus hard to assess and evaluate," the fact that even when "we agree fully about the kinds of considerations that are relevant [to value judgments], we may disagree about their weight," and that "there are different kinds of normative considerations on both sides of an issue and it is difficult to make an overall assessment."[29]

At this point we encounter a grave defect in Rawls's argument. He provides no further content to the idea of properly acknowledging the burdens of judgment. In particular, he says nothing to help us distinguish between a proper humility or appropriate caution in the light of the several sources of disagreement among reasonable people and a failure to exercise even rather minimal critical scrutiny regarding the quality of the reasoning we or others use to support conceptions of justice. In other words, Rawls offers nothing like a conception of *justificatory* (or epistemic) *responsibility*—minimal standards for what counts as acceptable reasons, apart from logical consistency or coherence and the suggestion that reasonable conceptions are "conscientiously" held. (Nothing Rawls says suggests that the latter implies anything more than sincerity.)

Thomas Christiano characterizes Rawls's conception of reasonableness as subjectivist.[30] This is almost correct. With the exception of the very minimal constraint on reasonable conceptions of public order imposed by the requirement of consistency or coherence and the requirement that they must exemplify a common good conception of justice (that everyone's good is to count), Rawls's conception is subjective. There is no trace of a requirement of minimal rationality (beyond logical consistency and coherence). Christiano correctly

[29] John Rawls, *Political Liberalism* (Columbia University Press, New York, 1993), 56–7.
[30] Thomas Christiano, 'Justice and Disagreement at the Foundations of Political Authority', review of Christopher Morris, *An Essay on the Modern State*, *Ethics* 110 (2000), 165–87.

observes that such a weak conception of reasonableness is itself as controversial as the comprehensive conceptions of human good that Rawls wants to avoid basing his principles of justice on.

Quite apart from that, there is another reason to reject Rawls's subjectivistic conception of reasonableness: If the goal is to show respect for reason, or for human beings so far as they are reason-givers and beings capable of choosing and acting on reasons, then why should we assume that mere logical consistency, coherence, and conscientiousness (along with implementation of a common good conception of justice and the requirement that social interaction is not coerced as it is in slave societies) are worthy of respect? Surely proper respect for reason—our own as well as that of others—demands that what are given as reasons must meet certain minimal standards beyond Rawls's largely subjectivistic criteria. For example, to count as a reasonable conception of public order a view must not rest on patently false empirical premises; nor can the 'reasoning' offered in favor of it rely on obviously fallacious inferences or blatant equivocations on key terms, or on flagrant overgeneralizations from scanty or unrepresentative evidence.

Why should we accept as reasonable a conception of society that 'justifies' a system of serious racial inequalities only by a combination of extraordinarily sloppy reasoning and patently false empirical premises about natural differences between untouchables and Brahmans or blacks and whites? And how could the fact that the system of inequalities is not quite so egregious as to require naked and pervasive force for its maintenance, but instead manages to reproduce itself through the systematic promulgation of misinformation about the natural characteristics of various groups, render acceptable what is so clearly unreasonable?

Respect for reason cannot require treating as reasonable views that are clearly irrational. And to ignore the most minimal requirements of rationality on the grounds that not everyone observes them would be to deny one's own reason the respect it is due and to take a patronizing view of others' capacities for reason.

At this juncture it is important to recall that our critical examination of Rawls's conception of reasonableness has a practical purpose. We are attempting to determine whether he is correct in asserting that some of what international law regards as human rights are not human rights at all. Rawls's claim is that if we are reasonable, in particular if we acknowledge the burdens of judgment with a proper humility, then we will limit our list of human rights to those he recognizes.

Rawls merely assumes without argument, then, that a richer set of human rights—one that includes a right against serious gender, ethnic, or racial discrimination for example—violates the reasonableness standard, and is an unreasonable imposition of the views of some upon others who can reasonably reject them. What he seems to overlook is that in the real world of human rights discourse those who advocate public orders of extreme inequality are quite reasonably expected to provide arguments for the inequalities they endorse and that these arguments typically do *not* meet minimal standards for justificatory responsibility.

Although I cannot canvass all of them here, I can sketch some of the more familiar justifications offered by the advocates of extreme inequality and suggest why I think one can criticize them effectively without failing to show proper humility and caution in the light of the burdens of judgment. My aim is to show that the arguments typically given in favor of regimes that discriminate on the basis of caste, ethnicity, or gender, or that reject democratic governance, fail to meet the minimal standards of rationality that respect for reason requires.[31]

Consider a standard argument frequently offered by dictators, oligarchs, or their spokesmen (including servile academics) in developing countries: There is no universal, that is, human right to democratic government because in some societies (including this one) democracy is incompatible with the kind of social discipline needed for effective economic development.

This argument, like most modern arguments for undemocratic government, rests on empirical generalizations about what does or does not facilitate economic development or other dimensions of the common good (rather than on appeals to divine right, as in early defenses of monarchical government, or to alleged natural differences among humans, as in Plato's Republic). The effective reply to such arguments is to challenge the empirical generalizations on which they rest, and they are very dubious generalizations indeed.

---

[31] This and the next paragraph draw on Buchanan, 'Justice, Legitimacy, and Human Rights'.

For example, there is substantial evidence that undemocratic regimes tend to be plagued by corruption, including ubiquitous rent-seeking (purely parasitic) behavior on the part of even the most lowly officials, that corruption retards economic development, and that undemocratic states are more prone to economic disasters, including famines.

In *The Law of Peoples* Rawls never scrutinizes arguments for inequality. Consequently, he pays no attention whatsoever to the role of false empirical generalizations in justifications for political or other inequalities. Instead he simply conjectures that these justifications meet his very minimal subjectivist standards for being reasonable views (coherence, sincerity, consistency, compatibility with everyone's good counting for something). Rawls is also on shaky ground if he believes that the reasonableness criterion does not rule out social orders that are deeply sexist, which systematically deprive women of rights that men enjoy without providing anything like compensating advantages for women in other areas of the social distribution of benefits and burdens.

Consider the fate of women under the Taliban theocratic regime in Afghanistan. Women reportedly were not allowed anything beyond the most basic education, if that; nor were they allowed to participate in political processes. They also had very limited rights regarding divorce, though men had substantial rights in this regard. They were also barred from almost all occupations outside the home.

Now Rawls might object that a society controlled by the Taliban does not meet his criterion for being decent. According to Rawls, decent societies, though not democratic, do include what he calls a "consultation hierarchy" and presumably women would be represented in this.

However, it is not clear that inclusion of women in the consultation hierarchy ensures that they will be protected from discrimination that is damaging to some of their fundamental interests as human beings, including the interest in being able to exercise some of what Nussbaum calls the central human capabilities. The first problem is that Rawls is not very clear about just what is entailed by the notion of a consultation hierarchy.

What is more, he gives no indication of the impact that the social context surrounding them may have on the representation of interests within consultation hierarchies. If the surrounding background social practices and institutions are sufficiently oppressive of women, the representation of women's interests, even by women, may be so inadequate that it is compatible with some of the severe inequalities that reportedly existed in Taliban society. To put the matter somewhat crudely, the women who participate in the consultative process may be brainwashed into submissiveness by being acculturated within a sexist framework of social institutions and practices. Furthermore, it is only a *consultative* process, which presumably means that even if women participate in it and accurately assert the fundamental interests of women, what they say may either be ignored or interpreted paternalistically, along lines that support grossly unequal social arrangements.

If the consultation hierarchy were embedded in the right sort of broader institutional scheme, these problems might be avoided. But it is hard to see how this could be accomplished without implementing a richer list of human rights than Rawls is willing to endorse. More specifically, rights to basic education, to freedom of association and expression, and rights regarding employment and property ownership that provide opportunities for women to have some degree of economic independence if they do not conform to traditional roles—all of these rights may be necessary if women's basic interests are to be effectively represented in the consultation hierarchy.

Again, let me emphasize that I believe that Rawls himself did not think that his notion of a decent society was compatible with institutionalized racism, or a caste system, or the rule of the Taliban. My point, rather, is that his notion of a common good conception of justice when combined with his conception of tolerance seems to commit him to an unpalatable view. Nor does the addition of the requirement that social participation is 'voluntary', not forced, guarantee that such *intolerable* inequalities will not exist.

To make this point clearer, it is necessary to understand just how problematic Rawls's conception of tolerance is. Surely a proper humility in recognition of the burdens of judgment does not preclude us from requiring that a positive defense of extreme inequalities among races or between men and women be provided by those who endorse them, nor from criticizing such a defense by pointing out that it rests either on unsupported assumptions to the effect that the "essential interests" of women differ from those of men or that women are not morally equal to men except in the very minimal sense that their good is to count for something, or else upon bogus generalizations about the licentiousness of women or the inability of men to control their lust when they find themselves in proximity to human beings that are recognizably female. My surmise is that in general the defenders of gender, racial, ethnic, or caste inequalities tend to make just these sorts of assumptions and that these assumptions are eminently criticizable—that they fail to meet the minimal standards for moral argument that are compatible with a proper recognition of the burdens of judgment and required by due respect for our own reason.

The example of racial inequalities is illuminating. It is sometimes said that advocates of racial inequalities believe that persons should be treated differently simply because of the color of their skin. This betrays a gross misunderstanding of racism. Racists believe that a darker skin is merely the external mark of an inner inferiority. When pressed to justify apartheid or Jim Crow laws, the racist appeals to a web of empirical generalizations about the moral and intellectual inferiority of blacks, assertions about the nature of black people. These generalizations can and ought to be challenged. (To take yet another example, proponents of the practice of clitoridectomy typically claim that it enhances fertility. Clinical evidence indicates that precisely the opposite is true: The procedure often results in infections that can scar the fallopian tubes, resulting in sterility.)

This is not to say that disagreement between racists and antiracists is always purely empirical, only that it invariably includes a significant empirical element without which the racist's justifications fail in their own terms. The racist may also be wrong, not only about his empirical generalizations concerning the moral and intellectual defects of blacks, but also about which sorts of differences among human beings provide a plausible basis for unequal treatment. The error of mistaken generalizations about the nature of blacks may be compounded by indefensible assumptions about which characteristics of human beings are relevant to their basic moral status. One such assumption is that those of lesser intelligence have no rights or only rights of an inferior character. This kind of view can be and indeed has been successfully rebutted by careful reflection on just what it is about persons that grounds their most basic rights.

It might be objected that some who advocate gender, racial, ethnic, or caste inequalities of the sort that are compatible with Rawls's lean list of human rights do not defend them on the basis of unsupported assumptions about which natural characteristics confer rights or patently false empirical generalizations (or uncontroversially fallacious patterns of inference). They simply claim that the inequalities are required by the revealed doctrines of their comprehensive religious conceptions of the good.

To this I would reply that it would be very implausible to hold that rejecting such a 'purely religious' justification for serious inequalities is intolerant. It is the person who refuses to give what I referred to earlier as humanistic reasons—reasons referring to the good of human beings as providing sufficient moral reasons in its own right—who fails to show proper respect for human reason by substituting alleged revelation for reasoning of the sort accessible to all humans of normal cognitive capacities.

Reasonableness, if this includes a proper recognition of the plurality of ethical views, secular as well as religious, and has anything to do with respect for human reason, cannot allow appeals to revelation when it comes to the justification of principles of public order. In other words, properly recognizing what might be called the burdens of reasonableness—what I referred to earlier as justificatory responsibility—in a world containing not only different religious conceptions of the good but secular ones as well, requires that argumentation concerning "the fair terms of cooperation" among human beings be framed in terms of the interests of human beings in their own right, as these interests can be known by anyone with normal capacities of human reason.

Rawls himself admits as much when he asserts that reasonableness demands at least that a public order must recognize the minimal commitment to the equality of persons captured by the idea of a common good conception of justice (that everyone's good is to count). But once we go this far, we are within the domain of humanistic reasons, and the burden of justification lies on those who support inequalities as to the weights that the goods of various individuals ought to be accorded.

That burden cannot be borne simply by making religious claims that are unconnected to an appeal to facts and patterns of inference available to all who possess human reason. And if that is so, then appeals to revelation do not meet the standard of justificatory responsibility that respect for reason includes.

We now have a response to the challenge posed by the Christian imperialist encountered earlier in this chapter—the individual who advocates religious persecution to establish a public order he believes to be necessary for protecting the most important human interest, the interest in salvation. His justification for violating what we believe to be the human right against religious persecution at best meets only a necessary condition for justificatory responsibility: It appeals to human good (asserting that the highest interest of human beings is salvation). But this is not sufficient for reasonableness. In addition, the conception of human good appealed to, and the assertion that a particular social order alone is conducive to the good understood in that way, must be capable of support by appeal to reasons that are accessible to all human beings by virtue of their human reason. Appeals to the revealed will of God do not meet this condition.

As noted earlier, Rawls supplies no account of what proper respect for the reason of human beings demands when it comes to assessing the reasonableness of comprehensive conceptions of the good beyond what Christiano calls the subjectivist epistemic notion. He provides no set of objective minimal epistemic standards, either for empirical claims or for the validity of inferences, so far as these are employed in justifications for principles of public order. In other words, Rawls assumes that reasoning is entitled to respect if it is coherent, consistent, sincere, and yields a conception of public order in which everyone's good is to count, even if it includes patently fallacious inferences without which its conclusions cannot be supported and relies crucially on unsupported generalizations about the nature of blacks, women, or untouchables.

The preceding discussion of the role of unsupported empirical generalizations in the justifications typically given for extremely inegalitarian public orders suggests that a conception of reasonableness that includes even rather minimal objective epistemic standards will rule out as unreasonable considerably more than Rawls thinks. If this is so, then it is possible to advance a considerably richer list of human rights than those Rawls endorses, without exceeding the proper bounds of tolerance.

The fundamental flaw in Rawls's account of toleration can also be put in this way: Rawls collapses respect for reason into an over-expansive conception of humility based on a subjectivistic view of what counts as a reasonable conception of public order, thereby sacrificing a commitment to equal consideration of persons to that flawed conception of reasonableness. But even if he were right (as he surely is not) in thinking that respect for the reason of persons mandates such extreme toleration (or, rather, near total suspension of critical judgment!), it would not follow that we should pare down the list of human rights and assert that arbitrarily inegalitarian public orders respect human rights. Instead, we should recognize that equal consideration for persons may sometimes require imposing protections for certain extremely important human interests even on those who reject them on the basis of views that are reasonable. Respect for the reason of persons—respect for their judgments about what is good or just—is not all there is to respect for persons; it is only one component of it, and perhaps not the most important at that.

Rawls thinks that we ought to refrain from interfering with those who strive to shape society to fit their conception of the good so long as that conception is coherent, consistent, sincerely held, and treats everyone's good as counting for something and so long as the social order is not maintained only by pervasive, naked force. But refraining from interfering with efforts to implement conceptions of the good that meet these extraordinarily weak criteria for reasonableness may result in some persons in that society not being treated with the equal respect that all persons are due.

Unless Rawls is willing to abandon the whole project of developing what he calls a political conception of justice—unless he is willing to rely on a comprehensive conception of the good that elevates respect for reason to the highest moral principle, higher even than respect for persons themselves or equal consideration for their well-being—he must recognize that respect for persons' reasons is not the be all and end all of morality. He must recognize that respect for persons' reasons may sometimes have to be subordinated to the demands of a more comprehensive principle of equal consideration of persons, whether this is spelled out as equal respect for persons or equal concern for their well-being.

To my knowledge Rawls offers no intimation of an argument to show that respect for persons' reasons has absolute priority over equal respect for persons all things considered or equal concern for the well-being of persons. To attempt to do so would be to base his moral theory of international law, and indeed his entire theory of justice, on a kind of hyper-Kantian comprehensive moral conception that focuses only on one dimension of personhood, the giving of reasons. This would mean the abandonment of political liberalism and a reversion to one of the more controversial comprehensive conceptions of the good imaginable. The idea that the supreme object of moral concern is respect for the reasoning of persons, even when their 'reasoning' fails to meet any standards of justificatory responsibility other than sincerity, coherence, and logical consistency (along with acknowledgment that everyone's good is to count where this is compatible with the good of some counting for almost nothing comparatively speaking) is if anything more controversial than the Kantian or utilitarian comprehensive moral conceptions that Rawls rejects as being unreasonable bases for international order.

The results of my critical examination of Rawls's position on the relationship between tolerance and the role that human rights ought to play in a moral theory of international law can be summarized. Rawls holds that human rights should play a major role in a theory of international law, but he offers a list of human rights that is much leaner than that found in the International Bill of Rights and even leaner than that which I believe should form the core of a justice-based moral theory of international law. Moreover, some of the rights absent from his list are thought by many to be important and relatively uncontroversial, such as the right against the more serious forms of discrimination on grounds of gender, race, ethnicity, or nationality and against exclusion from political participation in the higher levels of government on the basis of race. I have also argued, however, that the conception of tolerance that Rawls advances is so flawed that it poses no barrier to a richer role for human rights in moral theorizing about international law.

Rawls's fundamental insight about the moral theory of international law

Despite these criticisms of Rawls's views, I wish to emphasize that I am in complete agreement with the basic idea that grounds his approach to the moral theory of international law: it is wrong to require all societies to satisfy the same standards of justice that may be justifiably enforced in liberal democratic societies. I agree with him that what I call standards of transnational justice should not require what we, the citizens of liberal democracies, reasonably believe is perfect justice. My theory has that much in common with Rawls's variety of 'moral minimalism'. That is the chief reason why I am attempting to work out a moral theory of international law that is grounded in the conception of *basic* human rights.

My disagreement with Rawls concerns just how minimal the minimum is and, more importantly with how toleration shapes the minimum. I have already indicated why I think that Rawls's conception of human rights is too forgiving of at least some of the more damaging forms of inequality. In the next chapter I argue that Rawls makes a much more serious mistake in thinking that there is no place in the ideal moral theory of international law for principles of distributive justice that go beyond recognition of a right to subsistence. The chief conclusion I wish to draw at this juncture, however, is that Rawls's valuable insight that principles of justice suitable for a liberal democratic society cannot serve as standards of transnational justice does not preclude a foundational role in the ideal moral theory of international law for a more substantial conception of human rights than he imagines.

Walzer: respect for cultural integrity as a limitation on human rights or their enforcement

In his provocative and insightful book *Just and Unjust Wars* and in several subsequent papers, Michael Walzer develops a view of the importance of cultural integrity that he believes imposes very strong constraints on humanitarian intervention.[32] According to Walzer, what some theorists have called a comprehensive culture is a collective enterprise for the articulation of social meanings, including those that supply content for abstract notions of justice.[33] This collective cultural enterprise is of such great moral importance that it warrants extraordinary protections from intrusive forces that would disrupt its integrity.

[32] Michael Walzer, *Just and Unjust Wars: A Moral Argument with Historical Illustrations* (Basic Books, New York, 1977), 86–108.
[33] Avashai Margalit and Joseph Raz, 'National Self-Determination', 439–61.

Although Walzer is perhaps not wholly clear about this, he can be interpreted as a justificatory individualist, in spite of this emphasis on the collective enterprise. On this interpretation, Walzer believes that the integrity of the collective cultural enterprise warrants protection ultimately because participation in it is of such profound importance for individual human beings. He concludes that protecting cultural integrity requires a very austere rule regarding humanitarian intervention: Only when genocide or something very close to it is taking place or is imminently threatened is intervention justified, except in cases where another power has already intervened in an internal conflict and thereby disrupted the endogenous competition for control.[34]

If Walzer is correct, then all the human rights other than the right against genocide (and perhaps also the right not to be killed along with very large numbers of other persons) cannot function as legitimate requirements of international law because efforts to enforce them would interfere with cultural integrity. Understood in this way, Walzer is not only imposing severe limitations on military intervention, but upon *any* form of influence that threatens the integrity of the cultural project of a society. What should be important for Walzer is not the mode of intervention, but whether it threatens the integrity of the cultural project.

Walzer does not present his plea for tolerance for the sake of protecting cultural integrity as an argument about which rights are human rights. To my knowledge he never denies that rights beyond the right against genocide are human rights. He offers an argument about intervention, or rather an argument against intervention except in very extreme circumstances.

However, Walzer's cultural integrity argument for tolerance has serious implications for the role that appeals to human rights ought to play in the international legal order. Even if he acknowledges that there are human rights other than the right against genocide or perhaps other forms of large-scale lethal violence, he is committed to the view that it would be wrong for the international legal order to enforce a richer set of human rights principles or otherwise exert influence on states to conform to these principles, for example, by economic sanctions or refusal to bestow economic benefits such as

---

[34] Walzer, *Just and Unjust Wars*, 78–101.

participation in beneficial trade regimes. He believes that such actions would transgress the bounds of tolerance, so far as they pose a threat to cultural integrity.

Framed in slightly different language, Walzer's contention is that once we appreciate the importance of cultural integrity for individuals we should recognize a *principle of self-determination* for states that prohibits any form of intervention broadly construed, except in the extreme case of genocide or other large-scale lethal violence.[35] So it appears that the view about the value of cultural integrity that underlies Walzer's very restrictive position on humanitarian military intervention has the larger implication that there is little room in a moral theory of international law for a conception of human rights that goes beyond the right against genocide or other forms of mass murder.

However, Walzer's cultural integrity argument for toleration presents no serious barrier to a more ambitious role for appeals to human rights in the international legal order, because it is unsound. The major objection to Walzer's position is that states and comprehensive cultures—those groups whose collective cultural enterprises warrant noninterference—are not in one-to-one correspondence. Virtually every existing state (Iceland may be an exception) contains more than one such group. But if this is the case, then a rule according to which intervention in a state is only justified when genocide or other massive killing is under way or imminent may actually facilitate disruption of the collective cultural enterprise of minority cultural groups who are subject to serious oppression at the hands of the government.

For example, the collective cultural enterprise of the indigenous peoples of a Latin American state or of the Hungarian minority in the Slovak Republic may be seriously disrupted, even perhaps destroyed, by government oppression that falls short of genocide. Restricting intervention to cases of genocide (or large-scale killing) gives states free rein to disrupt or even destroy the cultural integrity of minority groups within their borders.

---

[35] In *Just and Unjust Wars*, Walzer qualifies this with the view that intervention in civil wars is permissible if another state has already intervened. I will not address this aspect of his view here, but will only note that my rejection of it is based on the theory of the right to secede developed in Chapter 8.

Walzer's view about the protection of cultural integrity from disruption by *external* forces is an argument for austere restraints on humanitarian intervention or other forms of international influence employed against states that violate human rights, then, only on the plainly false assumption that states encapsulate a single comprehensive culture. For the members of an indigenous group or a national minority, it is usually the state itself that threatens to disrupt their collective cultural project.

What Walzer needs to explain, then, is why those who appreciate the importance of cultural integrity would adopt a rule that places extreme limits on intervention into *states*. On the contrary, protecting minority or indigenous cultures might in some cases even require interventions to break up states, in order to allow these groups to gain the protection of their own state structure through secession.

Walzer is not alone in advocating a very austere constraint on humanitarian intervention. Others who do not accord cultural integrity the paramount importance he seems to nevertheless also assert that intervention across state borders should only be undertaken when violations of human rights become so massive as to approach genocide.[36] They defend this restrictive position on fallibilist grounds, arguing that the risk of error and abuse in application make more permissive rules of intervention unacceptable. Walzer could be seen as holding a particular version of this position: For him the chief risk that calls for a highly constrained rule of intervention is the risk that cultural integrity will be disrupted. Other proponents of the fallibilist argument would focus on other harms that result from intervention in the name of basic human rights.

The fallibilist position is not wholly implausible, but the argument typically given for it is radically incomplete. Whether a more permissive or a highly constrained rule of intervention is appropriate will depend upon what *other* features the international legal system has, including what political forces or institutional safeguards exist that limit the risks of error and abuse in applying a rule of intervention. Walzer's highly restrictive intervention rule would be more persuasive if it were embedded in a more complex argument

[36] Randall Forsberg, 'Creating a Cooperative Security System', *Boston Review* 17/6 (1992), 7–10.

that includes the assumption that intervention will be undertaken by individual states, and most likely by very powerful ones, rather than through a process of collective authorization, with procedural safeguards to minimize the risk of abuse and error. A more permissive rule of intervention that allowed action to protect a more inclusive list of human rights, if combined with a requirement of collective authorization embedded in a system of procedural safeguards, might actually provide better protection against error and abuse—and more protection for cultural integrity—than a simple austere rule that allows intervention only to curb genocide or other forms of mass murder, but leaves intervention up to the discretion of individual states.

The key point is that Walzer's discussion of intervention, like most, fails to consider the matter holistically. Whether a particular proposal regarding intervention is defensible will depend ultimately upon how it fits into a systematic moral theory of international law. In the absence of at least a sketch of an encompassing theory, Walzer's point that cultural integrity is an extremely important good excludes neither a more permissive rule of humanitarian intervention nor an ambitious role for a more inclusive conception of human rights in international law.

Conclusions concerning the bounds of tolerance

My strategy in this section has been to approach the question of whether tolerance places debilitating constraints on the project of grounding a moral theory of international law in a conception of basic human rights by examining two especially thoughtful and influential accounts of tolerance—those of Rawls and Walzer. My conclusion is that a proper appreciation of the virtue of tolerance is not so constraining as Rawls and Walzer believe. Nothing these theorists say about the nature and importance of tolerance rules out the sort of justice-based moral theory of international law I am attempting to develop in this book.

VII. The Ineliminable Indeterminancy of Human Rights and its Implications for the Moral Theory of International Law

Application indeterminacy

At the outset of this chapter I characterized human rights as abstract moral rights that impose constraints on how institutions should be, but without themselves providing concrete prescriptions for institutional design. I also noted that there are at least three sources of indeterminacy with regard to the legal implementation of these abstract rights. First, since institutionalizing rights requires resources, differences in the resources available in various societies may mandate different schemes for implementing protections for the interests that human rights accord special status to. Thus in a world in which there is nothing approximating global distributive justice, an extremely poor country cannot be faulted for failing to achieve the same level of health care as a wealthy one, even if it is true that health care is a human right. Second, which institutional schemes for implementing a particular human right are appropriate may depend on the nature of the dominant culture or cultures in a given state. An institutional scheme that in the abstract appears to be a more apt operationalization of a particular human right or set of human rights may in fact be less efficacious than one that is inferior from an ideal standpoint but more consonant with the culture and hence more likely to be conscientiously implemented and with lesser moral costs. Third, because at present most if not all societies fall far short of adequately protecting human rights, institutionalizing them is to a large extent a remedial process, a matter of reforming or eradicating those institutions that facilitate the violation of human rights. But these defective institutions will vary across societies, so implementation must vary accordingly. Together these three factors constitute what might be called the *application indeterminacy* of human rights.

Deep indeterminacy

There is a different type of indeterminacy that is more troubling. It has two sources: the fact that protection of basic human interests can be more or less robust and the fact that protection involves costs.

Granted that the protection of basic human rights can be more or less robust, in order to know what it is to respect human rights adequately we must know how much protection is required. But it appears that there is no single, uniquely correct answer to the question: "*How much* protection for the human interests at stake is morally required?"

Suppose, for example, that appropriate minimal requirements for justificatory responsibility are met during an institutionalized discussion about human rights in which none to whom these standards are to be applied is excluded from participating. A consensus may eventually emerge that freedom from religious discrimination is a human right. Suppose also that the same conditions of discussion eventually produce consensus as to the nature of the interests that the right against religious discrimination accords extraordinary protection to. Nevertheless, even the most ideal conditions for discussion—in which participation is completely open and minimal standards for justificatory responsibility are met—may not result in consensus as to whether freedom from religious discrimination requires outlawing a state religion of the relatively benign form found, say, in Norway, or the prohibition of "Christian Businessmen's" organizations that give their members special opportunities for advantageous networking in the United States. We may all agree that no one should be penalized for his religious affiliation, but on closer inspection we may disagree as to what counts as a penalty (as opposed to the mere lack of a benefit) or as to which sorts of costs rise to the level of a penalty. The history of U.S. Constitutional law is replete with examples of these types of deep disagreements about the content of rights (though it also contains disputes over application indeterminacy).

The difficulty of determining how much protection the interests correlated with human rights warrant results from the fact that supporting human rights is not costless. (If there were no costs, we might as well opt for the most robust protection possible.)

There are in fact two distinct cost problems. The first concerns the problem of assigning priorities in light of the fact that there is a plurality of human rights and that resources for improving respect for them are limited. It arises even within the perspective of a single individual and would be a problem even if there were no differences among reasonable people as to which human interests ought to be protected.

Suppose that you agree that the right not to be tortured is a human right. Suppose that in the year 2020 Human Rights Watch issues a report stating that both the incidence of torture and the severity of the torture still occurring have declined dramatically— that greater moral progress has been achieved with respect to this human right than anyone would have predicted. However, the report also predicts that to achieve further progress will be extremely difficult and very costly. (The marginal cost of torture reduction is steeply rising.) In the same report it is made clear that there are a number of other human rights, including the right to health care, and the right to freedom of expression, that have not shown such progress as is the case with the right not to be tortured. After painful deliberation, you decide that the best course of action would be to support a policy that concentrates the bulk of available resources on improving protection of these other human rights. However, since you think that the right not to be tortured is a very important right—even one torture session is too many—you concede that some resources should still be devoted to securing that human right. You also admit, however, that there is an ineliminable element of choice as to exactly how you would allocate resources between antitorture work and support for freedom of expression, etc.

Quite apart from whether others would agree with you, you have no rational, principled way of deciding just when the marginal costs of continuing efforts against torture are too high, given that every additional dollar spent in the antitorture campaign could be spent in support of other human rights. You cannot locate such a uniquely rational trade-off point because you have no rational way of commensurating the evil of n cases of torture with $n + m$ cases of interference with freedom of religion, etc.

My surmise is that you are not alone: No moral theory or theory of value we now have or are likely to have in the foreseeable future will eliminate this indeterminancy as to the relative costs we ought to bear in support of a plurality of human rights.

The second cost problem does not concern the relative value of improving compliance with one human right as compared with improving compliance with others. It would persist even if there were only one human right to be supported. This cost problem is one that is not unique to human rights but rather applies to every moral principle that requires us to bear costs for the sake of others.

The richest discussion of this issue occurred initially as a criticism of utilitarianism—that this ethical theory demands too much of us, that by requiring us to maximize overall utility it leaves too little room for us to pursue our own projects or to act for the welfare of those closest to us. But the problem of excessive demands applies to all ethical theories, or at least to all that require us to take the welfare of others seriously.

With regard to human rights, some have assumed that the problem arises only with respect to the view that human rights include so-called "positive," that is, economic or welfare rights—rights of distributive justice. This is a mistake, as I shall show in detail in the next chapter. Even so-called negative rights, such as the right not to be tortured and the right against religious discrimination, and even more clearly perhaps the right to equal protection under the law, require much more than that individuals refrain from committing certain wrongs. They also require "positive actions" that are capable of absorbing almost as much resources as we are able to devote to them.[37] For example, to establish a regime of "negative" rights to freedom from assault and violation of property rights requires resources for police, courts, prisons, etc. And the question will always remain: What costs are we obligated to bear to reduce violations of these rights?

Assuming that a plausible moral theory must make room for individuals to accord special weight to their own interests and to the interests of those close to them (their families, fellow citizens, co-religionists, etc.), there must be limits on our obligation to incur costs for the sake of greater compliance with human rights. Yet here, as in the case with the problem of how to decide when the marginal costs of further improvement regarding one human right justifies withholding resources from efforts to improve others, moral theory seems to yield no uniquely correct answer. At least the moral theories to which we have access at present do not.

In fact, moral theorizing in this area often is little more than the development of categories to mark off more from less plausible solutions to this cost problem. Thus, as I noted earlier, Samuel Scheffler identifies a type of moral theory that imposes some parameters on an answer to the second cost question, labeling as "Moderate Cosmopolitanism" the view that although we do have some special obligations to those near and dear to us, these are in some way constrained, though not entirely displaced, by obligations we have to all persons. This leaves entirely open exactly where the constraint imposed by our obligations to humanity at large falls. Hence it provides scant guidance as to how much cost we ought to

[37] Stephen Holmes and Cass Sunstein, *The Cost of Rights: Why Liberty Depends on Taxes* (W. W. Norton, New York, 1999).

bear in support of human rights and when appeals to our special obligations or interests provide a valid justification for not doing more to support human rights.

Coping with the two indeterminacies

The problem of application indeterminacy is in principle soluble given sufficient information about the relevant differences in culture, resources, and targets for remediation in different societies. Thus it might be thought that their solution requires a thoroughgoing *localization* of efforts to implement human rights: Those within a given society are more likely to know what the available resources are, which particular schemes of implementation are more consonant with the society's culture and hence more likely to be implemented effectively and without undue conflict, and which existing institutions and practices should be targets for remediation.

The difficulty with this initially charming suggestion is that in a society where there are serious violations of human rights—especially grave distributive injustices, political oppression, and restrictions on freedom of expression—those who are able to make the most politically effective claim to be the repositories of the concrete local knowledge needed to solve the problems of application indeterminacy are likely to be part of the problem, not the solution. Their view of what the relevant 'local' facts are will be biased and self-serving or at best honestly mistaken. As I shall presently argue, this problem cannot be solved, but it can be ameliorated by an appeal to procedural justice, understood as including democratic procedures for contributing to the specification of abstract human rights norms.

The problem of deep indeterminacy, in contrast, is not even soluble in principle, even under conditions of perfect information about differences among societies relevant to the task of institutionally implementing human rights norms, given the current state of moral theory. This is an indeterminancy of values at the deepest level, not a problem of how to implement agreed-upon values in different social circumstances. Although it cannot be solved, its intractability can be made more palatable by the same broad strategy that is needed to respond to the problem of application indeterminacy. That strategy is to rely upon the virtues of procedural justice by according a prominent role to democratic institutions broadly conceived.

A proceduralist response to indeterminacy regarding human rights

Even if there is no one correct answer to the question of how much protection, at what cost, is appropriate for the interests accorded special protected status by human rights, human rights principles must be specified to be applied. And some ways of specifying them are more morally defensible than others, even if none is uniquely correct. Here procedural justice, broadly understood, comes into its own.

I have already noted that there is a complex set of processes at the international and the domestic level by which efforts to implement abstract human rights norms yield a degree of consensus on an increasing specification of their content. I emphasized that more specific human rights conventions, such as the one on ending discrimination against women, international quasi-judicial agencies such as the International Human Rights Commission, and agreements explicitly designed to formulate guidelines and timetables for implementing the major human rights conventions such as the Helsinki Accords, play an important role in this process.

Specification is also achieved more indirectly when domestic courts apply international human rights norms on the assumption that they are incorporated into domestic law, whether through legislative acts or automatically according to constitutional provisions.[38]

---

[38] See the United States Ninth Circuit Court Opinion *Alvarez* v. *Machain*, 266 F.3d 1045 (9th Cir. 1991) for the various ways that international law is ascertained and incorporated into United States federal law: The Supreme Court has stated that the law of nations "may be ascertained by consulting the works of jurists, writing professedly on public law; or by the general usage and practice of nations; or by judicial decisions recognizing and enforcing that law." *United States* v. *Smith*, 18 U.S. 153, 160–1, 5 L. Ed. 57 (1820); *Filartiga* v. *Pena-Irala*, 630 F.2d 876, 880 (2nd Cir. 1980). See also *The Paquete Habana*, 175 U.S. 677, 700, 44 L. Ed. 320, 20 S. Ct. 290 (1900) (stating "where there is no treaty and no controlling executive or legislative act or judicial decision, resort must be had to the customs and usages of civilized nations, and, as evidence of these, to the works of jurists and commentators who by years of labor, research, and experience have made themselves peculiarly well acquainted with the subjects of which they treat. Such works are resorted to by judicial tribunals, not for the speculations of their authors concerning what the law ought to be, but for trustworthy evidence of what the law really is"). The Second Circuit also has used United Nations ("U.N.") declarations as evidence of the law of nations...*Filartiga*, 630 F.2d at 883.

Thus there is a kind of division of labor between international (and regional) and domestic institutions in coping with the problems of indeterminacy.

My proposal for how a morally defensible international legal system would respond to the problems of indeterminacy builds upon and refines the principles at work in this state of affairs. In Part Two I will argue that ideally the international community should recognize an entity as an independent, legitimate state, a member of the state system in good standing, only if it meets certain moral requirements. Whether this ideal requirement for legitimacy can be applied to existing states in the foreseeable future is debatable. There is much more to be said for the proposal, which I develop in Chapter 6, that *new* entities should only be recognized as states if they meet it.

Legitimacy, as I understand it there, means being morally justified in the attempt to make, apply, and enforce general rules within a jurisdiction. I argue that an international legal system that features justice-based criteria for recognition of entities as legitimate states can be a force for moral progress, by rewarding states that make a credible effort to achieve justice and penalizing those that do not.

Assigning a substantial role to individual states in the process of specifying human rights norms for application within their own borders becomes much more plausible on the assumption that the states in question meet certain minimal moral requirements of the sort laid down in the criteria for recognition I develop in Part Two. In particular, I argue that to be recognized as legitimate, states ought to satisfy a minimal democracy requirement and protect the most basic human rights of their citizens. If a state satisfies these criteria for legitimacy as a member of the international system, this provides some reason to regard its efforts to specify abstract human rights norms for purposes of domestic application as legitimate as well.

Among the rights of sovereignty acknowledged by recognition is included the right to enact domestic legislation and to operate courts that among other things render decisions that specify international human rights norms in order to apply them domestically. This view that democratic states ought to be recognized in international law as having the authority to specify human rights norms as they are applied within their own borders is developed more fully in a valuable recent work by Kristen Hessler.[39]

---

[39] Hessler, 'A Theory of Interpretation for Human Rights'.

This is not to say that a state that is recognized as legitimate has an unlimited right to specify the content of abstract human rights norms. In addition to setting criteria for legitimacy that act as a constraint on the character of the domestic institutions by which specification for domestic application is achieved, international law can and should, through its own agencies of specification, lay down constraints within which domestic specification processes may operate.

The fundamental question is this: What would an international legal system have to be like in order for it to be morally justifiable for it to empower domestic institutions that meet certain moral criteria to contribute substantially to the specification of human rights norms needed for implementation and at the same time limit their right to specify by setting an international standard for a universal minimal content for these rights? This is the question of system legitimacy I explore in Chapter 7 of Part Two. My aim at this juncture is not to anticipate that discussion but to suggest that the appropriate response to the indeterminacy of human rights norms must be institutional, and that which institutional arrangements for coping with indeterminacy are appropriate must be determined in part by an appeal to moral theory, in particular to the theory of legitimacy.

It may seem that this approach involves a vicious circle: If our moral theory is itself too indeterminate as to the relative importance of various human rights and the costs we ought to bear to secure them for others, then won't this same deep indeterminacy undercut efforts to appeal to moral theory to develop an account of just procedures for specification? The problem of circularity would seem to be most acute in the case of the right to democratic governance, if this is understood as something that ought to be an international legal human right. If there is no uniquely correct specification of the institutional arrangements necessary for democratic governance, then how can international law use democratic governance as a criterion for determining which entities may specify the content of the right to democratic governance for purposes of domestic application?

A closer look at how the division of labor proposal would play out in the case of the right to democracy shows that there is no problem of vicious circularity. Imagine the following scenario. International agencies and processes provide a minimal content for the right to democratic governance by specifying the basic requirements of representative institutions needed for accountability (including periodic free elections of a legislature by all citizens, and a multi-party system operating under conditions of freedom of the press and freedom of political association). States that satisfy these minimal requirements are then given considerable latitude under international law to specify human rights norms for appropriate domestic application.

It is important to understand that the internationally specified minimal content for the requirement of democratic governance does not appear from nowhere. It is based on several centuries of historical experience about what sorts of political institutions do the best job of protecting human rights through representation of basic human interests and the accountability that it makes possible. In brief, even if we initially have difficulty in formulating crisp, explicit criteria for democratic governance, international legal agencies should be able to appeal to current and historical examples to determine in a preliminary and minimalist way what international law should require of states by way of democratic governance. Even if we cannot give a fully explicit and ultimately satisfactory definition of democracy, within broad limits we know minimal democracy when we see it.

Next, the right to democratic governance, understood as having this minimal content, is used as a requirement of international law for legitimacy of states (along with the requirement that other basic human rights are respected). Then states that meet the legitimacy requirement are recognized under international law as having authority to determine further the specific content of the right to democratic governance within their own borders (along with the content of other human rights), so long as their doing so is consistent with the minimal international standard.

Such an arrangement would accomplish three important goals: (1) it would allow for the supremacy of international law as a limit on state sovereignty, for the sake of achieving justice understood primarily as protection of basic human rights; (2) it would create a protected space for diversity in the institutional implementation of human rights norms, thereby acknowledging that efforts to specify abstract norms should give weight to local conditions and values—more specifically, it would not require the imposition of one particular conception of democracy; and (3) it would steer a course between relativizing basic rights to such an extent that they no longer warrant the title of human rights, on the one hand, and pretending that human rights norms themselves contain concrete prescriptions for institutional design, on the other. The success of this proposal for a division of labor in coping with the indeterminacy of human rights norms depends ultimately upon the plausibility of the account of state legitimacy and system legitimacy offered in Part Two.

Before turning to these issues of legitimacy, I conclude Part One (Justice) with the following chapter, on distributive justice. There I address two main questions. First, should international law recognize rights of distributive justice for all individuals (beyond the currently widely recognized human right to resources for subsistence) and, if so, what is the content of those rights? Second, should international law recognize rights of distributive justice for entities that are not individual human beings, such as states?

CHAPTER 4

———

Distributive Justice

This chapter grapples with the most controversial topic in the discourse of human rights: distributive justice. The chief questions to be addressed are (1) whether a justice-based international legal order should include rights of distributive justice (sometimes called social and economic rights) for individuals that exceed the right to the means of subsistence that is already widely recognized in international and regional human rights instruments, and (2) whether international law should recognize not only individuals but collectivities such as states or "peoples" or nations as having rights of distributive justice. To situate these questions I begin by considering alternative explanations for widespread skepticism about the possibility that distributive justice can have a significant place in the international legal order.

Transnational and international justice

My discussion of distributive justice will be structured by a distinction between two types of principles, those of *transnational* and those of *international* justice.[1] Transnational justice concerns those rights and duties that obtain among members of the same state or between the government of a state and its members which ought to be recognized by international law as being universal, that is, as applicable to all states.[2] In brief, transnational justice theory articulates the principles of

---

[1] I am indebted to David Golove and Scott Shapiro for clarifying this distinction.
[2] I choose the somewhat awkward term 'members' because it is vague enough to encompass citizens and residents of states. One key issue in the theory of transnational distributive justice is whether noncitizen long-term residents of states have rights of distributive justice against the state.

justice that the international community ought to ensure are met by all states in their internal affairs.

The requirements of transnational distributive justice are minimal in this sense: They are all the international legal order should require of distributive relations within states. If a state determines through its own political processes that the distributive shares of some or all of its citizens should be more generous than what transnational justice requires, this is not the business of the international legal order. A regime of transnational distributive justice is therefore compatible with different states implementing different conceptions of distributive justice. To that extent the idea of transnational distributive justice can accommodate the belief that there is a degree of ineliminable pluralism with respect to views about distributive justice.

International justice includes the rights and duties of the subjects of international law so far as they are not members of the same state or do not stand in the relationship of government to governed within a state. (Notice that this special sense of the term 'international justice' is narrower than that in ordinary usage. Often the term 'international justice' is used in a way that would encompass both transnational justice and international justice in this special sense. To avoid confusion one might reserve the term 'global' justice to cover both transnational and international justice.)

International justice (in the special sense) includes the rights and duties of states to one another, but more than this. It also encompasses the rights and obligations of international organizations, global corporations, and nongovernmental organizations such as environmental and human rights groups so far as these operate across borders. International justice also includes principles specifying the permissibility and/or obligatoriness of intervention in support of principles of transnational justice. The distinction between transnational and international justice applies to both ideal and non-ideal theory, at least if it can be assumed that ideal theory will include a plurality of primary, territorially based entities—something like what we now call states.

Three theses about distributive justice

My aim in this chapter is to argue for three theses that clarify the proper role of distributive justice in the international legal order.

1. Contrary to theorists such as Rawls, Miller, and Walzer, an ideal moral theory of international law must include a prominent place for distributive justice, both as an individual human right and as a constraint on economic inequalities among states (to the extent that the ideal theory includes a primary role for states). Both transnational and international distributive justice will be prominent features of ideal theory.

2. However, due to current international *institutional incapacity*, which includes but is not restricted to a lack of enforcement capacity, there are serious limitations on the role that international law can now play in contributing to distributive justice. At present it is unrealistic to think that the international legal order can authoritatively formulate and implement comprehensive principles of distributive justice for relations among states or for assigning determinate distributive shares to individuals beyond a right to subsistence. This limitation has an important implication: A nonideal moral theory of international law should acknowledge that for now states must be the primary arbiters and agents of distributive justice.

3. In spite of this limitation, international law today can and should play a beneficial, largely *indirect* role in securing distributive justice, (i) by supporting other human rights, including the right against discrimination on grounds of gender, as well as democratic government within states, as essential conditions for economic development and equality of opportunity for economic advancement; (ii) by promoting more equitable trade relations, labor standards, environmental regulation, aid for development, and endeavors to preserve global commons as a "common heritage" to be used and preserved for all mankind, including future generations; (iii) by creating a global intellectual property rights regime that will preserve incentives for innovation while at the same time contributing to a more equitable distribution of the benefits of biotechnology, especially so far as these benefits have a positive impact on the health of those in the poorest countries; (iv) by supporting efforts to liberalize immigration policies to increase economic opportunities for the world's worst off; (v) by adopting principles regarding the right to secede that do not exacerbate problems of distributive justice by allowing richer parts of countries to secede simply in order to improve their economic prospects; (vi) by helping to ensure that states discharge their obligations to rectify injustices committed against indigenous peoples within their borders; and, perhaps

most importantly of all, (vii) by encouraging the development of the institutional capacities needed for the eventual formulation and implementation of comprehensive principles of transnational and international distributive justice.

Although at present it is unrealistic to expect that the international legal order can do much directly to achieve distributive justice by formulating and implementing comprehensive principles of distributive justice is nonetheless an important element of the ideal moral theory of international law. And despite the present limitations of institutional capacity, there is much the international legal order can now do to serve the cause of distributive justice.[3]

I. *The Place of Distributive Justice in International Law*

Doubts about distributive justice

In practice and in theory the place of distributive justice in international law is highly contested and deeply ambiguous. In practice, it has proved more difficult to get states to agree that human rights include rights of distributive justice—at least when they exceed the right to resources for subsistence—than to agree that they encompass the right against torture, genocide, racial and religious discrimination, and a number of the other standard civil and political rights. Due to this impasse, the struggle for distributive justice often takes place in areas whose connection to standard conceptions of human rights is unclear or at least indirect, in particular in the fields of environmental regulation, the regulation of conditions of employment (international labor standards), treaties governing trade relations between richer and poorer countries, conventions concerning the use of "global commons" such as outer space and the ocean floor, agreements for multilateral aid, including the provision of credits and loans, and in controversies over the right to immigrate to states that offer greater economic opportunities.[4]

---

[3] For an important very recent effort to develop ideal theory principles of global distributive justice, see Darrell Moellendorf, *Cosmopolitan Justice* (Westview Press, Boulder, CO, 2002).

[4] For an illuminating analysis of the role of considerations of distributive justice in all of these areas, see Thomas Franck, *Fairness in International Law and Institutions* (Clarendon Press, Oxford, 1995).

In the realm of theory attention has only recently begun to focus on the international dimension of distributive justice. Among moral theorists of international law and international relations there is a great divide between those who include substantial rights of distributive justice in their ideal theories (such as Charles Beitz, Darrel Moellendorf, Thomas Pogge, and Henry Shue) and those who do not (such as John Rawls, David Miller, and Michael Walzer).[5] Some moral theorists deny that there are any "positive" human rights, rights to resources or goods of any kind.

The mistaken rejection of positive rights

It is useful to distinguish worries about the role of distributive justice in international law from worries about distributive justice that apply to both the domestic and the international context. As I noted in the previous chapter, some libertarian moral-political theorists deny that there are any "positive" moral rights, including rights of distributive justice, while affirming that there are "negative" moral rights. They then conclude that the proper role of political authority at any level is restricted to the enforcement of the negative rights. By "positive rights" they mean those whose correlative obligations require not just that we refrain from doing certain things (for example, not killing or stealing) but that we do certain things (such as provide basic health care, basic education, or income support for the unemployed).

Two reasons are given for the conclusion that there are negative moral rights but no positive moral rights and hence no rights of distributive justice. The first is that while we may have a duty of charity to act affirmatively for the welfare of others, there is no such duty of justice; although we ought to provide aid to others, it is not owed to them, they have no right to it.[6] Call this the Charity, Not Justice Argument against rights of distributive justice. The second is that there are no positive rights because putative positive rights fail a necessary condition for rights, namely, that their correlative obligations impose clear and definite requirements.[7]

[5] Rawls, *The Law of Peoples*; Walzer, *Just and Unjust Wars*; and David Miller, *On Nationality* (Clarendon Press, New York, 1995).

[6] Maurice Cranston, *What Are Human Rights?* (Taplinger Publishing Co., New York, 1973), 68.　　　　　　　　　　　　　　　　　　　　　[7] Ibid.

The second objection assumes that positive rights, or at least those that are said to be rights of distributive justice, have as their correlatives obligations that are not only indefinite but open-ended and that this is incompatible with their being rights. A further assumption of the second anti-redistributive argument is that unless something is a moral right, it is unjustifiable to enforce the corresponding obligation by the power of the law.[8] Call this second objection the Indeterminacy Argument against rights of distributive justice.

Both arguments are unsound. The Charity, Not Justice Argument has two fatal defects. First, it grossly overstates the contrast between rights of distributive justice and what its proponents take to be the primary examples of negative rights, namely the standard civil and political rights found in liberal constitutions and in international human rights conventions. As I observed in Chapter 3, enforcing a right to freedom from assault or theft (the protection of so-called negative rights to security of the person and to property) or the right to due process under the law requires a host of "positive" actions, from raising taxes to fund a police force and a court system, to monitoring their performance and undertaking institutional reforms to make them function effectively.[9] For this reason the United Nations Human Rights Commission, which monitors compliance with human rights norms as specified in the two fundamental international Covenants, has found that in recognizing the right against torture all states thereby undertake obligations to perform a wide range of positive acts, to supervise the treatment of prisoners and to establish complaint procedures in which prisoners can protest against ill-treatment. The Human Rights Commission has also held that upholding the right to freedom of assembly requires states to take actions to ensure that private individuals or groups do not suppress unpopular demonstrations.[10]

In addition, the Charity, Not Justice Argument against rights of distributive justice assumes without justification that distributional equity is always a matter of charity, never of justice. Unless this is

---

[8] I criticize this assumption in detail in Allen Buchanan, 'Justice and Charity', *Ethics* 97 (1987), 558–75.   [9] Holmes and Sunstein, *The Cost of Rights*.

[10] Jeremy McBride, 'Reservations and the Capacity to Implement Human Rights Treaties', in J. P. Gardner (ed.), *Human Rights as General Norms and a State's Right to Opt Out: Reservations and Objections to Human Rights Conventions* (The British Institute of International and Comparative Law, London, 1997), 128.

to be dismissed as a question-begging definition of justice that restricts it to "negative" rights, we need a reason why the same concern for the basic interests of persons that requires us to recognize the basic civil and political rights as human rights does not also support the conclusion that rights of distributive justice are human rights.

In fact the most plausible and widely held human interest-based justifications for the basic civil and political rights also support rights of distributive justice. Our fundamental human interests in well-being and autonomy are served by freedom of speech and the right to political participation, but also by rights to basic health care and education. (Not having enough to eat can often be a greater threat to your well-being than interference with your freedom of expression, and disease can greatly restrict a person's sphere of autonomy.) But if this is so, then it is hard to see how, at the level of basic moral theory, one can coherently say that equal consideration of persons requires, as a matter of justice, that all persons be accorded these "negative" civil and political rights, but that they have no rights of distributive justice at all. Moreover, once one admits that securing the so-called negative rights requires positive actions, there is no obstacle to acknowledging that there are human rights of distributive justice.

Furthermore, quite apart from the fact that so-called positive rights serve the same basic human interests that are appealed to in order to justify so-called negative rights, it is undeniable that without some constraints on material inequalities among citizens, the effectiveness of the so-called negative rights in protecting those interests will be greatly impaired for the worse off. For example, if you and I both have the same ("negative") rights to property or to due process under the law or to political participation, but I am extremely wealthy and you are extremely poor, the effectiveness of your equal rights may be greatly reduced. I will be able to hire the best attorneys to press my claim to property in a dispute with you about ownership or to pay for prime media time to support the campaign of my political candidate, while you are unable to afford legal representation to present your claims effectively and may not be able to get your political message into the media at all. Rights of distributive justice are needed to constrain material inequalities among citizens so as to limit inequalities in the effectiveness of civil and political rights. And quite apart from whether I can exercise my rights more effectively than you (that is, apart from the *relative* effectiveness of rights), the same concern for basic human interests that justifies ascribing rights to you requires that you be able to use them effectively so as to protect those interests.

The force of this familiar Effectiveness of Rights Argument for distributive justice can be greatly augmented if one recognizes a feature of the legal enforcement of so-called negative rights that I have stressed on another occasion: The courts and police not only apply and enforce the law of property rights, the prohibition against assault and homicide, etc., they endeavor to do so *monopolistically*.[11] The courts claim the exclusive right to be the ultimate arbiter of what the law requires and the police claim the exclusive right to enforce the law. Furthermore, the resolution of conflicts prescribed by the law trumps other modes of conflict resolution. Thus any legal system—even one restricted to "negative" rights—not only protects individuals; it also imposes severe limits on their freedom to help themselves, penalizing those who attempt to protect their interests by means other than those approved by the legal system. (If you steal my property I must defend my interests as best I can in court, rather than depending on my own wiles or strength or that of my friends to get back what is mine.)

So it is a mistake to think of the rule of law as only bestowing benefits; it also imposes a burden of restraint, and not just upon would-be wrongdoers. It limits the law-abiding as to what remedies for wrongs they may pursue. And where material inequalities among citizens are so great as to produce gross inequalities in the effectiveness of individual rights, that burden of restraint is unfairly distributed. If my material wealth gives me a great advantage in using the rule of law to further my own interests, then the burden of restraint (the threat of penalty if one resorts to self-help) is much less for me than it is for one whose poverty or lack of education impairs his ability to work within the rule of law to protect his interests. So-called positive rights, rights of distributive justice, are required if the monopolistic legal system for protecting negative rights is to be fair.

---

[11] Allen Buchanan, 'Deriving Welfare Rights from Libertarian Rights', in Peter Brown, Conrad Johnson, and Paul Vernier (eds.), *Income Support: Conceptual and Policy Issues* (Rowman & Littlefield, Totowa, NJ, 1981).

I noted earlier that an often-unarticulated additional assumption of the Justice, Not Charity Argument is that only obligations of justice may be enforced. This assumption is also incorrect. In some cases it is justifiable to enforce compliance with rules requiring contribution to important public goods, even if no one has a right to a share of them, so long as enforcement does not violate rights. To assume that it is "a matter of definition" that only obligations that are the correlatives of rights may be enforced is to use definitional fiat to beg an important question about the justification of enforcement.[12]

The second argument for denying that there are rights of distributive justice, the Indeterminacy Argument, correctly notes that rights of distribution may have an ineliminable indeterminacy. But as we saw in Chapter 1, this is true of all human rights, including so-called negative human rights. The proper response to the undeniable indeterminacy of all rights is to develop morally defensible, authoritative political processes to move from abstract and therefore necessarily indeterminate rights principles to the specification and fair distribution of more definite (though perhaps never fully determinate) obligations.

Some theories of distributive justice may characterize rights of distribution in an open-ended way that exacerbates the inevitable indeterminacy of all human rights. For example, Rawls's Difference Principle might be interpreted as requiring that the prospects of the worst off are to be maximized, even if this means continually reorganizing social production so as to increase the stock of goods available for distribution. On this interpretation, the Difference Principle appears to countenance no limit on what must be done for the sake of justice (so long as additional efforts improve the prospects of the worst off), just as a utilitarian theory of distributive justice seems to require endless efforts to maximize utility.

This kind of unbridled expansiveness is troubling in a theory of distributive justice. But while that may be a reason for rejecting a particular theory, it is not a reason to jettison the notion of distributive justice. A theory of distributive justice that requires a constraint on distributive inequalities for the sake of limiting inequalities in effectiveness of basic civil and political rights, or to make everyone's

---

[12] For a more detailed exposition of this argument, see Buchanan, 'Justice and Charity'.

rights at least minimally effective by ensuring a "decent minimum" of the most important social and economic goods for all, is not inherently over-expansive, even though it is indeterminate to the extent that the notion of a decent minimum is inherently vague. The characterization of the right as the right to a decent minimum is an explicit acknowledgment that it is limited.

To summarize: If equal consideration of persons requires recognition of so-called negative rights in order to protect their fundamental interests in well-being and autonomy, then it also requires recognition of so-called positive rights of distributive justice, because (1) distributive justice directly serves the same fundamental interests that justify so-called negative rights, (2) because some limits on social and economic inequalities are needed to ensure that material inequalities do not seriously undercut the effectiveness of these rights for the worse off, and (3) because without rights of distributive justice, a system of legal enforcement of negative rights, which is inherently monopolistic, would impose unfair burdens of restraint on those who lack the resources to use their rights effectively. Furthermore, while it is true that rights of distributive justice are to some extent indeterminate, this is true of so-called negative human rights as well; and the problem of over-expansive obligations only applies to some theories of distributive justice, not all.

Given the weakness of the position that justice in general does not include rights of distribution, I turn now to the more interesting claim that even if distributive justice is a significant element of a just domestic legal order, it has little or no role to play *in international law*. The question before us, then, is whether the tendency to minimize the role of distributive justice in international law is justified in the case of international distributive justice, transnational distributive justice, or both.

II. *Reasons for Rejecting a Prominent Role for Distributive Justice in International Law Today*

Although there seems to be a considerable consensus, especially among international legal theorists, that the role of distributive justice in international law is rather minimal, there is less agreement on exactly why this is so, on whether the situation might change, and on whether change is desirable.[13] Those who take a dismissive stance toward the role of distributive justice in international law typically fail to make it clear whether they are making a point about nonideal theory (or nonideal theory in the short run) or ideal theory. This is regrettable, because different views about why the role of distributive justice in international law is rather minimal have different implications for the future of international law and for the enterprise of moral theorizing about international law.

Deep distributive pluralism

Three distinct reasons for minimizing the role of distributive justice in the moral theory of international law ought to be distinguished, so that each can be accurately evaluated in turn. First, there is the position that disagreements among societies regarding the demands of distributive justice are especially pronounced and intractable to rational resolution—more so than with the civil and political rights found in standard lists of human rights. This position, call it *Deep Distributive Pluralism*, is prominently displayed in the work of Michael Walzer. It supplies a reason for denying that either transnational or international distributive justice can play a significant role in the international legal system: If disagreements among societies about distributive justice are fundamental and not amenable to rational resolution, then there is no prospect of justifying either distributive standards to be met by all states in their internal affairs (transnational distributive justice) or principles to govern the global distribution of benefits and burdens among states (international distributive justice). So a defensible moral theory of international law will contain neither principles of transnational distributive justice nor principles of international distributive justice. The ideal moral theory of international law includes no significant role for principles of distributive justice.

Societal distributive autonomy

Second, there is the *Societal Distributive Autonomy* view, according to which distinct societies ought to be free to develop their own

---

[13] Thomas Franck is a conspicuous and important exception to this consensus. See his *Fairness in International Law and Institutions*.

principles of justice. Rawls's version of this view holds that distributive justice is inapplicable to relations among states because (1) states are both economically self-sufficient and distributionally autonomous (so there is no need for international distributive justice) and because (2) toleration prohibits the imposition of standards of transnational justice, at least on those states that are organized according to a reasonable conception of justice, what Rawls calls well-ordered societies, which includes both liberal and non-liberal but 'decent' societies. A state is economically self-sufficient if it can, at least under conditions of good government, produce all the goods its citizens need; it is distributionally autonomous if it can determine the distribution of goods among its citizens.[14]

The conjunction of (1) and (2), what might be called the Self-Sufficiency Plus Toleration View, is Rawls's complex reason for including neither transnational nor international distributive justice in his moral theory of international law, even at the level of ideal theory. The one exception, as we have seen in Chapter 3, is that Rawls does include a right to resources for subsistence in his truncated list of human rights, thus supplying a rather weak principle of transnational distributive justice.

Institutional incapacity

The third reason for minimizing the role of distributive justice in systematic accounts of how international law should be, the *Institutional Incapacity View*, is radically different from the first two. Unlike them, it does not rule out robust requirements of either international or transnational distributive justice *in principle*, that is, as a matter of ideal theory. Instead, it argues that under current conditions the international legal system lacks not only the political will but also the institutional resources to serve as a primary actor in the process of authoritatively determining what distributive justice requires and effectively enforcing those requirements.[15] According

---

[14] Charles Beitz, 'International Liberalism and Distributive Justice: A Survey of Recent Thought', *World Politics* 51 (1999), 269–98.

[15] The discussion that follows owes much to Thomas Christiano's perceptive published comments on my paper 'Secession, Federalism, and the Morality of Inclusion'. See Buchanan, 'Federalism, Secession, and the Morality of Inclusion', 53–63 and Thomas Christiano, 'Democracy and Distributive Justice', *Arizona Law Review* 37 (1995), 65–72.

to this third position, for now it is for the most part only individual states that have the institutional capacity to serve as the primary agents of distributive justice (though it is true that one transnational quasi-federation, the European Union, is apparently developing the needed institutional capacity).

Considering each of the three views in turn, I will argue that neither Deep Distributive Pluralism nor the Societal Distributive Autonomy view provide good reasons for excluding principles of distributive justice from the ideal theory of international law. I will also show that the Institutional Incapacity View supplies a good reason for assigning only a relatively minor role at most for comprehensive principles of distributive justice in the nonideal moral theory of international law at the present time. Determining the correct reason for minimizing the role of distributive justice matters, because the first and second views rule out a significant role for distributive justice even in ideal theory, while the third does not.

Moreover, the third view is compatible with the current institutional incapacity of the international legal system being only a temporary condition. The Institutional Incapacity View, then, unlike the other two views, allows for the possibility that in the future rather robust requirements of transnational and international distributive justice should be added to the agenda for reform. And because it affirms that distributive justice is an important element of the ideal theory of a just international order, the Institutional Incapacity View implies that we *now* have an obligation to work together to create international institutions that can function as primary arbiters and implementers of distributive justice.

The position I want to advance is that distributive justice, both transnational and international, is a major ingredient in a cogent ideal moral theory of international law, but that for the present nonideal theory should assign considerations of distributive justice a less prominent or at least more indirect role than considerations involving other basic human rights. I will also argue that rather than providing a reason for not pursuing the development of an ideal theory of global distributive justice, recognition of the current lack of institutional capacity should serve as a stimulus for ideal theorizing. Ideal theory can help us determine what we ought to do here and now, by providing compelling justifications for why these goals should be pursued, and by grounding obligations to help build the institutional capacities required to attain them.

III. *Deep Distributive Pluralism*

We encountered the more general version of this position earlier, when we examined the communitarian variant of meta-ethical cultural ethical relativism. According to the latter position, the most basic ethical values are rooted in and only justifiable by reference to the tradition of a particular society or encompassing culture. The position we are now considering simply limits this thesis to distributive justice, while acknowledging that there are other genuinely human, that is, universal, rights.

Questioning the extent and permanence of distributive pluralism

The obvious difficulty with this first reason for rejecting a significant role for distributive justice in the moral theory of international law is that it is hard to see why intersocietal disputes about distributive justice should be uniquely permanently intractable. Once we jettison the unrealistic picture of encompassing cultures as social billiard balls that are internally homogeneous in values and impervious to external influences, why should we assume that values concerning distributive justice are uniquely immune to revision in the direction of greater intersocietal consensus? In the end, whether or not disputes about distributive justice are so much more recalcitrant to rational resolution than disputes about human rights generally that there can be no significant role for them in the moral theory of international law is a matter of fact, to be answered by cross-cultural empirical research.

However, as I noted in Chapter 3, neither Walzer nor MacIntyre nor others who espouse the meta-ethical communitarian view have marshaled the needed empirical evidence to support it, either as a general claim about basic ethical principles or as a special claim about the most basic principles of distributive justice. I also observed that there are a number of instances in which an impressively broad international consensus on moral principles has been achieved (as with codes for the protection of human subjects in research). Indeed, there already is a broad consensus, reflected in many international and regional human rights instruments, that there is at least one human right of distributive justice, namely, a right of each individual to the resources needed for subsistence.

For the present, agnosticism is more reasonable than pessimism concerning the possibility of a global consensus on minimal standards of distributive justice that go beyond a right to resources for subsistence. Given that the interpenetration of cultures through the development of a global economy and through an evolving transnational civil society is such a recent and as yet incomplete phenomenon, and given that serious systematic theorizing about distributive justice is in its infancy, the assertion that disputes about cross-cultural distributive justice are rationally unresolvable is premature. To put this issue in perspective, recall that little more than fifty years ago anyone with even the most rudimentary knowledge of international affairs would have thought it naive to believe that states would ever publicly agree to the limitations on their internal sovereignty imposed by human rights conventions.

Especially in international law, predictions about the limits of consensus on ethical principles are risky business. The more reasonable position, as I argue below, concedes that for the time being the institutional incapacity of the international legal system is sufficient to rule out a prominent and direct role for distributive justice as compared with civil and political rights. This position does not assume that consensus on the content of distributive justice will ever equal that of consensus on the content of the right not to be tortured, but it does not rule out the possibility that a workable consensus on rights of distributive justice that exceed the right to resources for subsistence may eventually emerge.

The discourse of fairness in existing international law

Critiques of the international legal system tend to assume that it contains and indeed facilitates such gross unfairness that there is little reason to expect that distributive justice will ever be accorded a prominent role in it. Yet a closer look at the full range of international law reveals that fairness discourse, and in some cases explicit appeals to distributive justice, is far from absent, and that in some instances it actually appears to influence what transpires. In a masterful and erudite treatise entitled *Fairness in International Law and Institutions*, Thomas M. Franck provides a systematic overview of the various areas of recent international law in which considerations of distributive justice play a significant role. Especially striking instances discussed by Franck include: (1) multilateral compensatory financing (treaty-based commitments of wealthier states to compensate poorer trading partners for detrimental fluctuations in the prices of commodities the latter export), (2) multilateral lending institutions that provide subsidized loans and credits for economic growth and the reduction of poverty in the worse off countries, (3) international judicial interpretations of treaties governing the exploitation of continental shelves and seabeds and their subsoils that appeal to the notion that the allocation of these resources should be determined by considerations of equity where this is understood to imply giving special weight to the interests of poorer states, (4) treaties concerning outer space and Antarctica that recognize them as a "common heritage" from which all mankind is entitled to benefit, and (5) environmental agreements that impose obligations on states to take into account the conservation of resources for mankind generally, including future generations.[16]

Franck marshals compelling evidence that in all of these areas appeals to distributive justice are prominent and actually influence the character of the law, even if they do not take the form of the endorsement of explicit, comprehensive, overarching principles of transnational or international distributive justice. Thus he concludes that:

Bilateral and multilateral aid programs, concessionary lending, commodity [price] stabilization, trade preferences [for poorer trading partners], resource transfers and sharing, and the creation, and equal or equitable distribution, of new resources: these are the new entitlements which mark a global awareness that distributive justice...is never off the agenda, whether the subject is manganese nodules on the ocean floor, geostationary orbits in outerspace, or penguins and the Antarctic ice-cap.[17]

To Franck's list should be added (1) the growing international labor standards movement—the struggle for humane standards for wages, nondiscrimination in hiring, and worker safety, and for the right of freedom of workers to associate to try to improve their condition[18]—and (2) efforts to incorporate a right to immigration

---

[16] Franck, *Fairness in International Law and Institutions.*   [17] Ibid. 436.

[18] See e.g. Lance Compa and Stephen Diamond (eds.), *Human Rights, Labor Rights, and International Trade* (University of Pennsylvania Press, Philadelphia, 1996).

(including both a right to leave and a right to be accepted) that is more liberal than a right to seek refuge from political persecution into the framework of human rights.

Especially from the standpoint of the obligation to help ensure that all persons have access to institutions that protect their basic rights, there is much to be said for international recognition of a liberalized right to immigration, since this would both enable individuals to move to states where their rights are better protected and exert pressure on states that wished to limit immigration to support efforts to improve conditions in other states. A comprehensive nonideal moral theory of the international legal order presumably would provide a prominent place for a right to immigration as an indirect, though important, means of achieving distributive justice by increasing individuals' economic opportunities.[19] How liberal the right to immigration recognized in international law should be would depend upon many factors, including the possibility that unrestricted emigration of the better-educated members of less developed countries may make it more difficult for their governments to satisfy the demands of distributive justice. How serious this problem is will depend upon how effectively institutions of international distributive justice can compensate for the tendency of the immigration "brain-drain" to undercut the efforts of developing countries to satisfy the requirements of transnational justice.

Franck's use of the term 'entitlement' in the passage quoted above is warranted. His point is that, in all of these areas of international law, explicit recognition of the demands of justice, not charity or the *noblesse oblige* of the more fortunate states, has become an accepted component of the argumentative discourse. Of course the growing recognition that international law must take considerations of distributive justice into account does not constitute a consensus on what distributive justice requires beyond a right to resources for subsistence, much less proof that the international system is distributively just. But it does indicate a degree of confidence that convergence toward more determinate and comprehensive standards is attainable.

[19] I am grateful to Bill Edmundson for impressing upon me the importance of this point.

For example, when states agreed to the Law of the Sea Convention's provision that a portion of the benefits derived from mining seabed deposits in coastal waters are to be disbursed according to "equitable sharing criteria, taking into account the interests and needs of developing States, particularly the least developed and land-locked among them" they thereby endorse the process of treaty implementation and interpretation as a mechanism for giving substance to the notion of equitable sharing.[20] In doing so, they appear to assume that pluralism concerning distributive justice may not be a permanent barrier to the development of standards of distributive justice at least for certain aspects of the international legal order.

The upshot of Franck's analysis is that there is a growing consensus, concretely manifested in the substance of international law in a number of distinct areas, not only that distributive justice matters, but also that some policies and institutional arrangements are unacceptably unjust, even if there is no consensus on all that distributive justice requires. Although it is impossible to predict how much consensus on substantive standards of justice in any of these areas will emerge and how effective efforts to secure compliance with them will ultimately be, these developments at least cast serious doubt on the assumption that international agreement on distributive justice is forever an impossible dream.

Of course, the fact that the discourse of fairness Franck describes exists does not show that there is an international consensus on a comprehensive conception of distributive justice. But it does show that it is possible to make progress on distributive matters in the absence of that sort of consensus, through indirect means, and that it is mistaken to conclude that distributive justice considerations play no significant role in international law. Thus Deep Distributive Pluralism is doubly wrong: It gives no good reason to conclude that distributive justice is not an important element of the ideal theory of international law and it mistakenly assumes that the international legal order can do nothing of importance at present to advance the cause of distributive justice in the absence of a global consensus on a comprehensive conception of distributive justice.

---

[20] Franck, *Fairness in International Law and Institutions.*

IV. *Societal Distributive Autonomy*

Rawls's rejection of international distributive justice

The second position that purports to rule out a significant role for distributive justice in international law is exemplified in Rawls's *The Law of Peoples*. Rawls's moral theory of international law explicitly rules out a significant role for both transnational and international distributive justice in international law—even in the ideal theory of international law.

Rawls believes that tolerance for reasonable societal conceptions of distributive justice precludes imposing distributive requirements that every state is to meet in its internal affairs (beyond the right to subsistence). Although he is not altogether clear on this point, it appears that he also believes that tolerance rules out principles of international distributive justice (principles specifying rights and obligations of distributive justice among states), as opposed to a duty of charity on the part of better-off states to aid less fortunate ones. He seems to think that if international law imposed duties of inter- national distributive justice, it would wrongly interfere with the ability of states to distribute resources within their borders accord- ing to their "people's" distinctive conception of distributive justice.

In addition, Rawls holds that there is no *need* for principles of international distributive justice because states can produce what their citizens need (economic self-sufficiency) and ensure that it is distributed effectively according to the society's conception of dis- tributive justice (distributional autonomy). Under these conditions, principles of international distributive justice are otiose and an unnecessary intrusion into the internal affairs of a society. So long as states are well governed, Rawls contends, they do not need to rely on assistance from outside their borders.[21]

Rawls is mistaken on both counts. Tolerance does not rule out either transnational or international distributive justice; and even well- governed states are not economically self-sufficient or distributionally autonomous, because there is a global basic structure that has pro- found distributive effects both on individuals and on the ability of states to implement economic policies. Moreover, whether a state is

---

[21] Rawls, *The Law of Peoples*, 108; see my article, 'Rawls's Law of Peoples'.

well governed may depend upon how it is affected by the global basic structure. Each of these criticisms of Rawls's view is elaborated below.

Why tolerance does not rule out transnational distributive justice

My critique in Chapter 3 of Rawls's reasons for endorsing only a very lean list of human rights lays the groundwork for rejecting his assertion that tolerance precludes a prominent role for transnational distributive justice in international law. There I argued that Rawls mistakes excessive humility in refraining from criticizing persons' beliefs for respect for persons' reasons and hence for persons as having the capacity to reason, because he relies on a conception of reasonableness that lacks an appropriate account of justificatory responsibility.

In brief, Rawls's subjectivistic account of reasonableness demands too little of human reason. Once we abandon this defective account of reasonableness and the invertebrate conception of toleration that it attempts to support, we are free to demand more of those who endorse systems of extreme material inequality. We can and should demand justifications that meet minimal justificatory standards.

I argued in Chapter 3 that even in the absence of a comprehensive account of what the appropriate justificatory standards are, it is plausible to conclude that justifications for the most severe inequalities tend to be so deficient as to fail to meet any reasonable justificatory standards. For example, if a dictator argues that the economic development of his country is incompatible with democracy, we should require him to support this claim with good data (and to respond to data, marshaled by Sen and others, indicating that precisely the opposite is true). If apologists for female genital mutilation claim that this practice enhances fertility, we should not remain passive in the name of toleration, but confront them with the fact that clinical data show that it reduces fertility. Similarly a proponent of apartheid or of the caste system should be required to justify the social, political, and economic inequalities he endorses, and if, as is inevitably the case, he does so by appealing to alleged natural differences among groups, we should demand good evidence that these differences exist (and a cogent explanation of why, if they do exist, they are relevant to determining the fundamental civil and political status of persons). Thus it is a mistake to think that a society that systematically relegates certain classes to poverty because of their ethnicity or race or other alleged natural inferiority or that violates even the most minimal requirements of formal equality of opportunity through institutionalized discrimination should be of no concern from the standpoint of transnational justice, so long as that society provides all with the means of subsistence.

Here as in Chapter 3, I am not suggesting that Rawls himself would endorse such inequalities or regard societies that include them as being "decent" and hence not subject to interference from without. Rather, my point is that his notion of a common good conception of justice is so normatively thin that there are circumstances under which it would allow these sorts of inequalities.

In Chapter 3, on human rights, I suggested that those who do claim that such extreme inequalities should not be constrained by international law owe a justification for grossly unequal treatment. There are two reasons for thinking that this is the case. On the one hand, if they agree, as Rawls says they must if their view is to be reasonable, that everyone's good is to count, they owe us an explanation of why the good of some counts so much more than that of others, *and this explanation must be compatible with the justification they would accept for holding that everyone's good is to count.* Yet it is hard to see how one can make a convincing case that *everyone's* good should count for something that does not appeal to what is valuable about all human beings. Once such an appeal is made, surely there is at least a burden of argument to be borne to show why all human beings are not entitled to equal consideration. My surmise is that the advocates of extremely inegalitarian social orders typically do not bear that burden of argument, because the justifications they give fail to meet minimal justificatory standards.

On the other hand, if we begin, not with the weak presumption that the good of all is to count for something, but rather with the assumption that equal consideration for all persons should be reflected in the design of the most basic social institutions, then it is all the more obvious that the more extreme institutionally based inequalities we see in many societies around the world require a more robust justification than Rawls's weak standard of reasonableness permits: Coherence, logical consistency, and compatibility with the assumption that the good of each is to count for something, are not sufficient.

A sound justification for relegating some citizens to second-class status must be provided; and the sorts of justifications that are given typically fail to meet minimal justificatory standards. If this is so, then there is no reason to take the issue of transnational distributive justice off the table, at least so far as the ideal moral theory of international law is concerned.

The importance of the global basic structure

In *A Theory of Justice* Rawls emphasized the significance for distributive justice of the existence of what he called the "basic structure" of a society. If there is such a thing as a global basic structure—the international analog of the basic structure of a single society as Rawls understands the latter—then being well governed does not ensure either economic self-sufficiency or distributional autonomy. Being well governed does not guarantee that a society will be able to provide a decent and worthwhile life for all its members nor that its distinctive conception of justice or the good can be adequately implemented, because even a well-governed society may be seriously disadvantaged by the global basic structure, if there is one. The workings of the global basic structure may either prevent the society from being able to produce what is needed (economic self-sufficiency) or constrain its ability to determine the distribution of what it produces (distributional autonomy), or both.

In addition, the global basic structure—depending upon its characteristics—may either facilitate or impede a society's ability to achieve good government. For example, there are features of the existing global basic structure, including a practice of recognition that bestows great benefits upon even the most oppressive governments and a virtually unconstrained international market in arms and technologies of torture, that make it difficult to achieve good government in many societies.

Notice that in the second passage cited above Rawls simply assumes that it is "the basic structure of *their* political and social institutions" that is relevant to whether a people prospers or not (emphasis added). This assumes both economic self-sufficiency and distributional autonomy, in effect denying that the global basic structure is a significant influence.

Recall Rawls's introduction of the term 'basic structure' in *A Theory of Justice* in 1971 and his argument that the basic structure is the primary subject of justice. The basic structure is "the way in which the major social institutions distribute fundamental rights and duties and determine the division of advantages from social cooperation."[22] It is because of the nature of the distributional effects of the basic structure that it is the primary subject of justice.

The basic structure is the primary subject of justice because its effects are so profound and present from the start. The intuitive notion here is that this structure contains various social positions and that men born into different positions have different expectations of life determined, in part, by the political system as well as by economic and social circumstances. In this way the institutions of society favor certain starting places over others. These are especially deep inequalities.[23]

The global basic structure as a subject of justice in international law

If there is a global basic structure—a set of economic and political institutions that has profound and enduring effects on the distribution of burdens and benefits among peoples and individuals around the world—then surely it is a subject of justice and a very important one. Whether the basic structures of individual states are more important will depend upon whether or not their distributional effects are even greater than those of the global basic structure (and which is more important may change over time, as the global basic structure becomes more comprehensive). But in either case, if there is a global basic structure, principles of justice will be needed for it, just as they are for domestic basic structures.

There *is* a global basic structure. Its existence and major features are documented in a vast and growing interdisciplinary literature that goes under various headings: globalization, structural dependency, and theory of underdevelopment.[24] Among the elements of

---

[22] Rawls, *A Theory of Justice*, 7.   [23] Ibid.

[24] See Robert Wood, *From Marshall Plan to Debt Crisis: Foreign Aid and Development Choices in the World Economy* (University of California Press, Berkeley and Los Angeles, 1986); Andre Gunder Frank, *Latin America: Underdevelopment or Revolution: Essays on the Development of Underdevelopment and the Immediate Enemy* (Monthly Review Press, New York, 1970); Graham Hancock, *Lords of Poverty: The Power, Prestige, and Corruption of*

the global basic structure are regional and international economic agreements (including the WTO, NAFTA, and various European Union treaties), international financial regimes (including the International Monetary Fund, the World Bank, and various treaties governing currency exchange mechanisms), an increasingly global system of private property rights, including intellectual property rights that are of growing importance as technology spreads across borders, a set of international and regional legal institutions and agencies that play an important part in determining the evolving character of all the preceding elements of the global basic structure (the meta-structure of the global basic structure), and, as I have emphasized, a practice of recognition for states and governments that is bereft of normative standards.

The burgeoning literature on the global basic structure attempts to delineate its distributional effects. No attempt can be made here to summarize its complex findings. The chief point is that, like a domestic basic structure, the global basic structure in part determines the prospects not only of individuals but of groups, including peoples in Rawls's sense (groups organized in states). It is therefore unjustifiable to ignore the global basic structure in a moral theory of international law—to proceed either as if societies are economically self-sufficient and distributionally autonomous or as if whatever distributional effects the global structure has are equitable and hence not in need of being addressed by a theory of justice.

the International Aid Business (Atlantic Monthly Press, New York, 1989); Cynthia Enloe, *Bananas, Beaches, and Bases: Making Feminist Sense of International Politics* (University of California Press, Berkeley and Los Angeles, 1990). It has been suggested that global structures can also destabilize governments that might otherwise be effective, or reinforce and empower nongovernmental groups or other forces in civil society who have inegalitarian or otherwise unjust and exploitative agendas. If true, this would further undermine Rawls's claim. See Hedley Bull, *The Anarchical Society: A Study of Order in World Politics* (Columbia University Press, New York, 1977); Andrew Hurrell and Ngaire Woods, 'Globalisation and Inequality', *Millennium: Journal of International Studies* 24/3 (1995), 447–70; Laura Macdonald, 'Globalising Civil Society: Interpreting International NGOs in Central America', *Millennium: Journal of International Studies* 23/2 (1994), 267–85; Alexander Wendt and Daniel Friedheim, 'Hierarchy under Anarchy: Informal Empire and the East German State,' *International Organization* 49/4 (1995), 689–721; Cynthia Enloe, *The Morning After: Sexual Politics at the End of the Cold War* (University of California Press, Berkeley and Los Angeles, 1993).

Why good government is not enough

Rawls offers no support for his sweeping generalization that good government ensures that a society can provide a decent and worthwhile life for all its citizens. If there were no global basic structure, then this generalization would be plausible—but only because it would approach tautology. But since there is a global basic structure, Rawls's good government assumption needs a justification. And this is true, regardless of whether a "decent and worthwhile life" means one in which Rawls's truncated list of human rights is respected or a life that is decent and worthwhile according to the distinctive conception of justice or of the good of the society in question. There is simply no reason to believe that a global basic structure that is not regulated by principles of justice will allow all societies to meet either standard of prosperity. Rawls also fails to consider the possibility that an unjust global basic structure can prevent some societies from achieving good government, for example by allowing credits, loans, and military aid that keep murderous kleptocrats in power.

Aid to burdened societies

One of Rawls's principles for an international legal order addresses some of the inequalities among societies. As I noted earlier, he recognizes a duty of better-off societies to aid "burdened societies." Although he does not elaborate on the form such aid should take or on its extent and the costs the donor should be willing to bear, the use of the term 'aid' suggests transfers of food or funds or perhaps technology, or perhaps the provision of credit, not structural changes in the international social, political, and economic order. Furthermore, there is no suggestion that this duty of aid is the collective responsibility of the international community, to be discharged through international institutions, though this might be compatible with Rawls's overall view.

More important, there is no mention of a *right* on the part of poor societies to receive aid. In short, the duty of aid as Rawls conceives it seems to be an imperfect duty of charity, not an obligation of justice.

Be that as it may, if there is a global basic structure there is no more reason to believe that the fulfillment of such a duty of aid by individual states will achieve international distributive justice than there is to believe that acts of charity by individuals or groups will offset the injustices of the domestic basic structure. Once again, the same reasons Rawls gave in *A Theory of Justice* for insisting on principles of justice for the domestic basic structure speak in favor of including principles of international distributive justice in a moral theory of international law. Because the distributional effects of a basic structure are profound, enduring, and to a large extent unchosen and undeserved, justice requires systematic principles that are applied to the basic structure, not merely principles of aid to be applied by individuals, whether the individuals are persons or states.

However, it is quite another question as to what those principles are. Elsewhere I have shown how a Rawlsian hypothetical contract, with two stages, the first where the parties represent individuals, the second where they represent states (or the peoples of states), can generate ideal theory principles of transnational and international distributive justice respectively.[25] I will not repeat those arguments here because my objective in this chapter is not to develop an ideal theory of distributive justice for the international legal order. Instead my goal is only to show that ideal theory will include a prominent role for distributive justice and to explain why, at least for the present, nonideal theory should approach the issue of distributive justice in a largely indirect manner that need not rely on a full-blown ideal theory. In the next section I first summarize the argument of this chapter thus far and then articulate and endorse a view about the current character of international legal institutions that grounds this position.

V. *Institutional Incapacity and Lack of Political Will*

The state of the argument on the role of distributive justice in international law

This chapter began with the observation that most international legal theorists have serious doubts about the role of distributive justice in international law, but that the basis of this pessimism is unclear. So far I have articulated, examined, and rejected two distinct

---

[25] Buchanan, 'Rawls's Law of Peoples'. See also Moellendorf, *Cosmopolitan Justice*.

explanations of why distributive justice should not play a significant role in a moral theory of international law. The first, which is suggested by the work of Michael Walzer and other meta-ethical communitarians, is that there are such deep, unresolvable disagreements about the nature of distributive justice that no substantive principles of international or transnational distributive justice can be rationally justified. (The meta-ethical explanation for this conclusion is supposed to be that moral principles or at least principles of distributed justice are grounded in and meaningful only by reference to the traditions and forms of interaction of a particular community.) I have argued that this view rests on an unsupported, premature prediction of the impossibility of attaining a cross-cultural consensus on minimal requirements of distributive justice, and that its a prioristic pessimism is grounded in an unrealistic picture of societies as social billiard balls, impermeable to normative ideas from the outside. The second explanation, which is developed in the later work of Rawls, is that a proper toleration rules out anything but the most meager requirements of transnational justice (leaving only the right to subsistence) while the alleged self-sufficiency of individual societies (at least if they are well governed) makes principles of international distributive justice (as opposed to charity) superfluous.

I have also argued in this chapter that given a more appropriate account of what counts as a reasonable conception of justice—based on a more demanding understanding of respect for reason that incorporates minimal standards for justificatory responsibility— toleration does not rule out principles of transnational distributive justice that place further constraints on inequalities within societies than the bare right to subsistence. I have argued as well that once the existence of a global basic structure is acknowledged and the assumption that well-governed states are distributionally autonomous and economically self-sufficient is rejected, there is a strong prima facie case for principles of international distributive justice in ideal theory, at least so far as it is assumed that ideal theory will include a prominent role for states.

Quite apart from the fact that there is a global basic structure and that it is an important subject of justice, the Natural Duty of Justice for which I argued in Chapter 2 implies that obligations regarding distributive justice, like obligations of justice generally, are owed to all individuals, not just to those who happen to be our countrymen. There I argued that equal regard for persons requires that we help to ensure that all persons have access to institutions that protect their most basic human rights. This obligation would ground the enterprise of developing principles of transnational justice and international legal institutions to facilitate their implementation, even if there were no global basic structure connecting us to all other individuals and indeed even if we were not currently interacting at all with some people, much less interacting cooperatively with them.

The Natural Duty of Justice provides a basis for a prominent role for transnational and international distributive justice that is independent of the Interactionist assumption that we owe duties of justice only to those with whom we interact in a cooperative scheme. Yet the Natural Duty view can recognize the importance of the existence of the global basic structure. Acting on the obligation to help ensure that all persons have access to institutions that protect their basic human rights requires efforts to regulate and perhaps even transform the global basic structure because the latter profoundly affects the prospects of individuals for securing justice and the ability of states to deliver it. So even though the Natural Duty approach does not require cooperative interaction, or indeed any interaction at all, as a condition for the existence of obligations of distributive justice, it acknowledges the importance of the global basic structure, both as an obstacle to achieving justice for all and as a potential resource for progress toward that goal. Unlike the interactionist view of justice, it does not require the problematic assumption that the global basic structure is a cooperative scheme in any normatively significant sense.

The nature and consequences of institutional incapacity

The third explanation of why it is wrong to expect much at present of international law regarding the implementation of comprehensive principles of distributive justice is compatible with my rejection of the previous two explanations. It holds that although ideal theory will include substantive principles of transnational and international distributive justice, nonideal theory at present should not assign a primary and direct role to international institutions in efforts to achieve distributive justice because they lack the capacity to do so. The Institutional Incapacity View, unlike Deep Distributive Pluralism and the Societal Distributive Autonomy View, allows for the possibility that comprehensive principles of transnational distributive justice may come to occupy an important place in international law.

Of equal significance, the Institutional Incapacity View, again unlike the other two views, is compatible with a commitment to trying to build the institutional capacity needed for making transnational distributive justice a reality. Indeed, when combined with the Natural Duty of Justice it implies that we ought to honor this commitment.

Not just lack of enforcement capacity

It is important to understand that the needed institutional capacity does not consist solely in the inability to enforce principles of distributive justice, whether transnational or international. Equally necessary is the capacity to make authoritative pronouncements about what distributive justice requires and to adjudicate the application of these requirements. For this reason it would be more accurate to say that at present institutional resources are insufficient to assign the role of primary *arbiter and enforcer* of distributive justice to any international agency or collection of international agencies. Thomas Christiano makes this important point with admirable clarity in the following passage:

One view that might be attributed to Locke and Kant is that the state is a necessary *instrument* for the establishment of justice and the only such instrument [presently] available. Three reasons support this conclusion. [1] The state is the only entity that is capable of reliably *enforcing* the rights of persons. Only it has a sufficient concentration of resources and manpower to threaten punishment for injustice. [2] It is furthermore the only institution with any chance of impartially and even-handedly *judging injustice*. The state is able to establish courts wherein injustice can be judged by reasonably disinterested judges. [3] Most importantly, the state provides a context in which individuals can make *authoritative, collective decisions about what is to count as just or unjust* behavior among themselves. The state does this by making laws regulating behavior through some recognized authoritative decision procedure. The state performs executive, judicial and legislative functions which are essential to the establishment of justice...The chief insight here is that even if justice is itself not a conventional matter, the establishment of justice requires coordination among many different actors on a single set of laws coupled with judicial and executive institutions to back them up...On the other hand, the system of states does not have the kind of resources, at the present moment [to establish justice].[26]

Christiano makes this point in a discussion of *distributive* justice. Yet he traces its pedigree to Locke and Kant, who apply it to the whole of justice, and Christiano himself frames the argument in terms of what is required for justice generally, not just distributive justice. But if the problem of the institutional incapacity of the international legal system afflicted all matters of justice with equal severity, then the Lockean-Kantian point would eliminate any significant role for international law in protecting *any* human rights, not just rights of distributive justice, because the international legal system lacks the institutional capacity that states have.

Chapter 2 provides a basis for distinguishing between distributive justice and other human rights in this regard. There I argued that the international legal system has already made considerable progress in developing institutional capacity for specifying and applying some of the more important human rights, even if it lacks a central legislature and a hierarchy of courts with compulsory jurisdiction. What I wish to suggest now is that the international legal system's institutional incapacity is relatively more serious at present in the area of distributive justice. Therefore there is no inconsistency in the position I am advancing: that at present the nonideal moral theory of international law can include a basic role for human rights (other than rights of distributive justice that go beyond the right to resources for subsistence) but must assign a relatively minor or at least indirect role to more ambitious principles of distributive justice.

Institutional capacity, will, and consensus

The notion of institutional capacity can be understood in a narrower or a broader sense. In the narrower sense institutional incapacity is the lack of what we ordinarily think of as institutional structures for

---

[26] Christiano, 'Democracy and Distributive Justice', 65–72.

making and enforcing authoritative determinations of distributive justice. In the broader sense it includes both institutional structures and the support of key agents and constituencies needed to make those structures function effectively. This support in turn typically depends upon both some degree of consensus among the key agents and constituencies as to what goals ought to be pursued through the institutional structures, as well as sufficient political will to achieve them.

Institutional incapacity in the narrower sense—lack of appropriate institutional structures—can be both a result and a cause of lack of consensus: Institutional structures can provide mechanisms and forums needed for forging consensus, but where consensus is seriously lacking appropriate structures will not be developed. Similarly, lack of political will to achieve justice may hinder the development of appropriate structures and hence of the consensus that these structures provide mechanisms and forums for developing. And without appropriate institutional structures to facilitate the realization of moral goals, the pressures of self-interest may sap the political will to make justice a reality.

Because of the complex interactions between institutional structures, consensus, and political will, it is risky to focus on any one of these factors as being primarily responsible for the current inability to implement comprehensive principles of distributive justice in the international system. For this reason I utilize the broader notion of institutional incapacity, which enables me to highlight the lack of global institutional structures to serve as the arbiter and enforcer of distributive justice while leaving open the question of to what extent lack of consensus and of political will are largely the causes or the effects of the lack of institutional structures.

Sources of institutional incapacity

There are at least two factors that may explain this asymmetry as to the institutional capacity to determine authoritatively what distributive justice requires and implement those requirements: There is less consensus on distributive justice than on other basic human rights; and monitoring compliance with comprehensive principles of distributive justice is more difficult than monitoring compliance with the more important civil and political rights. Each of these factors warrants elaboration.

First, there does appear at present to be less consensus about what distributive justice requires than about the wrongness of violating the most basic civil and political human rights. This relative lack of consensus may be in part a result of the absence of international institutional structures that could help forge a consensus, but it is also highly likely that it in part explains why the needed institutional structures have not developed. That there is considerable disagreement on what distributive justice requires is not surprising: Justifying a conception of distributive justice requires taking a stand on a number of complex, interrelated moral issues concerning the roles of equality, need, merit, desert, and responsibility. In addition, issues of distributive justice raise in the most direct and obvious way the disquieting question that is perhaps the single most important source of what I referred to in Chapter 2 as Deep Indeterminacy regarding rights generally: What costs must one bear for the sake of others, especially those with whom one has no connections of sympathy, kinship, co-nationality, or citizenship?

It may well be, then, that the ineliminable indeterminacy that afflicts all abstract human rights norms is somewhat more pronounced in the case of the idea of distributive justice. This hypothesis gains some support when we look to theorizing about distributive justice: The range of disagreement seems exceptionally broad, when compared with the much greater convergence of views about the importance of the more basic civil and political rights.

The range of disagreement about distributive justice

Existing theories of distributive justice for the individual state (theories of domestic distributive justice) fall into two broad categories: anti-redistributivist theories (usually called libertarian or classical liberal) and redistributivist theories. Anti-redistributivist theories deny any significant scope for redistributive principles, except for the purpose of rectifying past unjust takings of goods to which people have become entitled through labor, voluntary exchange, or gift. In contrast, redistributivist theories assert that individuals have entitlements to goods and opportunities that are independent of the claims of rectification and that require the state to undertake redistributive policies such as subsidizing education, health care services, and income support.

At the beginning of this chapter I indicated some of the main reasons why the anti-redistributive view should be rejected. The central point is that the same equal regard for persons that grounds the so-called negative civil and political rights requires the recognition of so-called positive or economic rights as well.

Now if we reject the anti-redistributive view for the case of domestic distributive justice, and do so on the grounds that a proper equal regard for all persons requires that we do so, then the presumption should be that all persons, regardless of which state they find themselves in, have rights of distributive justice. But if that is the case, then there is also the presumption that an international legal order should help ensure that all persons, regardless of which state they find themselves in, enjoy these rights; in other words, that the principles of international law should include principles of transnational justice.

The Deep Distributive Pluralist and Societal Distributive Autonomy views are attempts to rebut this presumption. Those who hold these views do not reject the idea of redistributivism—they are not classical liberals or libertarians—rather, they embrace redistributivism but argue that it is improper for international institutions to require individual states to recognize redistributive obligations to their citizens or redistributive obligations among states. That is to say, those who hold these two positions reject the ideas of transnational justice and international justice, not only in non-ideal theory but also in ideal theory. But I have just argued that neither Deep Distributive Pluralism nor Societal Distributive Autonomy succeeds in showing that the international order should not include principles of transnational or international justice. So the presumption holds: If distributive justice in the single state case requires redistribution—if the citizens of a state, simply because they are persons, have rights to economic goods and opportunities—then at least so far as ideal theory is concerned, the international legal order should include principles of distributive justice.

However, it is one thing to reject the anti-redistributivist view both for the single-state case and for international institutions, another to determine exactly what positive or economic rights all persons have and which should supply the content for transnational and international distributive justice. How are we to determine which of the competing redistributive theories of distributive justice is the correct one?

This is not the occasion for a critical survey of the whole array of redistributive theories. However, this much can be said: All of the more plausible ideal theories insist that distributive justice requires more than a right to resources for mere subsistence. At bottom, all rely either upon (1) the Rawlsian thesis that so far as the basic structure of institutions influences persons' life prospects, any inequalities must be justified by the contribution they make to the good of the worst off, (2) the assumption that maximizing overall utility requires more stringent limitations on economic inequalities than a mere right to subsistence, (3) the "prioritist" view that the interests of the worst off should be accorded special weight (though not the same weight they are accorded by Rawls's Difference Principle), or (4) the notion that equal regard for persons requires that all have the opportunity for a "decent" life or a life consonant with the "inherent dignity" of human beings (including the exercise of their central human capabilities), and that this requires access to economic goods and opportunities that exceed the minimum needed for subsistence.

Among the various redistributivist theories, then, there is an overlapping consensus (to use Rawls's phrase) that among the human rights are positive or economic rights that are more generous than the right to subsistence; but there is much disagreement, with little prospect of rational resolution for the foreseeable future, as to the content of these entitlements.

It is important to understand that the current lack of consensus on the substance of redistributive entitlements need not preclude a significant role for distributive justice in the international legal order. Much will depend upon the depth and scope of the ineliminable disagreement on distributive justice. It is quite possible that a kind of least common denominator, a focus of overlapping consensus among rival conceptions of distributive justice, might eventually enjoy widespread support, and that implementing it would require major reforms in the global order. So even if what I referred to in Chapter 3 as the Deep Indeterminacy of human rights turns out to be more pronounced in the case of rights of distributive justice, this does not mean that no widely agreed-upon standards of global distributive justice will ever emerge.

Institutional incapacity for monitoring compliance

The second explanation of the relative lack of international institutional capacity regarding distributive justice pertains to the greater difficulty and complexity of monitoring compliance with distributive justice principles. Even if more consensus on the content of distributive justice as a human right is eventually achieved, monitoring compliance with principles of justice designed to apply to the basic structure of institutions, whether global or domestic, would be an exceptionally daunting task, if only because determining whether a basic structure as a whole satisfies some favored pattern of distribution requires agreement on a complex array of sociological and economic facts. Ascertaining that a portion of the population of a state lacks the means of subsistence, or that a particular government shot to death approximately 2,500 peaceful protestors in a public square, or that a military junta jailed much of the opposition press, or that a "nation-building" regime has forcibly deprived many indigenous children of their opportunity to learn their own language, is generally much easier than determining whether material inequalities work to the greatest benefit of the worst off or maximize overall utility.

The international legal order has only recently begun to develop the relatively simpler institutional structures needed to monitor compliance with basic civil and political human rights. It is far from being able to undertake the much more complex monitoring that would be required to determine whether comprehensive standards of transnational and international distributive justice are being effectively implemented. So quite apart from whether conceptions of distributive justice are afflicted by especially deep indeterminacy as a matter of theory, the lack of institutional structures capable of monitoring the complexities of implementing comprehensive principles of distributive justice greatly limits the role that distributive justice can now play in the international legal order.

*Working for distributive justice indirectly,
on a number of fronts*

It does not follow from this that international law at present can play no significant role in efforts to establish distributive justice, only that at present its role will be for the most part indirect and somewhat limited. Given the strategic importance for states of preserving their role as the primary arbiters and agents of distribution, the greatest hope for success at present lies with reforms that do not directly or transparently challenge that role. Among the most important of these are the development and implementation of global labor standards to improve the conditions of working people, those environmental reforms that ameliorate the inequitable flow of resources from underdeveloped to developed states, provisions in trade agreements designed to ameliorate the injuries that fluctuations in market prices inflict on poorer countries, multilateral commitments to development aid, and support for democratic government and basic civil and political rights so far as these enhance the accountability of government to all citizens, not just the rich. Just as important is the economic effect of achieving better compliance with existing international human rights norms against discrimination, especially discrimination against women.

Finally, especially in the era of antibiotic-resistant tuberculosis and AIDS-HIV, international efforts to reduce the most dramatic global disparities in health may do more to improve the lot of those in the poorest countries than policies that aim at the direct redistribution of income, even if states would agree to the latter and administer them effectively. Recent and anticipated advances in genomic science have the potential for significantly improving the health of people in less developed countries, by producing better diagnostics and vaccines for major infectious and parasitic diseases and through more effective countermeasures against crop destroying pathogens based on an understanding of the pathogens' genetics.[27] How widely these benefits are distributed will depend in part upon whether international law can develop an intellectual property rights regime that prevents the worst off from being left behind by the biotechnology revolution while at the same time preserving adequate incentives for the risk-taking that innovation requires.

In all of these areas, appeals to distributive justice—or at least pleas to avoid the most obvious injustices—can have a significant impact, even if comprehensive and determinate principles of

[27] Joint Centre for Bioethics, University of Toronto (2002), *Top 10 Biotechnologies for Improving Health in Developing Countries* [Internet, http://www.utoronto.ca/jcb/].

transnational and international justice are not explicitly articulated and endorsed.[28]

State-building

It is also crucial to emphasize that in many cases the most severe deprivations do not occur because there is a well-functioning state that refuses to help ensure that all its citizens enjoy the access to goods and opportunities to which all persons are entitled. Instead, the problem is that the state, if it can be said to exist at all, is far from being capable of being an effective agent of distributive justice. For this reason, the greatest contribution to achieving transnational distributive justice may lie, not in efforts to achieve the global enforcement of comprehensive substantive principles of transnational distributive justice (even if a consensus on their content could be achieved), but rather in international efforts to facilitate state-building.

Without a basic public health infrastructure and the security that the rule of law alone can provide, there is no prospect that international efforts to impose standards of distributive justice would succeed. By helping to build functioning states, and thereby creating the conditions in which people can improve their own economic conditions, the international community can do much to serve the cause of transnational justice, even if it lacks the capacity to specify, monitor, and enforce comprehensive principles of transnational justice. We may not be able to resolve disagreements as to whether distributive justice requires satisfaction of Rawls's Difference Principle or some more modest version of "prioritism," or whether equal opportunity mandates compensation not only for bad luck in the social lottery but for genetic disadvantages as well, but we do know that most people will not have a decent life in a society that lacks the rule of law, clean water, effective sanitation, and basic education for females.

---

[28] It is perhaps worth pointing out that in terms of practice for the foreseeable future, the indirect measures for promoting transnational justice that I have just described could be wholeheartedly endorsed by those, such as Miller and Walzer, who reject a substantial role for transnational justice in ideal theory. They might well recommend such measures as the best way to act charitably toward poorer countries.

Just as important is the task of expanding the global human rights culture to include a consensus on the proposition that a proper recognition of the equality of all persons requires limits on material inequalities, both in order to secure for all persons the resources needed for well-being and a significant sphere of personal autonomy, and in order to avoid excessive inequalities in the effectiveness of human rights generally. It is not inconceivable that particularistic struggles to inform international law with considerations of distributive justice in the diverse areas noted above, coupled with a growing awareness that rights of distributive justice are full-fledged human rights, will contribute to the eventual emergence of a significant consensus on comprehensive minimalist principles of transnational and international distributive justice and a commitment to develop institutional mechanisms for their implementation.

Finally, an important element of the needed institutional capacity (in the broader sense) for establishing international and transnational distributive justice is a secure and widespread perception that the international system that is attempting to establish distributive justice is itself legitimate. If, as I suspect, the problem of what in Chapter 2 I called Deep Indeterminancy is more pronounced for distributive justice than for some of the most widely acknowledged human rights, then procedural justice in the international processes by which the idea of distributive justice as a human right is specified for purposes of implementation will be all the more critical. For if there are significant limits on the consensus that can be obtained regarding the *substance* of distributive justice, either in its international or transnational dimensions, then consensus on the legitimacy of the *process* for making ideas of distributive justice sufficiently determinate to be implemented becomes all the more important.

The issue of system legitimacy, and of procedural justice as an element of system legitimacy, is the subject of Part Two of this volume. In Part Three, Self-Determination, I argue that considerations of distributive justice should play another indirect role in a moral theory of international law: Principles designed to prevent or ameliorate intrastate conflict by recognizing rights of self-determination for certain groups should be crafted in such a way as to reflect the fact that for the present, the state—with all its imperfections—is the primary arbiter and enforcer of distributive justice. One concrete implication of this point is that international principles regulating secession should not encourage secession of the "haves" from the "have nots," since this will undercut the ability of the state to redistribute wealth in the name of distributive justice. Also in Chapter 9 (Part Three) I argue that an international legal order that gives distributive justice its due must include principles of rectificatory justice regarding unjust taking or exploitation of lands to which indigenous groups have valid customary or treaty-based claims.

I noted at the outset of this chapter that the majority of international legal and political theorists would probably concur that at present distributive justice must be relegated to a relatively minor role in international law. I agree with this conclusion, but with three very important provisos. First, although it is true that international institutions currently lack the capacity to formulate, apply, and enforce comprehensive, determinate principles of distributive justice, it would be dogmatic to conclude that this will never change. Moreover, even if international institutional capacity to determine and implement such principles never develops, there is still a significant and expanding role for considerations of distributive justice in several important areas of global governance (including labor standards, environmental regulation, and aid for development, regulation of access to global commons, international financial regimes, indigenous peoples' rights, secession, immigration). Transnational justice also can be served through better compliance with international human rights norms against ethnic, racial, and gender discrimination so far as this facilitates individuals' economic advancement, through international efforts to facilitate the state-building that is a precondition for economic development, and through initiatives to reduce the worst global disparities in health.

Second, although institutional capacity is currently lacking for the authoritative formulation, application, and enforcement of comprehensive principles of distributive justice, there are some areas of distributive justice in which there is considerable institutional capacity. For example, in recent decades several states, including Australia and the United States, have made significant progress in rectifying past unjust takings of the lands of indigenous peoples. To some extent international legal support for this sort of progress in rectificatory justice can proceed in the absence of the more ambitious institutional capacity that would be required for implementing a comprehensive conception of distributive justice.

Third, it is a mistake to infer Deep Distributive Pluralism—according to which disagreements on distributive justice are so intractable to rational resolution that there can be no principles of global distributive justice—from current institutional incapacity or from the apparent neglect of explicit principles of distributive justice in international legal practice. From both the standpoint of the Natural Duty of Justice and Interactionist theories of justice, the international legal order is undeniably within the domain of distributive justice and hence a fit subject for ideal theory.

According to the Natural Duty of Justice we are obligated to help ensure that all persons have access to institutions that protect their most basic human rights, and doing this will require, among other things, developing consensus on what rights of distributive justice persons as such have and the creation of international institutions capable of helping to secure them. From the standpoint of Interactionist theories also, the fact that global institutions currently lack the capacity to regulate the global basic structure so as to achieve distributive justice is a deficiency to be remedied, not a reason to abandon the quest for formulating and eventually implementing ideal theory principles.

Furthermore, ideal theory has a practical function even if consensus on comprehensive global principles of distributive justice and the capacity to implement them are currently lacking. It is needed to guide efforts to forge consensus on what distributive justice requires and to make clear the basis of our obligations to develop the institutional capacity for achieving it.

PART TWO

Legitimacy

CHAPTER 5

Political Legitimacy[1]

Justice and legitimacy

In Part I began developing the idea of an international legal order based on justice, where justice is understood chiefly as the protection of basic human rights. In this second part, I turn to an examination of the conditions under which it is morally justifiable to exercise political power to enforce international law, in the pursuit of justice.

In our world, progress toward justice often requires the exercise of political power. But the exercise of political power is itself subject to the demands of justice. We need to know not only what political power should aim to achieve, but also when the exercise of political power is morally justified.

From the standpoint of a moral theory of international law, there are two chief questions concerning legitimacy: What justifies the exercise of political power by individual states, and what justifies the exercise of political power through the agencies of the international legal system itself? To answer these questions it is first necessary to answer the more general one: What makes the exercise of political power morally justified?

This chapter develops a justice-based conception of political legitimacy. I define 'political legitimacy' as follows: An entity has political legitimacy if and only if it is morally justified in exercising political power. The exercise of political power may be defined as the (credible) attempt to achieve supremacy in the making, application, and enforcement of laws within a jurisdiction.

---

[1] This chapter is based on Allen Buchanan, 'Political Legitimacy and Democracy', *Ethics* 112/4 (2002), 689–719.

I will argue that an entity that exercises political power is morally justified in doing so only if it meets a minimal standard of justice, understood as the protection of basic human rights. The conception of political legitimacy I offer is meant to be perfectly general. It applies to any entity that wields political power, whether at the state, regional, or international level.

This general conception of political legitimacy will serve as the basis in Chapter 6 for a proposal for an international legal practice of recognizing as legitimate states—as possessors of the full bundle of powers, liberties, rights, and immunities that constitute sovereignty—only those new entities claiming the status of state that are legitimate in the sense just defined. The same general conception of political legitimacy will also serve in Chapter 7 as the point of departure for an examination of the idea of the legitimacy of the international legal system as a whole. In Chapter 8 I will again rely on the conception of political legitimacy developed in this chapter to advance a theory of the right to secede, an account of when a state's claim to a portion of its territory can be voided to clear the way for the creation of a new state there.

I. *Political Legitimacy and the Morality of Political Power*

It is fair to say that the dominant view on the legitimacy of the state system is that it is secured by state consent. One important upshot of this chapter's analysis is that the dominant view ought to be rejected, for two reasons. First, state consent is of dubious moral significance in a system in which many states often do not represent all or even most of their citizens or take their basic interests seriously. Second, it is a credible commitment to the protection of human rights, not consent, that confers political legitimacy. Consent of the governed, I shall argue, is not necessary for the justified exercise of political power, whether within individual states or in the workings of international legal institutions. Nor is it sufficient.

Political legitimacy and political authority

The term 'political legitimacy' is unfortunately ambiguous. One source of confusion is the failure to distinguish clearly between political legitimacy and political authority.[2]

---

[2] For a more detailed analysis of the distinction between political authority and political legitimacy, as well as a view of the relationships of these concepts to that of authoritativeness, see ibid.

I will distinguish carefully between political legitimacy and political authority. I will also articulate two different variants of the notion of political authority. Having drawn these distinctions, I will argue first that political legitimacy, rather than political authority, is the more central notion for a theory of the morality of political power. My second main conclusion will be that where democratic authorization of the exercise of political power is possible, only a democratic government can be legitimate.

Although it is common to conflate the democratic choice of government officials and legislators with consent, they are distinct. Democracy is first and foremost a method for choosing who shall exercise political power and how it shall be exercised. Nothing is gained by assuming that when democracy exists the individuals who participate in it are thereby giving their consent to anything, much less to everything that results from the democratic process. Hence one can reject the consent theory of legitimacy and still consistently hold, as I do, that where democracy is possible it is required for legitimacy.

Another ambiguity is also a source of confusion. Sometimes it is unclear whether 'legitimacy' is being used in a descriptive or a normative sense. In this chapter and those to follow I am concerned exclusively with legitimacy in the normative sense, *not* with the conditions under which an entity is *believed* to be legitimate. This is a notable distinction, not least because much of the literature on international law uses 'legitimate' to mean 'is believed to be legitimate'.

Political power and political legitimacy

According to the terminology I am recommending, an entity has *political legitimacy* if and only if it is morally justified in wielding political power, where to wield political power is to (make a credible) attempt to exercise supremacy, within a jurisdiction, in the making, application, and enforcement of laws. The supremacy feature is necessary if we are to distinguish political power from mere coercion. A state not only uses coercion to secure compliance with its rules; it also attempts to establish the supremacy of those rules and endeavors to suppress others who would enforce its rules or promulgate their own rules without its authorization. Typically those who attempt to wield political power also claim that they do so rightfully and hence that they are justified in asserting supremacy.

Note, however, that supremacy does not imply that there are no limits on state power. Supremacy refers to the lack of a rival for the state's making, application, and enforcement of law within an assumed jurisdiction (typically understood as a territory). This is compatible with the scope of the rules it imposes being limited, for example, by human rights principles imposed by international law or by a bill of rights included in a constitution.[3]

This definition of political power is deliberately inclusive. It covers not only the actions of the government of a state within its own borders, but also those of an occupying military force. Some might think that the fact that the definition encompasses the latter shows that it is too inclusive. Recall, however, that the goal is to formulate a conception of political power, not a conception of a genuine or ideal political community, in which political power is wielded by a group of people over themselves. To object that the definition of political power offered here must be defective because it leaves open the possibility that a government of military occupation might satisfy the conditions for being legitimate, that is, for being morally justified in wielding political power, is to beg important questions about the conditions under which political legitimacy is possible.

The definition of political power I am operating with leaves open the possibility that entities wielding political power can be legitimate even if they do not achieve an ideal of democratic governance or are less than morally optimal in some other respect. It also leaves

---

[3] It might be thought that this conception of political power is not sufficiently political—that it does not capture what is distinctive of political as opposed to other forms of power. For it seems that it would apply to the administration of a prison or mental hospital, assuming that the administration promulgates rules and enforces them within the institution, and attempts to do so in a way that denies others in the institution the opportunity to perform these functions.

This is not the case, however. To the extent that institutions such as prisons or mental hospitals within society employ supreme coercive power within certain subdomains of the state's sphere of control, in principle they do so as agents of the state or at least with the state's permission to do so. If something further is needed to distinguish clearly between political power and the power wielded within such institutions as correctional facilities or mental hospitals, one may add that political power is the attempt to make, apply, and enforce rules with supremacy over the broadest class of citizens, including what might be called the "unencumbered" population, not just those in a special class, such as convicted criminals, the mentally infirm, or minors, whose civil and/or political rights are subject to special restrictions.

open the possibility that entities wielding political power can be legitimate even if the individuals over which political power is wielded do not constitute a political community in some normatively robust sense according to which all members of the group are said to have significant special obligations toward each other.

One reason to take this approach is to avoid conflating legitimacy with perfect justice (understood as requiring democracy) or with an ideal of political community at the outset of the analysis. Of equal importance, we need a conception of political power, and an account of the conditions under which wielding it is morally justifiable, that is not restricted to cases where a "genuine political community" already exists or where democratic government is feasible, because we need to know when it is morally justifiable to attempt to achieve supremacy in the use of coercion in order to build genuine political communities and develop democratic institutions under conditions of state breakdown.

I shall say that an entity has *political authority* if and only if, in addition to (1) possessing political legitimacy, it (2) has the right to be obeyed by those who are within the scope of its rules; in other words, if those upon whom it attempts to impose rules have an *obligation to that entity* to obey it. To say that X has a right to be obeyed by P implies that if P does not comply with X's rules P wrongs X, violates X's right to be obeyed.

Some who employ the term 'political authority' in this way are unclear as to whether the entity that is said to have the right to be obeyed is the state or the government; indeed one suspects that they use these terms interchangeably in some cases. However, there is a distinction and it is significant. The state is a persisting structure of institutions for the wielding of political power. Within this structure there are roles that empower their occupants to exercise power in various ways, and the government consists of the occupants of these roles or at least the more important of them. States typically persist through changes of government. Given this distinction, the more coherent view is that obedience is owed to the government, not the state, since the idea of owing anything to an institutional structure, as opposed to those persons who occupy roles in it, is problematic.

Some who use the term 'political authority' do so in a different way. The idea of the right to be obeyed is still crucial to the notion, but the subject of this right is not said to be the government, but rather one's fellow citizens. Locke, for example, is best interpreted as arguing that it is not the government, but one's fellow citizens to whom one owes obedience (in a properly constituted polity). On this view, where political authority exists, the right to be obeyed is owed to those in whose name and on whose behalf it is wielded, rather than those who actually wield power (except perhaps in the rather extended sense in which it can be said that the people wield power through the agency of the government).

In the analysis that follows, I will distinguish, where it is relevant to do so, between these distinct conceptions of who has the right to be obeyed. What the two variants of the notion of political authority have in common is that they both include the idea that citizens have an obligation to obey someone—that someone has a right to be obeyed—not just the idea that someone is justified in imposing rules on them. In the former variant the obligation is owed to the government, the actual (or at least proximate) wielder of political power; in the latter to one's fellow citizens. I will argue that if political authority is understood as including the obligation to obey the government, it is largely irrelevant to the question of what justifies the exercise of political power and what gives those over whom political power is exercised reason to comply with its demands.

Theorizing the morality of political power

My focus on political legitimacy and my skepticism about the significance of the idea that we owe compliance to the government are both based on a conception of what is needed for a theory of the morality of political power. The chief objective of such a theory is to answer two questions: (1) under what conditions is it morally justifiable for some agent or agents to wield political power (the agent-justifiability question), and (2) under what conditions do those upon whom political power is exercised have sufficient reasons to comply with its demands (the reasons-for-compliance question)? As will become clear shortly, answering these two questions does *not* require an account of political authority, where this is understood as including a right to be obeyed on the part of the government. Nor does answering them require recourse to the notion that we owe our fellow citizens compliance with the laws, except in circumstances where democratic authorization for the exercise of political power is feasible; and even in that case the obligation is only presumptive.

II. *The Irrelevance of the Idea that We Owe Compliance to the Government*

The relationship between political authority and political legitimacy

Political authority, understood as including the right of the government to be obeyed, entails political legitimacy, but not vice versa. An entity may be morally justified in attempting to exercise supremacy in the making, application, and enforcement of laws without it also being the case that those upon whom it enforces the laws owe *it* an obligation to obey. Whether an entity is politically legitimate depends only upon whether the agents attempting to wield political power in it are morally justified in attempting to achieve supremacy in the making, applying, and enforcing of rules. In other words, political legitimacy is an agent-justification notion, having to do solely with the normative sufficiency of the justification for imposing rules, not with whether those upon whom the rules are imposed have obligations to those who impose the rules. An agent can be justified in exercising political power even if no one owes it obedience.

Similarly, whether we have sufficient reasons for complying with rules does not depend upon whether those who impose them have the right to be obeyed. Of course it is true that *if* one is obligated to obey X, then this gives one a reason to comply with the rules X promulgates. But being obligated to obey X is not *necessary* for having good or sufficient reasons to comply with the rules. For as A. John Simmons and others have emphasized, we can have *other* good and sufficient reasons and indeed we can be morally obligated to comply, in the absence of any obligation to those who wield political power.[4] For example, we may have weighty prudential reasons (we are likely to be punished for noncompliance) or religious reasons (we believe the scriptures and the scriptures say to render

---

[4] A. John Simmons, *Moral Principles and Political Obligations* (Princeton University Press, Princeton, 1979), 29–38, 152–3.

unto Caesar what is Caesar's) or we may have weighty general moral reasons (the law codifies sound moral principles that prohibit killing, theft, etc.) to comply with the laws the government imposes. Yet none of these reasons implies that we owe compliance to the government (or to our fellow citizens).

So both the agency-justification and reasons-for-compliance questions can be answered without recourse to the notion that compliance with the laws is owed to the government. So the first variant of the concept of political authority, according to which obedience is owed to the government, is irrelevant to the two main tasks for a theory of the morality of political power.

III. *Explaining the Preoccupation with the Government's Right to be Obeyed*

The notable absence of political authority

In the past three decades there has been an extensive debate in political philosophy about political authority. Some of this literature has focused on the first variant of the notion of political authority, according to which we owe compliance to the government, but in some cases it may be the second variant, according to which compliance is owed to fellow citizens, that is assumed instead. I believe that the single most compelling conclusion to be drawn from the recent normative literature on political authority is that virtually no government possesses it, not because no government is morally justified in exercising political power nor because we have no sufficient reasons to comply with the rules governments impose, but because the conditions for citizens having an obligation to their government to comply with the laws are not satisfied and are not likely to be satisfied.[5] Given these disappointing results, there is all the more reason to ask whether analyses of the morality of political power should focus on, or even include, the issue of political authority.

If the conditions for political authority appear to be unattainable, one ought to ask: Why is political authority so important? I have argued that the answer cannot be "Because without political authority, the wielding of political power is not justifiable," nor "Because

---

[5] For the most detailed criticisms leading to this conclusion, see ibid., 7–190.

if the state lacks political authority we cannot have good reason to comply with the laws."

Sometimes the conclusion that virtually no governments have or are likely to come to have political authority is equated with the thesis that the state cannot be "justified." But that is unfortunate, because it either fails to distinguish not only between the government and the state but also between political legitimacy and political authority—or else wrongly assumes that the only "justification" of interest for the state is one that shows it to have not only political legitimacy but the more demanding characteristic of political authority.

Preoccupation with political authority overlooks the simple point noted earlier: We can have sufficient reasons (prudential, religious, and moral) to comply with the law, indeed we can have weighty obligations to do so, without it being the case that we owe obedience to anyone, whether it be the government or our fellow citizens. So lack of political authority need not raise the specter of anarchy, if by anarchy we mean a condition of general lawlessness. One would only conclude that general lawlessness is the likely result of the lack of political authority if one assumes that most people will not find the other reasons for compliance compelling (apart from being obligated to the government to obey it). But this assumption is dubious. Once we recognize how demanding the notion of political authority is, and how unconnected it appears to be with the important questions concerning the morality of political power (the agency-justification and reasons-for-compliance questions), it is puzzling that some recent political philosophers seem to have assumed that an account of political authority must be a centerpiece of a viable political theory.

Why political authority has seemed important

Perhaps the best explanation of the preoccupation with political authority has to do with the popularity of the theory of government by consent. The theory of consent flowered at a time when two key liberal notions were coming into their own: the idea that liberty is the proper condition of human beings and the idea of the fundamental moral equality of persons. If we are all equal, what can justify some persons (the government) making, applying, and enforcing rules on us? How can the justified wielding of political power be squared with the fundamental equality of persons? And if liberty is our proper condition, how can the use of coercion, which government essentially involves, be justified? To both of these questions the theory of consent provides an elegantly simple, but flawed answer: Those who wield political power over us are justified in doing so if and only if we consented to their doing so.

Often it is assumed that the chief virtue of consent is that it takes the sting out of coercion, reconciling individual liberty with political power, and this is surely part of its attractiveness. But the justification of coercion as such is of paramount concern only if one assumes that liberty in the sense of freedom from coercion is the only or at least the most fundamental value. However, as Thomas Christiano has observed, quite apart from the question of liberty, the consent theory is attractive simply from the standpoint of reconciling *equality* and political power. Consent theory has much to commend it from the standpoint of those who take equal consideration of persons to be the preeminent value, quite apart from any special preoccupation with the justification of coercion.[6]

Political power as a challenge to equality as well as liberty

Political power is problematic from the standpoint of equality (not just liberty) because it involves *some* persons imposing rules on others. In brief: If we are all fundamentally equal, why should only some of us wield political power? The answer consent theory gives is that I have authorized you to do so by my consent. To the question "How is the coercive nature of political power compatible with individual liberty?" the consent theory answers that we best preserve our liberty by the free choice of consenting to a political power to enforce a regime of individual rights. Even better, consent theory reconciles power with equality and liberty in a way that respects autonomy. For according to consent theory, it is not sufficient that the government secure my liberty for me by exercising coercion over me; rather, the state may coerce me even for my

---

[6] Christiano, 'Justice and Disagreement at the Foundations of Political Authority', review of Christopher Morris, *An Essay on the Modern State*.

own good only if I freely limit my own liberty by authorizing the state to impose rules on me.

Consent theory, the gold standard?

In fact, according to this venerable theory the answer to both of the most important questions about political power is the same. (1) It is our consent that morally justifies the government in wielding political power (the answer to the agent-justification question). (2) Our having consented to be ruled gives us sufficient reason to comply with rules issued by those wielding political power (the answer to the reasons-for-compliance question). In addition, consent theory provides an account of political authority. On one variant of the theory, the "contract of government" view, we are obligated to the government to obey it because we gave our consent to those who comprise the government; on the "social contract proper" variant we are obligated to our fellow citizens because we gave our consent to them.

Perhaps the ability of the consent theory to answer all of these questions has led political philosophers to treat it as a kind of gold standard, to assume that any adequate account of the morality of political power would have to do what consent theory purports to do—not only solve the agent-justification and reasons-for-compliance questions, but also provide an account of political authority, understood as including the right to be obeyed. In addition, as I have already suggested, the consent theory is at first blush very attractive, at least within the broadly liberal tradition, because it seems to reconcile political power with the preeminent values of liberty and equality.

The demand for consent as a denial of politics

Although the consent theory has the attraction of answering all these questions, it does so by virtue of a concept that is remarkably ill-suited to the political world and so extraordinarily demanding as to remain utopian in the worst sense. The idea of consent is ill-suited to the political world for this reason: Not only are there no existing entities or any that are likely to come about that will ever enjoy the consent of most of their citizens, but politics seems to be concerned, in some fundamental way, with how to get along when consent is lacking. Whether we assume that what is to be consented to is the system as a whole, its processes for generating laws, or all the particular laws themselves, some citizens, for good reasons or bad, will not consent even if presented with the possibility of doing so. Moreover, no existing states, including the ones we intuitively regard as the most legitimate, have developed mechanisms for even trying to obtain the consent of all their citizens.

The nonconsensual conditions for consent

When confronted with the fact that the consent requirement is utopian for any real political entity, instead of asking "Why is political authority so important?" (given that we can answer the agency-justification and reasons-for-compliance questions without it), some theorists, including Locke, have fallen back on the idea that citizens tacitly consent by simply remaining within the state. However, the idea of tacit consent rapidly runs aground on two difficulties. First, as Hume observed, for many people in many states the costs of exit are so high or the prospects of a better situation elsewhere so dim, that remaining in place cannot count as consent. This first objection by itself seems to doom the idea of tacit consent. Second, Simmons and Wellman have argued that to have the right to determine that a citizen's continued residence within the state counts as consent, someone would *already* have to have the authority or rightful power the consent theory is supposed to explain.[7]

The second objection can be elaborated as follows. The problem with taking continued residence as a sign of tacit consent is that there is no such thing as a natural act of consent, at least not in the case of consent to political power. For some bit of behavior—for example, saying "Aye" in an assembly—to count as consent there must be certain conventions already in place; for example, conventions establishing where and when groups must meet if they are to count as assemblies, who is qualified to participate, how something to be consented to must be stated, by whom, what noises or signs are to count as consent, how long consent will be regarded as binding, whether there are implicit exceptions to consent rooted in some

---

[7] See Simmons, *Moral Principles and Political Obligation*, 75–95; and Christopher Wellman, 'Liberalism, Samaritanism, and Political Legitimacy', *Philosophy and Public Affairs* 25 (1996), 211–37.

conception of intent, and so on. To think that there is some act that could count as consent prior to a process that establishes such conventions is as incorrect as thinking that an exchange of words between two people could count as a contract in the absence of a framework of legal institutions.

So before maintaining residence in the state can count as consent, there must be some process by which these conventions are established. But that process itself would have to be legitimate; otherwise, the problem of legitimacy would simply be pushed back to this earlier stage: Who is justified in imposing the convention that such-and-such behavior is to count as consent (for the sake of taking consent as conferring legitimacy)? In brief, the problem of justifying the exercise of political power must already be solved before the consent theory can get off the ground.

The Simmons–Wellman argument may not be as conclusive as it first appears. For it might be objected that there can in fact be "natural" acts of consent. Thomas Scanlon has argued that in the absence of any institutions or social conventions whatsoever certain acts can count as promises to reciprocate. Scanlon asks us to imagine two strangers in a situation in which there is the possibility of an exchange of simple acts of aid, and surmises that they could signal, by some simple gesture, an intent to reciprocate.[8] Similarly, one might argue, there can be natural acts of consent.

However, Scanlon's natural act of promising and the case of consent seem deeply dissimilar, mainly because what one agrees to in the case of the exercise of political power is not only much more complex than what the two strangers agree to in Scanlon's example, but disputable as well. To consent to the exercise of political authority, if this consent is to have normative force, presupposes agreement on some conception of the scope of political power—at least some rough idea of how and for what political power is to be used. Open-ended consent, agreement that someone, somehow, is to attempt to achieve supremacy in the making, interpretation, and enforcement of general rules, for wholly unspecified purposes, would be irrational. But quite apart from whether consent to an unspecified object of consent would be irrational, it is difficult to imagine how Scanlon's

---

[8] See Thomas Scanlon, *What We Owe to Each Other* (The Belknap Press of Harvard University Press, Cambridge, MA, 1998), 297–8.

strangers could by some simple act, in the absence of an established process or convention, signal such open-ended consent to the exercise of political power. (One can perhaps imagine a natural act of total submission—for example, prostrating oneself or kissing the other person's foot—but this would be more like agreement to become a slave than consent to the exercise of political power).

Presumably some sort of collective process would be needed to enable individuals to converge on at least a rough conception of the scope of the exercise of political power that is to be consented to. Without this, any gesture they might make would not succeed in indicating just what it is they are consenting to nor hence give any assurance that they were consenting to the same thing. And further, since what the scope of political authority should be is a contested issue, it makes perfectly good sense to ask whether the process that identifies the proper object of consent (the scope of political power), and that designates some particular act as consent to that object, is itself legitimate. But if this is the case, then there can be no natural act of consent to the exercise of political power. The Simmons–Wellman conclusion stands.

Another difficulty is that even if it were true that consent is necessary for political authority (the right to be obeyed), it cannot be sufficient for having reasons to comply, nor for being obligated to obey the government. The fact that I have consented to government cannot itself show that I am obligated to comply with its demands, because there are some things that no government should require of anyone (namely, acts that are grossly immoral), and the fact that I have consented to government cannot change this. But once we hedge our consent-based obligations by appeal to independent moral principles, especially principles of justice, the question arises as to whether we can dispense with consent and simply argue that we ought to comply with a system of laws if it promotes justice and does so in ways that are themselves just. To summarize: In its unconditional form the view that consent obligates us to comply is false, but qualifying it threatens to make consent superfluous as an account of reasons to comply with the law.

Once its flaws are appreciated, as well as its essential irrelevance in light of the fact that it is not important to show that governments enjoy political authority (as opposed to legitimacy), consent theory should no longer serve as the gold standard for a moral theory of political power. We should not assume that an adequate theory will do what consent theory would do if successful, namely, articulate realizable conditions not only for the justification for wielding political power, but also an account of the obligation to the government to obey it.

However, one of the virtues of consent theory ought to be exemplified by a theory of political legitimacy: the reconciliation of the inequality involved in the exercise of political power—the fact that it involves the imposition of laws by some upon others—with the fundamental equality of persons. In the next section I develop the main outlines of a theory of political legitimacy and then argue that it successfully reconciles political power with equal regard for persons.

IV. *Toward a Theory of Political Legitimacy*

Political legitimacy without political authority

My aim in this section is to develop a theory of political legitimacy that does not rely upon the notion of a right to be obeyed. The central idea is this: A wielder of political power (the supremacist making, application, and enforcement of laws in a territory) is legitimate (i.e., is morally justified in wielding political power) if and only if it (1) does a credible job of protecting at least the most basic human rights of all those over whom it wields power and (2) provides this protection through processes, policies, and actions that themselves respect the most basic human rights.[9]

The intuitive appeal of this view of legitimacy can be stated quite simply: The chief moral purpose of endowing an entity with political power is to achieve justice. Given the state's coercive and monopolistic character and the fact that it necessarily involves inequality of power, nothing short of this could justify creating an entity so capable of causing harm, infringing freedom, and creating or maintaining inequalities. A wielder of political power that does a credible job of achieving justice is morally justified in wielding that power, if it provides a reasonable approximation of justice through processes that are themselves reasonably just. This conception of

---

[9] My argument in this section draws on Buchanan, 'Recognitional Legitimacy and the State System'.

political legitimacy is founded on a liberal conception of what states are primarily for, namely, the provision of justice.[10]

The intuitive idea of the justice-based conception of legitimacy can be elaborated as follows. The Moral Equality Principle requires us to take very seriously certain basic interests that all persons have; it grounds both negative and positive duties of justice, as I argued in Chapter 3. One exceptionally important way of promoting these fundamental interests is by ensuring that the basic human rights are protected. Adequate protection of basic human rights requires the exercise of political power—an agency to make, apply, and enforce laws, and to approximate supremacy in doing so.

So long as political power is wielded for the sake of protecting basic human rights and in ways that do not violate those same rights, it is morally justified—unless those over whom it is exercised have a right not to be coerced to respect basic human rights. But there is no right not to be coerced to respect basic human rights, so long as coercion is used in ways that do not themselves violate basic human rights.[11]

---

[10] Of course this is compatible with the possibility that once a political entity satisfies the conditions for legitimacy it may justifiably pursue other ends than justice, including improving the general welfare, etc.

[11] This argument has the same structure as that advanced by Christopher Wellman in several papers on political obligation and samaritanism. There is a significant difference, however. Wellman begins with a much more limited moral principle than the Moral Equality Principle: a duty to rescue others from dire physical harm. His argumentative strategy in choosing this starting point is that he believes that the existence of this duty is more intuitively plausible than a more substantial moral premise such as the Moral Equality Principle. Notice, however, that Wellman's starting point is a positive obligation, a duty to prevent harm, not just a duty not to cause harm. In that regard, his argument and mine both reject the libertarian view that there are only negative obligations. The drawback to Wellman's approach is that it is incapable of justifying the liberal, as opposed to the libertarian or "police and nightwatchman state." Because he starts out with only the duty to prevent serious physical harm, he cannot by this argument justify the use of political power to ensure the protection of even a fairly lean list of human rights, so far as these exceed the right against serious physical harm. I believe that this is too high a price to pay. Once one has already acknowledged that there is one positive obligation, the duty to prevent serious physical harm, it is better to argue, as I have in Chapter 3, that there are other positive obligations as well, corresponding to a broader list of basic human rights. Moreover, unless one assumes something like the Moral Equality Principle, it is hard to see why we are obligated to all other persons to prevent serious physical harm to them. And once we explore *why* it is important to prevent serious physical harm to persons, it seems arbitrary to limit our concern for them to serving their interest in avoiding serious physical harm. In other words, preventing harm is obligatory because of how harm affects persons, but a proper regard for persons requires that we also acknowledge that they have other rights as well.

This argument provides a plausible answer to both of the chief questions a moral theory of political power should answer, the agency-justification question and the reasons-for-compliance question. It shows what an entity must be like to be justified in wielding political power, and it explains why we should comply with the laws an entity that meets that description imposes. The answer to both questions is that equal regard for persons requires us to promote certain basic interests that all persons have, and that doing this requires the exercise of political power, in order to ensure that their basic rights are protected.

V. *Why Should Some Persons Rather than Others Wield Political Power?*

Democracy and political legitimacy

Earlier I observed that a theory of political legitimacy must answer the egalitarian challenge to political power—it must explain why it is, if we are all fundamentally equal, that some should have the power to make, apply, and enforce laws on the rest of us. From the standpoint of a justice-based theory of political legitimacy that takes equal consideration of persons as fundamental, no justification for the wielding of political power—no conception of political legitimacy—can be complete unless it provides a convincing answer to this question.

It might be thought that the egalitarian challenge only applies to nondemocratic forms of political power. This is not the case, however. Even in democratic societies—including those that are much more democratic than what we now call democracies—some individuals (government leaders, judges, legislators, administrative officials, police officers) wield power that ordinary citizens do not. So even in a democracy we can ask: Is the wielding of political power compatible with a proper recognition of the fundamental equality of persons?

Democratic theory itself provides an answer to this question, and does so without invoking the fiction of consent. According to what may be the most plausible versions of democratic theory, the inequality that political power inevitably involves is justifiable if every citizen can participate as an equal in determining who will wield the power and how it will be wielded.

The egalitarian democratic theorist acknowledges, as he must, that government leaders, legislators, administrative officials, judges, and the police wield powers that ordinary citizens do not. Even in a direct participatory democracy in which every citizen has an equal vote on every law, government officials will wield powers ordinary citizens do not. It is this asymmetry of power that raises the question of whether political power is reconcilable with the fundamental equality of persons. The egalitarian democratic theorist attempts to achieve the needed reconciliation, not by denying the asymmetry of power, but by arguing that it is compatible with acknowledging the moral equality of persons—if all citizens participate as equals in public processes for determining who will wield political power.

Thus one of the chief attractions of democratic theory is that it purports to do what consent theory claimed but failed to do, but without the over-demanding requirement of consent: reconcile equality with the exercise of political power. Whether or not any form of democracy that could be reasonably approximated in something resembling a modern state can fully achieve this reconciliation is not clear. The more complex the system of laws and policies becomes, the more difficult it is to satisfy the requirement that all citizens are to participate as equals in the public processes that determine who wields political power.[12]

Nevertheless, if we take the equality of persons seriously, then a political order that not only honors the commitment to equal regard by respecting all citizens' human rights, but also does so by political processes that themselves express this commitment to equality by being democratic, would seem to provide the best answer available to the problem of reconciling political power and equality. In other words, if the wielding of political power is morally justifiable only if it is wielded in such a way as to recognize the fundamental equality of persons, and if democracy is necessary for satisfying this condition, then political legitimacy requires democracy, at least in circumstances in which democratic institutions are feasible.

However, one might question the assertion that legitimacy requires democracy as follows. It is true that to be morally justified,

---

[12] For an exceptionally valuable treatment of this problem, see Henry S. Richardson, *Democratic Autonomy: Public Reasoning about the Ends of Policy* (Oxford University Press, New York, 2002).

political power must be exercised in such a way as to manifest equal regard for persons. But this will be achieved if the *content* of the laws is sufficiently egalitarian, more precisely, if the regime of laws provides adequate protection for the basic human rights of all.

The difficulty with this reply is that it is unresponsive to the fundamental egalitarian challenge to political authority: If we are all equal, why should only some of us have control over the making, application, and enforcement of laws? The requirement of democracy at least goes some distance toward answering this challenge, even if it does not answer it fully due to the fact that even the most democratic society will still include inequalities in political power (because citizens at best only have an equal say in choosing legislators, vote directly only on "ends" not "means", have no direct say over the determination of rules for administering policies, do not participate in adjudication and enforcement of laws, etc.).

To put the same point differently: Democracy does not actually achieve equality in political power; but it does take seriously the idea that inequalities in political power are problematic from the standpoint of a commitment to equal regard for persons. It does this by offering an account of how majoritarian processes can contribute to equalizing power over the *allocation* of inequalities in political power (in particular by ensuring that all can participate as equals in determining who will occupy the highest government offices and who will make the laws). In contrast, a theory of legitimacy that does not include a democratic requirement faces an unanswerable objection: If the political system should express a fundamental commitment to equal consideration of persons, why shouldn't this commitment be reflected in the processes by which laws are made and in the selection of persons to adjudicate and enforce the laws, not simply in the content of the laws?

Here it is important to acknowledge an implicit but crucial assumption of the argument that democracy is a necessary condition for legitimacy. The argument assumes either that (1) democracy can do at least as well as alternative systems in producing laws that satisfy the requirement of equal regard for all persons' basic interests, or that (2) participating as an equal in the public processes for determining who wields political power is such an important dimension of equal regard for persons that democracy is required even if a non-democratic arrangement would do a better job of producing laws that achieve the goal of equal regard for all persons' basic interests. If (1) is true, then there is no reason why those who are committed to equal respect and concern for all persons should settle for laws whose content or effect evidences equal regard; they will also insist on participating as equals in the public processes by which it is determined who shall wield political power, since this is a further affirmation of equality and comes at no loss in terms of the protection of all persons' basic interests. If (2) is true then democracy is required even if it can result in laws that do not treat all equally.

Assumption (2) is clearly the more problematic one. Supporting it requires showing that participating as an equal in the public processes that determine who wields political power is such a profoundly important dimension of equality that it must be achieved even if doing so comes at the cost of losses in other dimensions of equality, namely, in laws whose content or effect is not appropriately egalitarian.

My aim here is not to advance a full-blown defense of democracy as being required by equal regard for persons. However, it seems to me that there is much to be said for the idea that all being able to participate as equals in the processes that determine who wields political power is presumptively required by equal regard for persons and that opponents of democracy have not defeated this presumption by showing that democracy is less likely than other systems to produce laws that achieve equal protection of all persons' basic interests. On the contrary, democracies seem to do better at protecting the basic human rights of all citizens than undemocratic governments. If this is correct, then assumption (1), and with it the argument for democracy as being required by equal regard for all persons, is plausible.

VI. *Democracy and Mutual Obligations among Citizens*

Democracy, political authority, and political community

I have argued that democratic theory provides a more satisfactory answer than consent theory does to the question of how to reconcile the equality of persons with the exercise of political power. I also observed earlier that consent theory—if it worked—would answer the question of political authority as well: If I have consented to your exercising political power over me, then I am obligated to you to comply with your directives.

Democratic theory, in contrast to consent theory, does not provide an account of political authority if by this is meant an explanation of the conditions under which we are obligated to the *government* to obey it. It could not and should not do this, because the whole point of the doctrine of popular sovereignty upon which democratic theory is built holds that states are merely institutional resources for the people and governments are merely agents of the people, chosen to employ those institutional resources on the people's behalf, and therefore do not themselves have a right to anything, including our obedience.

Instead, democratic theory provides an account of the conditions under which citizens can have an obligation *to one another* to take compliance with the laws seriously. In other words, the same commitment to the equal consideration of persons that requires democracy as a condition for the morally justified exercise of political power also gives citizens a weighty reason to comply with the laws that emerge from democratic processes, because these processes are the best available way to express the fundamental commitment to equal regard for persons.

This is a great advantage of democratic theory. It makes sense of the idea of the polity as a *moral community*, not merely an instrumental association of individuals, yet it does so without assuming that the basis of this community is ethnicity or nationality or religion or even ideology.[13] And in so doing, democratic theory demonstrates that there is another important reason to obey the law, beyond reasons of self-interest (to avoid penalty) and even beyond the fact that the law includes (some) sound moral principles that we ought to obey anyway. In a democratic state, each citizen's recognition of the equality of all citizens supplies a reason for compliance with the laws. And it is a weighty reason because it is grounded ultimately in the most fundamental moral principle of all, the principle of equal concern and respect for persons.

It does not follow from this, of course, that citizens in a democracy have an unconditional obligation to comply. No one can be obligated to comply with a law that is itself a clear and serious

[13] I am grateful to Thomas Christiano for clarifying this point.

violation of the principle of equal regard for persons, even if that law is the result of a democratic process.

Democratic theory and the particularity problems

In Section V I argued that the protection of basic human rights justifies the exercise of political power. However, from this it does not follow that any particular agent is justified in coercing us in the name of protecting rights. Nor does it follow that equal regard for persons requires us to support the particular coercive agent that is the government of the state in which we find ourselves.

In other words, a satisfactory account of the morality of political power must provide an answer to two distinct particularity problems: (1) what makes any particular wielder of political power justified in doing so, and (2) why should we comply with the rules imposed by the particular coercive power that happens to be the government of our state? Although any satisfactory account must solve the two particularity problems, they seem to be especially pressing and difficult for an approach to political legitimacy founded ultimately on the highly abstract idea of equal regard for persons.

It will not suffice to say that honoring the Natural Duty of Justice requires us to support whoever happens to be effectively wielding political power in our locale. If existing institutional resources allow for a way of choosing among aspirants for political power or for endorsing an existing wielder of political power that expresses equal regard for persons, then we can and should demand more than mere effectiveness.

In other words, where institutional resources exist for *democratic authorization* of a government, proper respect for the fundamental equality of persons requires that they be utilized. For as I have already argued, proper recognition of the fundamental equality of persons requires a convincing answer to the question "If we are all fundamentally equal, why should some persons enjoy the special control over our common life that the exercise of political power entails?" Democratic authorization of a wielder of political power answers this question.

If a wielder of political power can be chosen through democratic processes, then there is an answer to both of the particularity problems. First, this particular agent is justified in wielding political power over us—and in attempting to do so monopolistically—because it is *this* agent that has been chosen by our democratic processes. Once this selection is achieved, there is one and only one agent who can justify its efforts to impose rules on us, because any agent who attempts to impose rules on us without enjoying democratic authorization would not satisfy the requirement of reconciling the inequality that the exercise of political power involves with the fundamental equality of persons.

Second, when an agent has been authorized to wield political power over us by democratic processes in which we can participate, we have a weighty moral reason to comply with the rules *this* agent imposes on us, not just because it is capable of effectively protecting our rights (others may be equally capable), but because to fail to comply with the rules *this* agent imposes, in the absence of some weighty moral reason for doing so, would show a disregard for our fellow citizens as beings entitled to equal moral regard. The same act of democratic authorization that makes it justifiable for this particular agent to wield political power over us gives us a weighty reason to comply with *its* rules, rather than the rules that some other coercive agent might supply. We ought to comply with the rules this agent imposes on us because this agent was authorized by a process that is required by, and at the same time expresses, the fundamental equality that obtains among us.

Notice also that the democratic authorization solution to the second particularity problem avoids the unsavory conclusion that we owe compliance to the government as such. It solves the second particularity problem without embracing the noxious idea that the government is itself a subject of rights, rather than simply the agent through which the people act.

I observed earlier that consent theory, in one of its versions, in contrast answers the second particularity problem by asserting that we are obligated *to the government* (this particular government) to obey the laws. However, another version of consent theory holds that we are obligated to our fellow citizens to comply with the rules the government imposes on us. The question arises, then, as to whether the idea of democratic authorization implies that we have an obligation *to our fellow citizens* to obey democratically created laws.

This conclusion appears to be too strong if it means that whenever one violates a democratically created law one thereby wrongs one's fellow citizens. It is more plausible if it means only that we wrong our fellow citizens—by failing to take seriously the fact that equality requires democracy—if we violate democratically created laws without some morally weighty reason for doing so. The obligation we owe our fellow citizens, then, is not an obligation to obey every democratically created law, but rather to show proper respect for them as equal moral persons by taking the fact that a law is democratically created as a weighty reason for complying with it.

Notice, however, that to solve the second particularity problem, the account of democratic authorization need not even go as far as asserting this latter obligation to our fellow citizens. All that is required is the claim that the fact that this particular coercive agent has been authorized by democratic processes gives us a weighty reason—a reason grounded ultimately in equal regard for persons—for complying with *its* demands, rather than with those of some other, perhaps equally effective coercive agent. And recall that we can have a weighty reason for complying with the government's demands without owing obedience to the government.

Democracy as an element of justice

So far I have argued for an account of political legitimacy that is grounded in the moral equality of persons and that includes the idea of democratic authorization as a solution to the two particularity problems. For this approach to succeed, it is necessary to show that the Moral Equality Principle requires supporting or helping to create democratic institutions, and this in turn requires showing that democracy is either an element of justice or a necessary instrument for achieving justice. This is clearly not the occasion to establish either of the latter large claims. Here I can only indicate the kind of argument that is needed and which is developed in more detail by several current democratic theorists.

The core idea is that whatever its instrumental value for achieving justice, democracy is morally required by the commitment to equal consideration for persons. If justice requires recognizing the fundamental equality of persons, and if this in turn requires that there be institutional resources that make it possible for all persons to participate as equals in the public processes for determining who shall wield political power, then justice requires democracy. Thus the same fundamental moral principle that requires us to support a coercive order for the protection of persons' basic rights also requires us to support a process of democratic authorization that singles out a particular wielder of political power, and this gives us a weighty reason for complying with the rules imposed by that agent because we owe it to our fellow citizens to take seriously the results of democratic decision-making.

The limits of democratic authorization

There are two quite different situations in which the problem of political legitimacy arises and the second of them reveals the limits of democratic authorization. The first is where people are already successfully organized as a democratic political society—where the state as a structure of institutions exists and already includes democratic processes for identifying agents to wield political power. Under these conditions the only question is who shall be the agents, and democratic processes are capable of yielding an answer. Once the agents are identified, there will be a single answer to the question "Who is justified in wielding political power?" and to the question "Whom ought the people to support?"

In the second situation the institutional resources for democratic authorization are not available, either because the state has disintegrated or because the state exists but is undemocratic and recalcitrant to democratization. Here there may at first appear to be an unbridgeable gap between the commitment to acting on the Moral Equality Principle and the acknowledgment that acting on it requires institutions that protect basic human rights, on the one hand, and the justification of any particular agent's use of coercion to enforce the protection of rights, on the other.

In such conditions, individuals who strive conscientiously to help ensure that basic human rights are protected will find themselves in a painful predicament: It is necessary to establish and support some particular coercive agency that lacks the imprimatur of democratic authorization in order to achieve the modicum of order needed to develop the democratic institutions which alone make the exercise of political power fully legitimate. Reasonable persons may find themselves on opposite sides of the barricades because they may make different but not unreasonable predictions about which coercive agents to support, and for how long.

However, as Jeremy Waldron has rightly noted, matters may not always be so grim. In some instances one particular potential coercive agent may be salient—if only because it already enjoys more support than its rivals.[14] If this is the case, then persons who strive conscientiously to act on the Natural Duty of Justice will support the salient potential government, at least if they have good reason to believe it will do as good a job of protecting basic rights as its rivals.

Mere salience versus democratic authorization

However, the fact that a particular agent is salient among those capable of enforcing a regime of rights cannot serve to legitimate it if institutional resources allow for democratic authorization. For if democratic authorization is feasible (and is also likely to be achievable without excessive risks to persons' basic rights), then the same Moral Equality Principle that requires us to work to ensure that all persons have access to a rights-respecting regime also requires us to achieve democratic authorization of the exercise of political power to protect rights and also requires us to support only that agent that is selected by the process of democratic authorization. On this view, the core of justice, namely, equal regard for persons, requires democratic authorization where this is feasible (and can be achieved without excessive risk to persons' basic rights).

This account does not provide a solution to the problem of how we are to converge in our support for a particular coercive agent when the institutional resources for democratic authorization are lacking. It is not clear that it should. What the account does tell us, and all that it can be expected to tell us, is two things: First, that we have a Natural Duty of Justice, grounded in the Moral Equality Principle, to help develop institutions for the wielding of political power to protect individuals' basic rights; and second, that we should do this in such a way as to support, or where needed to create, processes for democratic authorization of agents to wield political power in the name of justice. In conditions in which institutional

---

[14] Jeremy Waldron, 'Special Ties and Natural Duties', *Philosophy and Public Affairs* 22 (1993), 3–30. See also Buchanan, 'Political Legitimacy and Democracy'.

resources for democratic authorization are not yet available, the best way—indeed the only way—we can honor the moral equality of persons is by helping to create a regime of law and order that protects basic rights and at the same time facilitates, or at least allows for the development of, democratic institutions. Where democratic authorization is not possible, it cannot be a requirement for legitimacy.

VII. *Conclusions*

I began this chapter with the observation that it is not enough to know that the international legal system should take justice as a primary goal. In addition, we need to know the conditions under which political power can be exercised for the sake of justice; we need an account of political legitimacy.

I have argued for a general conception of political legitimacy that is grounded in the liberal tenet that protection of basic human rights is the core of justice and the *raison d'être* for political power. I have also argued that although political authority is not required for political legitimacy, democratic authorization is necessary if institutional resources are available for the democratic selection of an agent to exercise political power and if attempting to achieve democratic authorization is not unduly risky from the standpoint of persons' basic rights.

According to this theory, we may distinguish between what might be called minimal and full political legitimacy. Where institutional resources for democratic authorization are lacking, an entity can be politically legitimate—can be morally justified in exercising political power—if it satisfies minimal standards for protecting individuals' rights by processes and policies that are themselves at least minimally just. However, this legitimacy is deficient or at least less than optimal: It fails to reconcile the exercise of political power with the fundamental equality of persons.

Where democratic authorization is possible (and can be pursued without excessive risks to basic rights), it is necessary for political legitimacy. Moreover, where political legitimacy is achieved through democratic authorization, genuine political community, not merely a rational association for mutual protection, can be attained. And democratic authorization of the exercise of political power is superior because it achieves or at least approximates equal regard for persons.

In the next chapter I adapt the foregoing account of political legitimacy to address an urgent issue in the nonideal moral theory of international law: What principles should guide the practice of recognizing *new* entities that claim the status of legitimate states (in particular those that emerge as the result of secession)? There I argue for a normativized practice of recognition according to which new entities ought to be incorporated into the society of states only if they satisfy justice-based criteria, that is, only if they do a credible job of protecting the basic human rights of their citizens and refrain from serious violations of the basic human rights of those beyond their borders.

Then in Chapter 7 I explore a surprisingly neglected question: Under what conditions is the international legal system itself legitimate? More specifically: What would the system have to be like for it to be true that efforts to exercise supremacy in the making, application, and enforcement of principles of both international and transnational justice is morally justified?

Drawing on the present chapter's argument, I conclude that so long as global democracy is not feasible, the international legal system can be legitimate if it does a credible job of protecting basic rights by processes that do not violate those rights, but that equal regard for persons requires efforts to make global democracy a reality, if this ideal can be pursued without undue risk to basic human rights. This sets the stage for an exploration of different conceptions of what it would be to democratize the international legal system.

CHAPTER 6

Recognitional Legitimacy

I. *The Concept of Recognitional Legitimacy*

Three subjects of recognition

In the preceding chapter I outlined an argument for a justice-based general conception of what might be called *internal* political legitimacy, the conditions under which the exercise of political power within a political entity's own borders is morally justified. I now want to use this conception of internal political legitimacy as a component of an account of recognitional legitimacy (also called international legitimacy).[1]

The concept of recognitional legitimacy plays a central role in international legal institutions and international affairs. States, governments, and insurgency movements may all be recognized or not recognized as legitimate by individual states, groups of states, or regional or international organizations. My primary focus will be on recognitional legitimacy as applied to states—that is, on the judgment that a particular entity should or should not be recognized as a member in good standing of the system of states, with all the rights, powers, liberties, and immunities that go with that status. The guiding idea of my approach is that recognition is an act with serious moral implications and as such ought to be governed by rules that are themselves morally justifiable.

The idea of a justice-based theory of recognition

My aim is to develop a justice-based account of the proper criteria for recognition of legitimate states and then to use this to address

---

[1] The following two sections are drawn from Buchanan, 'Recognitional Legitimacy and the State System'.

the often more practically urgent, if less conceptually primary, issue of recognition of governments as legitimate. The account I develop, especially regarding recognition of new claimants to legitimate statehood arising from secession, will have implications for the practice of recognizing insurgency movements other than those that aim at secession, but I will make no attempt to draw them here.

By a justice-based account I mean one according to which satisfaction of what I shall call the minimal requirements of justice is necessary for recognition. To defend the justice-based account I set out more explicitly the argument sketched in Chapter 2 for understanding the minimal requirements of justice as being respect for basic human rights, both within the state (as the chief criterion for internal political legitimacy) and in the state's interactions with those beyond its borders. Then I develop a view about the way in which a proposal for a morally defensible institutional practice regarding recognition ought to be justified.

This view of justification includes two elements: nonconsequentialist or so-called "rights-based" arguments and teleological arguments that ground criteria for legitimacy in a view about how a proposal for a principled practice of recognition would contribute to moral progress in the international legal system by furthering what in Chapter 2 I argued ought to be a primary goal of the system, justice. I will also argue that the justice-based theory of recognitional legitimacy is morally preferable from a "rights-based" perspective because it grounds a practice of recognition that helps us avoid being accomplices in injustice.

In arguing for this thesis I will lend further support to a methodological position that I endorsed in Chapter 1: Sound institutional moral reasoning—reasoning about how institutions ought morally to be—is significantly teleological. Such reasoning must be informed by an appreciation of what the goals of institutions are and of which institutional arrangements are most likely to facilitate their achievement.

The concept of recognitional legitimacy

It is useful to distinguish the function, criteria, and content of the concept of recognitional legitimacy. The *function* of the concept is to make or deny assertions about the status of entities under international law. The judgment that an entity is legitimate in the recognitional sense confers the status of being a primary member in good standing of the international system, a legitimate state, with all the powers, liberties, claim-rights, and immunities that go with that status.

In its primary application, recognitional legitimacy is typically asserted or denied when an entity not now recognized as a legitimate state claims to be one. There are two main circumstances in which this occurs. The first is when an existing state has disintegrated or been destroyed and there is an issue of *state succession*, as when the rump of the former Yugoslavia, consisting of Serbia and Montenegro, demanded to be recognized as the Yugoslav state. The second is that of *secession*. A seceding group typically issues a declaration of independence claiming the status of a legitimate state, while the state from which it is seceding typically not only denies that the secessionist entity is a legitimate state, but also justifies its attempts to block secession by appealing to its own right, as an entity recognized under international law as a legitimate state, to protect its territorial integrity. Other states, whether individually or collectively through regional or international institutions, either accord the secessionist entity recognition or not.

The *content* of the concept of recognitional legitimacy is the bundle of juridical characteristics that define independent statehood or sovereignty. The prevalent view among international legal theorists is that this includes the following:

1. the right to territorial integrity;
2. the right to noninterference in internal affairs, i.e., internal self-determination (subject to certain restrictions);
3. the power to make treaties, alliances, and trade agreements, thereby altering its juridical relations to other entities;
4. the right to make (just) war;
5. the right to promulgate, adjudicate, and enforce legal rules within its territory (subject to certain restrictions).

This rendering of the content of recognitional legitimacy is uncontroversial only to the extent that it is abstract. Disputes arise when the parenthetical qualifications in 2 and 4 are fleshed out in such a way as to determine the scope and limits of the rights in question.

Full specification of 2 requires a theory of human rights, while 4 demands nothing short of a theory of just war.

The concept of recognitional legitimacy requires *criteria* for its application—necessary and sufficient conditions for an entity to be recognized as a member in good standing of the state system. In what follows I argue for adoption of justice-based criteria. It will be useful to begin, however, with a brief survey of historical and existing criteria, both to show that the criteria I propose are morally progressive vis-à-vis the current practice and to deflect the objection that they are so radical as to be utopian.

The *traditional* criteria for recognitional legitimacy, formalized in the Montevideo Convention of 1933,[2] are purely descriptive: An entity is entitled to recognition as a state if and only if it possesses (1) a permanent population, (2) a defined territory, (3) a functioning government able to control the territory in question, and (4) the capacity to enter into relations with other states on its own account (not merely as an agent of another state).[3]

According to some understandings of the *modern* or current criteria, there is an additional element: (5) in coming into being, an entity that claims to be a state must not have breached a (basic) rule of international law. At present it is not clear how much of an additional constraint, if any, condition (5) represents. The dominant international legal opinion seems to be that in general entities that satisfy the traditional criteria, which are summarized under the title "the principle of effectivity," are independent states and should be recognized as such in international law.[4]

Nevertheless, the fifth condition appears to include what I have referred to elsewhere as a Nonusurpation Requirement; it implies that an entity is not legitimate if it comes into being by displacing or destroying a legitimate state by a serious act of injustice.[5] Later I will argue that a Nonusurpation Requirement should be included in the criteria for recognitional legitimacy of states.

---

[2] Seventh International Conference of American States (1933), 'The Inter-American Convention on the Rights and Duties of States (The Montevideo Convention of 1933)', repr. in Weston Burns, Richard Falk, and Anthony D'Amato (eds.), *Basic Documents in International Law and World Order*, 2nd edn. (West Publishing, St Paul, MN, 1990), 12.

[3] See Nii Lante Wallace-Bruce, *Claims to Statehood in International Law* (Carlton Press, New York, 1994), 19–92.

[4] Gerhard Von Glahn, *Law among Nations: An Introduction to Public International Law*, 7th edn. (Allyn & Bacon, Boston, 1996), 68–9.   [5] Ibid.

There is evidence that international legal doctrine and practice are gradually adding moral content to the criteria for recognitional legitimacy, so that mere "effectivity" eventually may not be regarded as sufficient. For example, resolutions of the UN General Assembly refused to recognize Rhodesia on the grounds that its basic political and legal institutions systematically discriminated against blacks. In addition, one eminent international legal theorist, Thomas Franck, has even suggested that the criteria for recognitional legitimacy are evolving toward inclusion of a requirement of democratic governance, understood as consisting of representative institutions, as well as a modicum of freedom of expression and association necessary for their functioning.[6]

The desirability of recognition

Being recognized as a legitimate state confers unique advantages. The most obvious is the ability to do the things that states do, including being a party to agreements, treaties, and alliances, with other states—relationships not ordinarily available to nonstate entities. Perhaps even more important, recognitional legitimacy implies international support for an entity's efforts to preserve its territorial integrity in the face of various threats as well as support for its efforts to direct its own internal affairs. If an entity is recognized as a legitimate state, then at the very least other states are prohibited from taking its territory or interfering in its internal affairs and are also prohibited from aiding others in doing so. (Whether they have positive duties to support recognized states against the threat of dismemberment is more controversial.)

A less obvious advantage of being recognized as legitimate is that legitimacy is both necessary and sufficient for being a primary participant in the processes by which international law is made and adjudicated and by which measures designed to increase compliance with international legal norms are devised and implemented.[7] For all of these reasons, recognitional legitimacy is highly prized. In some cases, the very survival of an entity will depend upon whether it receives recognition.

[6] Franck, 'The Emerging Right to Democratic Governance'.
[7] It can be argued that it is no longer true that states are the only entities that have standing to participate in the development of international law. Nevertheless,

The need for a moral theory of recognitional legitimacy

The decision whether to recognize an entity as a legitimate state has important moral implications: Entities recognized as legitimate states are legally entitled to support for their territorial integrity and to noninterference in their internal affairs, and ought to be allowed to participate (in theory as equals) in the basic processes of international law; entities that are not recognized as legitimate states ordinarily lack these entitlements. But whether any particular entity *ought* to have these legal entitlements is a moral issue. In particular, if the international community recognizes an entity as a legitimate state it thereby augments that entity's power to control those within the jurisdiction it claims. And if that entity treats those within its control unjustly, the international community is guilty of complicity in its wrongdoing.

Therefore, for any state or group of states to determine its relationships with other entities in accordance with the existing criteria for recognition is to take a moral position; to oppose the existing criteria is also to take a moral position. To say that recognition is not a moral matter, as some hard-bitten self-styled Realists do, can only mean that one has decided that the moral consequences of giving or withholding recognition do not matter, or matter less than the "national interest."

Given that the criteria for recognition have changed in the past and may now be changing again, it is important not only to evaluate the current criteria but also to evaluate potential changes in them. The fundamental question is this: Under what conditions, if any, is an international practice of recognition morally justified? To answer this question a moral theory of recognition is needed.

II. *Justifying the Justice-Based Theory of Recognitional Legitimacy*

The main elements of the justice-based theory

The criteria for recognitional legitimacy of states I propose include (1) a minimal internal justice requirement, (2) a nonusurpation requirement, and (3) a minimal external justice requirement.

even if other actors, including in some cases nongovernmental organizations, do participate, states still play a dominant role in the development of international law.

Requirement (1) is drawn from the conception of political legitimacy developed in the preceding chapter. Requirement (3) extends that conception to cover that the states act in ways that affect others beyond their borders, relying on the intuitively plausible idea that how they act externally matters as to whether they should be regarded as legitimate states.

Requirement (2) requires explication. It was not included in the conception of political legitimacy developed in Chapter 5. However, as I shall argue, including nonusurpation in the requirements for recognition in a morally defensible international legal practice of recognition is plausible. The reason for including a nonusurpation requirement in a normativized practice of recognition for the international legal system, even though it is not part of the general conception of political legitimacy, will become clear once we understand more fully the function of recognition in a justice-based international legal system.

I observed earlier that the modern criteria for recognition appear to include something like a nonusurpation condition—the requirement that the new state should not have come about through a (major) breach of international law. My suggestion is that to be recognized as a legitimate state an entity should meet minimal requirements of justice both internally and in its external relations and also should not have come about through usurpation, where this means forcibly displacing a legitimate state or unjustly taking part of the territory of a legitimate state.

Later I will defend the nonusurpation condition against the objection that it is too demanding. For now I simply want to state its chief rationale: The nonusurpation condition enables us to avoid becoming an accomplice to injustice, as we would be if we granted the benefits of recognition to those who unjustly destroyed a legitimate state, and at the same time it rewards legitimate states by offering them some protection against overthrow.

The internal and external minimal justice requirements are less controversial. They are to be explicated in terms of basic human rights, which, as I noted in Chapter 3, include the right to physical security, the right to resources for subsistence, minimal rights of due process and equality before the law (including the right against arbitrary seizure, the right to be apprised of the charges against one and to respond to them, the right to counsel, and a weighty presumption against retroactive criminal offenses), the right against at least the more serious forms of discrimination on grounds of race, religion, ethnicity, or gender, the right to freedom of expression as at least including the right to criticize one's government, the right against servitude and slavery, the right to freedom of association, and the right against torture.

This two-part (internal and external) justice requirement is called minimal to indicate that legitimacy does not require perfect or full justice, but rather a threshold approximation of justice, along with a credible commitment to progress toward greater justice. Although the view I am offering is justice based, it does *not* conflate legitimacy with justice.

The case for minimalism

In Chapter 2 I noted that the basic human rights can be justified from the perspectives of any of several distinct moral theories or ethical traditions. Since I left open the possibility that a more extensive list of human rights might also be justifiable, the question naturally arises: Why should the requisite for recognitional legitimacy be only respect for the basic human rights, rather than the full demands of justice?

The chief reason to opt for the minimalist requirement is that a nonideal moral theory of international legal institutions, if it is to provide useful guidance for practice, should not be so utopian as to be self-defeating. A justice-based theory of recognitional legitimacy whose justice standards were so stringent as to imply that even the most admirable existing states are illegitimate would not likely be taken seriously in the world of action, even as an aspiration.

More important, if no political entities that now exist or are likely to exist in the foreseeable future would meet its conditions for legitimacy, a theory cannot serve any useful function as a guide in the practice of conferring the benefits of legitimate statehood. Nor could it inform a practice of recognition that would provide effective incentives for improving state behavior. By setting its requirements too high it would set a goal that states would not take seriously.

Below I shall argue that the practice of recognition I recommend would create significant incentives for reform on the part of states.

The point here is that the prospect of gaining the benefits of recognition can only act as an effective lever for reform if conditions for being rewarded with recognition are not so demanding as to appear unattainable or not worth the cost.

The minimalist requirement is even more reasonable if we view the practice of recognition, like other features of the international legal system, as capable of improvement over time. Once we see that the justification for the principles that comprise a moral theory of international law is significantly teleological—that they are justified in part because their implementation would bring about moral improvements in the system—it becomes clear that the conditions for legitimacy can and should become more stringent if and when the system becomes capable of more progress.

The prospect that the justice requirements for recognition may and indeed ought to become more demanding over time is consonant with one of the key conclusions reached in Chapter 4. There I argued that at present international legal institutions lack the capacity to be the arbiter and agent of distributive justice. This current institutional incapacity, combined with the likelihood that agreement on principles of distributive justice is the most undeveloped area of the emerging global culture of human rights, implies that for the present there are significant limitations on the role that rights of distributive justice can play in international law. But if international institutions develop the needed capacity to serve as an arbiter and agent of distributive justice and if more substantive standards of distributive justice crystallize as part of a widely shared conception of human rights, then it may become appropriate to revise the conditions for recognition to include the protection of rights of distributive justice that exceed the right to resources for subsistence. Other revisions, in the direction of more demanding standards, may also become possible and morally compelling.

The internal and external justice requirements

In Chapter 5 I argued that an entity has internal political legitimacy— is morally justified in attempting to achieve supremacy in the making, applying, and enforcing of laws—if and only if it protects the basic human rights of those upon whom it enforces the laws within its jurisdiction and does so by means that respect those same basic rights. Now I want to show that the international community, acting through the international legal system, should require internal political legitimacy as a necessary condition for recognition of states.

As I observed earlier, there are two main arguments for this conclusion, one nonconsequentialist (or so-called "rights-based"), the other teleological. The nonconsequentialist argument, which I have already previewed, takes as a premise the obligation not to be an accomplice in serious injustice. If international law recognized as legitimate states entities that were *not* internally politically legitimate (that did not respect the basic human rights of those within their borders), then it would thereby confer legitimacy on entities that are not morally justified in wielding political power. But recognizing an entity as a legitimate state means conferring on it the rights and liberties of states, including the right to noninterference in its domestic affairs and the liberty to defend its control over its territory (for example, against revolutionary or secessionist forces or peoples striving to regain territory it has unjustly annexed). And recognition also implies that other states should regard as illegitimate any efforts by other parties to interfere with the entity's domestic affairs or to take its territory.

In other words, recognition *supports* and *enhances* the ability of an entity that is awarded this status to wield political power, which includes coercion, within its territory. But supporting and enhancing the political power of an entity that is not morally justified in wielding that power amounts to being an accomplice in injustice, since the morally unjustifiable exercise of political power is itself an injustice.

The key point is that to recognize an entity as a legitimate state is to confer legal powers on it, not simply to acknowledge a fact, and that conferring these legal powers has significant moral implications. If we confer legal powers that support and enhance the unjust exercise of political power, we act wrongly. The same holds true for the requirement of minimal external justice. If the international community grants recognition to states that engage in serious violations of the basic rights of those beyond its borders, it thereby not only tacitly condones such action, but confers rights and liberties on the perpetrator that support and enhance its ability to continue in these injustices. And by granting a right to noninterference in its domestic affairs unlimited by the requirement that it is to respect its own citizens' rights, such a practice of recognition would enable the state to ignore or crush internal opposition to its rights-violating foreign policies.

So in order to avoid a situation in which members of the state system would be accomplices in injustice, that system should recognize as legitimate only entities that are internally politically legitimate and that also satisfy the minimal external justice condition. Call this the Obligation Not to Support Injustice Argument. This is a nonconsequentialist or "rights-based" argument. It focuses on the necessity of avoiding being an accomplice in injustice as a constraint on action, including action to promote worthy goals.

The second argument is teleological. It focuses on the instrumental value of the practice of recognition for furthering what should be the chief goal of the system of international legal institutions, namely, justice, relying on the fact that the advantages of recognition provide powerful incentives for just behavior on the part of those who wield political power.

An institutional practice of recognition provides incentives for just behavior when it specifies criteria for recognition that reward with recognition's advantages only those entities that treat their own populations justly and refrain from violating the rights of those beyond their borders. Where such a practice exists, entities that respect basic human rights will be supported by the international community in two important respects. First, they will be recognized as having a right to their own territory and to noninterference in their domestic affairs. Second, they will be recognized as having a right to participate in the making, adjudication, and enforcement of international legal rules, and to enter into beneficial agreements with other states, rather than being excluded from these processes or relegated to a secondary role in it as is now usually the case with nonstate entities.

Other things being equal, a practice of recognition that provides incentives for just behavior is morally preferable. If in addition justice should be a chief goal of the international legal system, as I argued in Chapter 2, then the case for including the two minimal justice requirements in the criteria for recognition is that much stronger.

In one respect, the inclusion of the minimal external justice condition in the criteria for recognitional legitimacy is not controversial. International law already includes a prohibition against aggressive war (though the exact import of this prohibition may be hazy in some cases, due to disagreement about what counts as aggression). It also limits sovereignty by the need to respect human rights, and states that those who wage aggressive war necessarily violate the human rights of those they attack. What is novel about my proposal is the idea of including an external justice condition that entails the prohibition of aggressive war in the criteria for recognition.

Tying recognition to the external justice requirement provides powerful incentives for compliance with one of the most morally progressive existing rules of international law, the prohibition on aggressive war. In a system that currently lacks enforcement mechanisms of the sort that states have, this is a significant consideration.[8]

Secondary incentives to make the justice-based criteria for recognition effective

At present the act of recognition is viewed as a discretionary "political decision" on the part of individual states, not a matter of legal obligation. Moreover, there is no international institutional mechanism for penalizing states that recognize entities that should not be recognized. As a result, the potential for progress that the practice of recognition holds is not realized.

The case of the recognition of Croatia illustrates this point. In 1991 the European Union appointed a body that came to be known as the Badinter Commission (for its Chairman), which issued a recommendation that new claimants to statehood emerging from the dissolution of Yugoslavia should be recognized as legitimate states only if they supplied credible guarantees of equal protection for minorities within their borders.[9] This condition on recognition is

---

[8] An interesting question—and one to which I would not at this time venture an answer—is whether there are circumstances in which a government could be regarded as illegitimate if it persisted in making credible threats of aggressive war. I am more confident that in certain circumstances it is morally permissible and ought to be permissible under international law to engage in preventive military action against a state whose behavior creates a dire risk of human rights violations in other countries. For an argument to show that the justice-based, cosmopolitan view I develop in this book is compatible with there being cases of justifiable preventive war to alleviate wrongfully imposed dire risks, see Allen Buchanan and Robert O. Keohane, 'The Preventive Use of Force: A Cosmopolitan Institutional Perspective', unpublished paper.

[9] Conference on Yugoslavian Arbitration Commission (The Badinter Commission), 'Opinions on Questions Arising from the Dissolution of Yugoslavia', *International Legal Materials* 31 (1992), 1488–530.

entailed by the internal justice requirement I have proposed. The rationale for this recommendation was to use the incentive of recognition to reduce the risk of human rights violations.

Unfortunately, no provisions were made to ensure that the members of the European community of states or anyone else would withhold recognition if the criterion of equal rights protection was not met. First Germany and then the other European countries recognized Croatia as an independent state with the full knowledge that Serbs in Croatia were being persecuted and that the new Croatian state was not only condoning but actively participating in violations of the basic human rights of the Serbian minority.

If a justice-based rule of state recognition is to provide an effective force for improving state behavior, it must be accompanied by institutional mechanisms that make recognition a matter of legal obligation, not discretionary political judgment, and that impose significant penalties on states that grant recognition when it is not warranted by that rule. Given that both of these features are currently lacking, merely securing agreement among states that there are to be justice-based criteria, rather than the might-makes-right principle of effectivity, would not by itself accomplish much.

My proposal, however, is for more enlightened criteria for recognition coupled with institutional mechanisms to give them teeth. At the very least—and perhaps this is all that could be achieved in the short run—states that recognize as legitimate states new entities that fail to meet the minimal justice requirements could be censured by appropriate international bodies such as the Human Rights Commission and the UN General Assembly for aiding and abetting the violation of human rights. In the longer term the goal would be to impose more serious penalties.

It might be objected, however, that there is a fundamental problem with my proposal to create a normativized practice of recognition that makes recognition of new entities created by secession conditional on whether these entities give credible assurances that they will respect the rights of minorities. This proposal assumes that the international community can be effective in guaranteeing the rights of minorities in new states created by secession, either by threatening not to grant or to revoke recognition when they are violated, or in extreme cases, by intervening on their behalf. But, as Donald Horowitz asks, if the international community can guarantee the rights of minorities in states created by secession, why can't they avoid the need for recognizing a right to secede by protecting the rights of minorities in existing states so that secession is not necessary?[10] The fact that the international community has not been successful in protecting minorities within existing states indicates that it will not be effective in protecting them within states created by secession; so isn't the proposal for a normativized practice of recognition that requires new states to respect the rights of their minorities utopian?

What Horowitz's objection overlooks is that the international community has more leverage over groups seeking recognition than they have over existing states. The point, recall, is that the decision to recognize or not is an important window of opportunity for improving the behavior of would-be states. Secessionist entities generally crave recognition; existing states already enjoy the benefits of recognition.

Furthermore, at least for the foreseeable future, the prospects for creating an international practice of conditional recognition for new entities claiming statehood are surely better than for creating a practice of revoking recognition of existing states that are already recognized, when they violate minority rights. Also, new states are weaker and it is consequently easier to impose conditions on them. Finally, the attempt to impose conditions on new entities is not threatening to existing states and hence is more likely to be supported by the international community.

Horowitz is right to this extent: The best way to avoid secession and its upheavals and violence is to strive for more effective institutions of transnational justice to help ensure that states do not persecute their minorities. I have emphasized this point frequently.

However, as Horowitz himself acknowledges, the international legal order often fails to protect the rights of minorities within existing states. Under these conditions, it is expecting too much of persecuted minorities to wait patiently until states heed Horowitz's advice to accommodate their minorities by electoral schemes and other institutional reforms that reduce ethnic conflict. Recognizing a limited, remedial right to secede facilitates self-help on the part of persecuted

[10] Donald Horowitz, 'A Right to Secede', in Stephen Macedo and Allen Buchanan (eds.), *Self-Determination and Secession, Nomos* XLV (New York University Press, New York, 2003).

minorities in a legal system that often fails to protect their rights. A normativized practice of recognition, if embedded in the right sort of institutional arrangements to give it teeth, would reduce the chances that they would use their liberation from oppression as an occasion to persecute others.

The nonusurpation condition

This condition expresses a minimalist conception of procedural justice in the creation of states, mandating only that if a new entity is to be awarded the status of statehood it must not come about through the violent or otherwise unlawful overthrow of a recognitionally legitimate state. Notice that the nonusurpation condition is not as demanding as may first appear. It does not require that the new entity be morally pristine, only that it has not committed one particular offense, namely, the overthrow of a legitimate state. Thus the nonusurpation condition does not entail the unrealistic requirement that a secessionist movement should reach the point of seeking recognition without any breaches of international law or morality whatsoever.

Without the nonusurpation condition it would be possible for a group to achieve all the benefits of legitimate statehood *after* having unjustly overthrown a legitimate state. Including the nonusurpation condition in the criteria for recognitional legitimacy would contribute to peace by encouraging recourse to constitutional or other rule-governed, consensual processes for creating new political entities out of old ones that are legitimate while at the same time encouraging just behavior on the part of existing states by providing protection from violent overthrow so long as they satisfy the justice-based criteria. Other things being equal, a practice of recognition that encourages just and peaceful processes for the creation of new states is preferable.

The nonusurpation condition represents a significant revision of existing international law regarding legitimacy. Like the other justice-based criteria I am proposing, it rejects exclusive reliance on the principle of effectivity, denying that the mere ability to control a territory confers legitimacy if control was achieved by clearly unjust means.

Like the internal and external justice requirements, the nonusurpation condition is minimalist; it does not specify a particular process by which legitimate states may be created, leaving open the possibility of a plurality of just processes. More important, the nonusurpation condition only applies to the creation of new states from the destruction of legitimate states. It has no application to the creation of new states out of entities that were not legitimate. Nor does it apply to existing states that are already recognized as legitimate under international law.

Is the nonusurpation condition too demanding?

Earlier in this chapter and in Chapter 1 as well I observed that a moral theory of international law should steer a course between a pessimistic capitulation to the status quo and an unrealistic utopianism. Some might object that the criteria for recognition I am proposing, especially the nonusurpation requirement, are so demanding that they have little chance of being incorporated in international law. The worry is that because some of the states that exert the most influence on the shape of international law would not pass my test for recognition, they are hardly likely to help establish it as a matter of international law.

This worry is based on a misconception of my proposal. The nonusurpation condition is intended only to apply to the assessment of new claimants to legitimate statehood, not to existing states that are already recognized as legitimate.

A double standard of legitimacy?

Nevertheless, it might be objected that it is inconsistent to propose that new entities seeking recognition must satisfy the nonusurpation requirement while at the same time refusing to apply this condition to existing states, many of which came to be through nonusurpation. My first reply would be that in most such cases, the existing state may have come about through violence and injustice, but did not displace a legitimate state, since until very recently there have been few states that could qualify as legitimate.

A better reply to the inconsistency objection is to emphasize something I have noted repeatedly in this volume: The international legal system must be conceived diachronically, as a changing system that is capable of progress. Once the system is seen in this light, it cannot be assumed that criteria for recognizing new entities as legitimate states should be applied, without qualification, to the behavior of existing states throughout their histories. Especially if we view the practice of recognition as a lever for moral progress, we must take seriously the idea that different rules may apply to present as opposed to past behavior.

The commitment to working for justice within the international legal system assumes that there must be some system to work within, that the current state system is capable of meaningful reform, and that the moral costs of scrapping it entirely to start anew would be prohibitive. But if this is so, then there may be reason to strive for new and more stringent standards for legitimacy now without applying them retroactively if doing so would mean radically destabilizing the system or would undercut the goal of getting normative standards for recognition adopted.

The idea that a legal system should as Hart says be a "choice system"—and hence should avoid rules that make illegal acts that were legal at the time they were performed also lends some weight to the proposal to recognize a kind of moral statute of limitations on past state behavior that does not satisfy the justice-based criteria. Of course the difficulty lies in determining in a nonarbitrary way how recent behavior must be to count against a recognized state's continuing to be recognized.

The problem is greatly complicated by the question of identity: For purposes of international law is the entity called 'the United States' in 1850 the same as the one that bears that name today? If the basic character of the constitution of a state is essential to its identity, then the answer may be negative: The constitution of the entity called the United States in 1850 was radically different—at least insofar as it legally sanctioned slavery—from the constitution of the entity now called the United States. Without taking a stand on these complex issues, I would suggest that a proposal for a justice-based practice of recognition is more plausible than one that would be applied retrospectively, and that the proposal advanced here should not be dismissed as either utopian (because existing states that violate its criteria will not support it) or as inconsistent (if it recognizes as legitimate some entities that violated its conditions at some time in the past).

It is important to note, however, that the only options are not applying the justice-based criteria retroactively at the cost of withdrawing recognition from virtually all existing states, or ignoring all usurpations that occurred prior to the implementation of the justice-based criteria. It may be appropriate to place a statute of limitations on the nonusurpation condition while requiring existing states to redress or compensate for egregious and relatively recent violations of human rights as a condition of continuing to be recognized as legitimate. For the immediate future, efforts to reform the practice of recognition should focus mainly on implementing the justice-based criteria for *new* entities that seek recognition as states (as in the many cases of secession we now see) and withdrawing recognition from those states that at *present* persist in massive violations of basic human rights.

Minimal democracy as a condition for recognition

I remarked earlier that some international legal scholars detect a movement toward requiring democracy among the criteria for recognition. Without speculating as to whether the law is in fact moving in this direction, I now want to urge that it should do so—that the minimal internal justice requirement should be understood as including a minimal democracy condition.

As the discussion in Chapter 2 of the issue of whether democracy is a human right indicates, there are at least two distinct arguments for doing so. First, it can be argued that democracy is itself an important element of justice because justice requires equal regard for persons and this in turn requires that they can participate as equals in determining the most basic social rules and the allocation of the unequal political power that governance inevitably involves. According to this argument, the right to democratic governance should be included among the basic human rights and therefore included in the internal justice requirement. Second, it can be argued that even if democratic governance is not itself a human right or in some other way a direct requirement of justice, it is of such great instrumental value for justice, including respect for human rights, that it ought to be included in the criteria for recognitional legitimacy. This second argument is familiar from the human rights literature. The idea is that democratic institutions provide the most reliable protection for human rights.

The same considerations that weigh in favor of employing a notion of basic human rights rather than a comprehensive set of human rights also support the assumption that the democracy condition should be understood in a minimal fashion. By 'minimal democracy' I mean here what I described in Chapter 3 as the content of the basic human right to democratic governance: (1) there are representative, majoritarian institutions for making the most general and consequential laws (within appropriate constitutional constraints designed to protect basic human rights), such that no competent adult is excluded from participation; (2) the highest government officials are accountable by being subject to being removed from office through the workings of these representative institutions (with possible exceptions for purposes of maintaining the independence of the judiciary) under conditions of political competition; and (3) there is a modicum of institutionally secured freedom of speech and association required for reasonably free and informed deliberation about political decisions.

This minimalist conception allows for a wide range of different types of democracy, suited to different social, economic, and cultural conditions. An additional reason in favor of this minimal condition is that mechanisms for monitoring each of the three elements that comprise it are not beyond the current institutional capacities of the international legal system.[11]

If we include a minimal democracy condition, a second teleological argument for the internal justice requirement for recognition becomes available. Again, assuming that peace is a proper goal of the international legal system, in part because it is required for the protection of basic human rights, we can rely on the democratic peace hypothesis—the empirical generalization that developed democratic states tend not to go to war with one another. A practice of recognition that rewards democratic states and penalizes nondemocratic ones will, other things being equal, supply incentives for

---

[11] For evidence of increasingly sophisticated mechanisms for monitoring elections, see Geoffrey Gunn, *East Timor and the United Nations: The Case for Intervention* (Red Sea Press, Lawrenceville, NJ, 1997), 88–102; Yves Beigbeder, *International Monitoring of Plebiscites, Referenda and National Elections: Self-Determination and Transition to Democracy* (M. Nijhoff, Dordrecht, 1994); and Mark Rothert, 'U.N. Intervention in East Timor', *Columbia Journal of Transnational Law* 39 (2000), 257–82.

democracy and, if the democratic peace hypothesis is correct, thereby promote the goal of peace by increasing the proportion of democratic states in the system.

The analysis presented in Chapter 5 provides one final argument in favor of the minimal democracy requirement as a condition for recognition. There I argued that there is a sense in which a political entity cannot be fully legitimate unless those who wield political power within it are authorized to do so by democratic processes. Where democratic authorization is feasible, equal regard for persons requires it. By requiring that states be minimally democratic if they are to enjoy the full benefits of legitimacy, international legal criteria for recognition would help ensure that the constitutions of states, by virtue of being democratic, acknowledge the fundamental equality of persons.

Partial recognition: unbundling the attributes of sovereignty

I have argued that before new entities emerging through secession should be recognized as legitimate states they should be required to give credible assurances that they will respect the basic human rights of all within their borders. However, in some cases, the new entity may not yet be capable of providing such assurances, because the process of building institutions to secure equal protection for all will have only begun. Yet if the secessionist group has suffered severe violations of human rights at the hands of the state from which it is seceding, there can be no question of requiring it to remain subject to the sovereignty of that state until such time as it develops the institutions needed to supply a credible assurance that the rights of all will be respected.

This description seems to fit the situation of Kosovo. On the one hand, given the massive violations of their rights that have occurred, it would be unreasonable to expect the Kosovar Albanians to remain subject to the authority of Yugoslavia until they can develop institutions capable of providing equal protection for all, including the Serbian minority. (Moreover, there is little reason to believe they would be allowed to develop them if they remained subject to Yugoslavian sovereignty.) But on the other hand, an unqualified recognition of Kosovo's independence would be irresponsible, given the potential for further persecutions of Serbs (and Roma) by the Albanian majority.

Under these circumstances, Robert Keohane's suggestion to "unbundle" the attributes of sovereignty should be incorporated into the practice of conditional recognition I have outlined above.[12] In other words, sovereignty and hence recognition should not always be regarded as an all or nothing affair. Kosovo, and other secessionist entities that are similarly situated, should be accorded a transitional status that includes some but not all of the attributes of sovereignty, pending sufficient progress in building the institutions of justice that warrant full recognition. Sovereignty should be limited to the extent necessary to allow international forces to supply an interim guarantee of equal protection for minorities and to allow them to facilitate the building of institutions of justice that will eventually warrant recognition of the full range of attributes of sovereignty.

III. *Legitimacy of States Versus Legitimacy of Governments*

The conceptual priority of recognitional legitimacy of states

Often it is unclear whether ascriptions of legitimacy or illegitimacy are meant to apply to states or to governments. When the issue is whether to recognize a new entity that claims to be entitled to be recognized as a legitimate state, as in the case of secession, there is no ambiguity. But in the case of existing states, an allegation of illegitimacy might apply to either the state itself, the government of the state, or both.

So far I have concentrated on providing the basic outlines of a theory of recognitional legitimacy for states. Recall that by a state I mean an enduring structure of basic institutions for wielding political power, where this structure includes roles to be filled by members of the government. The government can be thought of as the human agency by which the institutional resources of the state are employed. In democratic states what Rawls calls the constitutional essentials, including separate legislative, executive, and judicial institutions, are the core of the enduring institutional structure that is the state. States ordinarily persist through changes of governments.

[12] Robert Keohane, 'Political Authority after Intervention: Gradations in Sovereignty', in Jeffrey Holzgrefe and Robert Keohane (eds.), *Humanitarian Intervention: Ethical, Legal, and Political Dilemmas* (Cambridge University Press, Cambridge, 2003).

From the standpoint of a moral theory of international law, recognitional legitimacy as applied to states is conceptually primary. The international legal system recognizes legitimate states, not governments, as having certain powers, liberties, immunities, and rights. Governments are recognized derivatively, only so far as they are regarded as the agents of legitimate states, not as entities possessing these juridical characteristics in their own right.

There is a sense in which recognitional legitimacy as applied to states is also morally primary. If a state is illegitimate because it fails to meet the minimal justice requirements, this means that there are grave flaws in some of the most basic institutions of society, and remedying them may require much more extensive changes than merely replacing an unjust government. For example, the flaws of apartheid South Africa or the pre-Civil War United States ran deeper than the defects of the respective governments. Remedying them required not just a change of government, but profound constitutional changes that transformed the state itself.

Because it is both conceptually and morally primary, I have begun the task of developing a moral theory of recognition with criteria for the recognition of states. A comprehensive theory must, however, say a great deal about the legitimacy of governments. Both because governments come and go more frequently than states, and because a concern for stability (and for protecting their own kind) leads states to be very reluctant to withdraw recognition from existing states, the issue of recognition arises much more often for governments.

Although I cannot at this point offer a comprehensive theory of recognitional legitimacy for governments, I hope at least to sketch its main contours. Building on the analysis of criteria for recognition of states, this much can be said. Like states, governments should not be recognized as legitimate if they usurp power from a legitimate predecessor or fail to meet the minimal requirements of justice in their external or internal relations.

In spite of the fact that the conditions for legitimacy of states and governments are essentially the same, it does not follow that if a state is legitimate its government is legitimate. The constitutional essentials that determine a state's identity might be exemplary from the standpoint of internal and external justice, and that state might have been created through a process that involved no unjust displacement of a legitimate state, yet the government, in defiance of the constitution, might violate human rights either internally or externally, or both.

On the other hand, if the state itself is illegitimate, then its government is thereby illegitimate. Because governments are to be understood merely as agents of states, the illegitimacy of a state infects its government. Thus, for example, if the Republic of South Africa under apartheid was an illegitimate state because its constitutional essentials institutionalized racism thereby violating the requirement of internal justice, then the South African government, whose status in international law should be strictly derivative on that of the state whose agent it is, was also illegitimate.

The distinction between the legitimacy of governments and that of states helps answer a potential objection to my proposal for a justice-based practice of recognition. The objection is that by withholding recognition, the international community disempowers the citizens of unjust states, depriving them of the only status that really counts in the international system. My response is that we need to distinguish clearly between recognition of states and recognition of governments. On my account, if a state is minimally just, then it is entitled to recognition, and this means that in recognizing a state as legitimate the international system affirms the status of the people whose state it is, even if the government is regarded as illegitimate. Since an illegitimate government is not entitled to be regarded as the agent of the people of a state, declaring that government illegitimate is no slur on the citizenry or their state. Indeed, international legal acknowledgment that the government is illegitimate can empower the international community to help the citizens of the state oust the government or at least pressure it to reform.

Just as important, to refuse to recognize a government as legitimate does not have either of the two implications the objection seems to assume. It does not follow that members of the international community should have no dealings with that government and it does not follow that those whose government is regarded as illegitimate would lack all representation in the international system. Each of these points warrants elaboration.

As I argued in Chapter 1, a commitment to seeking greater justice through the international legal system does not require self-defeating moral absolutism. Here Rawls's distinction between recognizing a government as legitimate and dealing with it through a mere modus vivendi is germane. In cases where refusing to deal with an illegitimate government would itself create an imminent threat to international peace—and hence to justice so far as war inevitably brings massive rights violations—a modus vivendi may be necessary.

Nevertheless, the principled distinction between legitimate and illegitimate governments remains, and it has practical implications. There are forms of censorship and condemnation that are permissible when applied to illegitimate governments that are not permissible when applied to legitimate ones. A modus vivendi with a powerful and potentially disruptive illegitimate government should constantly reassess the need to compromise for the sake of peace and be ready to institute more serious penalties or even coercive action as soon as a reasonable regard for peace allows.

Consider next the issue of representation. Is it true that if a government is not recognized as being legitimate, the people subject to it will lack a voice in the international legal system? The answer is plainly "no." The more seriously the international legal system takes human rights as a limitation on internal sovereignty, the less serious is the objection that by refusing to recognize unjust governments we thereby deprive citizens of their representation in the system. In a world without international support for human rights, individuals whose governments are not recognized are voiceless. But as the global culture of human rights grows, and as complex intergovernmental and nongovernmental networks for monitoring and securing compliance with human rights norms become more powerful, those who live under unjust governments no longer depend solely upon their own governments for representation. Moreover, the minimal internal justice criteria for recognitional legitimacy of governments I have proposed, including especially the minimal democracy condition, are designed to help ensure that governments actually do serve to represent their peoples.

Recognition as a rule-governed practice

In response to an article in which I initially presented the justice-based theory of recognitional legitimacy, Chris Naticchia asserts that "Given the extraordinarily high stakes involved in securing long-term peace and justice, the international community should confer recognition on the basis of judgments about the consequences for peace and justice and not impose any additional requirements, such as that entities must already be minimally just."[13] However, Naticchia's inference is invalid: From the fact that the stakes are high in an effort to promote some goal, it does *not* follow that the best way to promote it is to proceed in a case-by-case fashion, attempting to do what will best promote the goal. Nor does it follow, as Naticchia seems to assume, that the only thing relevant to a decision about how to promote a goal is whether what one does will best promote it. Especially in the design of institutions, there are many cases in which the most effective way to promote a goal is *not* to proceed in a case-by-case fashion, doing whatever can be expected as best to promote the goal, but rather to follow some substantive rule which, if generally adhered to, will do a better job of promoting the goal.

Furthermore, simply to assume that all that matters in deciding how to pursue it is whether what one does will effectively achieve the goal is to overlook the possibility that there may be moral constraints on the means one may employ to achieve it. In particular, there are some things one should not do even to promote justice. The acknowledgment that there are constraints on the means we may employ even for the worthiest ends, while entirely absent in Naticchia's discussion, is reflected in two features of the justice-based account of recognitional legitimacy. First, the internal justice requirement includes the condition not only that the wielder of political power is to protect basic human rights, but also that it must do so by actions and policies that do not themselves violate those rights. Second, the requirement that in order to be recognized as legitimate an entity must at least satisfy the (internal and external) minimal justice requirements and not be a usurper expresses the obligation to avoid being an accomplice in serious injustices and thereby places a limit on the instrumental use of the act of conferring recognition. Even if we had reason to believe that conferring recognition on a seriously unjust state would have good consequences, there are limits on the compromises we should make to

---

[13] Naticchia, 'Recognition and Legitimacy: A Reply to Buchanan'. For a response to other critical points advanced by Naticchia, see Allen Buchanan, 'Rule-Governed Institutions Versus Act-Consequentialism: A Rejoinder to Naticchia', *Philosophy and Public Affairs* 28 (1999), 258–70.

achieve good consequences, and the minimal justice requirement captures the idea that there are such limits, while not taking the absolutist, radically nonconsequentialist position that full justice is required for recognition.

I will not rehearse in detail the well-known arguments to show that in many circumstances the sort of case-by-case approach Naticchia recommends is likely to be self-defeating or at least less likely to promote the goals it pursues than a procedure that requires agents to act on substantive rules. Instead, I will focus on the practice of recognition, where I believe the liabilities of a case-by-case approach are especially pronounced.

What Naticchia fails to consider is that the required judgments would be extremely complex, long-term predictions about what will be conducive to peace and justice, but under conditions in which much of the data needed for the predictions is either unavailable or contested. Accordingly, there is ample opportunity for disagreement among members of the international community as to what the facts are, what their implications are for the predictions in question, and hence for whether or not to confer recognition in a particular case. Naticchia proposes his case-by-case procedure as the way in which "the community of states" should decide issues of recognition, but without acknowledging how serious the problem of disagreement is likely to be.

Under the actual conditions in which the non-rule-governed, case-by-case view would be implemented there is a serious risk, not only of failure to reach agreement, but also of fallibility, bias, and strategic behavior under the guise of sincere disagreement. Here, as in many other cases where what is at issue is the design of institutional practices, there is much to be said for reducing the complexity of the decision and hence the risks of fallibility, bias, and strategic behavior, by following substantive rules that in the long run are likely to be a more reliable path toward the desired goals of the practice. Especially in a world like ours, in which the legitimacy of the international system is constantly and quite reasonably challenged on the grounds that more powerful states manipulate the system to their advantage and grant recognition selectively and arbitrarily, it is important to constrain the process of making judgments about recognition by substantive rules. Under these conditions, agreement on whether to recognize an entity or not, and more important, agreement that is relatively unbiased, is more likely if the judgment is constrained by a substantive rule requiring minimal justice than if it is to be made simply on the basis of what is said to be conducive to peace and justice "in the long run."

When the minimal justice rule is employed, the task of reaching agreement on questions of recognition is greatly simplified. The international community has already made considerable progress in developing concrete standards and mechanisms for monitoring compliance with the most fundamental human rights. (Recall that one argument for the *minimal* justice requirement is that compliance with these basic rights may be more easily monitored. Thus for example it may be easier to reach consensus in the international community on whether a state is massively violating the right against torture or religious persecution than to determine whether it is respecting a rather demanding liberal-style right of freedom of expression or a very demanding, highly specific standard for democracy.)

It is not only regarding recognitional legitimacy that a rule-governed approach to the moral theory of international law is more attractive than a case-by-case approach. Virtually all theories of humanitarian intervention rely on substantive rules of intervention, rather than advocating a case-by-case judgment as to whether intervention would produce the best consequences in the long run. The dispute is mainly about *which* substantive rules are appropriate. (For example, should any serious violation of human rights trigger intervention, or should only the most serious wrongs, such as genocide?) Here, too, the assumption is that especially when what is sought is a morally defensible practice for a diverse community of states, some of which are much stronger than the others, substantive rules can reduce the risks of fallibility, bias, strategic behavior, and self-serving selectivity. An act-consequentialist (case-by-case) theory of recognitional legitimacy is no more plausible than an act-consequentialist theory of humanitarian intervention, and for much the same reasons.

We now have the main outlines of a moral theory of recognitional legitimacy. Its implications and attractions will be made clearer in Part Three, in the discussion of proposals for a principled international legal response to self-determination crises. The strategy there is to build an account of self-determination on the theory of recognitional legitimacy, arguing that legitimacy ought to be regarded as a shield against efforts to dismember states in the name of the right of self-determination. In particular, I will argue that the justice-based account of legitimacy supplies a needed premise for a remedial right only theory of the unilateral right to secede: Legitimate states as such have a strong claim to their territories, because territorial integrity is one of the attributes of legitimate statehood; so unilateral secession should only be permitted in cases where a persisting pattern of fundamental injustices robs the state of legitimacy. The same serious injustices that give credibility to secessionist demands also delegitimize the state, voiding its right to territorial integrity and thereby clearing the way for lawful unilateral secession.

In the next chapter, which completes Part Two, I explore the remarkably neglected question: Under what conditions is the international legal system itself legitimate? Utilizing the conception of political power introduced in Chapter 5, this question can be reframed with greater specificity as follows: What would the system have to be like for it to be true that efforts to exercise supremacy in the making, application, and enforcement of both international and transnational justice is morally justified? (Recall that transnational justice consists of the principles of justice that all states ought to be required to satisfy in their internal relations, while international justice consists of principles of justice that apply to relations among states or between states (or their citizens) and individuals or groups beyond their borders.)

CHAPTER 7

───

The Legitimacy of the
International Legal System

In this chapter, which completes the second part of the book, I rely on the conception of political legitimacy delineated in Chapter 5 to advance a justice-based, rather than a consent-based, account of system legitimacy—a set of criteria that the international legal system would have to meet in order to be legitimate. Building on groundwork already laid in Chapter 1 and Chapter 5, I show why, contrary to the dominant view among international lawyers, the consent of states cannot confer legitimacy on the international legal system. In addition, I argue that it is a mistake to assume that political equality among states is a necessary condition for system legitimacy.

Finally, I argue that the international legal system, like any system for the exercise of political power, ought to be democratic; but I also show that the idea of democratizing the international legal system is an ambiguous one and should not be equated with increasing state majoritarianism in the workings of the system. The charge that the international legal system has a "democratic deficit" is valid, but it is a mistake to assume that the remedy is to make the system conform more closely to the ideal of democracy as state majoritarianism. The most serious "democratic deficit" is not that states are unequal, but that a technocratic elite, lacking in democratic accountability to individuals and nonstate groups, is playing an increasingly powerful role in a system of regional and global governance. The fiction that international law is or ought to be a system of equal sovereign states, founded on state consent, is a distraction from the daunting task of developing and implementing a genuinely more democratic form of global governance in which those who make, apply, and enforce international law are account-able to individuals and nonstate groups, not only, or even primarily, to states.

In this book I have already given a number of reasons to reject the traditional conception of international law as a set of rules for the interaction of equal sovereign states, founded on their consent. The fact that this conception can tell us nothing about how to remedy the real "democratic deficit" that now exists in global governance is one more reason to reject it and to take seriously instead a conception of international law grounded in the ideal of protecting the basic human rights of all persons.

I. *The Question of System Legitimacy*

Distinguishing system legitimacy from other issues

In Chapter 5 I characterized the exercise of political power as the (credible) attempt to achieve supremacy in the making, application, and enforcement of laws, arguing that the two most basic questions a moral theory of political power must answer are (1) under what con-ditions are persons justified in wielding political power, and (2) under what conditions do those upon whom the laws are enforced have obligations or at least sufficient reasons to comply with the laws? The implication of this line of argument was that the political philosopher should concentrate on an account of political legitimacy rather than of political authority (understood as political legitimacy plus the right to be obeyed) because the latter is not necessary for answering these two most basic questions about the morality of political power.

The objective of the present chapter is to explore the notion of legitimacy for the international legal system as a whole, in order to answer two questions: (1) Under what conditions is it justifiable for agents to exercise political power through international legal institu-tions? and (2) what reasons do private individuals and repre-sentatives of states or other organizations have to comply with international law and support the international legal system? Question (1) focuses on the morality of the *agents* of international law—those who create, apply, and enforce it—asking for an account of the conditions under which they are justified in engaging in those activities. Question (2) focuses on the *subjects* of international law, those upon whom the agents of international law attempt to impose it, asking what sorts of considerations, if any, provide sufficient reasons for their complying with international law or for their being obligated to comply.

To answer question (1) we need to know the characteristics of an international legal system that would make it a framework within which agents may justifiably wield political power. I will argue that for the most part the same basic criteria of legitimacy that are appropriate for individual states are also appropriate for the international legal system, even though the latter is far from being a global state. Following the strategy articulated in Chapter 2, I will answer question (2) by asking: Does a sincere commitment to fulfilling the Natural Duty of Justice—the limited obligation to help ensure that all persons have access to institutions that protect their basic human rights—provide a good reason for complying with international legal rules and supporting the international legal system? In the final chapter of this book I will argue that even though the Natural Duty of Justice does provide a weighty reason for supporting the enterprise of international law, it does not rule out, but in fact in some cases may require, violating some existing international legal rules and not supporting certain existing international legal institutions.

The Natural Duty of Justice and system legitimacy

Granted, as I argued in Chapter 2, that all persons have a limited moral obligation to contribute to ensuring that everyone has access to institutions that protect their basic human rights, and granted that international legal institutions have a role to play in ensuring that all persons' basic rights are protected, taking the Natural Duty of Justice seriously requires an account of system legitimacy for international law.

Although we are obligated to try to bring about conditions in which all can obtain justice, there are moral constraints on the means by which we do this, including the institutional structures and processes by which justice is pursued. We need to know the conditions an international legal system must satisfy if it is to be legitimate—the features that make it an appropriate institutional framework within which to wield political power—in order to determine what moral stance we should take vis-à-vis the existing system. If we determine that it lacks legitimacy, we need to know how to improve it in this regard.

In Chapter 6 I distinguished between the legitimacy of states and of governments, states being enduring institutional structures for the wielding of political power, governments being the collections of individuals who fill key roles in that structure. We can also distinguish between the legitimacy of the international legal system, as an institutional structure, and the legitimacy of its 'government.' (Of course in the international case the 'government' is much more decentralized and less far-reaching in its control. The term 'governance' might be more appropriate since the international system includes no single governmental unit, no super-state.) Just as state legitimacy is conceptually prior to government legitimacy, so the legitimacy of the international legal system is conceptually prior to the legitimacy of international government. In both cases, the moral justification for agents acting in their institutional roles will depend in part upon the moral justification for the institutions within which they operate.

The justice-based account of political legitimacy gives a straightforward answer to (1), the agent-justification question: What morally justifies efforts to wield political power through the institutions of international law is what justifies the exercise of political power generally; not consent, but rather a credible commitment to achieving justice, understood primarily as the protection of basic human rights, and doing so in ways that do not violate those same rights. And when institutional resources for democratic governance are available, legitimacy requires democracy.

The beginning of an answer to question (2) has already been provided in Chapter 2, where I developed an understanding of the Natural Duty of Justice that provides a foundation for a commitment to developing and supporting legal institutions as one aspect of the task of providing all persons protection for their human rights. However, so far I have assumed, rather than argued, that the Natural Duty of Justice supplies good reasons for supporting and improving an *international* legal order. It is now time to ask a very basic question that is rarely if ever addressed by international legal scholars or political philosophers: Why should we have an *international* legal system, over and above a mere collection of domestic legal systems (perhaps supplemented by informal rules and practices that do not qualify as law)?

In terms of the Natural Duty of Justice, the question can be framed as follows: Why are *international* legal institutions necessary for ensuring that all persons' rights are protected? Note that this is not the same as the question: Why should we have legal institutions for the protection of human rights? The latter question, as we saw in Chapter 2, is answered rather easily in the affirmative: Fundamental rights are generally best protected within a regime of the rule of law, probably in any sizeable society, but at least in large-scale societies where individuals have diverse interests and goals. But it is one thing to recognize that legal institutions are needed to ensure that all persons' rights are protected, another to assume that an international legal system is needed.

II. *The Case for Having an International Legal System*

The Lockean case for a legal system

To approach this fundamental question, it is useful to recall in broad outlines the case for the state advanced by John Locke.[1] In contrast to Hobbes, Locke emphasizes not so much the need for an overwhelming coercive agent to enforce rules of peaceful interaction, but rather the need for a recognized authority to formulate and apply rules, in order to escape the problems that inevitably arise when individuals or subgroups of the population take it on themselves to do so independently. In other words, Locke can be understood as arguing for the need for a legal system, not for a state in Hobbes's spare sense. (Or if you prefer, Locke is arguing for the state as the rule of law.) His chief point is that where multiple agents independently formulate, interpret, and apply rules to their interactions, with no authority to which to appeal when conflicts arise, partiality and inconsistency of application are inevitable.

Although Locke's chief concern seems to be the problems of partiality and inconsistency that plague private application and

---

[1] John Locke, *The Second Treatise on Civil Government* (Prometheus Books, Buffalo, NY, 1986).

enforcement of rules, his case for the state as the rule of law can be strengthened by appealing to the need for coordination as well. In some cases coordination rules can arise spontaneously without being issued from an authoritative source, but the conditions under which this reliably occurs are rather narrow and unlikely to obtain in large-scale, "anonymous" societies, as opposed to small-scale, "face-to-face" groups.[2]

Without significant modification, Locke's argument for having a domestic legal system can be used to make the case for having an international legal system. But the international version of the argument does *not* in any obvious way cover the whole domain of international law. It only applies straightforwardly to international as opposed to transnational justice.

To avoid problems of partiality, inconsistency, and lack of coordination that would arise if there were only a plurality of domestic governments each with its own legal system, there is a need for an international legal system to govern *interactions among states and interactions between states or their citizens and individuals or entities in other states*. In the terminology introduced in Chapter 1, there is a cogent Lockean argument for a legal system that addresses issues of *international* (as distinct from transnational) justice.

However, the Lockean argument does not extend, in any obvious way, to the domain of *transnational justice* for this simple reason: States already have legal systems designed to avoid the problems that would arise from private interpretation and enforcement within their own borders. (Recall that international justice, as defined in Chapter 1, concerns interactions among states or among individuals or groups from different states, whereas principles of transnational justice are those minimal standards, preeminently basic human rights norms, that the international community may justifiably require every state to meet in its internal affairs.)

Absent common legal institutions, interactions among states and between individuals or groups in different states may be as prone to inconsistency, partiality, and lack of coordination as interactions among individuals in Locke's state of nature. Hence the need for an

---

[2] Robert Ellickson, *Order without Law: How Neighbors Settle Disputes* (Harvard University Press, Cambridge, MA, 1991); and David Lewis, *Convention: A Philosophical Study* (Harvard University Press, Cambridge, MA, 1969).

international legal order with principles of international justice. But where states exist, the problems of private interpretation, application, and enforcement are already addressed by the domestic legal systems so far as their internal affairs are concerned. The question, then, is this: Even if the Natural Duty of Justice requires the construction of a global legal system to deal with issues of international justice, why should that system also include norms and procedures for transnational justice? To put the same point differently: Even if, for Lockean reasons, it would be a bad idea to allow each individual state to formulate, interpret, and apply its own conception of proper rules of international justice, what reason is there to suppose that a global legal system would do a better job of articulating, applying, and enforcing principles of justice for interactions that occur exclusively within the borders of states than the domestic legal systems of those states?

Kristen Hessler has explicitly argued for what most international legal scholars implicitly assume: that with respect to the formulation, application, and enforcement of human rights norms, international legal institutions are preferable to domestic institutions, because states are likely to be biased when it comes to evaluating their treatment of their own populations.[3] After all, it is states that are the major violators of human rights, most commonly the human rights of their own populations. In my terminology, Hessler argues that there is a need for transnational justice, for a legal system beyond those of individual states, to ensure that states do justice within their own borders.

The difficulty with this simple application of the Lockean argument to the domain of relations within states is that there are some states whose legal systems provide better protections for human rights than the sum total of international human rights legal regimes. The same can be said for at least one regional human rights regime, the highly sophisticated system of protections found in the European Union. The fact that some states cannot be trusted to respect the human rights of their populations does not entail that *all* states should be subject to transnational human rights law. So we need a more complete explanation of why we need a regime of transnational justice.

---

[3] Hessler, 'A Theory of Interpretation for Human Rights'.

In fact, two questions must be squarely addressed. (1) What reason is there to believe that the best way to fulfill the Natural Duty of Justice is to have an arrangement in which global legal institutions, as opposed to individual states (or regional associations of states), have ultimate authority regarding the formulation, application, and enforcement of human rights norms within states? (Why should global law include not only international justice, but transnational justice as well?) (2) Even if it is a good thing that there be a global legal order that includes transnational justice, what reason do states that do an excellent job of protecting human rights within their borders have to recognize the supremacy of transnational legal norms within their own borders?

There are two answers to question (1). First, and most obviously, there are many states that do not do an adequate job of protecting human rights within their borders, and a regime of transnational justice can help improve their performance. Second, a global legal structure that includes international justice needs principles of transnational justice. The second point, being far from obvious, warrants elaboration.

Recall that the Lockean argument against private interpretation and enforcement of laws applies quite forcefully to the domain of *inter*national justice. States cannot be relied upon to behave impartially, consistently, and in a coordinated manner with regard to their interactions with one another, unless they are subject to a global legal framework within which political power can be exercised over them. So there is a strong case for a global legal regime that at least covers international justice. But a regime of international justice, which governs relations among states, must include principles for identifying which entities are legitimate states and this requires principles of transnational justice.

And as I argued in Chapter 6, in order to be recognized as legitimate states, entities should meet minimal standards of democracy and protection of basic human rights, both in their internal affairs and in their actions beyond their borders. But if this is so, then a morally defensible regime of international justice, in its normativized rules for recognitional legitimacy of states, will already include a domain of transnational justice, namely, the requirement that states must be minimally democratic and exhibit a credible commitment to the protection of basic human rights within their borders.

In this sense, international justice presupposes transnational justice. So a global legal order that includes only international justice is not an option.

If international justice presupposes transnational justice in this way, then we have an answer to the question: Why should states with well-developed legal systems *support* a regime of transnational justice? Even states with exemplary legal systems for the domestic protection of human rights have a moral obligation, grounded in the Natural Duty of Justice, to support a global legal system that includes principles of transnational justice as far as these are required for a normativized, justice-based practice of state recognition, even if that system contributes nothing to the protection of human rights within their own borders. More generally, even the most just states ought to support a regime of transnational justice that encourages less just states to improve and that provides a last-resort protection for individuals and groups when their own states fail to protect their basic rights.

We can now see why even states that enjoy the best human rights records ought to support a global legal order that includes principles of transnational justice. But we still do not have an answer to the question of why such exemplary states ought not only to endorse a system of transnational justice for other, less admirable states, but also recognize its supremacy over their own domestic law. To put the point bluntly: Why should Germany, or Norway, or France, or the United Kingdom, or the Netherlands, or any country that has a highly developed legal system with excellent protections for human rights, recognize the authority of the international legal system regarding matters of transnational justice as applied to itself, and what could justify the efforts of international legal agencies to assert the supremacy of international law in domestic matters within such states?

There are two reasons why states with excellent domestic protections for human rights ought not only to support a regime of transnational justice for others, but recognize its supremacy within their own borders as well. First, under certain circumstances, even states that generally do an excellent job of respecting human rights have lapses, and acknowledging the supremacy of transnational law can reduce the risk that this will occur or provide a remedy if it does. For example, the United Kingdom, a country that generally respects human rights, engaged in serious human rights violations during its armed conflict with the IRA, including extrajudicial killings of suspected terrorists on the territory of another sovereign state.

Quite apart from cases involving emergency conditions of armed conflict, even states with the most impressive overall records on human rights frequently are less scrupulous in protecting the rights of certain minorities (and in some cases women). Recognizing the supremacy of transnational justice equips domestic courts and advocacy groups with powerful means of preventing or remedying these lapses.

The second reason why states that do an exceptional job of protecting human rights ought to recognize the supremacy of transnational justice within their own borders is that by doing so they enhance their effectiveness as leaders in the cause of progress toward the fulfillment of the Natural Duty of Justice. Especially for the more influential states—which for the most part are those that have better overall human rights records—to apply transnational law to others but refuse to recognize its supremacy in their own case is damaging to the cause of developing a global culture of human rights.

Neither of these reasons for human rights-respecting states to recognize the supremacy of transnational law grounds an absolute commitment. Even if they are sufficient reasons for such states to recognize the supremacy of transnational law in general, there can still be particular circumstances in which the moral costs of acknowledging supremacy would be too high. The responsible approach would seem to be to recognize the supremacy of transnational law as a strong general presumption, but one that is defeasible in exceptional circumstances, while working to improve it so that the moral costs of acknowledging its supremacy are reduced.

My goal in this section has not been to argue for an absolute commitment on the part of all states to the supremacy of transnational law. More generally, my position throughout this book is to reject what might be called Legal Absolutism, the unfortunately widespread view among international lawyers that international law (or at least its most basic rules) ought to be regarded as sacrosanct by all who value the rule of law in international relations. In the final chapter of this book I will argue that a sincere and consistent commitment to the enterprise of international law, grounded in the Natural Duty of Justice, does *not* require states, individuals, or groups to comply with every law of the existing international system, any more than respect for the rule of law excludes civil disobedience in the domestic case. There I explore the justifications for conscientious violation of international law in some detail.

Supporting the enterprise of international law versus supporting particular international legal institutions

I have argued that those who take the Natural Duty of Justice seriously will be committed to the enterprise of international law where this includes principles both of international and of transnational justice. But supporting the enterprise of international law is compatible with refusing to endorse and participate in efforts to establish particular legal institutions or refusing to support particular existing institutions, just as it is compatible with refusing to comply with a particular international law.

The argument thus far has only shown that there is a strong case for supporting the enterprise of an international legal system that includes both international and transnational elements, but little has been said thus far about what such a system would have to be like to be legitimate. A clearer conception of legitimacy is needed to guide decisions about which aspects of the current system deserve our support and which do not, and what sorts of new institutions for international law ought to be developed.

III. *A Justice-Based Conception of System Legitimacy*

The justification of institutions for wielding political power

The previous section focused chiefly on the reasons-for-compliance question—why should individuals, groups, and states support the enterprise of international law? This section addresses the agency-justification question—what justifies the wielding of political power in and through the institutions of international law?

In Chapter 5 I offered a justice-based general conception of political legitimacy: The exercise of political power is morally justified if and only if the entity exercising it achieves a minimal standard of basic human rights protection through means that are themselves at least minimally just. In addition, if democratic governance is feasible, then legitimacy also requires democracy.

It appears that this general conception of legitimacy should apply to any set of institutions for the exercise of political power. So it should serve as well for the international legal system as for a particular state.

Legitimacy, not perfect justice

On the view I am advancing, then, system legitimacy is justice-based. Yet this view does not conflate legitimacy with justice, because legitimacy does not require full compliance with principles of justice. The theory of legitimacy I have developed articulates a minimal moral standard that an institutional structure must meet if it is to provide a framework for the morally justified exercise of political power.

Legitimacy cannot require full compliance with principles of justice for another reason: In order to bring us closer to full compliance with principles of justice, the exercise of political power is necessary. To capture this point I have said that to be morally justified in exercising political power, an agent must exhibit a credible commitment to protecting basic human rights, not that it must achieve full or perfect justice. Yet two questions remain unanswered: (1) How just must an institution for wielding political power be, and (2) how well suited must it be to bring about significant advances toward full compliance with principles of justice, in order for it to be morally justifiable for persons to wield political power within it in the pursuit of justice?

Notice that answering only the second part of the question (i.e., (2)) is not sufficient. Even if an institutional system is capable of making significant progress toward the goal of satisfying principles of justice, we need to know whether the methods and processes by which it does so are sufficiently just to make it legitimate. If an institutional system includes features that facilitate egregious injustices in the name of advancing toward justice, our support of it makes us accomplices in injustice. The point made in Chapter 6 regarding recognitional legitimacy holds for the legitimacy of legal systems generally: A justice-based conception of legitimacy must include a nonconsequentialist constraint requiring that the institutional system as it now exists should not be so unjust as to make using it for the pursuit of justice morally impermissible.

It is important to understand that there is no unique, *general* answer to the question "How just must the international legal system be for the exercise of political power in it to be morally justifiable?" How just is just enough will depend chiefly upon two factors: What are the feasible and morally accessible alternatives to the system in question and how well do they approximate the requirements of justice, and what are the system's capacities for improvement in the direction of greater justice?

The international legal system as it now exists contains some elements that are resources for moral progress and some that are impediments to it. Moreover, because the 'system' is extremely decentralized and even fragmented, those who take justice seriously are not faced with an either/or choice, a decision either to reject international law as a whole or accept it *in toto*. To that extent, the question of whether the 'system' is legitimate may assume more coherence than exists.

Nevertheless, there is much to be gained by exploring the options for understanding what the system would have to be like for it to be clearly morally justifiable to exercise political power within it. *If* the system becomes more coherent—and if its ability to exercise political power increases—the question of legitimacy will become both more applicable and more morally urgent. Keeping that in mind, what is needed is not a moral yardstick to determine whether we ought to support the existing international legal system as a whole or reject it, but rather a forward-looking but realistic standard to guide our efforts to improve the system and to know which elements of it are the most suitable venues for the pursuit of justice.

In the remainder of this chapter my aim is to show that a justice-based conception of legitimacy best serves these purposes. To do this, I offer what I believe are fatal criticisms of the dominant view of what makes the international legal system legitimate, namely, state consent.

IV. *The Consent Theory of System Legitimacy*

System legitimacy as adherence to the super-norm of state consent

By way of supplying a context for the attempt to develop a justice-based account of system legitimacy, it should be said that there is remarkably little available by way of explicit, systematic theorizing on this fundamental topic. There is a considerable literature that points out deficiencies in the international legal system and then assumes, more than argues, that these deficiencies impugn the system's legitimacy. Yet such suggestions are less than convincing in the absence of an explicit, principled account of what would make the system legitimate. Nor is there even a clear statement, to my knowledge, of system legitimacy as a normative concept.

Instead, attention has focused primarily if not exclusively on two other questions: (1) Under what conditions is the international legal system, or particular norms within it, believed to be legitimate, and (2) what makes international law binding on states? The former question is descriptive, not normative. The latter focuses on the reasons the subjects of law have for complying with it—a question already addressed in the preceding section of this chapter—rather than on what makes the exercise of political power in the international system morally justifiable.

There is, of course, the dominant traditional view according to which state consent is both necessary and sufficient for the legitimacy of norms within the international system. Some theorists apparently assume that this consent theory of the legitimacy of *norms* yields a theory of *system* legitimacy when combined with the assumption that the legitimacy of the system is reducible to the legitimacy of the norms that it includes. On this latter version of the state consent theory, the international legal system is legitimate so far as it observes the super-norm (or constitutional principle) that all international legal norms must be created through the consent of states. In other words, norms are legitimate if and only if they enjoy state consent, and the system is legitimate if and only if all (or most of?) its norms are legitimate, that is, if they have been consented to by states.

I will refer to the assertion that the system is legitimate if its norms (or the majority of them?) are legitimate as the Reducibility Thesis. To clear the way for a discussion of the justice-based account of system legitimacy, I will first explain why I believe the idea of state consent cannot provide an adequate theory of system legitimacy for the international legal system, even if the Reducibility Thesis is granted.

I will resist the temptation to make short work of the state consent theory of legitimacy by simply observing that it is, after all, a consent theory, and therefore is vulnerable to the same objections that apply to the idea that consent makes an individual state's government legitimate. Instead, I will explore the difficulties of the consent theory as applied to the consent of states in international law. This should forestall the objection that the peculiarities of the international legal system make state consent the appropriate criterion for system legitimacy even if the consent of individuals is not the appropriate criterion for the legitimacy of the individual state.

Is state consent to norms sufficient for system legitimacy?

The idea that adherence to a super-norm of state consent to international laws is *sufficient* for system legitimacy is quite implausible for several reasons, especially if it is supposed to provide a basis for saying that the existing system or anything remotely like it is legitimate. First, the super-norm of state consent, as it actually operates in the international legal system, is too morally anemic to confer legitimacy, either on individual norms or on the system as a whole. For one thing, what counts as consent in the system is not qualified by any requirement of voluntariness that would give what is called consent normative punch.

Thus, for example, when the losers in a war sign a peace treaty literally at gunpoint, this can count as state consent under international law. Now it is true that Article 52 of the Vienna Convention on Treaties states that "A treaty is void if its conclusion has been procured by the threat or use of force *in violation of the principles of international law as embodied in the Charter of the United Nations.*"[4] But the italicized phrase allows the possibility that "consent" extracted by duress is valid for purposes of international law, for example, if the victors in a defensive war or a humanitarian intervention authorized by the UN Security Council impose a peace treaty on the vanquished (as occurred with the Dayton Accords that ended NATO's humanitarian war against Yugoslavia).

Regardless of whether this is the proper interpretation of Article 52, in practice there has been a marked reluctance to recognize duress

---

[4] The United Nations (1969), 'Vienna Convention on the Law of Treaties', repr. in Carter and Trimble (eds.), *International Law: Selected Documents*, 55–80, 70.

as invalidating state "consent" in international law.[5] (Recall that what determines whether a rule is an international law depends upon the practice of states, not just the wording of texts.)

To hold that "consent" under duress bestows legitimacy (understood as moral justifiability of enforcement) is absurd. Without the fulfillment of background conditions that place constraints on extreme inequalities in bargaining capacity or which at least rule out the more extreme forms of duress, state consent cannot confer legitimacy; yet the current international legal system lacks such constraints. Notice that the question we are asking here is not whether state consent confers *legality* on norms, that is, whether a state's consent to a norm makes that norm legally binding on those that consent to it, but whether the fact that states have consented to norms makes it morally justifiable to enforce them.

Second, it is false to characterize the current system as one in which the state consent super-norm is satisfied. In the area of customary law, it is not true that norms enjoy the consent of all states, unless one is willing to stretch the notion of consent to the point that it is so normatively inconsequential as to provide no connection with the moral justification for wielding political power. Stronger states have a disproportionate influence on the creation and revision of customary international law and weaker states must, for the most part, play by the customary rules. Opting out—publicly and persistently dissenting from customary norms—is simply not a viable option in many cases, especially for weaker states. So it is scarcely more plausible to say that the existence of a customary norm proves that it satisfies the super-norm of state consent than it is to say that by remaining within the boundaries of a state, the individual citizen has given his tacit consent. Furthermore, once a customary norm has been created, states are bound by it whether they dissent from it or not, even if they had no opportunity to dissent from it during the process of its creation.

Third, to assume that state consent to norms confers legitimacy in a system in which many states do not represent the interests of their citizens is to indulge in the now thoroughly discredited view that Charles Beitz calls the Autonomy of States—the error of treating states as if

---

[5] Henry Steiner and Philip Alston (eds.), *International Human Rights in Context: Law, Politics, Morals. Text and Materials* (Oxford University Press, Oxford, 2000), 106.

they were moral persons in their own right, rather than merely being institutional resources for human beings.[6] Until all or at least most states come to represent all their citizens, state consent cannot serve to legitimate particular norms or the system as a whole, even in cases in which that consent is genuinely voluntarily given by state leaders.

Despite its implausibility, the position that state consent is sufficient for the legitimacy of norms and that adherence to the super-norm of state consent is sufficient for system legitimacy is probably the dominant view about system legitimacy (if only because there is so little explicit theorizing about system legitimacy). What, apart from the very implausible Autonomy of States view, might account for the popularity of the state consent theory?

Here is one possible explanation. Some legal theorists are highly critical of international acts that seem to violate the consent super-norm (for example, armed human rights interventions within states without the state's consent). These theorists suggest that the super-norm is a basic or constitutional principle of the international legal system. Perhaps their assumption is that a system is legitimate if its practices adhere to its own basic or constitutional principles. In the form of an explicit argument, this position, which I will call Constitutional Positivism, would go like this.

1. The principle that state consent is sufficient for the legitimacy of a norm is a basic or constitutional principle of the international legal system.
2. If a principle stating that a certain condition is sufficient for the legitimacy of a norm is a basic or constitutional principle of a legal system, then norms that satisfy that condition are legitimate.
3. (Therefore) if the norms of the international legal system enjoy state consent, then those norms are legitimate.
4. The legitimacy of a system of law is reducible to the legitimacy of its norms: If the norms of a system are legitimate, then the system is legitimate.

---

[6] Beitz, *Political Theory and International Relations*, 71; Teson, *A Philosophy of International Law*; and Teson, 'The Liberal Case for Humanitarian Intervention', in Jeffrey Holzgrefe and Robert Keohane (eds.), *Humanitarian Intervention: Ethical, Legal, and Political Dilemmas* (Cambridge University Press, New York, 2003).

5. (Therefore) the international legal system is legitimate if its
   norms satisfy the requirement of state consent (state consent is
   sufficient for system legitimacy).

The Constitutional Positivist Argument, however, must be rejected.
Its most obvious flaw is premise 2, which is a simple equivocation on
the term 'legitimacy'. The question we are asking is this: What conditions must the international legal system satisfy if it is to be an institutional structure within which it is morally justifiable to wield
political power, that is, to attempt to exercise supremacy in the making, application, and enforcement of laws? We are *not* asking what
makes a norm a law or what makes it legally binding. Premise 2, however, if true, can only be understood as a statement about what makes
a norm a law or what makes it legally binding, that is, what makes it a
law in the system, not about moral justifiability—unless one is willing
to endorse the false and abhorrent view that it is morally justifiable to
enforce a norm simply because it is a law or simply because it is a
basic or constitutional law.

Premise 2 in effect says that the super-norm according to which a
norm is international law only if it enjoys state consent is the rule of
recognition (in Hart's sense of that phrase) in the international legal
system. But from this it only follows that norms that enjoy state
consent are international laws, not that it is morally justifiable to
enforce them, and not that a system in which the state consent
super-norm is adhered to is a legitimate system. But given this reading of premise 2 (according to which we substitute 'legality' for
'legitimacy'), premise 3 should read: If the norms of the international legal system enjoy state consent, then they are legally valid
norms in the international legal system. This is hardly informative
and, more important, when combined with the assertion that the
legitimacy of a legal system is reducible to the legitimacy of its
norms, does *not* imply the conclusion that the international legal
system is legitimate if its norms enjoy state consent. Recall that the
conclusion the argument was supposed to support is an assertion
about the moral justifiability of the international legal system
understood as an institutional structure for monopolistic efforts to
create, apply, and enforce law.

To summarize: The Constitutional Positivist Argument makes
the mistake of sliding from a statement about what constitutes legal

validity in the international legal system (combined with the Reducibility Thesis, 4) to a conclusion about what makes the system legitimate (the question of moral justifiability). The irony is that the Constitutional Positivist Argument commits the very error that positivists generally delight in exposing in the thinking of Natural Law thinkers: the confusion of law with morality.

Is state consent necessary *for system legitimacy?*

Given that the facts of the existing system preclude state consent from being a sufficient condition for legitimacy (in particular the fact that much state consent is less than voluntary and does not represent citizens' preferences even when it is), and given the flaws of the Constitutional Positivist Argument, it is hard to see what basis there could be for holding that state consent is even a *necessary* condition for system legitimacy. The assertion that state consent to norms is a necessary condition of system legitimacy might be somewhat more plausible if all states really represented their citizens (either by taking their interests to heart or acting on their preferences). But even if this ideal condition were satisfied, it is not at all obvious that state consent would be necessary for legitimacy.

After all, requiring state consent to norms is one possible supernorm (constitutional requirement) for an international legal system, but whether it is a uniquely appropriate requirement all things considered is highly disputable. As I observed in Chapter 5, consent of individual citizens is not a necessary condition for the legitimacy of domestic legal systems. So why should one think that state consent is a necessary condition of the legitimacy of the international legal system?

As a possible answer, but one that ultimately will prove unsatisfactory, consider the Simple Positivist Argument.

1. According to international law, state consent is necessary for a norm to be legally valid in the international legal system (i.e., to be an international law).
2. Only if a norm is legally valid in the international legal system is it legitimate (i.e., morally justifiable to enforce it).
3. (Therefore) only if a norm enjoys state consent is it legitimate.
4. A system of law is legitimate if and only if the norms comprising it are legitimate (the Reducibility Thesis).

5. (Therefore) the international legal system is legitimate only if the state consent super-norm is satisfied (i.e., its norms enjoy state consent). So state consent to norms is a necessary condition of system legitimacy.

The hypothesis that they espouse this argument explains why Legal Absolutist critics of humanitarian interventions they regard as illegal are so vehement in their condemnation: According to the Simple Positivist Argument, to violate the norm of state consent by engaging in humanitarian intervention is not simply to act illegally, it is to undermine a necessary condition for the legitimacy of the international legal system, namely, state consent.

The Simple Positivist Argument, however, is no more successful than the Constitutional Positivist Argument. The first difficulty is that, for reasons already explained, premise 1 is highly dubious at best. Treaty-created norms apply to states that fall within their scope regardless of whether they consent or not (e.g., treaties concerning peaceful uses of international waterways apply to newly created states that include stretches of waterways and to existing states that come to have territory adjacent to international waterways due to shifts in the courses of rivers). In addition, as has often been observed, peremptory norms of international law (*jus cogens*) apply to all states regardless of their consent to the treaties or conventions or practices that contributed to their creation. And finally, customary norms apply to states that did not consent to them and that may now denounce them, so long as those states did not dissent from them during the process by which the norms "crystallized." So unless one is willing to take the extreme view that a considerable portion of what we ordinarily take to be international law is not legally binding because it does not enjoy state consent and there are no *jus cogens* norms, premise 1 must be rejected.

V. *Moral Minimalism and the Consent Theory of System Legitimacy*

State consent as a substitute for a shared core conception of justice

We have already encountered, in Chapter 1, another argument that has been employed to try to show that state consent is a necessary condition of legitimacy for the international system: the Moral Minimalist view. According to the Moral Minimalist, consent is the only thing that can make the enforcement of norms across borders morally justifiable because so-called international society is a mere association of moral strangers. The idea is that there are no shared substantive ends or shared core conception of justice (such as is available in liberal societies according to Rawls) that can serve as a basis for justifying enforcement in the absence of the consent of those upon whom the law is enforced.

Objections to the Moral Minimalist state consent view of system legitimacy

The immediate and most obvious problem with the Moral Minimalist argument for state consent as necessary for system legitimacy is this: It asserts that state consent serves to justify enforcement absent the consent of those upon whom norms of international law are enforced, that is, those whose liberty is constrained by enforcement. But in many cases international law constrains the liberty of individuals and nonstate collective entities, not just states. So, given that states often do not represent their citizens and do not act with their consent, how could the fact that states consent to international legal norms show that their enforcement on other collectivities and individuals is morally justified? Quite apart from this, the Moral Minimalist view upon which this putative justification for state consent is a necessary condition of system legitimacy is afflicted by the deficiencies of that view.

I will not rehearse here in detail the objections I raised in Chapter 1 to the Moral Minimalist view. The single most serious of these is that Moral Minimalism assumes, without sufficient evidence, not only that there are no shared substantive values or no core conception of justice capable of providing the basis for justified enforcement, but that there never will be. The expanding global culture of human rights, which is imperfectly institutionalized in international law, gives reason to hope that a shared core conception of justice may emerge, if it does not already exist.

Indeed, the Universal Declaration of Human Rights, as well as other central human rights conventions, explicitly endorses the idea that the inherent dignity of free and equal individuals entitles them to be treated in certain ways—and this sounds very much like a widely shared, core conception of justice. So the Moral Minimalist view does not appear to provide a conclusive reason to believe that without state consent to norms the international legal system cannot be legitimate.

Notice, however, that even if the problem of global consensus on values turns out to be as severe and intractable as the Moral Minimalist assumes, and even if it were true that in the absence of consensus nothing other than consent could serve to legitimate the international legal system, it would not follow that the international legal system is or is likely to be legitimate. Instead, given the fact that the existing system contains many norms to which at least some states have not consented, the proper conclusion to draw from the Moral Minimalist view is that the international legal system is not legitimate and will never become so.

The Moral Minimalist view, therefore, cannot be invoked to support the widely held assumption that the existing system is legitimate because based on state consent. On the contrary, if Moral Minimalism were true, one would simply have to admit that the existing international legal system is not legitimate because a substantial proportion of its norms do not enjoy state consent. Such a result would hardly be palatable to those who invoke Moral Minimalism to try to show that humanitarian intervention is illegitimate because it violates the norm of state consent and thereby threatens to undermine the legitimacy of the system.

To summarize: Moral Minimalism, when combined with a sober recognition both of the extent to which the existing system is not consensual and of the normative impotence of what passes for consent in the system, implies that there is no legitimacy for such non-consensual action to undermine. So if we accept the Moral Minimalist justification for state consent as a necessary condition of system legitimacy, the widely held belief that only state consent can confer legitimacy has the unintended radical implication that the international legal system is illegitimate, not the intended conservative implication that those who value legitimacy should steer clear of changes in the system that states do not consent to.

VI. *The Instrumental Argument for State Consent as a Necessary Condition for System Legitimacy*

State consent as a protection against predation

One final argument for the conclusion that the legitimacy of the international legal system depends upon adherence to a super-norm requiring state consent remains to be considered. It can be outlined as follows. Call it the Predation Prevention (or Instrumental) Argument.

1. To be legitimate the international legal system must provide an adequate approximation of equal protection under the law for all states.
2. An adequate approximation of equal protection under the law exists only if there are adequate constraints on predation by stronger states on weaker ones.
3. The requirement of state consent to norms is a necessary element of any system of adequate constraints on predation by stronger states on weaker ones.
4. (Therefore) state consent to norms is a necessary condition for the legitimacy of the international legal system. (Without adherence to the norm of state consent the international legal system cannot provide an institutional structure within which the making, application, and enforcement of laws can be morally justified).

Limitations of the predation prevention argument

Premises 1 and 2 are unexceptionable. Premise 3 is dubious. First, it is not at all clear that adequate constraints on predation can *only* be achieved by a requirement that all norms must enjoy state consent. For example, a significant reduction of the risk of predation might be achieved by giving clearer content to the existing prohibition on aggressive war, combined with an arrangement by which humanitarian intervention is permitted only through a process of collective authorization that features a number of safeguards to prevent stronger states from using humanitarian intervention as an excuse for domination. (For example, if weaker states were included in the permanent membership of the Security Council, they could veto decisions that would authorize the more powerful states to intervene.)

Second, the costs of achieving constraints on predation by adherence to the norm of state consent may be exorbitant. The requirement of state consent—which if taken seriously is a veto right for every state or at least a requirement of approval by the majority of states—is a formidable obstacle to improving a system whose greatest defects lie in the behavior of some of the states whose consent is required in order to create and enforce norms that would prohibit their wrongful behavior. So even if adequate protection of weak states is a necessary condition of system legitimacy, and even if adherence to the state consent norm provides adequate protection to weak states, it does not follow that the system can be legitimate only if there is adherence to the norm of state consent. That conclusion would follow only if state consent were the only way, or the least costly, effective way to achieve adequate protection for weak states; but this very strong claim has not been established.

State consent and the formal equality of states

We saw in Chapter 1 that Benedict Kingsbury employs an instrumental argument to support the conclusion that the formal equality of states under current international law provides a significant obstacle to predation of strong states upon weak ones. By the formal equality of states here is meant the attribution to all states, large or small, weak or strong, of the same rights, immunities, liberties, and duties.

Kingsbury's conclusion is about the instrumental value of the formal equality of states, not about the super-norm of state consent. However, some who hold that adherence to the super-norm of state consent is necessary for system legitimacy in the case of the international legal system may do so because they hold that system legitimacy depends upon the formal equality of states while wrongly assuming that the formal equality of states is equivalent to or entails the state consent super-norm.[7] The difficulty with this view is that the formal equality of states is neither equivalent to nor entails the state consent super-norm.

To say that states are equal under international law is only to say that they all have the same rights, duties, liberties, and immunities. Whether they must all give their consent if norms are to be binding on them is another question, one that has to do with what is included in the rights of states, not with the issue of whether the rights are the same for all.

State consent as one constitutional option among others

I have argued that for a number of reasons state consent to norms is not defensible either as a necessary or as a sufficient condition for

---

[7] Alfred Rubin seems to fall into this category. See his *Ethics and Authority in International Law* (Cambridge University Press, Cambridge, 1997).

system legitimacy. Instead, the state consent super-norm is best regarded as an instrument for curbing predation by stronger states on weaker ones. But I have also suggested that how best to curb predation is a complex issue of constitutional design for the international legal system. There is no more reason to think that there is only one way to achieve adequate constraints on potential predators, namely, by adherence to the state consent super-norm, than there is to think that the only way to prevent stronger individuals from preying on weaker ones is to require that each citizen have a veto over any potential legislation. Consequently, pointing out that the state consent requirement has some effectiveness in curbing predation is not sufficient to show that the international legal system could not be legitimate without it.

However, a case might be made that through most of its history the international legal system has had such meager institutional resources that adherence to the state consent super-norm has been a crucial instrument for curbing predation. The lesson to draw from this is that until more robust institutional resources are developed, it would be best to continue to rely on the state consent super-norm as a curb on predation. (This seems to be Kingsbury's point.)

This may be so. But it would be much less persuasive to say that additional resources cannot or will not be developed. So even if it were true that adherence to the state consent super-norm, as an instrument for curbing predation, is now a necessary condition for system legitimacy, this might well change. What is necessary for system legitimacy now may no longer be required in the future, if alternative protections for weak states can be established.

Before turning to a further exploration of the justice-based conception of system legitimacy, a word of caution is in order. I have argued that adherence to the state consent super-norm is not defensible either as a necessary or a sufficient condition of system legitimacy and that it may not be the best instrument for reducing the risk of predation. From this nothing follows about how we ought to regard existing norms to which states have in fact consented. It certainly does *not* follow that such norms should not be treated as legally binding, nor that they should not be regarded as legitimate. (Recall the distinction between the legality of norms (whether they are international law), the legitimacy of norms (whether it is morally justifiable to enforce them), and the legitimacy of the system (whether it is an institutional structure within which it is morally justifiable to wield political power).)

A legitimate system may include provisions for more than one way to create laws, and state consent will surely be one of them. Moreover, even if a reformed, more legitimate system did not count as valid some of the agreements among states that are now regarded as fulfilling the consent requirement, it would not follow that the reformed system would regard them as void. Considerations of fairness and stability might provide conclusive reasons for "grandfathering in" norms that do not meet the new, more defensible consent requirement.

VII. *Is Democracy a Necessary Condition of System Legitimacy?*

The limits of the domestic analogy

My approach thus far has been to reject the idea that system legitimacy must be based on state consent and to suggest that a more satisfactory account of system legitimacy can be developed by beginning with the core elements of the general theory of legitimacy developed in Chapter 5. The rationale for this strategy is straightforward: In both cases we are seeking conditions that an institutional structure must satisfy if it is to be a framework within which the morally justifiable exercise of political power can take place.

So far I have focused on the core idea that legitimacy depends upon credible efforts to achieve protection of basic human rights through means that respect those same rights. But in Chapter 5 I also argued that where the resources for democratic governance exist, legitimacy requires democracy as well. The question I now want to explore is whether—or in what sense—democracy is required for the legitimacy of the international legal system.

Democratizing the international legal system

In fact, critics of the existing international legal system frequently suggest that its legitimacy is in question precisely because it is not sufficiently democratic.

For some who complain of the "democratic deficit" in the international legal system, the problem is that the system seems to be rapidly moving further away from the ideal of a system of equal sovereign states that is the core of the traditional conception of international law. For others, the concern is not that states are losing power, but that individuals and nonstate groups are increasingly denied it. What they have in common is the conviction that global governance is becoming increasingly a matter of control by technocratic elites—economists, financiers, and international lawyers ensconced in the bureaus of the European Union in Brussels and the World Trade Organization—who lack democratic authorization and hence accountability. I will argue that the first "democratic deficit" complaint is a distraction because increasing the role of state majoritarianism in the international legal system would not make it more legitimate. The second "democratic deficit" complaint, in contrast, is a fundamental challenge to the direction the enterprise of international law seems to be taking at present.

The notion of democratizing the system to make it more legitimate is ambiguous. Democratizing the system could mean any of the following: (1) increasing the scope and importance in the international legal system of decision-making through majoritarian voting by states (augmenting the scope of state majoritarianism); (2) making states more democratic, so that their governments can better function in the system as agents that genuinely represent all their citizens (thus giving more normative punch to state consent); or (3) making international institutions more representative of individuals, more accountable to individuals both as individuals and as members of nonstate groups that are important for their well-being and in some cases their identities.[8] (For reasons that will become clearer shortly, (3) has the best claim to the title "democratization of the international legal system", though it may turn out to be achievable only after significant advances in democratization in sense (2), democratization of states.)

In the preceding chapter I have already suggested how the incorporation of normative criteria for recognition can help implement (2) above, namely, by providing incentives for states to become more democratic in the sense of better representing all of their citizens.

---

[8] My discussion in this section draws on Allen Buchanan and David Golove, 'Philosophy of International Law', in Jules Coleman, Scott Shapiro, and Kenneth Himma (eds.), *The Oxford Handbook of Jurisprudence and Philosophy of Law* (Oxford University Press, New York, 2002), 930–4.

In this chapter I will focus on the other interpretations of democratizing the international system, (1) and (3). My main conclusion will be that the legitimacy of the international legal system depends ultimately on (3), not (1).

State majoritarianism

Consider the assertion that a larger role for state-majoritarian voting is required for system legitimacy, or at least that this would make the system significantly more legitimate. Just as democracy in a particular state does not require that every citizen has a veto over all legislation, so it does not require the consent of all states in a system in which states rather than individuals are the principal lawmakers. In the domestic case, individuals' rights and interests can be protected—and at less cost—by majority voting institutions combined with entrenched individual rights that constrain the domain of issues over which majority rule holds sway.

Given that state majoritarianism is neither a necessary nor a sufficient condition for system legitimacy, would increasing the scope of state majoritarianism in international law make the system more legitimate? The initial appeal of the idea of reform in the direction of state majoritarianism lies in the perception that the current system is unfairly dominated by powerful states. Democratization, understood here as an increasing role for state-majoritarian voting procedures, is proposed as the obvious mechanism for diminishing the morally arbitrary inequality of political power among states and thereby enhancing the legitimacy of the system.

But instituting a rule of state majoritarianism for the making, application, and enforcement of international legal norms is only one way of reducing this putative morally arbitrary imbalance of power among states. Again, the issue is one of constitutional design, and it would be rash to pronounce that the only practicable and morally defensible constitution for the international legal system must include a simple rule requiring that all or even most decisions concerning the making, application, and enforcement of law are to be made by state-majoritarian voting.

The attraction of the proposal to democratize the system by adopting state majoritarianism lies in the fact that the current system encompasses extreme inequalities of political power among states, in spite of the formal equality of states. However, to some extent the preoccupation with inequalities among states may be due to the unquestioned, highly traditional assumption that international law is exclusively the law of states. Once we acknowledge that international law now encompasses subjects and actors other than states, and that this change represents progress, it is no longer clear that equality of states itself—apart from whether it is the best means of protecting weak states from predation—is an overriding desideratum.

Much will depend upon how successful democratization in the second and third senses ((2) and (3) above) is. Unless states become more democratic, and unless the system further empowers nonstate actors, increasing the democratic equality of states in the workings of the system may do little to increase system legitimacy. After all, as I have argued, the touchstone for system legitimacy is justice, not the equality of states.

In brief, whether state majoritarianism would enhance system legitimacy will depend, among other things, upon how important states are in the system. If the system continues to make progress in empowering individuals and groups to help shape international law without being so dependent upon representation by states, then the political inequality of states becomes correspondingly less important. Finally, whether increased state majoritarianism would enhance system legitimacy will also depend upon whether there are other equally effective but less costly constitutional arrangements for decreasing the morally arbitrary political inequality among states that characterizes the existing system.

I have just emphasized that the attraction of the state majoritarianism proposal rests to a large extent on the framing assumption that states are the primary actors in the international legal system and I have noted that we cannot assume that this assumption will continue to hold true into the indefinite future. Nonetheless, as a matter of nonideal theory for here and now, the statist framing assumption is appropriate. So the question before us is whether state majoritarianism is now (and for the foreseeable future) the appropriate mechanism for reducing morally arbitrary inequalities in the existing system.

It might be thought that this is not quite the way to pose the question. If, as I have argued, democracy is a necessary condition for recognitional legitimacy of states in the system, and if, as I have also argued, the problem of morally justifying the exercise of political power is fundamentally the same whether it is wielded in one state or in the system, shouldn't we begin with the *presumption* that the system should be democratic? And in a system in which states are the main makers of law, mustn't being democratic mean state majoritarianism?

The fundamental flaw in this line of reasoning is that the two main arguments for democracy, understood as including individual-majoritarian voting procedures in the case of a particular state, do not apply to the case of the international legal system. The first type of argument would have to present state-majoritarian voting procedures as an expression of equal consideration for *individuals*; the second would have to show that state-majoritarian voting procedures are the most reliable safeguard for human rights.

In order to adapt the two chief arguments for individual majoritarianism to serve as arguments for state majoritarianism, additional premises are needed, and they are problematic. With regard to the first argument, one would have to establish that equal consideration for individuals requires that their states have an equal say in international lawmaking. If the identity of persons were as closely bound up with the international power and prestige of their states as some nationalists fantasize and if states were mononational, this premise would be more plausible than it in fact is. Due to the fact that many states systematically disregard the well-being of many of their citizens and that in many cases individuals do not identify with the state, but are in fact alienated from it because they belong to groups that are marginalized if not persecuted by the government, it is far from clear that the only way, or the best way, to express equal consideration for individuals is to adopt state majoritarianism.

Similarly, it is not at all obvious that state majoritarianism is the best instrument by which the international legal system can secure individuals' human rights. In a system in which many states systematically violate individuals' human rights, state majoritarianism in fact may be the single greatest impediment both to the effective institutional expression of equal consideration of persons and to the protection of human rights.

Consider more closely the second argument, according to which state majoritarianism is held to be the most reliable protection for human rights. Whether this is so will depend on how the majority of states will act regarding the protection of human rights. If there is a minority of states that are both more zealous in protecting human rights and also so powerful that they can exert a disproportionate influence in the world, then increasing the scope of state majoritarianism may actually be a setback for human rights.

Indeed, some would argue that by and large the most powerful states in the system today have much better than average records on human rights (China being a notable exception and, at least in its policy toward Chechnya, Russia as well). Hence it could be argued that at this point in time—when a robust human rights culture is not firmly rooted in many states—state majoritarianism is *not* the most reliable mechanism for protecting human rights. (I, for one, would be much more comfortable if the members of the European Union had the power to determine the character of international law than if the UN General Assembly did.)

This last argument is likely to be much more palatable to those who happen to be citizens of the more powerful states than to those whose states are weak. And here it is important to remember that an almost invariable concomitant of power is an extraordinary ability to rationalize self-interested action as being the expression of moral superiority. Nevertheless, this much is true: Whether state majoritarianism will provide the best protection for human rights will depend upon how committed the majority of states are to human rights, and in a system in which the institutional recognition of human rights is barely a half-century old and states are still the chief violators of human rights, the depth and extent of this commitment is questionable, to put it mildly.

The central point is that the argument that individual majoritarianism within states is the most reliable protection for human rights is much stronger than the corresponding argument for state majoritarianism in the international governance system. So one cannot argue from the fact that democracy is a necessary condition for the legitimacy of a state to the conclusion that democracy, understood as state majoritarianism, would enhance the legitimacy of the international legal system.

Equality of states, inequality for persons

There is one more reason to temper enthusiasm for trying to increase system legitimacy by "democratizing" the system in the sense of increasing the scope of state-majoritarian decision-making: There is no correlation between democratic representation of individuals and state majoritarianism because states contain vastly differently sized populations. A system in which all important international legal determinations are made by a majority vote among states, under the ideal condition that states accurately represent the preferences or interests of their citizens, would give much greater weight to the preferences or interests of some individuals, namely, those who are members of states with small populations. Enthusiasts for enhancing system legitimacy by augmenting democratic equality among states should ponder the fact that a system in which Slovenia has the same number of votes as China cannot be justified in any direct way, if at all, by appeal to the equality of persons.

The key point is that state majoritarianism, unlike individual majoritarianism, is not an institutional arrangement that is directly required by a basic moral principle. Individual majoritarianism, according to the first argument for democracy, is required by equal regard for persons, and this is a fundamental moral principle if anything is. But the connection between state majoritarianism and equal regard for individuals is more tenuous and problematic because there may be other arrangements that satisfy the demand of equal regard for persons, because states often do not represent their citizens, and because if they did, a system in which every state regardless of population size has an equal vote gives some persons a greater say than others.

To summarize: Neither of the two chief arguments for democracy (understood as individual majoritarianism within the state) translates into an argument for democracy in international governance (understood as state majoritarianism). So democracy, *understood as state majoritarianism*, does not appear to be a basic condition for legitimacy of the international system as it does for the individual state. There may be other reasons for state majoritarianism in international governance, including most obviously the need to constrain abuses by powerful states. Whether the international legal system should accord a larger or a smaller role to state majoritarianism as a method of decision-making (and for which domains of decisions) is a complex matter of constitutional design.

Domestic constitutions not uncommonly include bicameral representative institutions with one house based on population (individual majoritarianism) and the other based on equal numbers of votes for each federal unit regardless of their relative populations (federal unit majoritarianism). So even if a reformed international legal system would have a place for state-majoritarian voting, it is not clear what its scope should be, simply because it cannot be assumed that reducing existing political inequalities among *states* is the sole or the overriding desideratum for a morally defensible system. Under current conditions, providing better protection for basic human rights is the most pressing moral objective, and it is far from clear that increasing state majoritarianism is the best strategy for achieving it, rather than a major obstacle.

System legitimacy and political inequality

According to the justice-based conception of system legitimacy, what counts is whether the system provides institutional resources for the morally justifiable exercise of political power in the pursuit of justice. The primary condition for legitimacy, then, is that the system must have the capacity to further this goal and that the processes by which it does so should not themselves violate basic human rights or other important constraints of justice. So far we have explored the attractions and limitations of state majoritarianism as one way of pursuing political equality among states. It is only one way because political equality encompasses more than equal voting rights.

Once we abandon the dark fiction that states are moral agents in their own right, entitled to equality as a matter of basic moral principle, it becomes evident that political equality among states is of value *only* so far as it contributes to justice as goal or as process. Political equality among states is not valuable for its own sake, and certainly cannot be regarded as a necessary condition in its own right for system legitimacy.

Nevertheless, so long as states play a crucial role in the system, reducing existing *morally arbitrary political inequalities* among states, whether through the device of state majoritarianism or by other means, may significantly enhance the legitimacy of international law. My point, however, is that state-majoritarian democratization is only one mechanism for reducing morally arbitrary political inequalities among states and that how important the problem of political inequality among states is depends upon how important states are.

Furthermore, the assumption that the current inequality of states is "morally arbitrary" and for that reason unacceptable should be treated with more caution than it is usually accorded. If it could be argued persuasively that the current inequality among states actually contributes to improving the system by enabling the more powerful states, most of which happen to be strong proponents of human rights, to impose higher standards for human rights, then it would not be accurate to say that the inequality of power is morally arbitrary. Instead, it could be justified, at least in part, by appeal to the fact that for the time being it is a necessary condition for moral progress in a deeply defective system.

VIII. *The Pursuit of Justice in an Imperfect System*

In this chapter thus far I have pointed out the flaws of the dominant traditional view that the international legal system is legitimate if and only if it adheres to the super-norm of state consent and I have argued that instead the general, justice-based account of international legitimacy should serve as the core of an account of system legitimacy. I have also argued that simple proposals for enhancing legitimacy by achieving state-majoritarian "democratization" are much more problematic than is often assumed, even though morally arbitrary inequalities among states are prima facie a legitimacy-challenging feature of the existing system.

I have suggested that the general theory of political legitimacy I developed in Chapter 5 can provide the basis for an account of legitimacy for the international legal system. But my sketch of a theory of system legitimacy as yet provides no clear guidance for how we are to flesh out a global legal system analog of the minimal democracy requirement that is included in the conditions for the internal legitimacy of states. State majoritarianism, at least under present conditions, does not seem to be the proper way to capture the minimal democracy requirement.

In contrast, there is much to be said for the idea that equal consideration of persons requires some sort of global *individual* democratic governance—that each person should be able to participate as an equal in at least *some significant aspects of global governance*, through some meaningful system of representation, just as they ought to be able to participate as an equal in the governance of their own state.

Progress toward democratization in this sense would alleviate the true "democratic deficit"—the increasing influence of an unelected, unaccountable global technocratic elite. This third conception of enhancing the legitimacy of the international legal system by democratizing it has the best claim to being simply called the democratization of global governance, because here as in the case of the individual state, democracy contributes to legitimacy by what it does for individuals—it is generally the most reliable instrument for ensuring that their basic human rights are protected and it inherently expresses equal regard for all who are subject to the system of governance.

But it is very difficult to imagine that much headway on achieving genuine (i.e., individual) democratic global governance can be made at present, for at least three reasons. First, given that we still have a state system, to make sense of the idea that individuals have an equal say in global governance it seems that we must think of the latter as the global counterpart of a democratic federal state; yet the current international system is very far from even approximating a loose federal system and the prospects for changing it in this direction seem slight for the foreseeable future. Second, if states are to be thought of as the units of a global democratic federation, many of them will have to be radically transformed. Being undemocratic, they cannot serve as intermediate links between the individual and the global governance institutions in a democratic global federation. Thus democratization in the second sense, making states more representative of their citizens, seems to be a prerequisite for (individual) democratization of the international legal system, at least so long as states play an important mediating role between individuals and global governance structures.

Third, the problem of actually achieving anything like "an equal say" or political participation "as equals" for all in a system of global governance is even more daunting than achieving domestic democracy. Democratic theorists have noted that in the case of the single modern state, the need for a broad sphere of bureaucratic discretion based on technical expertise—and the growing asymmetry of knowledge between administrators and citizens—threatens to undercut the political equality that is supposed to be essential to democracy.[9] If anything this problem seems even more daunting, given the complexities of global governance.

[9] Richardson, *Democratic Autonomy*; and Christiano, *The Rule of the Many*.

Nevertheless, it would be a great mistake to dismiss the idea of global individual-democracy as wholly utopian. The oft-remarked processes of globalization, especially the growing worldwide access to electronic communications, may eventually provide the basis for at least a limited sphere of global individual-democratic decision-making. After all, the European Union has already made some gains in the creation of individual democracy at the super-state level (though "democratic deficit" critics rightly point out that at present power lies mainly not in the European Parliament, the most democratic element of the Union, but in its least democratic elements, the Council and the Commission). The same Natural Duty of Justice that requires us to support the enterprise of international law requires us to explore the possibility of developing institutions for individual global democratization, rather than to dismiss it as utopian.

Significant (individual-) democratization of the international legal system is nowhere near possible, given present international legal institutional resources. However, this does not entail that the international legal system is illegitimate, because, as I argued in Chapter 5, democracy is only a necessary condition for legitimacy where it is possible. This means that for the immediate future the most accurate measure of the legitimacy of the international legal system, as well the most pressing goal for improving it, is the protection of basic human rights. Nevertheless, as greater power over the lives of the world's population comes to be exercised through institutions of global governance, especially in economic matters, democratization will become a more pressing concern—and its lack will be an increasingly serious challenge to the legitimacy of the system. The burden of argument is on those who dismiss progress toward democratization as utopian, not upon those who recognize that democratization is a requirement of legitimacy where it is possible. The Principle of Moral Equality requires us to try to develop democratic governance (understood as including participation in governance by individuals) because democracy alone provides a satisfactory answer to the question: Why should some rather than others exercise political power if we are all fundamentally equal?

In this volume I make no attempt even to scratch the surface of the question "What sorts of institutional changes would be required, here and now, to move toward (individual-) democratization of the international legal system?" Instead my aim in this chapter has been to clarify the relationship between democracy and system legitimacy and to clear the way for taking the possibility of democratic global governance seriously, by showing that the ideal of state majoritarianism that has played such a central role in the traditional philosophy of international law is not the proper target for reforms designed to enhance the legitimacy of the system, but a muddled distraction from the real task.

Despite the lack of a satisfactory account of what global individual democracy would be like and our current inability to achieve anything that resembles it, the justice-based account of system legitimacy I have provided may suffice for now. Recall that there are two functions an account of system legitimacy should perform. It should give us a target to shoot for in improving the system, and it should help us determine whether the existing system is so far from being fully legitimate that efforts to work within it for reform are morally impermissible.

I believe the justice-based account of system legitimacy I have developed from Chapter 5's general account of legitimacy performs both of these functions adequately. It gives general guidance as to how to improve the system from the standpoint of legitimacy, by focusing on the fundamental idea that in the international legal system, as in any institutional framework for wielding political power, doing a credible job of moving toward justice for all by processes that are themselves just is the only thing that can justify political power. Equally important, it warns us against mistakenly assuming that some current features of the system, such as reliance on state consent, are necessary for legitimacy.[10]

The implications of my analysis of the problem of system legitimacy are far from encouraging. I have argued that although any system of governance can only be fully legitimate if it is democratic, the international legal system is far from even approximating the most minimal democracy. Furthermore, at present it is difficult even to know how one would go about creating a system of representation linking individuals to a system of global governance through participation in their domestic political processes, quite apart from

---

[10] I am indebted to David Luban for urging me to place more emphasis in this chapter than I initially did on the complaint that the problem of a technocratic elite is the greatest challenge to the legitimacy of the international legal system.

the fact that many states are not themselves democratic, making them unsuitable to serve the needed mediating function.

The most important implication of my analysis is that for the present the main standard for gauging the legitimacy of the system must be whether it does a creditable job of protecting basic human rights. Despite my belief that international law has played a role in improving the protection of human rights and my hope that it may continue to advance further toward the goal of justice, I would not deny that it is not nearly as effective in meeting this crucial standard for legitimacy as even some of the less than fully developed domestic legal systems. In this light, the demand for democratization of global governance seems even more utopian, unless it turns out, as I am convinced that it will, that further progress in the protection of basic human rights through international law ultimately depends on making some gains in democratizing the system. After all, one of the chief arguments for democracy—as I have emphasized in Chapter 3 and elsewhere—is that it is the most reliable form of governance for protecting basic human rights, and I see no reason to think that global governance is an exception to this general principle.

Nevertheless, at least in the short run, there can be a conflict between improving the capacity of the international legal system to protect basic human rights and building its capacity for democratic governance. In Chapter 11 I consider such a conflict in an exploration of the morality of reforming the international law of humanitarian intervention. There I argue that at present the best prospect for increasing the capacity of the international legal system to protect persons from violent violations of their most basic human rights may require the creation of a liberal-democratic, rule-governed, treaty-based coalition for humanitarian intervention that would be "elitist" at least in its initial form, insofar as it would bypass the more inclusive UN-based system of law.

To that extent, the conclusion of my discussion of system legitimacy must be postponed until Chapter 11, where I take up the issue of the morality of international legal reform by focusing on the example of reforming the international law of humanitarian intervention. There I argue that in a system whose legitimacy is as problematic as that of the existing international legal system, responsible efforts at making the system more just may allow and even require illegal action and indeed illegal action undertaken by a small group of states, in the absence of democratic accountability to humanity at large. That discussion completes my analysis of system legitimacy by examining the relationship between our evaluation of the system's legitimacy, our commitment to the rule of law in international affairs, and our willingness to engage in illegal acts directed toward legal reform.

In the next chapter I begin the third part of the book, developing an agenda for reform of the international law of self-determination, advancing a principled case for reforms that would make the system more substantively just, if not more democratic.

PART THREE

Self-Determination

CHAPTER 8

―――

Self-Determination and Secession

This chapter begins the task of applying the justice-based conception of political legitimacy developed in Part Two to the practically urgent and theoretically vexing issues of secession and self-determination. Two main theses are advanced. (1) International law should recognize a remedial right to secede but not a general right of self-determination that includes the right to secede for all peoples or nations. From the standpoint of international law, the unilateral right to secede—the right to secede without consent or constitutional authorization—should be understood as a remedial right only, a last-resort response to serious injustices. Accordingly, the international legal order should support states' efforts to preserve their territorial integrity so long as they do a credible job of protecting basic human rights, but deny that states have the right to suppress secession when secession is a remedy of last resort against serious injustices. In affirming a remedial understanding of the right to secede, international law should unambiguously repudiate the nationalist principle that all nations (or "peoples") are entitled to their own states. (2) The international legal order should encourage alternatives to secession, in particular by working for greater compliance with existing international human rights norms prohibiting ethno-national and religious discrimination and in some cases by supporting intrastate autonomy regimes, that is, arrangements for self-government short of full sovereignty. Restricting the unilateral right to secession to cases of severe and persisting injustices would encourage states to take a more flexible stance toward intrastate autonomy arrangements, because it would dispel the fears of a slippery slope toward state-breaking that a general right of self-determination for all peoples or nations understandably evokes.

I. *Introduction*

The need for a comprehensive theory of self-determination

In 1919 U.S. Secretary of State Stanton observed that the phrase "self-determination" is "loaded with dynamite." A moral theory of international law should provide practical guidance for defusing the self-determination bomb, while at the same time giving legitimate interests in self-determination their due.

The need for a principled stance on self-determination has never been greater. Most large-scale violent conflicts now occur within states rather than between them, and in many cases of large-scale intrastate conflict, self-determination is an issue—sometimes *the* issue.[1] In this chapter and the next, I draw the outlines of a moral theory of self-determination for international law grounded in on the justice-based account of legitimacy developed in Part Two. The result is a proposal for an international legal response to claims and counter-claims regarding self-determination that is grounded in the commitment to protecting basic human rights, rather than any putative fundamental "right of self-determination" of peoples or nations.

Self-determination and secession

Secession is the most dramatic form assertions of self-determination can take. Nevertheless, as I shall argue, focusing exclusively or even primarily on secession distorts theory and impedes progress in practice. Achievement of independent statehood is in many cases the least feasible or appropriate exercise of self-determination. A comprehensive theory of self-determination, therefore, must include not only an account of the right to secede but also a broader normative framework for evaluating and responding to claims to self-determination, and one that does not assume that independent statehood is the natural goal or inevitable culmination of aspirations for self-determination.

James Anaya has distinguished usefully between two modes or dimensions of self-determination.[2] (1) *Constitutive self-determination*

---

[1] Ted Gurr, *Minorities at Risk: A Global View of Ethnopolitical Conflict* (United States Institute of Peace Press, Washington, DC, 1993).

[2] James S. Anaya, *Indigenous Peoples in International Law* (Oxford University Press, New York, 1996), 81.

occurs when a group makes a fundamental choice concerning its political status, for example, opting for or rejecting independent statehood or inclusion in a state other than the one it is currently a part of. (2) *Ongoing self-determination* is self-government, though it need not be full independence. To be self-governing a group must exercise some independent political control over some significant aspects of its common life. With regard to at least some matters of importance, it must wield political power in its own right, rather than merely power delegated by a higher political unit and subject to being overridden or revoked by the latter.

Thus self-determination (or autonomy) implies an independent domain of political control. But this characterization leaves open (1) the nature of the domain of independent control (what sorts of activities and institutions the group exerts control over in its own right), (2) the extent of its control over items in the domain (which may vary from item to item), and (3) the particular political institutions by which the group exercises political control over its domain of control. Given the indefinitely large set of self-government arrangements made possible by various combinations of different ways of specifying these three variables, it is extraordinarily unhelpful to talk about "the" right of self-determination (or autonomy). Yet existing international law contains dangerously ambiguous references to "the right of self-determination of all peoples."

The status of secession in international law

The prevailing opinion among international legal scholars appears to be that at present there is no international legal right to secede except in two rather specific circumstances: (1) "classic" decolonization (when an overseas colony seeks to liberate itself from metropolitan control), and (2) (perhaps) the reclaiming of state territory that is subject to unjust military occupation.[3] (Some scholars would add a third circumstance: where a racial group has been denied meaningful access to participation in government.)

By a right to secede here is meant a claim-right: a liberty-right or permission, plus a correlative obligation. To say that a group has the

[3] Antonio Casesse, *Self-Determination of Peoples: A Legal Reappraisal* (Cambridge University Press, Cambridge, 1995), 37–78; and Hannum, *Autonomy, Sovereignty, and Self-Determination.*

right to secede, then, implies at least this much: (1) it is permissible (not forbidden) for it to attempt to establish its own legitimate state, and (2) others, including the state in which the group is now located, are obligated not to interfere with the attempt.

The ambiguity of 'the right to secede'

At this point a complication emerges. There is a difference between saying that (1) a group has a right to *attempt* to establish its own legitimate state and saying that (2) it has a right *to* its own legitimate state. The international legal system might recognize that under certain conditions, such as colonization or unjust military occupation, a group is entitled to *attempt* to constitute a fully independent, primary political unit that will be recognized as such by the international system, but might leave it up to existing states to accord legitimate statehood status to the group depending upon whether the new unit it constitutes meets certain requirements.

To say that the group is entitled to attempt to constitute a legitimate, fully independent political unit, would only be to say that in making this attempt it acts permissibly, with the implication that the group's claim to the territory is valid at least in the sense that it is not voided by any claim the state from which it is seceding might make. Understood as a claim-right, this would also include the obligation on the part of states not to interfere with the group's attempt to achieve independence. Indeed this is probably the most accurate interpretation of existing international law: that in cases of decolonization and perhaps unjust military occupation it establishes a right of a group to repudiate the authority of the existing state and to attempt to achieve recognition of independence, but that this does not entail that the group has the right to a legitimate state, in the sense of being entitled to recognition as legitimate, since recognition is a matter of discretion for existing states.

This distinction between the right to secede understood as (1) a right to throw off the existing state's control and attempt to achieve the status of being a legitimate state and as (2) the right to be recognized as a legitimate state under international law is often ignored in moral theorizing about secession. But when secessionists claim a right to secede *they* typically understand this to mean—and expect others to understand it to mean—that they are entitled to their own legitimate state, not just that they are entitled to attempt to establish their own state.

The distinction is important because it reveals two distinct options for how international law should respond to secession. According to the first option, a morally defensible international law of secession would only recognize a right to secede understood as the right of a group to throw off the state's authority and attempt to constitute an entity that will be recognized as a legitimate state; according to the second, the right to secede is the right of a group to have its own legitimate state. On the second option, the right to break away and the right to recognition go together; on the first they do not.

The proposal for international legal reform I am advancing is the first option. If the state persists in certain serious injustices toward a group, and the group's forming its own independent political unit is a remedy of last resort for these injustices, then the group ought to be acknowledged by the international community to have the claim-right to repudiate the authority of the state and to attempt to establish its own independent political unit. But this by itself does not imply that the new entity ought to be recognized as a legitimate state in international law.

Acknowledging the group's right to secede, where the right is understood in this weaker way, as only encompassing the right to attempt to create a new state, is far from vacuous. It implies a profound change in institutional status, namely, that the state's right to territorial integrity no longer encompasses the area in question, because the injustices the state has perpetrated have voided its claim to a part of the state's territory. It also accords legitimacy to the secessionists' attempt to create an entity that will be recognized as a legitimate state, making it clear that in attempting to do so the secessionists do not commit a wrong. But acknowledging the right to secede in this weaker sense does not imply that the secessionists have a right to recognitional legitimacy. It does not imply that states are obligated to recognize the entity in question as a legitimate state, only that they are obligated not to interfere with the secessionists' efforts to gain recognition.

Whether the international community should in addition recognize the new entity as a legitimate state, with all the rights and privileges that go with that peculiar status, should depend upon whether the group provides credible commitments to satisfying the appropriate normative criteria for recognition of new entities as legitimate states, in particular whether its constitution and other relevant documents (such as a declaration of independence) evidence a clear commitment to equal rights for all within their borders, including ethno-national minorities. Chapter 6 developed the case for such a normativized, conditional practice of recognition in some detail.

The rationale for separating the right to repudiate state control over a portion of the state's territory and to attempt to establish an independent state, on the one hand, and the right to legitimate statehood, on the other, is straightforward: The grounds of the two rights differ. The ground of the former right is that by persisting in grave injustices toward the group the state has voided its own claim to that part of its territory, and this makes it permissible for the group to repudiate the state's authority and to attempt to exert their own control over the territory with the ultimate goal of achieving recognition of statehood. By recognizing the right to secede understood in this weaker sense, as the right to attempt to form an independent state, the international community would do two things: empower oppressed groups to use separation as a means of self-defense against their oppressors, and at the same time withdraw support for the territorial integrity of the existing state on the grounds that the state has failed to satisfy the conditions upon which its rightful control of the territory depends.

The ground of the right to recognitional legitimacy, in contrast, is that the entity in question has satisfied appropriate justice-based criteria, those for which I argued in Chapter 6. By ascribing the right to be recognized as a legitimate state to a new political entity, the international legal order signals that it is ready to take its place in the system of states, discharging the functions that only states have and enjoying the rights, liberties, privileges, and immunities peculiar to states.

The point of distinguishing between the right to repudiate the state's control over the territory and to attempt to form a political unit that will be recognized as a state, on the one hand, and the right to be recognized as a state, on the other, is to make clear that there is a difference between (1) the conditions under which a group may defend itself against serious and persistent injustices by wresting control over a territory and in which other states should no longer recognize the oppressing state's right to that territory, and (2) the conditions that a new entity ought to satisfy if it is to be recognized as a legitimate state.

Marking this distinction in international law has a point. By distinguishing the right to secede from the right to recognition as a legitimate state and by making the recognition of the new entity as a legitimate state dependent upon its satisfaction of justice-based criteria, the international community would tie the practice of recognizing new states to what I argued in Part One should be a primary goal of the system, namely, justice—and thereby reduce the risk that the seceding group will escape oppression by the state only to become the oppressor of its own minorities.

The importance of the territorial claim

A state in the context of issues of secession is understood as a territorially based primary political unit. Thus, as Lea Brilmayer has rightly emphasized, every assertion of a right to secede includes a claim to territory.[4] Furthermore, the claim is to a portion of the territory of an existing state—a primary political unit that itself claims the territory to which the secessionist lays claim. From this it follows that to make a case that a group has a right to secede one must show that the group's claim to the territory in question is valid and therefore that it trumps or supercedes or negates the state's claim to that territory.

This simple point has large implications for evaluating rival theories of the right to secede. *Unless a theory can provide a plausible account of the validity of the claim to territory by those to whom it ascribes the right to secede, it fails.* I will argue in Section II that there is only one type of theory of the *unilateral* right to secede that can provide a convincing account of the territorial claim that is essential to secession—what I have elsewhere called a Remedial Right Only Theory.[5]

According to this type of theory the right to secede unilaterally, like the right to revolution, is a right to a remedy of last resort

---

[4] Brilmayer, 'Secession and Self-Determination'.
[5] Buchanan, 'Theories of Secession' and 'Recognitional Legitimacy and the State System'.

against serious and persistent injustices. These injustices must be of such consequence as to void international support for the state's claim to the territory in question.

Unilateral versus consensual or constitutional secession

The statement that international law only recognizes a right to secede in the case of classic decolonization and (perhaps) unjust military occupation applies only to the *unilateral* right to secede—that is, to the right of a group to attempt to establish a fully independent territorial political unit without state consent or any other form of negotiated or institutionally sanctioned process of separation. Nothing in international law prohibits—or should prohibit—negotiated agreements to allow secession between the state and the secessionists, as occurred with the secession of Norway from Sweden in 1905.

Nor does international law prohibit secession by constitutional provision. The latter could proceed in either of two ways: (1) by the exercise of an explicit constitutional right to secede (an example of which is included in the current Ethiopian Constitution), or (2) by a process of constitutional amendment (for example, as outlined by the Supreme Court of Canada in its recent Reference on Quebec Secession).[6]

The unilateral right is the right of a group to attempt to form its own independent territorial political unit and seek recognition as a legitimate state in a portion of the territory of an existing state absent consent or constitutional authorization; the consensual right to secede is generated by a process of negotiation or exercised in accordance with constitutional processes.

Some might argue that while international law only includes a unilateral right to secede in the two special circumstances of classic colonization and military occupation or annexation, it does not include any clear prohibition of secession either. They would assert that since what is not forbidden is permissible in international law, secession is permissible—that there is a Hohfeldian liberty-right (a mere permission) to secede for a group that seeks to do so.

However, one could argue that if it is true that in international law "what is not forbidden is permissible," this has traditionally

---

[6] *Reference re Secession of Quebec* 1998. 2 SCR.

applied only to the actions of states, not to nonstate groups and so is irrelevant to the question of whether secession is permissible, except perhaps in the case when secession is simply the taking back of unjustly taken state territory (as with the secession of the Baltic Republics from the U.S.S.R). In addition, one could argue that international law's long-standing emphasis on supporting the territorial integrity of existing states implies a strong presumption against the permissibility of unilateral secession in situations other than the two cases in which there is a legal claim-right (the cases of classic colonization and military occupation), or at least imposes obligations on third-party states not to aid secessionists, except in those two cases.

My aim is not to settle definitively this dispute about what the international law of secession is, but only to show that even the statement that international law does not prohibit secession is controversial. This uncertainty is only one indication of the inadequacy of international law regarding secession.

The flaws of the existing international law of secession

The most obvious deficiency of existing international law regarding unilateral secession is the apparent arbitrariness of the restriction to classic decolonization. Presumably what justifies secession by overseas colonies of a metropolitan power is that the colonized are subject to exploitation and unjust domination, not the fact that a body of salt water separates them and their oppressors. But if this is so, then the narrow scope of the existing legal right of self-determination is inappropriate. The existing right to secession as decolonization appears to be justice-based, yet the idea that serious injustices can justify secession points to a more expansive right.

Furthermore, international law provides little or no guidance for how the international community ought to respond to many, perhaps most, of the cases of secession that have occurred recently, are now occurring, or are likely to occur in the coming years—cases that do not involve decolonization in the classic sense. The secessions of Slovenia, Croatia, and Bosnia-Hercegovina from Yugoslavia are not addressed by the highly restrictive international legal right to secede, nor is that of Nagorno-Karabakh, or that of Chechnya, to take only a few examples among many.

The ambiguity or silence of international law concerning cases of secession other than those involving classic ("saltwater") decolonization (and perhaps unjust annexation or military occupation) is not merely a theoretical deficiency. It contributes to the human misery that almost always has attended secession, by failing to provide a defensible basis for institutional responses that would avoid or mitigate the violence of unconstrained secession.

As I noted in Chapter 1, the confused and ineffectual international response to the break-up of Yugoslavia and to the wars of Chechen secession shows not only a lack of political will but also an absence of consensus on principles. In the case of Yugoslavia the Western powers vacillated between proclaiming the conflict to be an internal dispute protected from intervention by the veil of Yugoslav state sovereignty and attempting to constrain what soon came to be seen as the inevitable process of disintegration by applying the international legal principle of *uti possidetis*, rather implausibly, to a situation quite different from that in which the principle had previously been recognized.

According to *uti possidetis*, borders are to remain intact, except where changed by mutual consent. This principle had been invoked to a limited extent in the processes of decolonization in South America and was later affirmed by the Organization of African Unity during the period of African decolonization in the 1960s and 1970s. In these contexts, *uti possidetis* prescribes that when colonial liberation occurs, the new states that emerge should take as their boundaries the pre-existing colonial boundaries, unless changes are made by mutual consent of contiguous former colonies.

In the case of Yugoslavia the principle was applied, not to boundaries of colonial states, but to the internal boundaries of a fully sovereign federation. (Elsewhere I have argued for a much more limited interpretation of *uti possidetis* and explained in detail the shortcomings of the recent application of the principle to the case of Yugoslavia.[7])

In the case of Chechnya, the most influential members of the international community have tended to proceed, without any credible justification, as if that conflict is an "internal matter," without

[7] Allen Buchanan, 'Secession, State Breakdown, and Intervention', in Deen Chatterjee and Donald Scheid (eds.), *The Ethics of Intervention* (Cambridge University Press, Cambridge, 2003).

explaining either why the internal boundary that encompasses Chechnya in the Russian Federation is so different from the boundaries of the seceding Yugoslav federal units or why the well-documented—and continuing—history of violent oppression of Chechnya by Russia is irrelevant to the evaluation of Chechen claims to independence. Furthermore, given that the distinction between Union Republics and Autonomous Republics of the former Soviet Union was drawn largely on instrumental grounds to further Soviet-Russian imperial interests, it would be difficult to argue that according to *uti possidetis* Union Republics such as Georgia had the right to secede but Autonomous Republics do not.

President Clinton plumbed the depths of confusion (assuming his statement was sincere) when he likened Yeltsin's suppression of Chechen secession to Lincoln's preservation of the Union. Such statements obscure the moral issues, failing to distinguish between secession by a colonized people with whom the colonial power had made and then broken a series of autonomy agreements (the Chechens) with the effort to suppress a secession undertaken at least in large part to preserve and extend the institution of slavery (the Southern secessionists).

The tendency of the United States and other Western Powers to take the line that the wars of Chechen secession are "internal matters" for Russia also glides over another important distinction regarding the international legal response to secession. It is one thing to assert that the Chechens have no right to secede; it is quite another to say that if they have no right to secede then the means by which Russia resists their secession are strictly an "internal matter," of no legitimate concern to the international community.

In my judgment a very strong case can be made that the pattern of colonial injustice and the violation of autonomy agreements confers on the Chechens a unilateral right to secede. But even if I am wrong about this there is ample evidence that Russia has violated international law by the brutal and indiscriminate means by which it has attempted to crush the secession. Although existing international law, as I have argued, fails to provide an adequate basis for a principled response to the question of whether a group should be accorded the unilateral right to secede, it does supply a substantial normative structure for controlling the character of secessionist conflicts, at least from the standpoint of the state's role in them.

Of course having a coherent and morally defensible *theory* of the unilateral right to secede would not be sufficient for a more effective and humane international legal response to crises of secession. But it may well prove necessary. For as I noted in Chapter 1, it is true that the international community lacked the political will to respond credibly to the Yugoslav and Chechen conflicts. However to rest content with the diagnosis of a failure of will is to overlook the role that principled belief can play in mobilizing political will. Coherent principles can contribute to constancy of will.

The status of intrastate autonomy in international law

Current international law also fails to provide coherent conceptual and institutional support for forms of self-determination short of full independence and for a principled way of ascertaining when more limited modes of self-determination are appropriate. Thus in her excellent systematic analysis of the range of alternative self-determination arrangements short of secession, Ruth Lapidoth concludes that "except for 'peoples' [in the international legal right of self-determination of peoples, which applies unambiguously only to classic colonial domination and perhaps military occupation], international law has not yet established a right to autonomy."[8]

This statement requires a significant qualification: In the field of indigenous peoples' rights (which Lapidoth explicitly excludes from her study), international law may be coming to recognize that various forms of intrastate autonomy are appropriate, and may even eventually acknowledge that in some cases some groups have an international legal right to them.[9]

However, even there, talk about "the" right to self-determination is profoundly misleading so far as it suggests a single, one-size-fits-all entitlement. Moreover, international law concerning indigenous peoples is very much in the formative stages and it is at present

---

[8] Ruth Lapidoth, *Autonomy: Flexible Solutions to Ethnic Conflicts* (United States Institute of Peace Press, Washington, DC, 1996), 177.

[9] Anaya, *Indigenous Peoples in International Law*; Benedict Kingsbury, 'Sovereignty and Inequality', *European Journal of International Law* 9 (1998), 599–625; and Douglas Sanders, 'The Re-emergence of Indigenous Questions in International Law', *Canadian Human Rights Yearbook* 3 (1983), 12–30.

unclear whether the rights of self-determination toward which it seems to be headed will have application beyond the special case of indigenous groups.

While there is a broad consensus that international law on self-determination (including secession) is deficient, there is much controversy as to how it should be improved. In this chapter I will argue that what at first might seem the obvious way to develop a more comprehensive international law on self-determination is not the proper remedy. The task is *not* to develop a more comprehensive international right to self-determination that would encompass the right to secede but also include an entitlement to intrastate autonomy if the right-holder chooses that less drastic option. Instead, a coherent, practical, and morally defensible international legal system would *uncouple* secession from other forms of autonomy and deny that recognition of a group's right to autonomy within the state entitles it to opt for full independence if it chooses.

Because there are so many possible forms of intrastate autonomy and such a variety of considerations that must be brought to bear to make a case that any particular group is entitled to any one of them, misleading talk of *the* right to autonomy and *the* right to self-determination should be avoided. A more theoretically perspicuous and politically efficacious discourse would feature a rather limited and exceptional right to secede while acknowledging that there are diverse legitimate interests in autonomy that can best be served in different circumstances by a correspondingly broad range of intrastate autonomy regimes.[10]

A strategy for developing the needed theory

In this chapter and the next I develop a way of rethinking the international law of self-determination (where the latter term covers both secession and various forms of intrastate autonomy).

[10] Henry Steiner, 'Ideals and Counter-Ideals in the Struggle over Autonomy Regimes for Minorities', *Notre Dame Law Review* 66 (1991), 1539–60, 1557; and Morton Halperin, David Sheffer, and Patricia Small, *Self-Determination in the New World Order* (Carnegie Endowment for International Peace, Washington, DC, 1992).

The core idea of the strategy is captured by the slogan "isolate and proliferate": Isolate a limited right to unilateral secession under- stood as a remedial right only—that is uncouple the unilateral right to the most extreme form of self-determination from the question of intrastate autonomy—and then proliferate the options for intrastate autonomy arrangements.

The strategy I am proposing also includes the uncoupling of the right to secede from nationality. To adopt the Remedial Right Only Theory of the unilateral right to secede is to reject the claim that nations as such have a right to secede.[11]

The core idea of my approach to self-determination is not novel.[12] However, others who have endorsed what I label the "isol- ate and proliferate" strategy have not systematically articulated its moral foundations; nor have they drawn its implications for inter- vention. My goal is to develop the "isolate and proliferate" strategy more systematically, integrating it with a justice-based conception of legitimacy, making a more explicit and persuasive case for a lim- ited unilateral right to secede, and arguing that in some cases inter- vention may be justified to support intrastate autonomy agreements as alternatives to secession and, in exceptional circumstances, to intervene to help sustain them.

The objective of Part Three of this book, then, is to develop the isolate and proliferate strategy in detail, grounding it in the justice- based theory of legitimacy developed in Parts I and II. The key to achieving this objective will be to refine the theory of a limited right to secede I first explored in *Secession* (1991), to argue for the superi- ority of the refined theory over several rival theories, and then to show that the international legal order ought to complement the constrained stance on unilateral secession that the Remedial Right

[11] Omar Dahbour also advocates the uncoupling of self-determination and nationality in his 'Self-Determination in Political Philosophy and International Law', *History of European Ideas* 16 (1993), 879–84.

[12] It is explored, to take a few examples, by Halperin, Sheffer, and Small in *Self- Determination in the New World Order*; by Lapidoth in *Autonomy*; by Hannum in *Autonomy, Sovereignty, and Self-Determination*; and by Christian Tomuschat, 'Self-Determination in a Post-Colonial World', in Christian Tomuschat (ed.), *Modern Law of Self-Determination* (M. Nijhoff Publishers, Dordrecht, 1993), 1–20. I also endorsed it many years ago in 'The Right to Self-Determination: Analytical and Moral Foundations', *Arizona Journal of International and Comparative Law* 8/2 (1991), 41–50.

Only Theory recommends with a much more permissive and supportive posture concerning intrastate autonomy agreements.

II. *A Justice-Based Theory of Secession*

Institutional moral reasoning

As I noted in Chapter 1, the proper way to determine what the international law of secession ought to be is to engage in holistic thinking about what sort of legal right to secede best harmonizes with the other main elements of a morally defensible international legal system. This approach is in stark contrast to that of those political philosophers who proceed by trying to determine the conditions under which a group has a right to secede by consulting "our moral intuitions" about particular hypothetical cases, abstracted from any institutional context, and without any connection to the idea of a law-governed practice of recognition that determines the status of new entities that emerge through secession.

Often such theorists attempt to develop a conception of the moral right to secede without taking institutional considerations into account at all and then simply say that existing institutions ought to be changed so as to embody the moral right to secede they recommend. Somewhat more sophisticated practitioners of this method of appealing to moral intuitions independently of institutional considerations acknowledge that the principles abstracted from moral intuitions evoked in response to isolated individual noninstitutional examples must then pass a feasibility test—it must be possible to incorporate them into the international legal order.[13]

This latter version of the noninstitutional approach is closer to the mark but still deficient. Whether a group has the right to its own state, or even the right to attempt to get its own state, must depend, *inter alia*, not only upon whether the right *could* be implemented, but also upon whether implementing it would be consonant with the proper goals of the system in which statehood is defined and in which the practice of recognizing entities as legitimate states takes place. A particular conception of the right to secede might be feasible, yet implementing it might detract from rather than enhance the

---

[13] One example is Moellendorf, *Cosmopolitan Justice*.

morally attractive features of the system. Such dissonance might occur, for example, if the proposed norm regarding secession interacted with existing norms to create incentives for states to act unjustly or which encouraged armed conflict. (I will argue later that this is the case with nationalist theories of secession, those that ascribe the unilateral right to secede to nations as such.)

The "moral right" theorist might reply that his conception of the right to secede *is* institutional: He or she is making a moral argument for including a certain conception of the unilateral right to secede in an *ideal* international legal order. The idea is that one first develops a theory of the ideal institutional right to secede that takes into account the proper goals of the system and then considers whether it would be feasible to implement it.

If this is what is meant by saying that we must first develop an account of the moral right to secede and then proceed to the question of what principles ought to be incorporated into international law, then pumping intuitions about individual cases abstracted from institutional considerations looks even less credible than before. Whether a particular principle specifying the right to secede for an ideal institutional order is defensible must depend upon how well that principle fits with the other principles that comprise the ideal theory. But to my knowledge, those who suggest that they are proposing a right to secede for ideal theory have not produced so much as a sizeable fragment of the larger set of principles of which the right to secede is to be a part.[14] Instead they have proceeded as if it is possible to give a freestanding theory of the right to secede.[15]

It is important not to misunderstand the nature of my criticism of what might be called the noninstitutional, moral right approach, the attempt to justify a principle specifying the right to secede without taking institutional considerations into account and without integrating the theory of secession with a more comprehensive moral theory of international law. I am not denying the distinction between ideal and nonideal theory. My point, rather, is that both ideal

---

[14] See e.g. Wellman, 'A Defense of Secession and Political Self-Determination'.

[15] Moellendorf in *Cosmopolitan Justice* offers principles for an ideal theory of global distributive justice, but he does not discuss principles of recognitional legitimacy; nor does he distinguish between the right to secede and the right to recognition as a legitimate state.

and nonideal theory must be institutional because the right to secede is inherently institutional (as I argued at length in Chapter 1).

A second potential misunderstanding is also worth noting. I am not denying that there is a distinction between the conditions under which a group is morally justified in attempting to throw off the state's control over the territory they occupy and to establish their own state, on the one hand, and what sort of principles regarding the right to secede ought to be incorporated into international law. In this volume I am interested in the latter, not the former.

One must acknowledge, of course, that here as in other cases, there can be a conflict between the way the law ought to be and what some individual or group is morally justified in doing in a particular case. Even the best law may not be wholly congruent with morality. Sadly, there can be times when there are conclusive moral reasons for enforcing a law that it would be morally justifiable for someone to break under exceptional circumstances.

Some philosophers writing about the right to secede disclaim any direct implications of their views for how international law ought to be. They would protest that they are providing only a theory of "the moral right to secede," leaving it open whether this moral right ought to be formulated as a legal right in the system. Call this the dualist position.

There are two problems with the dualist position. First, it is quite untrue to the actual political discourse of secession. When a group asserts the right to secede, it means by this that it at least has the right to attempt to form its own legitimate state, if not that it is entitled to its own legitimate state, and that, as I have just argued, is to make an institutional claim, and hence one that can only be evaluated by taking into account the proper goals of the system. Second, and more important, if the dualist denies that the moral concept of the right to secede he is working with has any institutional implications and hence that congruence with institutional goals is irrelevant to the justification for his characterization of that right, then we have no reason to think that the right as he conceives it is relevant to determining what the international law of secession should be. The more radically separate the justification of the alleged moral right to secede is from institutional considerations, the wider is the gap between that justification and support for any proposal concerning what the international legal right to secede should be.

To summarize the key methodological point: Whether a particular account of the right to secede is defensible will depend upon whether embodying its principles in the international legal order would, all things considered, promote the proper goals of the system. That is why an account of the right to secede, if it is to provide guidance for reforming international law, must be embedded in a more comprehensive moral theory of international legal institutions.

III. *Theories of Secession*

Criteria for evaluating rival theories

Before one tries to evaluate rival theories of the right to secede, one ought to be clear about what the criteria for comparative evaluation are. Surprisingly, discussion of the criteria for comparative evaluation of rival theories is largely absent in the existing normative literature on secession.

The following criteria appear to be the most crucial. Spelling them out makes even clearer the fact that a theory of the right to secede requires institutional moral reasoning.

1. First and foremost, as I have already noted, the theory must provide a cogent account of the territorial claim that is essential to assertions of the right to secede. Recall that, as Lea Brilmayer stresses, secession is not merely the repudiation of the state's political authority over a group of persons, nor merely the attempt to form a new political association among persons; it is the attempt to appropriate territory claimed by an existing state and to exercise the functions characteristic of states within that territory, with the implication that the state's claim to this territory is invalid. Accordingly, a theory of the right to secede must explain why those to whom it ascribes the right to secede have a valid claim to the territory in question, in spite of the fact that the state lays claim to the territory.

2. The theory ought to possess the virtue of "progressive conservatism." The principles it proposes ought, if implemented, to achieve an improvement of the existing system (ameliorating at least some of the more serious defects in the current system's conceptual and normative resources for responding to secessionist conflicts noted at the beginning of this chapter).

Other things being equal, if two rival theories each would achieve moral progress if implemented, but one is consistent with some of the best features of the existing system and the other is not, the former is preferable. The rationale for this criterion is that the overall moral theory of international law of which the theory of secession is to be a part should at least be coherent, and preferably should exhibit mutual justificatory support among its elements, and that the guiding goal of reform should be the overall improvement of the system.

3. The theory ought to possess the virtue of moral accessibility.[16] It is not enough that it is possible to implement the theory; it also should be possible to do so by means and transitional processes that do not involve unacceptable moral costs. This criterion was first articulated in Chapter 1 as a desideratum for moral theories of international law. It applies also to the components of such theories, including theories of the right to secede. For example, a theory of the right to secede whose principles could only be implemented at the price of violent changes in state boundaries with massive violations of human rights would not be acceptable. Of course, no substantive theory of the right to secede is likely to be free of moral costs, even when conscientiously implemented; but other things being equal, a theory whose implementation runs a lesser risk of human rights violations is a better theory.

4. The theory ought to possess the virtue of incentive compatibility, or at least should minimize perverse incentives. Implementation of the principles it recommends should not create perverse incentives— incentives to act in ways that are counter-productive either with regard to the goals the principles are supposed to promote or other important goals of the system into which the principles are to be incorporated. For example, a theory of the right to secede that ascribed to federal units the right to secede if a majority of their populations desired independence would create an incentive for the governments of centralized states to resist efforts at decentralization, fearing that they would be the first step toward disintegration.

Yet, not infrequently a strong case can be made for decentralization, either on grounds of efficiency, or as a means of achieving

---

[16] In 'Theories of Secession' I used the term 'moral accessibility' for what I now label moral convergence.

autonomy for groups within states, as a way of increasing participatory democracy, or for other reasons. Therefore, other things being equal, a theory whose implementation would create incentives to resist federalization is deficient. Similarly, if the implementation of a theory of the right to secede would tend to undermine the processes of deliberative democracy by introducing powerful incentives for strategic behavior on the part of citizens (unprincipled threats of "exit" by secession), then other things being equal, this is a strike against the theory.

5. The theory ought to possess the virtue of moral convergence. Other things being equal, a theory whose principles can be affirmed from the perspectives of a number of different existing ethical views, both secular and religious, is preferable. At least from the standpoint of nonideal theory for a system that currently lacks powerful enforcement mechanisms, there is much to be said for principles that can command voluntary allegiance. To use Rawls's terminology, it is a point in a theory's favor if it is the focus of a broad overlapping consensus.

In my judgment, this fifth principle should *not* be understood as a meta-ethical constraint on legitimacy, that is, as being based on the notion that it is morally justifiable to enforce only those principles that all upon whom they will be enforced could agree to from the standpoint of their own ethical views. I have already criticized the Rawlsian conception of tolerance that this meta-ethical view implies, in Chapter 3 (Human Rights). Instead, I understand the fifth theoretical virtue as a condition whose satisfaction contributes to compliance with the principles of a theory that satisfies it, on the assumption that likelihood of compliance is an important consideration in nonideal theory. Moral convergence is an especially compelling theoretical desideratum in a system in which widespread allegiance to the principles a theory proposes is crucial because there is no effective enforcement mechanism.

Two types of theories of the unilateral right to secede

Moral theories of secession can be divided into two main types: Remedial Right Only Theories and Primary Right Theories. The proponents of these rival types of theories do not always make it clear whether they are offered as accounts of (1) the conditions under which groups have a moral right to secede or of (2) the conditions under which international law ought to recognize a group as having a right to secede. (They also frequently fail to distinguish between the right to secede as the right to attempt to form an independent state and as the right to recognition as a legitimate state.)

My focus will be on (2), since my goal is to integrate an account of secession into a more comprehensive moral theory of how international law should be. I will also proceed on the assumption that these two theoretical approaches are accounts of the *unilateral* right to secede. (What international law should say, if anything, about negotiated or constitutional secession is another matter, with its own complexities, some of which I have addressed in other publications.[17]) My aim, then, is to evaluate Remedial Right Only and Primary Right Theories as accounts of how the international legal order ought to respond to attempts at (unilateral) secession, on the assumption that the principles these theories recommend are to be embedded in a system of principles constituting a comprehensive moral theory of international law.

Remedial Right Only Theories conceive of the right to secede as analogous to the right to revolution as understood in the mainstream of liberal political theory: as a remedy of last resort for persistent and grave injustices. Revolution aims at the overthrow of government; secession only at severing a portion of the state's territory from its control. What is common to Remedial Right Only Theories of the (unilateral) right to secede and the mainstream liberal position on the right to revolution is that in both cases the right only exists under conditions of serious, persisting injustices.

Different Remedial Right Only Theories provide different accounts of the sorts of injustices for which secession is the appropriate remedy of last resort. One major division along these lines is between Remedial Right Only Theories that recognize only (1) genocide or massive violations of the most basic individual human rights and (2) unjust annexation, as each being sufficient to generate a right to secede; and those that also recognize (3) the

---

[17] See Buchanan, *Secession*, 127–43; and Allen Buchanan, 'The Quebec Secession Issue: Democracy, Minority Rights, and the Rule of Law', a paper commissioned by the Privy Council, Government of Canada (1998), repr. in Stephen Macedo and Allen Buchanan (eds.), *Self-Determination and Secession*, Nomos XLV (New York University Press, New York, 2003).

state's persistence in violations of intrastate autonomy agreements. The type of Remedial Right Only Theory I will advance includes (3) as well as (1) and (2), thereby correcting what I now take to be a serious flaw in the theory of the right to secede I advanced in *Secession*, which failed to recognize (3).

It is important to note that Remedial Right Only Theories only concern the conditions under which there should be an international legal right to *unilateral* secession. They are compatible with the view that international law should take an entirely permissive stance toward negotiated or constitutional secession. For this reason, Remedial Right Only Theories are not as conservative as they might first appear. Furthermore, understood as proposals for reforming international law, rather than as comprehensive moral theories of secession, Remedial Right Only Theories do not rule out the possibility that there may be some cases in which a group would be morally justified in seceding even if its doing so would violate the international legal rule they recommend. As I observed earlier, even the best laws may not achieve a complete congruence between the legal and the moral. Nevertheless, for reasons that will become clear below, I believe that the Remedial Right Only approach to the international law of secession is highly congruent with the morality of secession; and this is a point in its favor.

Primary Right Theories, in contrast, have a more permissive view about what international law should say about (unilateral) secession. They reject the thesis that international law should only recognize the (unilateral) right to secede as a remedy of last resort for persisting, serious injustices. The term "Primary Right" is appropriate to signal that these theories recognize a right to secede that is not remedial and hence not derivative upon the rights whose violation its exercise is supposed to remedy.

Primary Right Theories divide into two main types: Ascriptivist (Nationalist) Theories and Plebiscitary Theories. The former hold that certain groups whose memberships are defined by what are sometimes called ascriptive characteristics should have the (unilateral) international legal right to secede, simply because they are such groups, independently of whether they have suffered any injustices. Ascriptive characteristics include being of the same nation or ethnicity or being a "distinct people". (Such characteristics are called 'ascriptive' because they are ascribed to individuals independently of their choice.) The most common form of Ascriptive Theory is the view that *nations* should be recognized under international law as having a right of self-determination that includes the (unilateral) right to secede. Accordingly, my criticism of Ascriptive Right Theories will focus on what might be called the nationalist theory of the unilateral right to secede.

In contrast, Plebiscitary (also called voluntarist or associative-group) Theories assert that international law should recognize a (unilateral) right to secede where a majority of persons residing in a portion of a state's territory wish to form their own state there, regardless of whether the secessionist group's members are united by any characteristics other than the desire for independence. On this view, the secessionists need not be a nation or ethnic group (or be members of a "distinct society" or people or cultural community).

What Ascriptivist and Plebiscitary Theories have in common is that they do not *require* injustice of any sort, much less large-scale and persistent basic injustices, as a necessary condition for the (unilateral) right to secede. However, both types of Primary Right Theories *allow* the possibility that injustice justifies (unilateral) secession as well. Primary Right Theories, then, are not Primary Right *Only* Theories; they allow secession as a remedy, but hold that it can be justified on nonremedial grounds as well.

Remedial Right Only Theories

In *Secession* (1991) I argued for a fairly simple version of Remedial Right Only Theory, one that primarily recognized two sorts of injustices as being sufficient to generate a (unilateral) right to secede: (1) large-scale and persistent violations of basic individual human rights, and (2) unjust taking of a legitimate state's territory.

Injustice of type (2) is illustrated by the case of the Baltic Republics' secession from the Soviet Union. Lithuania, Latvia, and Estonia were independent states, recognized as such in international law when the Soviet Union forcibly annexed them in 1940. An example of injustice (1) is the massive human rights violations suffered by the population of East Pakistan, for which the secession of East Pakistan in 1971 to become the independent state of Bangladesh can be seen as a justifiable remedy.

I will not rehearse in detail the arguments I have advanced elsewhere for including (1) as a sufficient ground for international legal acknowledgment of a group's (unilateral) right to secede.[18] Granted the justice-based theory of political legitimacy developed in Chapter 5, the central idea is simple: Individuals are morally justified in defending themselves against violations of their most basic human rights. When the only alternative to continuing to suffer these injustices is secession, the right of the victims to defend themselves voids the state's claim to the territory and this makes it morally permissible for them to join together to secede. This is not surprising, given that the basis of the state's claim to territory in the first place is the provision of justice, understood primarily as the protection of basic human rights.

States and governments

One clarifying point should be added to this basic argument, however. The Remedial Right Only Theory I am advocating takes seriously the distinction between the state, the government, and the people.[19] The state, as I noted in Chapters 5 and 6, is the persisting structure of institutions through which the people, the ultimate sovereign, exercise their will. The government is composed of persons who occupy certain roles in that structure and whose duty it is to serve as the agents of the people.

Suppose that a state is legitimate according to the justice-based criteria I articulated in Chapter 6. The problem is not that the constitution (written or unwritten) denies the rights of a certain portion of the citizenry. Instead the difficulty lies with the behavior of the government. If a government persists in violating the fundamental rights of a group of citizens living in a portion of the state's territory, then that group has the right to secede, as a remedy of last resort against these injustices. But this does not mean that the government's unjust behavior voids the state's (more accurately the people's) claim to the *rest* of its territory.

---

[18] Buchanan, 'Theories of Secession'.

[19] I am indebted to David Golove for making the importance of this point clearer to me.

This way of understanding the basis of the secessionists' claim to territory is attractive because it avoids the unacceptable implication that a bad *government's* actions are sufficient to undermine the legitimacy of the *state*. Such a view is implausible because it would impose an unjust penalty on the people of the state as a whole—especially when they oppose the government's unjust policies.

When a group secedes in circumstance (1), where the government persists in inflicting violations of basic individual human rights upon it, the people as a whole do lose a portion of the territory that had been theirs; but this loss is justified on the grounds that in choosing secession as a last-resort remedy against these injustices the secessionists are exercising a fundamental right of self-defense. The intuitive idea is that it is fairer for the people of a state whose government is persisting in profound injustices toward a subset of the people to lose part of their territory than for the victims to be barred from availing themselves of the only remedy they have for persistent and grave violations of their basic human rights. Yet the right of the injured group to avail themselves of this remedy does not affect the state's claim to the remainder of its territory.

Secession as the recovery of unjustly taken sovereign territory

At first blush the argument for including condition (2) among the sufficient conditions for a group having the (unilateral) right to secede seems even more straightforward. The secessionists are simply taking back what was lawfully theirs, rectifying the injustice of the wrongful taking of what international law recognized as their territory. For this reason many found the secession of the Baltic Republics from the Soviet Union in 1991 to be the paradigm of a just secession, the Soviet Union having unjustly annexed those states in 1940.

Note, however, that from the standpoint of a human rights-based conception of state legitimacy, the case for including unjust annexation as a ground for the unilateral right to secede is not quite so straightforward as that for including massive violations of human rights.[20] Of course unjust annexations usually involve massive

---

[20] I am grateful to Andrew Valls for pointing this out to me.

violations of basic human rights, as when those whose territory is annexed are killed or suffer violations of their civil and political rights in the process of conquest. But why should unjust annexation in itself be regarded as a ground for acknowledging a unilateral right to secede in international law?

The most obvious answer is that international legal recognition of a right to secede in order to reclaim unjustly annexed territory would serve as a deterrent to unjust annexations and would to that extent reinforce the existing international legal restrictions on the aggressive use of force by states. And there are a number of considerations that speak in favor of limiting the aggressive use of force.

One has already been noted: Aggression typically involves violations of basic human rights. In addition, at least in a system in which the existence of states is taken as a provisional given, the citizens of legitimate states ought to be regarded, at least with a very strong presumption, as being entitled to govern themselves. Hence international law should protect them against violations of their right to self-government. One way to do this is to acknowledge an international legal right to secede to reclaim unjustly annexed territory, both to deter violations of their right of self-government and to empower the remedy of self-help when that right is violated.

Condition (2) becomes more problematic, or at least more complicated, when two questions are considered. First, was the sovereignty of the entity in question disputable at the time it was forcibly annexed? If so, then the claim of the secessionists that they are simply taking back what was theirs is to that extent also disputable. This problem is exacerbated if there is no authoritative international court with compulsory jurisdiction to settle such disputes. Thus to be fully effective an international legal principle recognizing unjust annexation as a sufficient condition for a group coming to have the right to secede would need to be accompanied by an authoritative procedure for adjudicating disputes about whether the territory taken belonged to a legitimate state. Here we have only one example of a more general point: Proposals for legal reform should include not only proposals for principles, but also for the institutions needed to make them practicable. Admirable principles, if they lack appropriate institutional support, may be ineffective or even counter-productive.

Second, do legitimate interests in the stability of the state system argue for a statute of limitations on unjust takings of territory?

Some international legal theorists have suggested, for example, that since aggressive war, including wars of territorial conquest, was not unambiguously prohibited by international law until 1945 (some would say 1928),[21] it would be reasonable to treat unjust annexations before and after that date differently. Both stability and the principle of avoiding retroactive laws would speak in favor of some such statute of limitations.

Here it is important to note that the only alternatives are not an open-ended principle that might justify secession by present-day descendants of peoples whose territories were forcibly annexed hundreds of years ago or utterly ignoring all claims against unjust annexations that occur before some particular recent date such as 1945, including those that occurred just before that date. A third, more reasonable alternative is a principle that recognizes a statute of limitations (perhaps taking 1945 as a presumptive cut-off point for claims) but allows principled exceptions to it, to be identified by an appropriately constituted international legal body.

Violations of intrastate autonomy as a ground for secession

I now wish to expand the Remedial Right Only Theory to include a third set of conditions under which international law ought to recognize a (unilateral) right to secede: (3) serious and persisting violations of intrastate autonomy agreements by the state, as determined by a suitable international monitoring inquiry. Condition (3) is suggested by reflections on the case of Chechnya, but many other similar cases as well. Consider the brutal secessionist conflicts that have occurred in Sudan, Eritrea, the Kurdish region of northern Iraq, and Kosovo. What these otherwise disparate cases have in common is the following sequence of events: Pressures from a minority group eventually result in the state agreeing to an intrastate autonomy arrangement; the state breaks the agreement; in response to the broken autonomy agreement autonomists become secessionists; and then the state violently attempts to suppress the secession.

The response of the international community to this familiar pattern has been sorely inadequate. Only when the breakdown of an

---

[21] See the Kellogg–Briand Treaty [Internet, http://www.yale.edu/lawweb/avalon/imt/kbpact.htm]

autonomy agreement has already occurred, and the dynamic of secessionist and counter-secessionist violence has produced massive violations of human rights, have there been serious attempts to intervene, and then to intervene militarily.

The time is ripe for serious consideration of a more proactive approach. As a key element of what I have called the "isolate and proliferate" strategy, the international community should (1) help broker intrastate autonomy agreements as an alternative to secession, (2) monitor both parties' compliance with such agreements, (3) support the agreements' viability by holding both parties accountable for fulfilling their obligations, and (4) provide an impartial tribunal for adjudicating disputes over whether either or both parties have failed to fulfill their obligations.

The case of Kosovo dramatically illustrates the relevance of the fourth condition. There is no doubt that Serbia, under Milošović's leadership, unilaterally revoked Kosovo's autonomy in 1989. But there is dispute about who violated the terms of the autonomy agreement first. According to those who supported the revocation of autonomy, the Kosovar Albanians had abused their right of autonomy, by using the Kosovar Communist Party as a corrupt patronage system that excluded Serbs and by engaging in violent attacks on Serbs.

Whether a group that escalates its demands from autonomy to independence, as the Kosovar Albanians did, has a valid claim to attempt to set up its own state is a complex matter. But one factor relevant to the evaluation is whether they sabotaged a legitimate autonomy agreement or were victims of the state's destruction of it. Unless the international community is willing to press for serious monitoring of intrastate autonomy arrangements, at least in cases where the risk of a breakdown of the agreement is significant, it would be irresponsible to hold states accountable for continuing to recognize a group's rights of intrastate autonomy regardless of how those rights are being exercised. Furthermore, states are unlikely to enter into autonomy agreements if they believe they will suffer international censure or intervention if they rescind the agreement, regardless of whether the group that is granted rights of self-government violates the terms of the agreement.

I wish to emphasize that I am not recommending that international law should at this time acknowledge a unilateral right to secede when the state has seriously and persistently violated an intrastate autonomy agreement. I am advocating that such a legal right be recognized if two other conditions are satisfied: There has been a formal international legal determination (1) that the state is responsible for the breakdown of the autonomy arrangement and (2) that secession is the remedy of last resort. At present there is no international institutional mechanism for satisfying either condition, though there may be existing institutional structures, such as the Committee of Twenty-Four of the United Nations, that could be adapted to perform these functions.

Institutionalizing the remedial right to secede

There is much to be said for requiring some such impartial international adjudicative procedure for any exercise of the right to secede on remedial grounds, not just for cases where there has been a serious violation of an intrastate autonomy agreement. Requiring a group to make a convincing case to an impartial international body that the conditions for a remedial right to secede are satisfied would serve several purposes. First, it would reduce the risk of groups attempting unilateral secession when the conditions for their having a remedial right are not in fact satisfied. Second, and of equal importance, by erecting a hurdle that must be cleared before there is international legal recognition of a unilateral right to secede, this procedural requirement would reduce the risk that groups will resort to secession too quickly, instead of making a sincere effort to gain redress for their grievances while remaining within the state.

Suppose, for example, that a minority group G within state S has recently suffered grievances of the sort that ordinarily would justify unilateral secession, but that there has just been a fundamental change of regime in S, so that G now has an opportunity for full participation in governance and good prospects for making its case for redress of its grievances. Under these circumstances, there is a need for some mechanism to give the members of G an incentive to try to work things out—to cooperate to create conditions in which it is no longer true that their only remedy for injustice is secession—rather than to invoke the unilateral right to secede. The requirement of adjudication of grievances by an impartial international body is one such mechanism. Institutionalizing the right to secede in this way would also help counter the charge that permitting secession undermines deliberative democracy by making exit too easy.

Requiring a minority group to make its case for a remedial right to secede to the state that they view as the author of the injustices they seek to remedy is unreasonable; expecting them to make their case to an impartial international body is not. Even if the unilateral right to secede is to be a "self-help" device, international society has a legitimate interest in imposing some constraints on the recourse to self-help here as elsewhere.

Getting the incentives right

Essential to the "isolate and proliferate" approach, as I have already noted, is the uncoupling of secession from other, less drastic forms of self-determination. States will be reluctant to enter into intrastate autonomy agreements if they fear that by so doing they are implicitly recognizing a right to secede on the part of the group in question. Discontent minority groups will be equally unlikely to find the rather constrained Remedial Right Only approach to unilateral secession acceptable unless they are assured that by forgoing claims to independence except in cases of serious and persistent injustices they will gain meaningful forms of self-determination short of full independence. Thus the "isolate and proliferate" strategy is designed to create the right incentives for both parties, by assuring the state that so long as it avoids major injustices it will retain international support for its full territorial integrity, and by assuring potential secessionists that by relinquishing claims to full independence they will increase their prospects of gaining significant forms of self-determination through a peaceful process in which the international community both facilitates, and protects the integrity of, intrastate autonomy agreements.

The problem of the permanent minority

There is a fourth condition that arguably can justify unilateral secession as a last resort: the situation in which a group finds itself a permanent minority on fundamental issues of value within the proper scope of democratic decision-making.

To clarify the problem, a highly idealized hypothetical situation will be useful. Suppose that state S is thoroughly democratic, indeed more democratic than any existing state, and that the members of minority group G within it do not suffer discrimination or violations of other human rights. Each citizen, including all the citizens of group G, has the right to vote on every major legislative proposal, and each has the right to run for office. Suppose in addition that the members of group G suffer no unjust disadvantages in the distribution of resources for political discourse (access to the media, etc.), and the democratic process is entirely free of fraud and corruption, and that whatever differences there are in wealth in the society do not significantly influence the outcome of elections or legislation.

G, a minority, is free to attempt to change the majority's mind, enjoying not only rigorous legal protections for free speech but also special accommodations in public forums to ensure that its views are heard. But suppose that nevertheless the members of group G have good reason to believe that they will continue to be outvoted on matters of fundamental importance.

The situation under scrutiny is not one in which the majority is violating the minority's human rights or reneging on agreements that accord them autonomy within the state. Nonetheless, the minority group has a complaint that is not easily dismissed. They can argue that the same fundamental principle that requires democracy in the first place, the principle that all are to be accorded equal regard, is being violated in their case, because in fact they do not participate as equals in any meaningful sense in the processes for determining the fundamental rules of public order, even if they are formally equal citizens. The fact that the outcome of votes on fundamental issues can be reliably predicted without waiting to count votes shows that they do not in fact have "an equal say."

It is difficult to evaluate this objection. To be compelling it must be restricted to the case of a permanent minority regarding *fundamental* issues of value within the proper democratic decision-making. For surely it would be wrong to say that the mere fact that a group is a permanent minority on any issue, no matter how inconsequential, generates a unilateral right to secede.

The difficulty lies in articulating what counts as a fundamental issue—and who is to judge it to be so. Proposals for what counts as an objective standard of importance are likely to be hotly disputed and it seems equally wrong to allow what counts as fundamental to be decided by the majority or by the minority. This much seems clear, however: A minority's preference for having its own state should not itself count as a disagreement on fundamental issues of value.

The "isolate and proliferate" approach recommends an initial response to the problem: Create an intrastate autonomy arrangement that gives the minority more influence over the fundamental issues in question. This approach was in fact followed in Canada: In an effort to block its secession, Canada granted Quebec special powers of self-government not enjoyed by other provinces. Suppose, however, that for one reason or another this response is not feasible. What then is the proper response to the complaints of the permanent minority?

Perhaps the best reply to the permanent minority argument would run as follows. It is unrealistic to think that democracy can function in such a way that no group will ever be a permanent minority on any issue of importance. If democracy operates within its proper scope—constrained by entrenched individual rights and in such a way as to honor the terms of intrastate autonomy agreements with minorities—and if special accommodations are made to provide resources with which minorities can attempt to persuade the majority to change its mind, then it does not violate the minority's rights to expect them either to accept their situation or to limit their efforts to *consensual* secession. To think otherwise is to expect too much of democracy and too little of citizens. This conclusion is strengthened once it is admitted that secession may create new permanent minorities.

Some may think this rejection of the permanent minority condition as a justification for unilateral secession too harsh. Here perhaps theory can borrow from practice, to mitigate this concern. In 1998 the Canadian Supreme Court issued a "Reference" on the question of Quebec secession. It concluded that although Quebec does not have a right to secede (because it does not satisfy the conditions for what I have called a remedial right to secede and does not have a constitutional right to secede), nevertheless the Canadian government has an obligation to enter into negotiations over possible secession, if a "clear" majority in Quebec votes in favor of secession in response to a "clear" referendum question on secession.

It is true that the Court does not state or imply that Quebecois (or the majority of Quebecois) are a permanent minority on any issue of importance other than that of whether Quebec should be independent. Nevertheless, let us assume *arguendo* that there are fundamental issues other than that of independence on which the majority of Quebecois are a permanent minority within the Canadian state. The virtue of the Court's position is that it enjoys the attractions of a Remedial Right Only Theory by stopping short of according a unilateral right to secede for a permanent minority, but at the same time captures the idea that the majority ought to take seriously the desire of a permanent minority to have its own state. Note that the Canadian Supreme Court held only that the Canadian government had an obligation to enter into negotiations if a clear majority in Quebec voted in favor of secession in response to a clearly worded referendum question, not that the Canadian government had an obligation to allow Quebec secession under those circumstances.

It may well be the case, as the Canadian Court suggested, that a state is morally required to enter into negotiations concerning the possibility of secession in the case of a permanent minority on fundamental issues of value, and that the ultimate ground of this obligation is the same commitment to equality in the political sphere that justifies democratic government. However, it is another question whether the international legal order should recognize a right to unilateral secession for such minorities.

My sense is that the difficulties of forging reasonable agreement on what counts as fundamental issues of value makes the proposal for international legal recognition of such a unilateral right to secede unworkable. Reformist zeal would be better directed toward (1) supporting secessionists who are victims of clear and persisting injustices, by (2) pressuring states to protect the individual rights of members of minority groups to reduce the probability that secession will become an issue, (3) helping to ensure that the views of minority groups are effectively represented in public deliberations, (4) supporting intrastate autonomy regimes, and (5) providing assistance, including non-binding arbitration for a process of consensual secession by permanent minorities. I conclude, then, that the predicament of being a permanent minority should not in itself—in the absence of unambiguous injustices—count in international law as a justification for unilateral secession.

Conscientious secession

So far I have suggested that there are three types of injustices that international law should regard as grounds for recognizing a unilateral right to secede: (1) large-scale, persistent violations of basic human rights, (2) unjust annexation of the territory of a legitimate state, and (3) states' persistent, serious, and unprovoked violations of intrastate autonomy agreements. I have taken a more cautious view as to whether international law should recognize a unilateral right to secede for permanent minorities.

Two cases, one historical, one contemporary, suggest that there is yet another type of injustice worth considering as a ground for unilateral secession. In the second decade of the nineteenth century a faction of the American abolitionist movement, the Garrisonians, endorsed the slogan "No union with slavery." They believed slavery to be such a great evil that it was morally wrong to remain within a political entity that recognized its legality and actively supported the institution by enforcing the rights of slaveholders. Instead of arguing that they had the right to secede because *they* were the victims of injustices, the abolitionist secessionists argued that they had the right to secede to avoid complicity in gross injustices committed against *others*. Call this "conscientious secession."²²

Consider next a possible contemporary example of conscientious secession. Some Montenegrins expressed dismay at the policies of Slobodan Milošović. Enthusiasm for Montenegrin secession from Yugoslavia may have been based primarily on prudential considerations—in particular, the fact that Montenegrins were suffering from sanctions imposed on Yugoslavia as a result of Milošović's actions. But it is not inconceivable that a significant number of Montenegrins wanted to separate for more principled reasons.

At least at the time of this writing, the impetus for Montenegrin secession appears to have been diminished by the removal of Milošović from power and the negotiation of a looser association between Serbia and Montenegro. However, suppose that Milošović

---

²² The idea that the Northern states should secede also had strategic appeal to those who wished to extinguish slavery, because it was believed that the institution would be undermined by massive flights of slaves from Southern states across the new international border to an independent state that would not recognize the rights of their masters to recover them.

had not capitulated in the face of the NATO bombing campaign in the spring of 1999 and that NATO's intervention had escalated to include a ground war. Suppose that at that point Montenegro had seceded. Or suppose that at an earlier point, in moral revulsion to Serbian ethnic cleansing of Kosovar Albanians, Montenegro had seceded. In either case, it seems that Montenegrins would have had a strong moral case for unilateral secession from Yugoslavia on the grounds that the latter was engaged in a persistent pattern of gross human rights violations in which they refused to be complicitous.

This additional type of justification for a right to secede, "conscientious secession," has considerable moral appeal. It represents an expansion of the Remedial Right Only Theory I have hitherto endorsed. However, it is very much in the spirit of the Remedial Theory and of the justice-based theory of legitimacy upon which the latter rests. What "conscientious secession" has in common with secession as a remedy of last resort against persistent large-scale violations of the human rights of the secessionists and against the unjust taking of territory is the idea that by violating important rights a government can lose legitimacy and weaken the claims of the state to a part of its territory.

Should a morally enlightened international legal order recognize a right to "conscientious secession"? One might argue that the appeal to such a right is more likely to be abused than in the case of a remedial right that is restricted to the first two types of injustices (persistent large-scale violations of the basic human rights of secessionists and unjust annexation of the territory of legitimate states). The worry is that some group within a state might use the pretext of violations of the rights of others as a cover for secession that really was undertaken for altogether different reasons. There is also the concern that a group might be too ready to secede on the grounds that the government was oppressing another group rather than investing in attempting to change the government's policy.

Whether or not international law ought to recognize a unilateral right to "conscientious secession" is a difficult issue. Even if the answer is negative, one can still imagine cases where a morally sensitive international community would in effect make an exception to the law and not penalize a unilateral secession that was undertaken as a last-resort strategy for a group to dissociate itself from an evil state.

In other words, the reasonable approach might be for the international community to recognize a liberty-right, but not a claim-right to conscientious secession, either formally through a modification of the international law of secession or informally, by simply not supporting the state's claim to preserve its territorial integrity.[23] My inclination is to conclude that this approach is preferable to attempting to create an international legal right to conscientious secession.

Failed states and sauve qui peut separation

I now want to introduce a distinction that I and many others have tended to neglect: the distinction between separation from a functioning state and the attempt to form a new state in a situation of state breakdown, where there is no functioning state.

The contrast between the secession of Slovenia and Croatia from Yugoslavia and the possible secession of Quebec from Canada illustrates the distinction. At the time Slovenia and Croatia declared their independence, the constitutional order in Yugoslavia was already dissolving—Yugoslavia broke down before it broke up. Key constitutional processes, including the rotation of the Federal Presidency, had ceased to function. Increasingly there was good reason to believe that the delicate system of checks and balances to reduce the threat of discrimination against minorities was no longer reliable.

In short, the breakdown of the constitutional order created a situation of radical insecurity in which people understandably feared that their most basic rights, as individuals and as members of ethno-national groups, were imperiled. In these circumstances, secession by Slovenia and Croatia could perhaps be seen as an act of self-defense—what I shall call *sauve qui peut* separatism.[24]

Some might argue, however, that Yugoslavia was still a functioning state—though an impaired one—when Croatia and Slovenia declared their independence. (In fact some argue that Slovenia deliberately took actions aimed at undermining Yugoslavia's ability to function.)

---

[23] I am grateful to Russell Shafer-Landau for clarifying this option.

[24] The next paragraphs draw on Buchanan, 'Secession, State Break-Down, and Intervention'.

If the examples of Croatia and Slovenia seem less than fully persuasive, consider the current state breakdown in the Democratic Republic of Congo. *Sauve qui peut* separation may well prove to be a reasonable last-resort exercise of the right of self-defense for any of several regions in this failed, violently chaotic state.

I choose the term 'separatism' here to signal that the attempt to form a new political entity capable of protecting one's rights under conditions in which one can no longer rely on the previous political order is quite different—normatively speaking—from what ordinarily goes under the heading of 'secession'. The latter term is usually employed to characterize breaking away from a functioning state.

In an international system in which no third party can be relied on to shore up the disintegrating state in a way that gives credible assurance that basic rights will be protected, attempting to form a new state in a portion of the territory may be a reasonable strategy. Morally speaking, self-defensive or *sauve qui peut* secession seems justifiable under conditions of state breakdown in an international legal system that is still to a large extent better able to authorize self-help than to provide aid to failing states.

In contrast, consider the possible secession of Quebec. Canada is a functioning state, and one that does an exemplary job of protecting individual and minority rights. Here, unlike the Yugoslav case, it would be implausible to appeal to self-defense as a justification for separation.

With only minor modification, a Remedial Right Only Theory can properly recognize the normative force of the distinction between secession from a functioning state and *sauve qui peut* separation under conditions of state breakdown. According to the Remedial Right Only Theory, secession from a basic rights-protecting state is not justified (absent agreement or constitutional process), but is justified as a remedy of last resort for violations of basic rights. Such a theory can be extended to justify *sauve qui peut* separation by adding the principle that where there is no functioning state, and a situation of radical uncertainty exists in which basic rights are seriously at risk, groups are justified in attempting to form their own states in order to protect their basic human rights. This addendum coheres with the fundamental idea of a Remedial Right Only Theory: that unilateral secession from a rights-respecting state is not permissible and that only the need to protect basic rights can justify something so radical as unilateral secession.

Elaborating this addendum would require articulating an account of the scope and limits of the right of self-defense. Presumably a group's right to form its own state as a means of self-defense is a limited right, just as the individual's right of self-defense is. (For example, generally speaking, I am not permitted to infringe the basic rights of innocent persons in order to defend myself from attacks by others. Similarly, I cannot claim that I acted in self-defense in killing another person if I provoked him to attack me.) Here I can only issue a promissory note that such elaboration could be successfully achieved, but the central point is this: the fact that determining the limits of the right of self-defense is a complex and disputed matter does not show that there is no right of self-defense, either for individuals or for groups. It only shows that the right is qualified.

I have just argued that there is a strong moral case for saying that a group can be morally justified in trying to set up a new state in a portion of the territory of a failed state. But whether, and if so under what conditions, a group's right to attempt to set up a new state in the portion of the territory of a failed state should be recognized in international law is a vexing question.

One difficulty is that recognizing such a right would provide an incentive for a scramble to capture resources. To revert to the example of Congo again: the best prospects for establishing a viable state would presumably lie in the portion of that country that holds the greatest mineral wealth. International support for a new state in that territory presumably would make it even more difficult for a regime of law and order to emerge in the portion of the state that remained.

Even worse, those in a richer portion of the state might help create state failure in order to have a legally recognized justification for what is really a secession of the haves from the have-nots. (In fact some Serbs accuse Slovenian leaders of doing precisely that.) In Chapter 4 I emphasized that in a world in which the only thing approaching an effective agent of distributive justice is the individual state, international legal rules regarding separation should not generate incentives that undermine what little distributive justice there is.

There is, then, a dilemma. On the one hand, under conditions of violent anarchy it seems justifiable for those living in a portion of the territory of a failed state to seek to establish a haven in which their basic human rights are respected; so it seems excessive to demand that they choose instead the much more risky or even impossible task of creating a rights-respecting regime in the full extent of the failed state's territory. On the other hand, international legal recognition of a right of *sauve qui peut* separation runs the risk of worsening the problems of state failure, both by encouraging the sabotage of functioning states by people in resource-rich regions who prefer not to share the wealth and by allowing groups who happen to be in wealthier regions to deprive their fellow citizens of resources that are needed to rebuild failed states.

The problem of *sauve qui peut* separatism deserves more extensive consideration as only one element of a principled approach to a wider range of problems that arise when states fail. In particular, there is the need for an examination of the morality and feasibility of the long-term interventions that would be needed to help rebuild shattered states, and this would require a moral theory of international legal stewardship regimes.

Any attempt to draw even the broad outlines of such a theory lies beyond the scope of this book. Here I can only suggest that as in the case of conscientious secession the options are not limited to either recognizing a claim-right or condemning. For now, in the absence of anything approaching an adequate international response to state failure, the most reasonable course may be to stop short of recognizing an international legal claim-right to *sauve qui peut* separation, while remaining open to the possibility that in some cases the international legal community should tacitly endorse efforts to make new states from fragments of states by turning a deaf ear to the governments of failed states when they claim a right of territorial integrity that can no longer reasonably be ascribed to them.

Strengths of the Remedial Right Only approach

Now that the main outlines of the Remedial Right Only approach have been drawn, its attractions can be reviewed. Perhaps the most obvious virtue of the Remedial Right Only Theory is that it accords with the intuition that unilateral secession, like revolution, is a very serious matter, requiring the most weighty justification. Given the tendency of secession to provoke massive violence and cause severe political instability, the strength of the Remedial Right Only approach is that it recognizes the gravity of the matter by placing a significant constraint on unilateral secession: The international legal system should recognize a unilateral right to secede only when independence is the remedy of last resort against serious, persisting injustices.

A second and at least equally important virtue of the Remedial Right Only approach is that it provides a straightforward and compelling account of the claim to territory that is essential to secessionist demands. According to the justice-based theory of legitimacy on which the Remedial Right Only Theory is grounded, a state's claim to territory can be voided by a persisting pattern of serious injustices, because it is the provision of justice that justifies state power in the first place.

Third, the Remedial Right Only Theory gets the incentives right. On the one hand, states that protect basic human rights and honor autonomy agreements are immune to legally sanctioned unilateral secession and entitled to international support for maintaining the full extent of their territorial integrity. On the other hand, if, as the theory prescribes, international law recognizes a unilateral right to secede as a remedy for serious and persisting injustices, states will have an incentive to act more justly. The incentives for just behavior will be strongest if the remedial right to secede is understood to coexist with a right to recognition on condition that the normative criteria for legitimacy are satisfied—in other words, if recognition is not left, as it now is, to the discretion of states.

The Remedial Right Only Theory also appears to score high on the desiderata of moral progressivity, progressive conservatism, and moral accessibility. Its incorporation into international law would reduce the risk that responses to secessionist crises would exhibit the vacillation and inconsistency that characterized the international community's response to the dissolution of Yugoslavia, and this would surely count as moral progress. And, as I have already noted, the incentives its institutionalization would create would exert pressure on states to improve their behavior. So the theory has the virtue of moral progressiveness.

Although institutionalizing the theory would require changes in international law, they would be changes that build on the most progressive constituent of the existing system, the evolving law of human rights. Tying recognitional legitimacy and the right to territorial integrity to the protection of human rights would strengthen the system's commitment to the latter. To that extent the Remedial Right Only Theory exhibits the virtue of progressive conservatism as well.

The Remedial Right Only approach also scores high on the desideratum of moral accessibility. Unlike Primary Right Theories, and especially the nationalist version of Ascriptivist Theory, incorporating the Remedial Right Only Theory into international law would not pose a risk of large-scale violence and instability. The force of this last point will become clearer below, when we explore Primary Right Theories in detail.

Finally, the Remedial Right Only approach to the unilateral right of secession exhibits the virtue of moral convergence. A wide range of moral views support the commitment to human rights, recognize the right to take back unjustly taken sovereign territory, and acknowledge the importance of the keeping of agreements, including autonomy agreements. In contrast, Primary Right Theories appear to depend upon much more controversial moral assumptions about what can generate a valid claim to territory, whether it is the existence of an ascriptive group (the idea that all nations have a right to their own state) or the mere will to have an independent state (in the case of Plebiscitary Theories). From the standpoint of providing an explanation of the validity of the secessionists' claim to territory, Remedial Right Only Theory seems to require less morally controversial assumptions than its rivals.

The statist bias objection

Some critics have complained that my presentation of the Remedial Right Only Theory in *Secession* (1991) assumed a bias in favor of the status (i.e., statist) quo by requiring secessionists to bear the burden of argument by establishing a grievance against the state. Why, they asked, should the burden of argument fall on the secessionists? Surely—as I myself explicitly conceded—a liberal political theory must accord a presumption to the free choice of individuals regarding what polity they wish to belong to.

I believe I have convincingly answered this objection in Part Two of this book, where I articulated the main outlines of a theory of the legitimacy of states. There I argued for a justice-based conception of legitimacy, according to which only states that meet or exceed a minimal justice standard with respect to their internal and external actions have a valid claim to their territory. Against the background of this conception of legitimacy, the Remedial Right Only Theory does *not* embody an arbitrary bias in favor of the status quo. On the contrary, the Remedial Right Only view is founded on a theory of what gives a state a valid claim to territory, a theory that is a natural fit with the Remedial Right Only view's position that by persisting in serious injustices a state can void its claim to a part of its territory. Furthermore, those who raised the status quo objection did not distinguish between unilateral and consensual secession and therefore overlooked the fact that the Remedial Right Only Theory (which applies only to the former) can allow for secession without requiring that the secessionist prove that they are victims of injustice.

The irrelevance objection

Other critics have complained that the Remedial Right Only Theory is disturbingly irrelevant to the concerns of most groups seeking self-determination, because in most cases it is *nationalism* that fuels the quest for self-determination, not grievances of injustice that can be stated independently of nationalist claims.[25] I have two replies to this objection. First, because national minorities are frequently the targets of the state's worst human rights abuses, in many cases the Remedial Right Only Theory will ascribe the right to secede to national groups. The Remedial Right Only theorist does not reject claims to independence on the part of nations, but only the stronger—and in my view unjustified—claim that nations *as such* (in the absence of serious injustices) have a unilateral right to secede.

Second, and more important, the Remedial Right Only Theory I am endorsing in the chapter is only a theory of the *unilateral right to secede*, not a comprehensive theory of self-determination. Consequently, it must be evaluated as an element of a larger theory that takes the value of self-determination—or rather the plurality of values that self-determination serves—very seriously.

[25] Margaret Moore, 'Introduction', in Margaret Moore (ed.), *National Self-Determination and Secession* (Oxford University Press, New York, 1998), 6.

Recall that secession is only the most extreme form of self-determination. Short of independent statehood there is a broad range of self-determination arrangements, with varying degrees and dimensions of autonomy within the state. In the end, the plausibility of the Remedial Right Only Theory of the unilateral right to secede depends upon the credibility of the overarching theory of self-determination of which it forms a part, and in particular upon whether the latter gives legitimate nationalist aspirations their due.

The most promising way to achieve the needed theoretical integration is to embed the Remedial Right Only Theory of the unilateral right to secede within what I have called the "isolate and proliferate" strategy. The only alternatives, in other words, are not recognizing a unilateral right to secede for nations (as Ascriptive Right Theory would have it) or ignoring the phenomenon of nationalism. If international law decisively uncouples secession from other forms of self-determination, it can support a variety of intrastate autonomy arrangements, including those tailored to the needs of national minorities, without embracing the disastrously destabilizing and normatively unsupported notion that every nation has a right to a state of its own. In the next chapter I explore the ways in which the international legal order should support self-determination for groups within states.

Plebiscitary (Primary Right) Theories of secession[26]

The initial appeal of the Plebiscitary variant of Primary Right Theory is that it appears to make the determination of boundaries a matter of choice or, more accurately, majority rule. Thus Plebiscitary Theorists attempt to support their views by appeals to the value of liberty and that of democracy.

However, this is extremely misleading. The liberty in question turns out to be exclusively the liberty of those who happen, at a given time, to be the majority in a portion of the state's territory unilaterally to sever it from the state and unilaterally to change the citizenship of those residing in that region who do not wish to be

---

[26] This section draws on Buchanan and Golove, 'Philosophy of International Law', 909–16.

part of a new state. Thus the "majority rule" involved in the exercise of the putative Plebiscitary unilateral right to secede is not the rule of the majority of the citizens of the state, but rather the rule of the present majority within a portion of the state's territory to override the rights of the citizenry as a whole to the entire territory of the state.

Recall that according to the doctrine of popular sovereignty, which lies at the core of liberal political theory, the state's territory is more accurately described as the people's territory, the point being that it is the territory of the people as a whole, not just a collection of parcels of territory each owned by those who at a particular time happen to reside in them.

In other words, according to the doctrine of popular sovereignty, the people as a whole stand in a special relationship to the whole territory of the state. It is *their* territory in two distinct senses. The laws that are applied there are (1) supposed to give priority to their benefit and (2) it is they who ultimately are to determine who makes, applies, and administers those laws. Granted this view of the relationship between the people of the state and state territory, it makes no sense to say, as the Plebiscitary Theory does, that a subset of the people, those who happen to reside in a portion of the territory at a particular time have the right to lop it off and set up a new, independent jurisdiction there, simply because a majority of them wish to do so. Were they to attempt to do this, all the other citizens of the state would have a just grievance against them. So a plebiscitary unilateral right to secede is incompatible with the rights that are included in popular sovereignty.

As the Remedial Right Only Theory stresses, the right of the people as a whole to the whole territory of the state is not unconditional. Persistent violations of human rights can undermine the claim to territory and thereby justify secession where secession is the remedy of last resort for these injustices. The Plebiscitary Theory, in contrast, repudiates the rights associated with popular sovereignty *tout court*, even in the case of fully legitimate and even perfectly just states.

The Remedial Right Only view I am advancing endorses the commonsense understanding of popular sovereignty while explaining what makes it plausible. According to the Remedial Right Only view, there is no right of unilateral secession against a legitimate state because a legitimate state has a valid claim to its territory. The Remedial Right Only Theory I am proposing is to be understood as being embedded in the larger moral framework for international law I have developed in earlier chapters. On the assumption that the international legal system is to be regarded provisionally as a state system, it makes sense to hold that the people of a legitimate state, which on my view is one that is at least minimally democratic and does a credible job of protecting basic human rights, are entitled to exercise jurisdiction over the territory of their state. But this means that no portion of the citizenry, simply because it decides to create its own state, has a unilateral right to take away part of that territory to create a new jurisdiction.

It is no doubt true that at bottom there is something morally arbitrary about assuming that even the people of a democratic, human rights-respecting state are entitled to exclusive control over the territory that happens to be within the borders of their state and all the resources it contains. Democratic states, like other states, now enjoy near complete dominion over the resources within their borders and an almost unlimited ability to prevent noncitizens from enjoying them by immigrating there, and this surely contributes to distributive injustices.

As I argued in Chapter 4, as international institutional capacity for determining and implementing principles of distributive justice improves, it is to be hoped that various elements of the bundle of rights now lumped together under the sovereignty of the people will be unpacked and limited in the name of the basic moral equality of all persons. But from the fact that the control over resources that the citizens of particular states presently enjoy is problematic from the standpoint of justice, it does not follow that there is much of anything to be said for instituting an international legal rule that allows a majority of persons in a portion of such a state unilaterally to create a new state there!

At least as long as we are operating in a system in which states play a significant role, there are two reasons to deny that a plebiscite in a portion of a legitimate state should suffice to sever the territory. First, from the standpoint of a fundamental concern about justice, there is much to be said for having international legal rules that protect from dismemberment states that have done a decent job of protecting human rights within their borders. After all, in a world like ours, even the local achievement of minimal democracy and the protection of basic rights is a rare accomplishment, and most likely a rather fragile one. Second, again taking justice as the primary value, it seems much more plausible to say that the provision of justice grounds the claim to territory than the mere desire of the majority of persons who happen to reside there to have a state there.

The most serious and obvious weakness of the Plebiscitary Theory of the unilateral right to secede, then, is its account of what grounds the secessionists' right to the territory on which they seek to establish a new state. Just how deficient this account is becomes fully apparent when one recalls that, according to the Plebiscitary Theory, the state from which unilateral secession occurs can be a perfectly just one. As a general account of what grounds valid claims to territory, the Plebiscitary Theory looks dubious indeed: valid claims to territory come and go as majorities in favor of independence in a region wax and wane. Plebiscitary Theory thus makes state boundaries liable to extraordinary instability and hence can hardly be regarded as a progressive proposal for changing international law. (And this is quite apart from the fact that such a view is unfeasible due to the fact that it is very unlikely ever to be incorporated into a system in which states currently play a major role in determining what the law is to be.)

My objection that Plebiscitary Theory is committed to a very implausible account of what gives a group a valid claim to territory (namely, their mere presence in the territory coupled with a desire for independence) of course assumes a different theory of political legitimacy as a basis for the claim on the part of the whole citizenry to the state's whole territory. I have delineated the main contours of that theory in Part Two. The Plebiscitary Theory of the unilateral right to secede can be understood as assuming its own theory of political legitimacy; but it is a very deficient one. For to make sense of the Plebiscitary Theory one must assume some version of the Consent Theory of political legitimacy or authority and then argue that unless unilateral secession by a majority in a portion of the state is permitted, it cannot be said that all the citizens consent to government.[27]

---

[27] Beran, *The Consent Theory of Obligation*; and Harry Beran, 'A Democratic Theory of Political Self-Determination for a New World Order', in Percy Lehning (ed.), *Theories of Secession* (Routledge, New York, 1998), 32–59.

I have already argued in Chapter 5 that the notion of political authority is irrelevant to the question of political legitimacy and also rehearsed there the all-too-familiar objections to the consent theory of political legitimacy. Here I will only add one more. If consent of all the citizens is necessary for political legitimacy (for the state to be justified in making, applying, and enforcing laws), then how could a majority vote of only those in a portion of the state's territory, as opposed to a unanimous vote, establish a new legitimate political entity?

The problem can be stated as a dilemma. If the consent of all really is necessary for political legitimacy, then a unilateral right to secede by plebiscite is a dead letter, because there are virtually no cases in which everyone in a region of the state will wish to secede. But if the consent of all is not necessary, then why should the will of those who happen to be a majority in a particular portion of the state, rather than the will of the majority of the citizens as a whole, determine whether the state's territory shall remain intact or be divided?

In addition, the Plebiscitary Theory of the unilateral right to secede scores poorly on the desideratum of incentive compatibility. As Donald Horowitz and I have both observed, incorporation of a Plebiscitary Right to unilateral secession in international law would most likely undermine strategies for increasing governmental efficiency, increasing local self-determination, and reducing intrastate conflicts through decentralization, including various forms of federalism and consociationalism.[28] If state leaders know that unilateral secession will be considered a right under international law for any group that can muster a majority in favor of it in any portion of their state, they will not be receptive to proposals for decentralization. They will view decentralization as a first step toward secession, because creation of internal political units will provide the basis for future secessions by plebiscite.

International recognition of a plebiscitary unilateral right to secede would also create perverse incentives regarding both immigration

---

[28] Horowitz, 'Self-Determination: Politics, Philosophy, and Law', 435–6; and Allen Buchanan, 'Self-Determination, Secession, and the Rule of Law', in Robert McKim and Jeff McMahan (eds.), *The Morality of Nationalism* (Oxford University Press, New York, 1997), 316.

and economic development. States that did not wish to risk losing part of their territory (which includes virtually all of them) would have a strong reason for limiting immigration (or internal migration) that might result in the formation of a pro-secession majority in a portion of the state's territory. And to deter secession by existing internal political units, the state might even seek to prevent them from becoming sufficiently developed to be economically viable. (The Soviet Union's policy of dispersing major industries among the Republics was very likely motivated at least in part by precisely this consideration.)

I observed earlier that although some proponents of Plebiscitary Theory tout it as following from the principle of democracy, in fact this theory arbitrarily confers a unilateral democratic right to change state boundaries on those who happen to reside in a portion of the state's territory, thereby ignoring the democratic rights of the citizenry as a whole, in effect repudiating the principle of popular sovereignty. Elsewhere I have explored in considerable detail the relationship between democracy and secession.[29] That analysis reinforces the conclusion that it is an error to try to justify the Plebiscitary Right to unilateral secession by invoking the principle of democracy. Here I will only indicate some of the reasons why this is so.

It is a mistake to think that the commitment to democracy requires recognition of a plebiscitary unilateral right to secede, because the chief *justifications* for democratic governance within given political boundaries do *not* support the thesis that boundaries may be redrawn by majority vote. One chief justification for democracy contends that it is required, as a matter of equal regard for persons, that they should have an equal say or participate as equals in the decisions that determine the fundamental character of the polity in which they live. Yet clearly this justification for democracy does not imply that the decision whether to change boundaries should be made unilaterally by a majority in favor of secession in a portion of an existing polity rather than being determined by a majority of all the citizens.

[29] Allen Buchanan, 'Democracy and Secession', in Margaret Moore (ed.), *National Self-Determination and Secession* (Oxford University Press, New York, 1998).

In other words, the first justification for democracy tells us that all who live within the jurisdiction of a system of rules that determine the fundamental character of social life should participate as equals or have an equal say in deciding what those rules are. But this does not tell us what the boundaries of the polity should be, since in order to implement the principle of democracy we must have already fixed the boundaries of the polity.

The second, or instrumental, justification for democracy holds that democratic governance is the most reliable protector of basic human rights. Here, too, the force of the justification for democracy depends upon the assumption that what is being justified is a decision-making process for a polity, the whole polity. The key idea is that where *all* citizens have a voice in the process, basic human rights will be more likely to be protected. But if so, then this argument clearly cannot support the claim that only *some* citizens (namely, those in a particular portion of the polity) ought to be able unilaterally to decide a matter that will affect all citizens. So the instrumental argument for democracy cannot support a plebiscitary unilateral right to secede either. Moreover, in the real world the exercise of a plebiscitary right would make the human rights of minorities vulnerable to violation because it would enable a majority in a region of the state to create its own ethnically exclusive state and then cheerfully go about the business of persecuting minorities within it. For all of these reasons, the first type of nonremedial or Primary Right Theory of the unilateral right to secede, the Plebiscitary Right Theory, ought to be rejected as a basis for reforming international law on secession.

Ascriptivist (Nationalist) Theories

This type of Primary Right Theory confers a right to secede on ascriptive groups, variously referred to as peoples, distinct peoples, encompassing cultures, or, more commonly, nations. In its dominant form, this normative approach to unilateral secession has a long pedigree, reaching back at least to nineteenth-century nationalists such as Mazzini, who proclaimed that every nation should have its own state.

Before proceeding we must fix on a definition of 'nation' that is at least roughly serviceable for present purposes. Doing so is not without risk, considering the multitude of definitions that have been proposed. Nevertheless, we can begin with a useful character-ization proposed by Margalit and Raz, according to which nations are "encompassing cultural groups" defined as large-scale, anonym-ous (rather than face-to-face) groups that have a common culture and character that encompasses many important aspects of life and which marks the character of the life of its members, where mem-bership in the group is in part a matter of mutual recognition, is important for one's self-identification, and is a matter of belonging, not achievement.[30]

In addition, like most theorists of nationalism, Margalit and Raz emphasize that the identity of the encompassing cultural group includes a historical attachment to a particular territory, a home-land. This last element is significant. Without it the distinction between nations and non-national, for example, ethnic or religious groups that sometimes have the other features of encompassing cul-tural groups would be lost. Furthermore, any conception of nations that omits this crucial connection with a homeland, a particular piece of land, runs the risk of sliding over one of the most troubling features of the alleged right of national self-determination—the fact that in virtually every case more than one nation claims the same piece of territory. Thus as Jacob Levy has observed, Yael Tamir makes her project of reconciling nationalism with liberalism—and with international stability—seem much easier than it is by omitting the territorial aspect of nationalist aspirations.[31]

What is still lacking in this characterization of nationalism, even if the connection to a homeland is added, but which is emphasized in the preponderance of scholarly writing on nationalism, is that among the members of the group there is an aspiration for some form of self-government for the group. As David Miller aptly puts it, nations are inherently political in their aspirations.[32]

[30] Margalit and Raz, 'National Self-Determination'.

[31] Jacob Levy, *The Multiculturalism of Fear* (Oxford University Press, New York, 2000), 198–9.

[32] Miller, *On Nationality*, 11. For brevity we could then say that nations are encompassing cultural groups that associate themselves with a homeland and in which there is substantial (though not necessarily unanimous) aspiration for self-government of some kind (though not necessarily full independence) in that homeland.

There is a more serious flaw with this conception of nations, however. As Brian Barry, Margaret Moore, and others have noted, not all groups that identify themselves as nations and seek political self-determination using the discourse of nationalism are distinct cultural groups in any significant sense.[33] For example, there is such a thing as Scottish Nationalism, but those who seek political independence for Scotland are not united by anything that could reasonably be called a distinct Scottish culture. Similarly, nationalism in Northern Ireland is not based on a distinct Catholic or Irish cultural identity. In the context of the conflict in Northern Ireland, the terms 'Catholic' and 'Protestant' do not refer to distinct cultural groups, much less "encompassing cultures" in Margalit and Raz's sense. Of course, entrepreneurs of nationalist identity often attempt to foster the illusion that their group is a distinct culture, but that is a different matter.

For the purposes of this chapter, I will not harp on what I take to be the mistaken assumption that national groups, as such, are cultural groups in any interesting sense. My criticisms of the nationalist ascriptivist view will not rely on the premise that nations are sometimes not cultures. Instead I will attempt to assess various justifications for the claim that nations have a right of self-determination, including a right to secede, focusing on assertions about the normative significance of cultural identity where appropriate.

However, I will note that if Moore and Barry are correct in holding that not all national groups are distinct cultural groups in any significant sense, the case for a right of self-determination for nations is even more difficult to make. For as will become clear from what follows, attempts to show that nations are entitled to their own states or at least to some significant sphere of self-government typically depend upon the assumption that members of nations are connected with one another in something very much like the way in which participants in a culture, or at least an "encompassing culture," are related to one another.

---

[33] Margaret Moore, *The Ethics of Nationalism* (Oxford University Press, New York, 2001), 57–8; and Brian Barry, *Culture & Equality: An Egalitarian Critique of Multiculturalism* (Harvard University Press, Cambridge, MA, 2001), 82.

The infeasibility objection

Critics of the Ascriptivist Primary Right Theory have argued that it would legitimize virtually unlimited unilateral, forcible border changes because it confers an entitlement to its own state on every nation, and virtually every state contains more than one nation. Proponents of the theory quickly reply that it does not require every nation to *exercise* its unilateral right to secede and conjecture that were the theory incorporated into international law not every nation would in fact choose to secede. Nevertheless, given the horrific historical record of ethno-nationalist conflict, the worry remains that institutionalizing the principle that every nation is entitled to its own state could only exacerbate ethno-national violence, along with the human rights violations that it inevitably entails. Thus the moral costs of incorporating the Ascriptivist version of Primary Right Theory into international law appear prohibitive—at least if there are less risky ways to accommodate the legitimate interests of nations, such as better compliance with existing human rights norms, including those that prohibit discrimination on the basis of nationality, and recourse to intrastate autonomy arrangements that provide meaningful self-government short of independent statehood. The greater the extent to which these measures can satisfy the needs of national minorities, the more dubious the nationalist version of Primary Right Theory looks from the standpoint of the desideratum of moral accessibility explained earlier.

Weakening the nationalist thesis

Variants of nationalist Primary Right Theory typically attempt to allay the worry that acceptance of the theory would add fuel to the fires of ethno-national conflict by qualifying the unilateral right of secession for nations in various ways. For example, the theory may hold that there is a *presumption* in favor of each nation having a right to its own state or a prima facie unilateral right to secede, rather than a right to secede, but that the international community is justified in requiring some groups to settle for intrastate autonomy rather than full independence, in order to avoid dangerous instability or to accommodate similar claims by other groups to the same territory.

This way of responding to the worry about fueling ethno-national conflict comes at a price, however. What was originally billed as a unilateral right of every nation to its own state now turns out to be a highly defeasible presumption in favor of independence. In particular, if the strength of a nation's claim to statehood depends upon the compatibility of satisfying that claim with satisfying the similar claims of other nations within the same state, then this will in effect render the Ascriptivist right practically inconsequential, for the simple reason that in the vast majority of cases there will be more than one nation advancing a claim to statehood in the same territory. If one nation's claim to statehood is only to be satisfied when doing so is compatible with other nations' equally valid claims being satisfied, then nationalist claims to statehood will rarely be valid. And unless a fairly concrete account of the realistic conditions under which the presumption is not defeated is provided, it is hard to know what the practical implications of this qualified view are, or to know exactly what changes in international law would count as implementing it.

Two types of nationalist arguments

Earlier I noted that critics of nationalist (Ascriptivist) Primary Right Theories tend to focus on the potential costs of implementing this view in terms of ethno-national conflict. Proponents of nationalist Primary Right Theory would reply that it is not enough to note the potential costs; it is also necessary to appreciate the expected benefits of having a system in which the right of nations to their own states is acknowledged. David Miller, in his thoughtful and provocative book *On Nationality*, has usefully distinguished between two ways in which nationalist Primary Right Theories can be supported: by arguments to show that nations need their own states and by arguments to show that states need to be mononational.[34]

The first type of justification has two variants: One can argue that nations need to have their own states either (1) in order to be able to protect themselves from destruction or from forces that would damage their distinctive character, or (2) in order for co-nationals to

---

[34] Miller, *On Nationality*, 82.

have the institutional resources required for fulfilling the special obligations they owe to one another as members of the "ethical community" that a nation constitutes.

Notice that (1) appears to assume, mistakenly, that nations are cultural groups, since it bases the case for national self-determination on the need to protect the distinctive character of the group. It is hard to understand why the preservation of a distinctive character should be so important unless this refers to the survival of important cultural goods.

In contrast, the notion of an ethical community employed in (2) need not be that of a cultural group. All that is necessary is that the members of the group be related in ways that generate substantial special obligations among them.

Accommodating nationalist interests within the state

Both of these considerations ((1) and (2)) can, under certain circumstances, weigh in favor of *some* form of political independence for nations, but neither is sufficient to ground a general unilateral right of all nations to full independence and hence a unilateral right to secede for nations as such. Miller recognizes this point, drawing only the weaker conclusion that nations have a "strong claim" to self-determination, by which he may mean something like a presumption of a right or prima facie right. In fact, Miller does not even propose that international law should recognize such a presumptive or prima facie right. However, since my concern is with international law, I will consider the merits of this proposal.

There are two serious problems with the idea of incorporating into international law even a presumptive or prima facie right to unilateral secession for nations as such. First, nationalist Primary Right theorists have generally failed to take seriously the possibility that the legitimate interests of nations in most cases can be sufficiently realized by intrastate autonomy arrangements (combined with better enforcement of the human right against discrimination on grounds of ethnicity or nationality). Instead, they have tended to proceed as if the only alternatives are full independence for nations or the absence of any significant forms of self-government. This may be a consequence of the tenacious grip of statist thinking, in particular the tendency to think of states as both highly centralized and unitary and as the only sort of political unit worth having. Once one understands that the attributes of sovereignty can be unbundled, the idea that nations need their own states becomes much less plausible.

Second, how important it is for a nation to have its own state will depend upon two factors: (1) how important states are and (2) how effective institutions of transnational justice are in ensuring that human rights and rights conferred by intrastate autonomy agreements are respected. In a world in which there are manifold forms of self-determination, and in which effective international institutions pierce the veil of sovereignty to help ensure that states respect the rights of all their citizens and honor intrastate autonomy arrangements, the distinction between having and not having one's own state would not only be less significant, but difficult to draw.

Of course the fact that there is a wide range of possible forms of autonomy for nations within states does not by itself show that nations will be adequately protected without having their own states. This will depend upon whether the international community effectively supports meaningful intrastate autonomy arrangements for nations and, perhaps even more important, whether it comes to do a better job of ensuring that states respect the human rights of all their citizens, including those who belong to national minorities. But as the efficacy of transnational justice grows, the case for statehood for all nations, which is already problematic for all the reasons I have already adduced, becomes weaker still.

Earlier in this chapter I argued for incorporating into international law a Remedial Right Only account of the unilateral right to secede that recognizes serious and persisting violations of intrastate autonomy arrangements as a justification for secession under certain conditions. Implementing this principle would go a long way toward providing support for intrastate autonomy arrangements, and in some instances a strong case can be made for providing national minorities with intrastate autonomy. To that extent, my rejection of proposals for incorporating a unilateral right to secede for nations as such in international law is grounded in a more comprehensive moral theory of international law that nonetheless does take the aspirations of national minorities seriously. In the next chapter I begin to develop an account of when intrastate autonomy should receive international support.

There is another reason to challenge the assumption that nations need their own states: it is simply not the case that having its own state always contributes to a nation's security. In some cases, the insistence of smaller nations on sovereignty may work to their disadvantage, simply because they do not have the economic or military capacity to make a success of independence. The difficulty with Margalit and Raz's assumption that nations need their own states to protect their interests and ultimately the interests of their individual members is that it is an overgeneralization from a limited historical sample. "Stateless peoples"—including perhaps most prominently the Jews—have sometimes suffered because they lacked their own state. But there are also many cases in which less powerful nations fell prey to domination or annexation because they insisted on maintaining their independence rather than coalescing into a larger, more defensible political unit. Thus it is not surprising that the dominant opinion in many indigenous groups seems to be that intrastate autonomy rather than independence is necessary for the survival and flourishing of these nations.

Clearly then, whether nations need to have their own states will vary with circumstances. What I find surprising is that most proponents of nationalist Primary Right Theory tend to proceed as if the strength of the case for national independence does not depend upon circumstances and in particular upon how effectively the international legal system supports the legitimate interests of national minorities. Instead, they seem to operate within a very conservative framework that assumes that states are unitary, rather than containing autonomy regimes within them, and that in effect dismisses any significant role for institutions of transnational justice, working on the assumption that having their own state is the only way for nations to achieve adequate protection. To assume uncritically such a framing assumption is yet another example of the common failure to distinguish between ideal and nonideal theory and the failure to take a diachronic view of the international system that allows for the possibility that unitary states may not continue to be as important as they have been.

The nationalist Primary Right theorist would no doubt reply that the existing system is and is likely to continue to be statist for a long time. Institutions of transnational justice that would protect the interests of national minorities within states are not well developed and are not likely to be for some time, if ever. So at least from the standpoint of a nonideal theory that is relevant to the realities of our world, independence is the only reliable way for nations to be secure and to have the institutional resources needed for their members to fulfill their special obligations to one another.

The problem with this reply is that it tacitly assumes something that is almost certainly false, namely, that implementing a unilateral right to secede for all nations is currently more feasible than building more effective institutions of transnational justice and facilitating intrastate autonomy arrangements in order to help ensure that the legitimate interests of nations are accommodated within states. This assumption is extremely dubious because the international institutional system lacks, and is never likely to develop, effective mechanisms for sorting out the conflicting claims of various nations to the same territories and providing a relatively peaceful implementation of the prescription that every nation that wants its own state is entitled to one.

In addition, states are more likely to agree to a Remedial Right Only approach than to a principle of nationalist secession because the former allows them to continue to exist intact, so long as they meet minimal standards of justice, while the latter condemns many of them to disintegration no matter what they do. So even if it were the case that for the present the best way for a nation to protect its interests is to have its own state, it does not follow that the international legal order should recognize a right of nations to have their own states and hence to secede unilaterally from states in which they find themselves.

Do states need to be nation-states?

The second type of justification for the view that nations should be recognized as having a unilateral right to secede comes in two variants. The first holds that nation-states are required for democracy; the second makes a parallel claim about distributive justice. Both claims are ambiguous. Is the assertion that democracy can only function or deliberative justice only be achieved in a nation-state or that democracy and distributive justice are *best* served in a nation-state (leaving open the possibility that multinational states can achieve acceptable levels of democracy and distributive justice)?

The stronger claim, I shall argue, is very dubious. The weaker claim, though less implausible, is far from well supported. But even if it is true that a nation-state *best* serves democracy or distributive justice or both, it would not follow that nations as such should be recognized as having a unilateral right to secede or even a presumptive right, simply because maximizing democracy or distributive justice are not the only values that bear on whether international law should recognize a nationalist unilateral right to secede.

In an earlier essay I criticized in detail the assertion that nation-states uniquely further democracy or distributive justice.[35] Here I will only sketch the major points of that discussion and bolster them with some further thoughts.

Democracy, distributive justice, and nationalism

Consider first the very strong claim, advanced by J. S. Mill, that democracy can function only where the nationalist principle that every nation ought to have its own state is satisfied.[36] Before we go any further, we need to be very clear about what it means for a nation to "have its own state," what it is for a state to be a nation-state properly speaking. There appear to be only two sensible ways in which this latter phrase can be understood. It means either that (1) no one who is not a member of the nation is allowed to be a citizen, with full civil and political rights, or that (2) even if non-nationals have full citizenship rights, being a member of the nation is the dominant form of political identity, with nationality providing the frame for politics, in the sense that the state is viewed at least primarily as a resource for expressing the distinctive character and pursuing the goals (or destiny) *of one national group among others* within the state.

Given that virtually every state includes more than one nation and that there is not a ghost of a chance for changing this without

---

[35] Allen Buchanan, 'What's So Special about Nations?', in Jocelyne Couture, Kai Nielsen, and Michel Seymour (eds.), *Rethinking Nationalism* (University of Calgary Press, Calgary, 1998). For additional and related criticisms, see Harry Brighouse, 'Against Nationalism', also in *Rethinking Nationalism*; and Dahbour, 'Self-Determination in Political Philosophy and International Law'.

[36] John Stuart Mill, *Utilitarianism, Liberty, and Representative Government* (E. P. Dutton and Co., New York, 1951), 487–9.

genocide or ethnic cleansing, (1) is so repugnant that it requires no explicit refutation. Where states contain more than one nation, one nation "having its own state" in sense (1) means that all those who are not members of that favored nationality do not have equal rights and are not within the scope of democracy. Whites in apartheid South Africa had their own state in this sense.

Suppose instead that (2) is the proper interpretation of the idea of the nation-state as it occurs in the claims about the connection between democracy or distributive justice and the nation-state. Is it true that where the dominant form of political identity is nationality and public institutions embody the idea that the state is uniquely a resource for the life of one national group, this is likely to be especially conducive to democracy and/or distributive justice, much less indispensable for them?

Consider first the claim about democracy. *If* (which is never the case in our world) every citizen were a member of the same national group, this might in fact promote the spirit of common enterprise that facilitates the well-functioning of democratic institutions. But even in this fictional case, whatever benefits a single shared nationality might bring to the democratic process might well be offset by other, less fortunate concomitants of operating on the assumption that the state is in some fundamental way a resource for the nation. For example, political discourse may be distorted by the tendency of those seeking political power to claim that they are the authentic voice of the nation, with the result that those who disagree with them are traitors to the nation. The danger is that what are or should be disagreements over principles or how best to apply principles become debates over loyalty to the nation. (Consider the allegation that certain policies or attitudes are "Un-American".)

In the real world, where there are hardly any states that contain only members of one nation, using national identity to frame politics—treating the state primarily as a resource for furthering the life of one nation only—is a recipe for discrimination, exclusion, and marginalization of all who are not part of *the* nation. "Nation-building"—which involves nation-destroying so far as other groups are concerned—has proved to be one of the major sources of ethnic conflict in the past several decades.

Similarly, *if* a state contained only members of one nation, then that common nationality might help motivate the better-off citizens to cooperate in the distribution of wealth to the worse off, other things being equal. But recall that there are virtually no mono-national states. To the extent that distributive justice has anything at all to do with fairness and impartiality in the distribution of resources, it is hardly likely that those who are not members of the favored nation—the nation whose well-being is supposed to occupy a privileged position in politics—will receive their due. So on the face of it the claim that making the state a nation-state will promote distributive justice for all citizens is far-fetched.

In addition, there is ample historical evidence that nationalism and a commitment to redistributing wealth *within* the national group often do not go hand in hand. (As Marxists have rightly observed, appeals to nationalism are often made to block redistributive efforts within a state.) Whether the ascendance of the idea of the nation in politics will serve the cause of distributive justice even within the national group or impede it will depend upon the character of the nationalist identity—or, more accurately, upon who succeeds in being recognized as the arbiter of what counts as the "authentic" national identity.[37]

Premature pessimism about multinational democracy[38]

Consider now Mill's assertion that democratic institutions cannot function in multinational states. Interestingly enough, Mill stops short of the conclusion that nations as such have a right of self-determination, including a right to an independent state, even though his argument seems to require it. Perhaps he did not think that every nation was entitled to a state—only the 'great' ones. Members of lesser nations (including Bretons and Basques), he tells us, should be content (indeed grateful) to be absorbed into the great nations.[39]

This latter view, redolent with national chauvinism as it is, is no easier to square with the liberal principle of equal regard for persons

---

[37] Arthur Ripstein, 'Context, Continuity, and Fairness', in Robert McKim and Jeff McMahan (eds.), *The Morality of Nationalism* (Oxford University Press, New York, 1997), 209–26.

[38] This section is drawn from Buchanan, 'What's So Special about Nations?', 304–5.

[39] Mill, *Utilitarianism, Liberty, and Representative Government*, 490.

than would be the claim that members of minority religious sects should throw in their lot with large, well-organized religions. But it would probably be a mistake to assume that Mill thought members of lesser nations *ought* to assimilate into great nations. Instead it is more likely that he believed that it was inevitable that the lesser nations would disappear. His point is that this is not to be lamented, even from the standpoint of the members of the lesser nations, for they will gain by being assimilated into great nations.

Assuming that only the relatively few great nations among all the nations of the earth will require their own state is wonderfully convenient for the proponent of rights of national self-determination. This assumption takes much of the sting out of the Infeasibility Objection encountered earlier. If members of lesser nations will bow to the inevitable and assimilate willingly into the great nations, then perhaps there will eventually be a harmonious world in which every nation has its own state, and democracy can flourish.

However, if we do not assume that the disappearance of minority nations is historically inevitable (or that their deliberate destruction is morally justifiable), the matter is not so neat and simple. We are faced with a painful dilemma if we accept Mill's view of the connection between democracy and mononationality: either we must acknowledge that some nationalities will not have their own states, but instead will be sacrificed to create mononational states so that democracy can flourish, or we must forgo progress toward democracy in the name of equal consideration for nations by recognizing the multinational character of most existing states.

The painfulness of this dilemma should lead us to question its premise more closely than Mill and his contemporary followers have done. Is it in fact true that democratic institutions cannot flourish where the state contains more than one nation?

Those who doubt this generalization can point to apparent exceptions: Canada, Belgium, and perhaps Switzerland (depending on whether one thinks the latter is multinational or merely multiethnic). One might also add the United States, since a number of American Indian tribes have a legal status that approaches that of independent statehood and at least approximate the definition of nations as encompassing cultures associated with a particular territory.

Of course, modern-day proponents of the Millian view might be quick to point out that the continued unity of Belgium and Canada is very much in doubt. (Actually, at present the prospects of Quebec seceding look slim.) They might also argue that the circumstances of American Indians are so anomalous as not to constitute a serious exception to the generalization that democracy cannot flourish in multinational states.

The best reply to the Millian argument, however, is not only to cite these apparent exceptions to its premise, but to point out that it is simply too early to tell whether the politically acknowledged presence of more than one nationality within the borders of the state undermines democratic institutions. The lamentable fact is that until very recently there have been almost no serious attempts to develop democratic states that recognize a plurality of nations within them— that is, that do not discriminate against minority nations and treat them as equal citizens. (Here one is reminded of Chou En Lai's reply to a journalist who asked him what he thought the most important effect of the French Revolution was: "It's too soon to tell.")

Given that we can no longer console ourselves, as Mill may have done, with the belief that the number of nations will conveniently diminish to the point at which it will be feasible to have only one nation per state, and given that general acceptance of the presumption that each nation must have its own state is therefore likely to perpetuate if not inflame existing conflicts, we had better have very good reason to believe Mill's generalization. Since we do not, the responsible course is to explore the possibilities for multinational democratic states more fully than has been done before.

Before scrapping the idea of multinational democracies as unworkable, much more should be done to eliminate the more obvious sources of discontent among national minorities within states. This means working harder to eradicate legal and extra-legal discrimination against minorities in education, employment, health care, and access to the benefits of the legal system. It also means reducing, as far as possible, the culturally exclusive aspects of state policy and public life (enabling the use of minority languages in legal proceedings and legislative processes, and the removal of culturally exclusive symbols from public spaces, etc.). Such reforms are not novel, but their cumulative effects may be great.

The central point is that efforts to eliminate discrimination against minorities and to reduce the exclusive cultural content of state policy and public spaces are preferable to the alternative of trying to create separate political states for every "encompassing culture" or nation. Not least among the difficulties with this latter strategy is that instead of solving the problem of cultural or national minorities who are disadvantaged by a state apparatus that excludes them and devalues their culture, it replicates the problem.

If one is concerned with the effects of states on cultural or national minorities, the solution is not to give those minorities their own states, since in virtually every case this will result in a new version of the original problem: The formerly disempowered minority will simply become the disempowering majority. For example, if Quebec were to secede from Canada to achieve the full political empowerment of Francophone culture, this would come at the price of creating a new political unit that systematically disempowers all other cultures and nationalities, including those of immigrants and of Native Peoples.

*Summing up: the weakness of the case for nations
as such having a right to secede*

There are two main types of argument for the thesis that nations (as such, independently of remedial reasons) have a right to secede or at least a presumptive or prima facie right to unilateral secession. The first, perhaps best exemplified in the work of Margalit and Raz, is based on the premise that the security and flourishing of a nation is best insured by its having its own state, and that individuals have fundamental interests in the flourishing of the nation to which they belong. The second, which in its most cogent form is advanced by David Miller, is based on the premise that when citizens are co-nationals they will be better motivated to make democracy work and to achieve distributive justice.

These types of arguments do show that, under some circumstances, there are important advantages to nations (or rather, their members) in being self-governing. However, they fall far short of establishing that nations as such, independently of remedial reasons, have a moral right to their own states and hence to unilateral secession when they find themselves within a state that is not "their own." Nor is either type of argument capable of showing that international law ought to incorporate a unilateral right or even a presumptive or prima facie unilateral right of nations to secede.

This completes my criticism of the two rivals to the Remedial Right Only Theory of the unilateral right to secede. Having shown the attractions of the Remedial Right Only Theory, rebutted criticisms of it, and explained the deficits of the Plebiscitary and Ascriptivist (Nationalist) versions of the rival Primary Right Theory, I will now show how my account of the unilateral right to secede connects with my view on recognitional legitimacy.

IV. *Recognition and the Right to Secede*

In Chapter 6 I offered the main outlines of a normative theory of recognitional legitimacy, grounding a proposal for improving existing international legal doctrine and practice regarding the admission of new entities into the society of legitimate states. According to that theory, a new entity's claim to legitimate statehood ought to be accepted by existing states only if the former offers credible commitments to internal and external justice, understood respectively as respect for the basic human rights of its citizens and of the citizens of other states.

In this chapter I have argued that groups should be accorded the right to secede under international law only if secession is a remedy of last resort for three types of grave injustices: (1) unjust taking of the territory of a legitimate state, (2) large-scale and persistent violations of the human rights of members of the seceding group, or (3) major and persisting violations of intrastate autonomy agreements by the state, when a suitable formal international legal inquiry has determined that the state is responsible for the violations and when secession is the remedy of last resort. (I took a somewhat skeptical stance on whether international law should acknowledge a unilateral right to secession by a group that is a permanent minority on issues of fundamental values and/or "conscientious secession," whereby a group secedes from a state because of its persistent violations of the basic human rights of others, either within or outside the state.)

I now wish to link more explicitly the theory of recognitional legitimacy and the Remedial Right Only Theory of unilateral secession. On the view I am proposing, international law should accord the unilateral right to secede (i.e., to attempt to form an independent state in a portion of the territory of an existing state and seek recognition) to all and only those groups for whom secession is a remedy of last resort for one or more of the three specified injustices (violations of human rights, unjust annexation of a legitimate state's territory, or serious and persisting violations of an intrastate autonomy agreement). International law should recognize as legitimate states only those secessionist entities that (1) have a unilateral right to secede and (2) make credible commitments to internal and external justice. Furthermore, international law should unambiguously hold that (i) when these conditions for a unilateral right to secede are satisfied and a group exercises the right, all states are legally obligated to recognize the new entity as a legitimate state and (ii) all states are legally obligated not to recognize secessionist entities (in cases of unilateral secession) as legitimate states unless these conditions are satisfied.

Incorporation of this proposal into international law would constitute a significant change in two key respects. First, it would expand the right to secede beyond the context of classic decolonization recognized in various international legal documents under the heading of "the right of self-determination," thereby eliminating the arbitrary restriction of the right to secede, a limitation that has been rightly criticized for ignoring the fact that injustices as grave as those of classic, "saltwater" colonialism can be perpetrated on subgroups within the state.

My proposal for reforming the international law of secession would eliminate this arbitrariness *without* creating an over-expansive right of self-determination, because it would recognize only a remedial right of unilateral secession. As part of an "isolate and proliferate" strategy that would uncouple the right to secede from legitimate interests that groups have in various forms of intrastate autonomy, international legal acknowledgement of a remedial right of unilateral secession would avoid the dangerously open-ended rhetoric of a "right of self-determination of all peoples," while at the same time clearing the way for a more permissible and supportive stance toward intrastate autonomy. It would also uncouple self-determination from nationality, by making it clear that nations as such do not have a right to self-determination or to secession.

Second, by making recognition (and nonrecognition) obligatory, not discretionary, this proposal represents a significant erosion of state sovereignty. However, it should be remembered that the most laudable reforms of international law of this century—including preeminently the prohibition of genocide, slavery, and aggressive war and the protection of human rights generally—have required erosions of state power. Moreover, the justification for limiting the discretion of states to recognize entities created through unilateral secession is the most compelling possible: constraining states in this way is a vital element of a system that acknowledges both that the state's claim to territory can be voided by serious and persisting injustices and that state-breaking is a high-risk enterprise that itself can endanger human rights.

Having clarified the connection between my accounts of secession and of recognition, I now want to show how they can accommodate the conclusions I drew about the place of distributive justice in international law in Chapter 4.

V. *Secession and Distributive Justice*

In Chapter 4 I defined principles of transnational distributive justice as those that specify a distribution of important social and economic resources and opportunities that the international legal system ought to require states to satisfy in their internal relations. I then argued that transnational distributive justice can at present only play a relatively minor or at least a largely indirect role in international law, chiefly because the international legal system currently lacks the institutional capacity to determine comprehensive, substantive standards of transnational justice and to monitor states' compliance with them, let alone enforce them. I also argued that it is a mistake to infer Deep Distributive Pluralism from current disagreement on standards of distributive justice and thereby exclude distributive justice from any significant role in the ideal moral theory of international law. Finally, I argued that if greater international consensus on such standards develops in the future, transnational distributive justice could come to play a larger role in international law.

These conclusions were grounded in the assumption that at present it is the individual state that is the only entity capable of being the principal arbiter and enforcer of distributive justice. This assumption also has an important implication for proposals to reform international law regarding secession. International law should handle the problem of secession in such a way as to avoid encouraging the "haves" to secede from the "have-nots," since this would undermine the redistributive function of the state in conditions under which, with all its imperfections, the state is the only entity capable of discharging this function.

Sometimes secessionist movements appeal to the idea of distributive justice to justify their attempt to exit the state. Basque secessionists and members of Italy's Northern League proclaim that state policy systematically works to the economic disadvantage of their respective groups and in ways that are morally arbitrary and discriminatory. And if there was a sound justification for the secession of the American colonies from the British Empire it was at least in part that Britain's mercantile policy constituted discriminatory redistribution.

Discriminatory redistribution, at least in its more egregious forms, is a grave injustice. By pursuing policies that systematically discriminate against a group in the distribution of wealth, the state is violating a fundamental condition of its legitimacy, failing to function as an institutional structure for mutual benefit under the requirement of equal regard for persons. It would seem, therefore, that in addition to the three types of injustices articulated earlier in this chapter (persistent violations of basic human rights, unjust annexation, persistent and major violations of autonomy agreements), we should add discriminatory redistribution to the list of grievances that can morally justify unilateral secession according to the Remedial Right Only Theory.

In *Secession* (1991) I included discriminatory redistribution among the grievances that justify unilateral secession. I now take a more nuanced view, chiefly because I am more clearly focused in the present work on articulating principles that could be effectively incorporated into international law in the near to medium term and because I am now more appreciative of the international legal system's current lack of capacity to formulate, monitor, and enforce authoritative comprehensive, substantive standards of transnational distributive justice.

Under these conditions of institutional incapacity, an international law concerning secession that recognized a right to unilateral secession on grounds of discriminatory redistribution would not be feasible, *unless* it were interpreted narrowly to count as discriminatory redistribution only extremely egregious economic discrimination that would be regarded as such under a wide range of differing views on distributive justice. Failure to meet such a minimal standard of distributive justice would fit under the first grievance included in the Remedial Right Only Theory I am advancing, because it would count as a violation of basic human rights—specifically the right to subsistence and the right against discrimination.

Going beyond this, to include discriminatory redistribution as an additional, distinct ground for an international legal unilateral right to secede at the present time, would probably be unwise for two reasons. First, it would embroil international legal agencies in controversies about the substantive content of transnational distributive justice that they are not presently equipped to resolve in any principled and legitimate way. Second, it might encourage groups to claim that they are subject to discriminatory redistribution and are therefore justified in seceding when in fact they desire to have their own state simply in order to better their own economic situation at the expense of their fellow citizens. In brief, it would encourage secession of the "haves" from the "have-nots".

Even if international law presently cannot determine substantive principles of transnational distributive justice much beyond the requirement that all citizens of every state have a right to the material requisites of a decent life and a right against discrimination, it can at least support the role of the state in meeting this minimal standard. An international law of secession that facilitated the secession of the better-off groups of citizens would enable the latter to escape their redistributive obligations to their worse-off fellow citizens and thereby dismantle the redistributive state. Thus there is yet another advantage of the Remedial Right Only Theory I am proposing: (1) it bars secession by a local majority who are simply trying to avoid sharing their wealth with their fellow citizens, and thereby (2) reduces the risk that members of a better-off group will try to divest themselves of redistributive obligations under the cover of an allegation that they are suffering discriminatory redistribution.

In contrast, the Plebiscitary version of Primary Right Theory, if incorporated into international law, would provide a dangerous vehicle for secession of the better off from the worse off and hence for undermining the only effective agent for distributive justice we currently have, the redistributive state. Similarly, incorporating into international law the view that nations (as such, apart from any valid remedial claims) have a right or a presumptive right to secede would provide an opportunity for better-off national minorities to press for secession when their main concern was really economic self-interest rather than any lofty vision of the nation as an entity entitled to political independence.[40]

My suggestion then is that for the foreseeable future efforts to develop a more just and responsive international law concerning unilateral secession should not include discriminatory redistribution as a distinct justifying ground for secession. Instead, it should include a conception of the violation of human rights as a justifying ground that is comprehensive enough to include extremely (and relatively uncontroversial) discriminatory distributive policies. This proposal seems all the more attractive if it is combined with vigorous international support for democracy and the indirect approach to mitigating the worst distributive injustices discussed in Chapter 4.

The importance of democracy for distributive justice should not be underestimated. As Sen and others have argued, democratic governments are much less likely to engage in or at least persist in disastrous economic policies, and where democratic government is augmented by intrastate autonomy rights for especially vulnerable minorities the risk of at least the more extreme forms of discriminatory redistribution is appreciably lessened. In the next chapter I take up the matter of intrastate autonomy rights.

In addition, as Franck emphasizes, indirect support for transnational distributive justice can be achieved by building on current efforts in the areas of more humane international labor standards, trade agreements designed in part to mitigate the disadvantages of poorer countries, policies regarding donations and favorable loan terms for developing countries designed to ensure that the benefits are spread among all citizens, international laws that distribute the

---

[40] The Northern League in Italy is perhaps a good illustration of (perceived) economic self-interest clothed in an ensemble of nationalist fervor and grievances of discriminatory redistribution. The rhetoric of the League claims both that northern Italians are victims of unjust economic policies and are an ethnically or even "racially" distinct people of Celtic origins. Those of a more cynical or less gullible cast of mind regard the movement as a tax revolt utilizing secessionist rhetoric with an undeniable odor of racist nationalism.

burden of environmental protection fairly, rather than penalizing developing countries, and by creating an international intellectual property rights regime that encourages the wider distribution of biotechnologies that contribute to human health. These measures, taken together with international support for the state-building that is a prerequisite for economic improvement, along with efforts to overcome educational and economic discrimination against women, will do much to eliminate the need for international recognition of discriminatory redistribution as a distinct ground for justified unilateral secession.

VI. *Conclusions*

In this chapter I have drawn the broad outlines of a theory of how international law should deal with issues of secession and self-determination, developing and refining the views I first advanced in an earlier book and a number of articles. The core idea of my approach is to ground a Remedial Right Only Theory of the right of unilateral secession in a justice-based conception of legitimacy, to uncouple the unilateral right to secede from other, less drastic modes of self-determination and from issues of consensual or negotiated secession, to uncouple self-determination from nationality, and to advocate a vigorous role for international legal institutions in negotiating and supporting intrastate autonomy agreements as an alternative to secession. To make the case for the approach to secession I advocate, I have articulated criteria for evaluating rival theories of the unilateral right to secede and applied them to the comparative evaluation of the main types of theories of the unilateral right to secede.

In the next chapter I consider further the role international legal institutions should play in promoting intrastate autonomy as an alternative to secession, filling out the "proliferate" part of the "isolate and proliferate" strategy for responding to demands for self-determination. There I argue that the domain of transnational justice should include not only international support for individual human rights, but also for intrastate autonomy agreements.

CHAPTER 9

Intrastate Autonomy

I. *Intrastate Autonomy and Transnational Justice*

The isolate and proliferate strategy

In the preceding chapter I argued for combining a rather restrained, justice-based view of the unilateral right to secede, the Remedial Right Only Theory, with a much more supportive stance toward forms of self-determination within the state. Uncoupling the right to secede from the legitimate interests that groups may have in various forms of intrastate autonomy is liberating. It allows groups to get what they need without the risks involved in secession, and it should make states more receptive to legitimate claims for autonomy by assuring them that they can respond to these without implicitly recognizing a minority group's right to secede.

Here I want to elaborate the second prong of the isolate and proliferate strategy by clarifying what it means to say that the international legal order should support intrastate autonomy. The chief question I seek to answer in this chapter is this, then: Under what conditions should the international community involve itself in the creation, maintenance, or restoration of intrastate autonomy regimes?

This chapter should forestall the charge that the normative theory of secession set out in the preceding chapter gives short shrift to the value of self-determination. What that theory rejects is the conflation of self-determination and independent statehood, *not* the importance of self-determination. In this chapter I argue that the international legal order ought to acknowledge the importance of self-determination by supporting intrastate autonomy. I also wish to make it clear that quite apart from the role that international law should play, I believe that individual states should generally give serious consideration to proposals for intrastate autonomy, for a number of different reasons. For one thing, as I have argued all along in this volume, there is nothing normatively or practically privileged about the idea of the unitary state. Breaking the grip of the unitary state paradigm enables us to explore various forms of political differentiation within existing state boundaries.

I will begin with a more specific question: When, if ever, do intrastate autonomy regimes fall within the domain of transnational justice? The former and latter questions are distinct for this reason: Principles of transnational justice lay down the standards that the international legal order ought to *require* states to meet in their internal affairs as a matter of international law; but international actors may have legitimate interests in influencing what goes on within states, even when it is not a matter of transnational justice. The chief difference is that the principles of transnational justice limit and thereby partly define sovereignty, and therefore can provide grounds for forcible intervention in extreme cases. Beyond the domain of transnational justice there may be cases in which it would be permissible and even commendable for the international community to exert diplomatic efforts in support of intrastate autonomy, but in which the use or threat of force would not be justified.

I will first make the case for including in the domain of transnational justice the monitoring and enforcement of intrastate autonomy regimes under certain rather exceptional circumstances. Then, in the last section of this chapter, I will suggest that even where principles of transnational justice do not require it, there are cases in which the international community might play a constructive role by providing diplomatic support and economic inducements or pressure to encourage the creation and well-functioning of intrastate autonomy regimes.

When aspirations to autonomy are not valid claims of justice

The arguments of the preceding chapter show that it is important to distinguish between legitimate interests that groups may have in securing various forms of intrastate autonomy and valid assertions of the right to autonomy. Even when a group does not have a valid claim of justice to intrastate autonomy, there may be good reasons for it to seek it. Decentralizing government functions can be more efficient, can make for more meaningful democratic participation, and can better serve the interests of minorities that believe they have insufficient influence in the broader, state-wide political processes. For all of these reasons and more, intrastate autonomy is often a worthy goal.

However, for an aspiration to intrastate autonomy to be a candidate for being supported by a legal regime of transnational justice, it must express a valid claim of justice. It is important to distinguish then between cases where the international legal order may support or even ought to support intrastate autonomy and cases in which the commitment to justice obliges the international legal order to include a demand for intrastate autonomy within the realm of transnational justice and therefore to require the state to accept the arrangement.

The analysis of the preceding chapter indicates that there are several circumstances in which a group's claim to some form of intrastate autonomy ought to be acknowledged as a valid claim of transnational justice in international law. The first is where the group is entitled under international law to secede, but chooses instead to opt for self-determination that falls short of full independence. The second is where the state has granted self-government to a group within the state, but an appropriate international legal process has determined that the state has persisted in wrongly violating the autonomy arrangement in some fundamental way.

A third circumstance in which intrastate autonomy arrangements may fall within the domain of transnational justice is where the granting of autonomy to a group within the state is the best prospect for stopping persistent and serious rights violations by the state. In an imperfect system in which more direct attempts to end discrimination against a minority group have failed, it may be justifiable for the international legal order to demand that the state grant the group autonomy, even if the rights violations have not reached a level of severity sufficient to justify the group's seceding. (Thus it is conceivable that the worst ethnic cleansings of Kosovar Albanians by Serb forces and the death of many Serbs during the NATO intervention of 1999 might have been prevented if the international community had acted earlier to require Serbia to reinstate the autonomy status of Kosovo, which had been revoked by the Milošović government.)

Later in this chapter I will argue that there is a fourth circumstance that can justify international legal acknowledgment of a right to intrastate autonomy: the need to honor the valid claims of indigenous peoples to rectification of past injustices and their continuing effects.

Distinguishing the grounds for a right to autonomy from those for a right to secede

From the perspective of institutional design that takes incentives seriously, there is much to be said for making the remedial grounds for international legal acknowledgment of a group's right to intrastate autonomy somewhat less demanding than those for the international legal right to secede. For one thing, if the standards were the same, discontent minorities would be prone to conclude that they might as well opt for secession. This would be unfortunate, given the international legal order's legitimate interest in stability and the greater risk of violence that secession usually entails. For another, as Donald Horowitz rightly emphasizes, secession often simply creates a new problem of minority oppression, as the dominant group among the secessionists now have their own state with which to oppress minorities within it.[1] In contrast, where a group that is a minority within the state achieves autonomy rather than full independence, the state will usually still be able to exert some control over how the autonomous region treats its minorities and the majority in the autonomous region will have incentives not to oppress its minorities. For both of these reasons, it makes sense for the international community to require a lesser level of minority rights violations for the recognition of a right to autonomy than for a right to secede. By recognizing a right to autonomy, it may be possible to avoid the issue of secession.

Intrastate autonomy and the protection of individual rights

It is disappointing that the growing literature on intrastate autonomy regimes and power-sharing arrangements is seldom clear as

[1] Horowitz, 'Self-Determination', 433–7.

to whether such arrangements are needed only because current political structures are not effectively protecting minorities against violations of their individual human rights, especially their rights against discrimination on ethnic or religions grounds, or for other, nonremedial reasons.[2] There are in fact two quite different ways to regard intrastate autonomy and power-sharing regimes and to justify support for them by principles of transnational justice.

On the one hand, as I maintain, so far as justice is concerned they could be regarded as largely or even exclusively a remedial matter, as responses to failures to protect minorities from various forms of discrimination and violations of other human rights. On the other hand, they could be regarded as being required as a matter of justice even in the absence of human rights violations. The general thrust of my critiques in the previous chapter of various arguments for self-determination for nations and cultural groups as such is that the international legal order ought to regard intrastate autonomy regimes as remedial devices, as backups for failures to protect individual human rights (and as an optional remedy in the case of forcible annexations of sovereign territory), not as something to which groups have a right simply because they are nations or partake of a distinct culture or are distinct "peoples."

Again, to avoid misunderstanding, let me stress that I am not saying that demands for intrastate autonomy ought only to be taken seriously when they are claims of justice or that self-determination is valuable only as a remedy for injustice. Self-determination can be extremely valuable for many reasons, as I have repeatedly observed. My point is a much more focused one about what international law should require of states. It is a point about the scope of transnational justice, not about the value of self-determination.

There are many things that states can do that would largely obviate the need for instrastate autonomy regimes, or at least would undercut the claim that groups have a claim of *justice* to such arrangements. First and most important, states can provide better protection of individual human rights against discrimination, especially in

---

[2] Timothy Sisk, *Power Sharing and International Mediation in Ethnic Conflicts* (United States Institute of Peace Press, Washington, DC, 1996); Arend Lijphart, *Democracy in Plural Societies: A Comparative Exploration* (Yale University Press, New Haven, 1977); and Lapidoth, *Autonomy*.

employment, education, and basic health care and public health measures, but also against discrimination in access to political participation. Second, for some groups it will be necessary to undertake measures to counteract the continuing effects of past violations of these individual human rights, for example through special subsidies for education or employment, various types of affirmative action programs for minorities, and so on. Third, as I noted in the preceding chapter, states can and should do much more to jettison the particular cultural baggage attached to public ceremonies, holidays, and other items in the public space that minority cultural group members find alienating if not insulting. Even if it proves impossible for the state to be completely "culturally neutral," the more egregious instances of favoring one culture or religion or ethnic group or nationality over others can be eliminated and in some states already have been.

I am not denying that in some cases the individual rights of members of minority groups can best be protected by some form of intrastate autonomy for the group. I shall argue below that this often may be the case for indigenous peoples. But if the case for autonomy is that the minority group is suffering human rights violations, it is a mistake to *begin* with proposals for intrastate autonomy. Instead, the presumption should be that more must be done to protect minorities by respecting their individual rights, including those individual rights that empower and protect communities, such as the right to religion, to wear distinctive cultural dress, and to engage in cultural rituals and ceremonies, as well as the right against all forms of political, educational, and economic discrimination and exclusion.[3]

There are several weighty reasons for concentrating first and foremost on the protection of individual human rights. First, respect for rights generally is not likely to be enhanced by proliferating rights unnecessarily. If conscientious efforts to strengthen protections of individual human rights will do the job, there is no reason to create new autonomy rights. There is also the risk that by shifting our attention to the problem of choosing from a large and complex menu of alternative autonomy regimes we will be distracted from the

---

[3] Hurst Hannum emphasizes the importance of better compliance with individual human rights norms in *Autonomy, Sovereignty, and Self-Determination*, 4, 73, 103, 118.

crucial task of holding states accountable for their primary role of protecting the basic human rights of all their citizens. Furthermore, the creation of autonomy regimes does not itself guarantee that human rights will be respected; in some cases it merely creates a new locus of political power in which those who were the oppressed can become the oppressors. (Recall, for example, that in the century between the end of the American Civil War and the passing of key Federal Civil Rights legislation in 1964 and 1965, the autonomy of Southern states within the federal system legitimized the creation of a regime of institutionalized racism.)

Finally, there is the additional risk, which I explored in some detail at the end of Chapter 8, that if autonomous units within the state have considerable control over revenues and other resources within their boundaries, they will act in ways that impede state efforts to implement distributive justice. In a world in which the state is the only thing approaching an effective agent for distributive justice, this is a serious consideration.[4]

The many forms of intrastate autonomy

A rich and burgeoning literature catalogs the varieties of extant, as well as feasible but yet untried, intrastate autonomy regimes.[5] These range from consociationalism to various forms of symmetrical and asymmetrical federalism to forms of "personal" rather than territorially based rights of self-government. There is in fact an indefinitely broad range of what might be called political rights or rights of collectivities in which rights of self-administration shade off into genuine rights of self-government and rights to participate in decision-making regarding economic development in a group's region shade off into state-like jurisdictional rights to create rules defining property rights.

Nothing general can be said about which sort of autonomy regime is appropriate. Understood as remedies for failures to protect human rights of minorities, intrastate autonomy regimes must be

---

[4] Buchanan, 'Federalism, Secession, and the Morality of Inclusion'.

[5] Donald Horowitz, *Ethnic Groups in Conflict* (University of California Press, Berkeley and Los Angeles, 1985); Sisk, *Power Sharing and International Mediation in Ethnic Conflict;* Lipjhart, *Democracy in Plural Societies;* and Hannum, *Autonomy, Sovereignty, and Self-Determination.*

selected and modified to provide an appropriate response to the particular violations that have occurred, given the social and cultural context and the resources available. The point is that once we realize that the various elements of sovereignty can be unbundled, there is in principle a very wide range of alternative intrastate autonomy regimes.

II. *Indigenous Peoples' Rights*

Indigenous peoples' rights and the philosophy of international law

There are two reasons why a moral theory of international law should address the topic of indigenous peoples' rights (apart from the fact that advocacy of indigenous peoples' rights is becoming more prominent in international legal discourse). (1) Some advocates for indigenous peoples' rights see them as including *group* rights that constitute a challenge to the fundamentally individualistic framework of the dominant individualist conception of human rights. (2) The need to protect the interests of indigenous peoples provides perhaps the strongest case for international legal support for intrastate autonomy. Unfortunately, many international legal theorists—especially those who are Europeans—have tended to underemphasize the importance of indigenous peoples' rights. This chapter is designed in part to help remedy that deficiency.

With regard to (1) I will show that although a proper protection of the rights of indigenous peoples will require changes in international law, it is an exaggeration to say that achieving this protection requires a radical revision of the conceptual framework of human rights theory and practice. There is no reason to conclude that taking indigenous peoples' rights seriously requires abandoning the idea that the international legal order should be grounded in individual human rights or requires embracing the view that a new conception of group rights must be incorporated in it. The main thrust of this section, however, is to support (2), by showing how international legal support for intrastate autonomy for indigenous groups can serve the goals of rectificatory justice.

Rights of peoples, not just of persons

Consider first the thesis that the case of indigenous peoples shows that the conceptual framework of individual human rights that I have employed in earlier chapters is inadequate. Key documents in the discourse of indigenous peoples' rights seem to proceed on this assumption. Throughout the UN Draft Declaration on the Rights of Indigenous Peoples, various rights are ascribed to indigenous *peoples*, not to individual indigenous persons. This choice of words is deliberate; it implies that at least some of the rights set forth in the document are *group* rights. Because it interprets the Draft's reference to rights of peoples as signaling the assertion of group rights, the United States government has argued for revising the wording of the declaration so that only individual rights are recognized.[6]

The putative group rights of indigenous people are of at least two sorts: rights of self-government, usually understood as rights to intrastate autonomy rather than as rights to independent statehood, and rights to "cultural integrity," understood to include not only rights against interference with cultural activities, but also rights to positive actions by states to help indigenous peoples not only to preserve but "strengthen" their cultures and determine the direction of their cultural development.[7]

My concern in this chapter is primarily with rights of self-government, because the goal is to understand the role that support for intrastate autonomy regimes should play in a theory of transnational justice. Since the justice-based approach to the moral theory of international law I have advanced in this volume rests on a conception of individual human rights, it is necessary to clarify and evaluate the charge that such a normative framework cannot accommodate the legitimate claims of indigenous peoples.

Group rights in international law[8]

During the League of Nations period, between the two World Wars, international law included what might be regarded as group rights,

---

[6] Working Group Established in Accordance with United Nations Commission on Human Rights Resolution 1995/32 (1998), 'Report of the Working Group', UN Doc. E/CN.4/1999/82 at 40. See also Cindy Holder, 'Cultural Rights in the U.N. Draft Declaration on the Rights of Indigenous Peoples', unpublished manuscript (University of Victoria, British Columbia).

[7] Articles 15, 29, 33, and 34 of the UN Draft Declaration on the Rights of Indigenous Peoples relate to intrastate autonomy and articles 9, 10, 12, 13, 14, 16, 17, 24, 25, and 26 relate to cultural integrity. For discussion of these articles, see Holder, 'Cultural Rights'.

[8] This subsection is drawn from Buchanan and Golove, 'Philosophy of International Law', 892–7.

chiefly in the form of cultural rights for certain national minorities, but lacked clear norms specifying individual rights. Partly because the concept of minority rights was discredited by Hitler's appeal to the alleged violations of the rights of ethnic Germans in Czechoslovakia and Poland as a pretext for invasion, minority rights were at first accorded at best a minor role in the new international legal order forged by the United Nations in 1945.

Instead, until very recently the domain of transnational justice in the UN Charter era consisted almost exclusively of individual human rights, combined with the recognition of a "right of self-determination of peoples" that in practice has been restricted to "saltwater" decolonization. (The category of international, as distinct from transnational, justice has traditionally consisted until recently of the rights of states, which at least according to the notion of popular sovereignty might be described as group rather than individual rights.) There is some indication, however, that greater attention to the rights of minorities is emerging, especially in the area of indigenous peoples' rights.

The chief issue for a moral theory of international law, then, is whether the Charter era's near exclusive focus on individual rights is defensible, or whether in addition to the rights of states and the right of self-determination of colonized peoples, it ought to be supplemented with a richer menu of group rights. More specifically, if new group rights are to be included in international law, should they be understood as basic rights, coordinate with the most fundamental individual human rights, or as being in some way derivative? And if group rights and individual human rights conflict, which should be accorded priority?

Different senses of 'group rights'

My aim here is not to provide a comprehensive theory of group rights or even a catalog of all the different rights that are sometimes referred to as group rights. It is necessary, however, to clarify what is meant by group rights in the present context.

Unfortunately there is no fixed usage for the term. The following quite different senses can be distinguished.

(1) Group rights are those that cannot be wielded (i.e., exercised, waived, or alienated) by an individual as an individual, on his own

behalf. They can only be wielded on behalf of a collectivity through some collective mechanism, either through a majority vote in the case of a direct participatory democracy, or by the authorized representatives of a collectivity. When such rights are wielded by authorized representatives of a collectivity those representatives do not wield the rights as individuals, on their own behalf. The paradigm example of a group right in sense (1) is a right of self-government enjoyed by a state or by a federal unit or municipality or some other collective entity within the state.

(2) Group rights are those that are ascribed primarily to groups, rather than to individuals—group rights are said to be rights possessed by groups. Thus if a group right in sense (2) is violated, it is to the group as such, not to its members as individuals, that apology, restitution, or compensation is owed. The first concept of group rights, (1), distinguishes them from individual rights according to who or what wields the right; group rights in this sense cannot be wielded by individuals as such. The second, (2), distinguishes them from individual rights according to whom the possessor of the right is.

Although senses (1) and (2) are logically distinct, they usually go together. Thus the reason that a right of self-government for a collectivity such as an Indian tribe or the people of a canton or province is a group right in sense (1), a right that cannot be wielded by an individual as such, on his own behalf, is that it is a right possessed by the collectivity. If no individual possesses the right, then no individual can wield it as an individual, on his own behalf.

(3) A group right is one whose justification appeals to the interests of all or most of the members of a group, not just to the interests of an individual.[9] For example, a right to vote might be ascribed to each individual in a polity (individuals are possessors of the right and wielders of this right), but the justification for this ascription might appeal to the interests that all members of the polity have in having broadly-based participation in government. Appeals to the interests of any given individual or subset of the group might not be sufficient to justify ascription of the right.

For a right to be a group right in sense (3) one need not assume that groups have interests that are not reducible to the interests of

[9] Joseph Raz, *The Morality of Freedom* (Clarendon Press, Oxford, 1986), 207.

their members. The point of sense (3), rather, is that the justification for the right appeals to the interests of all or most members of the group. Furthermore, (3) leaves open the question of whether the right is a group right in sense (1), that is, whether it is to be wielded by individuals as such, on their own behalf.

It is important to recall, as I noted in Chapter 3, that international law, like all domestic legal systems, already includes group rights in sense (1). All the rights of states are group rights in the sense of rights that cannot be wielded by individuals as individuals, on their own behalf. No individual, as an individual, can exercise the sovereignty-constituting rights of the United States, or France, or Thailand, and so on.

So it is preposterous to say that the recognition of group rights in sense (1) for indigenous peoples or any other collectivities such as national minorities challenges the framework of international law. Indeed, until this century international law consisted almost exclusively of group rights in sense (1)—namely, the rights of states. Nor is there anything conceptually novel about saying that individual states or international law, or both, ought to recognize that indigenous groups or national minorities have group rights in sense (2), that is, that they should be regarded as possessors of rights of self-government. This is no more problematic, from a conceptual point of view, than saying that the people of the United States have rights of self-government.

So if what indigenous peoples or national minorities are asking for when they demand group rights is rights of self-government, there is nothing conceptually radical about this. They are simply demanding that some of the rights that states traditionally possess should be ascribed to them and wielded by their authorized agents, on their behalf.

As noted above, advocates of indigenous peoples' rights typically call for recognition not only of rights of self-government, but also a right to cultural integrity, and frequently regard the latter as a "group" or "collective" right. If this means that the right to cultural integrity is a group right in sense (3), then, as with senses (1) and (2), no radical revision of the individualist framework of the justice-based conception of international law is required. Perhaps it is true that the justification of the right to cultural integrity appeals not just to the interest of any single indigenous person but rests on the cumulative moral weight of the interests of all or most individuals in the group. The same may be true of various rights ascribed to the people of the United States or the people of France, including, for example, the right to exercise some control over who becomes a citizen and perhaps the right to vote as well.

The ascription of group rights to indigenous peoples could only challenge the conceptual framework of an individualistic moral theory of international law if group rights are understood in sense (2)—if groups are understood to be the *possessors* of the rights in question, where the reference to groups is not simply shorthand for saying that the right is a right of each member of the group. To understand why this is so, it is important to emphasize that the so-called individualist conceptual framework is only individualistic in a *justificatory* sense: According to moral individualism in the justificatory sense, all justifications for ascriptions of moral and legal rights (and duties) must be grounded *ultimately* on consideration of the well-being and freedom of individuals.

Justificatory individualism is compatible with the view that groups are 'real'—that not all the properties of groups can be reduced to the properties of individuals who are members of the groups.[10] As I emphasized in Chapter 1, it is a justificatory, not an ontological, view. In addition, individualism as a view about justification of rights assertions is also obviously compatible with the ascription of rights in both sense (1) and sense (3): having institutions that allow certain rights to be wielded only by representatives of collectivities, not by individuals on their own behalf (including rights of self-government), can be justified exclusively by appeals to the well-being and freedom of the individuals who are members of the collectivities; and justifications for rights assertions that appeal to the interests of all or most members of a group are nonetheless justifications that rest on considerations of the freedom and well-being of individuals.

The only remaining question is whether individualism in the justificatory sense is compatible with group rights in sense (2), rights whose possessors are groups. It clearly *is*, if the sense (2) group rights are *legal* rights; but not if they are *moral* rights.

---

[10] Buchanan, 'Assessing the Communitarian Critique of Liberalism'; and Allen Buchanan, 'Liberalism and Group Rights', in Jules Coleman and Allen Buchanan (eds.), *In Harm's Way* (Cambridge University Press, New York, 1994).

There are sound individualistic justifications for having laws that designate certain collectivities as possessors of rights. For example, business corporations are possessors of rights in all Western-style domestic legal systems, but this does not entail that corporations are moral entities in their own right and hence proper subjects for the ascription of moral rights. But to assert that a collectivity, as opposed to an individual, is a possessor of a *moral*, as distinct from a legal, right is incompatible with justificatory individualism because regarding a collectivity as a possessor of moral rights assumes that collectivities are moral subjects, and hence the kinds of things that have interests that can serve as the ultimate ground for moral justifications.

Justificatory individualism rejects this latter view, asserting instead that only the interests of individuals can serve as the ultimate ground of moral justification, that only individuals are moral subjects. But this only shows that justificatory individualism is incompatible with groups possessing moral rights, not that it rules out moral justifications for designating groups as possessors of legal rights or as wielders of rights.

There are, then, two quite different ways to understand the assertion that the rights of indigenous peoples include group rights in sense (2), rights that are possessed not by individuals but by collectivities. It can be understood as an assertion that international (and domestic) law should designate indigenous collectivities as possessors of legal rights. This is the view I endorse. Or it can be understood as claiming something further and much more problematic: that indigenous collectivities ought to be designated as the possessors of legal rights *because* they are the possessors of corresponding moral rights. That is the view I reject. Only the second assertion, not the first, is incompatible with the justificatory individualism that underlies the justice-based approach of this book.

Justificatory individualism rightly rejects as implausible if not outright incoherent the notion that groups are possessors of moral rights and hence on a par, morally speaking, with individual human beings. When the justificatory individualist speaks of the interests of groups this is shorthand for the interests of the members of the group.

This is quite compatible, however, with understanding that individuals can have certain interests only by virtue of being members of a group. And it in no way implies that the interests of the individuals who are members of the group are exclusively individualistic interests in the sense of being egoistic.

To assert that indigenous collectivities, or any collectivities, are the possessors of moral rights is not only implausible; it is also entirely *unnecessary* from the standpoint of devising institutions for protecting the interests of indigenous peoples. To see why this is so, in the next section I sketch the main arguments for according indigenous peoples rights of intrastate autonomy under international law. Once the force of these arguments is appreciated it becomes evident that there is a strong case for including intrastate autonomy, and therefore legal group rights of self-government, for indigenous peoples, within the domain of transnational justice. But nothing in these arguments depends upon the problematic assumption that indigenous groups are subjects of moral rights.

III. *Justifications for Intrastate Autonomy for Indigenous Peoples*

There are four distinct and mutually compatible justifications for developing international legal rights to intrastate autonomy for indigenous peoples. First, the creation of intrastate autonomy regimes for indigenous peoples can be required as a matter of rectificatory justice, in order to restore the self-governance of which these peoples were deprived by colonization. Second, intrastate autonomy can provide a non-paternalistic mechanism for protecting indigenous individuals from violations of their individual human rights and for counteracting the ongoing detrimental effects of past violations of their individual human rights or those of their ancestors. Third, it may be necessary to establish or augment institutions of self-government for indigenous groups in order to implement settlements of land claims in cases where lands that were held in common were lost due to treaty violations. Fourth, rectificatory justice can require measures to protect indigenous peoples from the detrimental effects of the disruption of the indigenous customary law that defined and supported their ways of life. However, the best remedy may not be to incorporate indigenous customary law into the state's legal system. Instead, equipping indigenous peoples with powers of self-government that include the right to make new laws for themselves better accords with the fact that their cultures are dynamic and should not be frozen by attempts to restore customary law that no longer best serves their interests.[11]

As these four arguments are explained below it will become clear that they all fall under the category of remedial justifications. None of them assumes that nations or peoples or "distinct societies" or cultural groups as such have moral rights to intrastate autonomy. And none implies that there is a special, *sui generis* category of indigenous peoples' rights. In each case the argument could also apply to groups that are not classified as indigenous. It just so happens that the circumstances that make the arguments applicable probably most often obtain in the case of indigenous peoples.

These four justifications for intrastate autonomy for indigenous peoples appeal to the need to remedy violations of individual human rights, including the rights to property held with others in systems of customary property rights, and to restore self-governance that was unjustly destroyed. It follows that the case for international legal recognition of intrastate autonomy for indigenous peoples does not require anything approaching a fundamental revision of the basic conceptual framework of the international legal order. Instead of being seen as a radical challenge to that framework, the struggle for self-government for indigenous groups should be seen as a long-overdue reformist movement aimed at achieving a more consistent and impartial application of the existing international legal system's most normatively appealing principles, those that emphasize the importance of individual human rights.

Restoration of self-government

In some cases the destruction of indigenous self-governance by colonial incursions is both relatively recent and well documented. Here the case for intrastate autonomy is in basic principle no more problematic than the case for restoring sovereignty to states that have been unjustly annexed. Although it may be true that the sort of self-governance enjoyed by indigenous peoples was not statehood in the sense defined by international law, rectificatory justice requires that they be restored to some form of self-government.

---

[11] See Levy, *Multiculturalism of Fear*, 161–96.

And to the extent that previous indigenous self-government was territorially based, rectification requires intrastate autonomy over a portion of the state's territory. As Margaret Moore has noted, the wrong done to indigenous peoples is the same as that perpetrated against colonized peoples generally: They were forcibly incorporated into a polity controlled by another group, even though they already enjoyed their own governance institutions.[12]

However, as Jeremy Waldron and others have argued, it is one thing to say that rectificatory justice requires the restoration of some forms of territorially based autonomy, but quite another to say that the right to control a portion of territory trumps all considerations of distributive justice and is impervious to all claims based on long-standing expectations under the principle of adverse possession.[13] Waldron's point is that it is unreasonable to hold that vast lands upon which millions of people who had nothing to do with the destruction of indigenous self-government now depend should be returned to the exclusive control of a relatively small indigenous group, even if it is true that the indigenous group previously exercised some sort of control over all of that territory and was the victim of unjust conquest. The need to rectify injustices to indigenous peoples must somehow take into account the demands of distributive justice regarding the larger society in which indigenous peoples find themselves.

This is not to say that the claims of indigenous peoples to restoration of some sort of territorially based self-government can be dismissed. The problem is how to reconcile the competing claims of rectificatory and contemporaneous distributive justice.

It should be emphasized that moral limitations on claims of restoration are not unique to the case of indigenous peoples. They apply equally to cases where states recover their sovereignty after having been unjustly annexed. Neither the reasonable expectations of persons who had nothing to do with the annexation nor the requirements of distributive justice can be ignored in the process of restoring sovereignty. A proper balancing of rectificatory and

---

[12] Margaret Moore, 'The Right of Indigenous Peoples to Collective Self-Determination', in Stephen Macedo and Allen Buchanan (eds.), *Self-Determination and Secession, Nomos* XLV (New York University Press, New York, 2003).

[13] Jeremy Waldron, 'Superseding Historic Injustice', *Ethics* 103 (1992), 4–28.

contemporaneous justice claims will result in some, perhaps many cases in the conclusion that an indigenous group is entitled to intrastate autonomy as the best means of rectifying the unjust destruction of their self-government, though the scope of self-government may be limited by the need to take legitimate expectations and the demands of distributive justice into account.

Self-government as a nonpaternalistic mechanism for preventing human rights violations and for combating the continuing effects of past human rights violations

Indigenous individuals often suffer violations of their human rights, especially in the form of economic discrimination and exclusion from political participation. In some cases the state is the violator of their rights, but perhaps more frequently nowadays the state allows private entities and individuals within the state to violate them. In addition, indigenous individuals frequently complain that they are not accorded equality before the law, suffer discrimination at the hands of the police, and face special difficulties in using legal processes to defend their rights and interests.[14] At least for the foreseeable future, there are likely to be circumstances in which according indigenous groups rights of self-government is the most effective way, or even the only practicable way, to reduce violations of individual human rights, combat more subtle forms of discrimination, and guarantee effective access to legal processes.

Like African-Americans and members of other groups that have undergone centuries of human rights violations, indigenous individuals frequently suffer the ongoing ill effects of past injustices. The most cogent rationale for affirmative action policies in employment and in admission to institutions of higher education is that these measures are needed to counteract the continuing effects of past injustices. The same basic rationale can support the establishment or strengthening of intrastate autonomy for indigenous peoples, in cases where the groups in question (unlike African-Americans) are territorially concentrated on lands whose occupation and use is an

---

[14] See Holder, 'Cultural Rights'.

important aspect of their ongoing efforts to throw off the burden of a history of injustices.

Establishing or strengthening indigenous self-governance, including tribal courts, in order to reduce current human rights violations and counteract the effects of past violations has the added virtue that it responds to the problem in a *nonpaternalistic* fashion, by equipping indigenous peoples themselves with the institutional resources to ensure that their rights are protected and to strive to overcome the disadvantages resulting from historical injustices. Too often in the past even the better-intentioned efforts of others have been ineffective or even counter-productive because of a failure to understand the needs of indigenous peoples or to identify the measures for preventing violations of their rights that are feasible, given their distinctive cultural beliefs and practices. Thus the case for intrastate autonomy as a mechanism for preventing human rights violations and counteracting the continuing effects of past violations rests both on the severity of the problem of discrimination and its ongoing effects and the demonstrated deficiencies of nonindigenous governments to respond adequately to it.

Self-government to facilitate the implementation of land claims settlements

When indigenous peoples succeed in their struggles to regain lands that were taken from them in violation of treaties, institutions of self-government may be needed to determine the ultimate disposition of the lands. Since the lands were typically in some sense held in common, it would be inappropriate to return particular portions of the land to individual members of the group.

It would be a mistake, however, to assume that if the lands that were unjustly taken in the past were held in common, they must ultimately be held in common after they are returned. Instead, it may be in the best interests of the members of the group if the land is allocated in a system that includes both some common property and some individual ownership.

The group's customary rules of common ownership (assuming they are known or can be recovered) may not be a suitable guide for making these crucial decisions about how the hard-won resource is to be used effectively under modern conditions. If the group lacks the institutions of self-government needed to make fair and effective decisions about how to dispose of land returned as a rectification of treaty violations, it may be necessary to create them. For these institutions to function effectively, they must receive legal recognition by the state. If the right to self-government under these circumstances is recognized in international law, this may encourage states to accept and even help facilitate the creation of institutions of self-government for indigenous peoples.

Self-government as a superior alternative to the incorporation of indigenous customary law in the state's legal system[15]

The fourth and final justification for international legal support for indigenous intrastate autonomy flows naturally from the third. Generally speaking, self-government appears to be a more suitable device for indigenous peoples to protect their legitimate interests, including their interests in protecting their cultures, than incorporating indigenous customary law into the state's legal system. In the intact traditional societies in which they are found, customary legal systems change over time through the cumulative actions of the members of those societies. But when such societies have suffered severe disruption and the ordinary processes by which custom evolves have been destroyed or damaged, to attempt to incorporate into the state's legal system what are said to be customary rules at a particular time is to treat the indigenous culture as frozen and fixed.

Intrastate autonomy regimes that include significant powers to create new laws are more consonant with the fact that indigenous cultures, like all other cultures, can and must change in response to new situations. Moreover, there is another risk attendant on attempting to incorporate indigenous customary rules into the state's legal system: Such a strategy typically underestimates the degree of disagreement that can exist in indigenous groups about what the customary norms are or should be, especially when these groups have suffered severe cultural disruption.

Here state actors who propose to protect indigenous groups by incorporating their customary rules into the state's legal system face

---

[15] Levy, *Multiculturalism of Fear*, 61–4.

a dilemma. If they rely on some persons within the indigenous group to determine what the existing customary rules are, without ensuring that the opinion they glean is representative, they may unwittingly support one subgroup (a self-styled elite, or the self-proclaimed interpreters of the authentic culture), and fix within the state's legal system a conception of indigenous life that does not serve the interests of all members of the group. But if they rely upon some institution of representation within the group in order to determine authoritatively what the customary rules are that are to be incorporated in the state's legal system, then they can be accused of undercutting the ability of the group to continue to make and revise its rules and thereby impose unacceptable constraints on future generations. This uncomfortable dilemma can be avoided if the group is accorded the rights of self-government needed to make and revise laws as the culture develops over time.

It is no doubt true that the institutions of self-government that states are likely to accord indigenous peoples will be at least somewhat alien to them, even if they are offered a wide range of alternatives, including some that are more consonant with their culture and traditions. However, if the severe cultural disruption that indigenous people typically have suffered has already gravely damaged their system of customary law or prevents it from evolving to adapt to an environment that is radically different from that in which it was formed, self-government may still be the lesser evil.

IV. *Basic Individual Human Rights as Limits on Intrastate Autonomy*

When the case can be made that intrastate autonomy for indigenous groups or for other minorities is necessary for protecting their members' human rights, or for rectifying past injustices, or for counteracting the ongoing effects of past injustices, international law ought to recognize a right to self-government. This is the most straightforward, justice-based case for international legal acknowledgment of the right to instrastate autonomy for indigenous peoples.

However, some have worried that granting intrastate autonomy might lead to exercises of political power within indigenous communities that violate individual members' human rights. They tend to be especially concerned about violations of rights against gender discrimination.

It would be disingenuous to deny that rights of intrastate autonomy will ever be exercised in ways that violate basic individual human rights. What I would like to point out, however, is that this is a problem of government in general, not of indigenous or minority self-government. Wherever there is political power, there is the risk that it may be exercised in such a way that the rights of some individuals within the political community may be violated. In that sense there is no special problem of a conflict between individual rights and indigenous self-government.

I have argued that in cases where effective protection of the individual human rights of indigenous persons requires it, international law should support indigenous self-government as a matter of transnational justice. But as I argued in Part One, the core of transnational ustice is the requirement that all states do a creditable job of respecting the most basic individual rights.

On that view the same rationale that provides the strongest case for intrastate autonomy for indigenous peoples, the protection of basic human rights, also imposes limits on the ways in which the powers of self-government may be exercised by anyone, including indigenous peoples. International law should hold the state responsible, as a matter of transnational justice, for seeing to it that the exercise of powers of self-government by indigenous peoples or other groups within the state is compatible with discharging its responsibility for ensuring that all its citizens enjoy basic human rights.

Thus the nature of the justification for intrastate autonomy for indigenous peoples makes a difference as to how to respond to conflicts between the exercise of powers of self-government and respect for individual human rights. If, as I have suggested, the rationale for intrastate autonomy is remedial, where the chief concern is the rectification and prevention of human rights violations, then at least in principle the limits of intrastate autonomy are clear. If, in contrast, one argues—as I have not—that international law ought to support intrastate autonomy for indigenous peoples because doing so is necessary to preserve their cultures, there can be a fundamental conflict of values between respect for cultural preservation and respect for individual human rights, with no indication of how it might be resolved even in principle.

V. *International Support for Intrastate Autonomy: Beyond the Requirements of Transnational Justice*

So far I have advanced a view about the circumstances in which international law should acknowledge legal rights to intrastate autonomy for groups within states, including self-government for indigenous peoples. This view is much more supportive of intrastate autonomy and to that extent much more sympathetic to self-determination than existing international law. I will conclude this chapter by suggesting that beyond the realm of what should be required as a matter of transnational justice, international law should even further encourage self-determination for minorities within states.

The crucial point is that the establishment or maintenance of intrastate autonomy may be valuable both to those who seek autonomy and others, even if the group in question has no *right* to self-government. In such cases, though it would be unjustifiable for the international community to infringe sovereignty by forcing the state to institute an autonomy regime, it may nevertheless be fitting to apply diplomatic pressure and economic inducements.

Given the potential of intrastate autonomy regimes for (1) improving efficiency and meaningful democratic participation, for (2) avoiding situations in which minorities believe they are a permanent minority without significant political influence, and for (3) preventing conflicts between groups within the state from escalating to the point of serious human rights violations (including those that typically occur when secession is attempted), there may be a substantial number of cases in which the international community, utilizing the resources of international legal institutions, should encourage autonomy agreements while refraining from seeking to mandate them.

There are several ways in which international legal institutions can encourage states to take seriously the possibility of intrastate autonomy arrangements. For example, the UN High Commissioner on National Minorities and the UN Working Group on the Rights of Indigenous Peoples could continue and increase their efforts in this regard, and regional organizations could also play a beneficial role.

If, as I have suggested, international law distinguished more clearly between the limited (remedial) right to unilateral secession and the various legitimate interests that groups can have in intrastate autonomy—and if loose talk about "the right of self-determination of peoples" is gradually expunged from international legal discourse—such efforts might well bear fruit. Uncoupling secession from self-determination, as I proposed in the previous chapter, would pave the way for a more supportive role for international law regarding intrastate autonomy.

This chapter completes Part Three, Self-Determination, and with that the theoretical core of the book. In Part Four, I first summarize the central argument of the book and list the major proposals for reform that I have advanced in earlier chapters on the basis of it (Chapter 10). I then begin to explore the complex and neglected issue of the feasibility and morality of international legal reform (Chapter 11).

PART FOUR

Reform

CHAPTER 10

Principled Proposals for Reform

This chapter briefly restates the central argument of the book and then summarizes the main proposals for reforming the international legal system that the preceding chapters have developed on its basis. It sets the stage for Chapter 11, which explores morally accessible ways of undertaking the proposed reforms.

I. *A Justice-Based Approach*

The foundation of the moral theory of international law to which this book is a contribution is the commitment to justice for all: the limited obligation each of us has to help ensure that every person has access to institutions that protect his or her basic human rights. This obligation is more robust than the Rawlsian obligation "to support *just* institutions *that apply to us*."[1] It requires us to strengthen existing rights-protecting institutions that are often far from just and in some cases to create new ones, for the sake of other persons, independently of whether those institutions affect us and regardless of whether we are already interacting with those persons.

Yet, as I have emphasized, this obligation to promote just institutions for all persons is not an unlimited one, and nothing I have said about it implies that it ordinarily requires sacrifices. It is important to remember that where resources for collective action in fulfillment of the Natural Duty of Justice already exist—and in particular where there are already developed domestic legal systems in wealthy and powerful states and an international legal system—the

---

[1] Rawls, *A Theory of Justice*, 115.

burden individuals must bear to further the cause of justice is greatly lessened.

Institutional resources not only multiply the effect of individual actions; if properly designed, they also distribute equitably the burdens of honoring the commitment to justice. At least for those of us fortunate enough to be citizens of affluent and politically developed states, the costs of improving others' access to institutions that protect their basic human rights need not be exorbitant if we use our collective institutional resources effectively.

It might be thought that the Natural Duty of Justice is too indeterminate to be of much practical import. But by utilizing existing institutional resources and building new ones, those who try to honor the Natural Duty of Justice can impose upon themselves more determinate duties through a principled division of labor. The more determinate these duties become, the more feasible it becomes to take effective measures to see that they are fulfilled. As I have argued in detail elsewhere, the creation of appropriate institutions can perfect imperfect duties.[2] Helping to ensure that all persons have access to just institutions requires modifying existing institutions, both domestic and international, and building new ones.

Of course to say that one must contribute toward the creation of basic rights-protecting institutions for all when one can do so without "excessive costs" is vague. And beyond the apparent truisms that a sincere commitment to justice for all persons requires that we bear significant costs, that significant costs do not ordinarily involve sacrifice of our most morally important interests, and that the required effort should be proportional to one's resources, I have had little to say about what would count as "excessive costs." (However, in the next chapter I add something of substance to my discussion of excessive costs in the context of armed intervention.)

As I argued in Chapter 3, in discussing the possibility of what I called Deep Disagreement on the specification of human rights norms, existing moral theory provides nothing like a determinate resolution to the question of how much we owe others. Indeed it is not an exaggeration to say that this is a glaring deficiency at the core of the enterprise of moral theorizing. I certainly have not tried to remedy that deficiency in this book (and not simply because

---

[2] Buchanan, 'Justice and Charity'.

I am concerned with the morality of international law, not the foundations of ethical theory).

Even if it is difficult to say how much cost we should bear for the sake of protecting the basic rights of persons generally, it is not so difficult to determine that some of us have not done enough. In a world in which most if not all states, including the astonishingly rich, single superpower, often act internationally as if they owe nothing to anyone other than their own citizens, one can safely say that the danger is not that of unwittingly exceeding the "reasonable costs" limitation of the obligation to promote just institutions.

That is why I have been more concerned to argue that there is such an obligation and to draw its broad implications for what the international legal order should be like, than to try to specify just how demanding it is. The key point is that the same equal concern and respect for persons that any moral theory worth serious consideration regards as fundamental requires that we take seriously the project of ensuring that all persons have access to institutions that protect their basic human rights.

We believe that persons as such have certain basic rights because of the exceptional moral importance of certain fundamental interests all persons have. We are able to identify these fundamental interests because we have a clear enough idea of what the requirements for a decent human life are.

In the case of so-called negative human rights (like the right not to be killed and the right to security of one's personal property), a proper recognition of the moral importance of these fundamental interests places what can turn out to be momentous constraints on our actions, in extreme cases even requiring us to sacrifice important interests—or our very lives. For example, even if my happiness or even my survival depends on your death or upon having something that is yours, I am still obligated to not kill you or appropriate what is yours, because you have human rights. Those who try to restrict the realm of morality to so-called "negative" obligations by emphasizing the costliness of honoring "positive obligations" overlook this fact. The belief that rights can trump appeals to social utility also indicates the profound moral priority we accord to those basic human interests that are served by respect for rights.

But if persons' fundamental interests are so morally important that they can mandate such onerous constraints on our actions and block efforts to maximize overall utility as well, how could it be that a proper regard for those interests is compatible with our having no significant obligation to help ensure that persons have access to the institutions that are needed to protect them? To recognize that persons as such have rights while denying that we are obligated to bear significant costs to help ensure that those rights are respected is to manifest a practically incoherent attitude toward the fundamental interests of persons. So, even if the Natural Duty of Justice is a limited obligation, it has implications for how we should live.

II. *An International Legal Order Grounded in Obligation, not Mere Permissibility*

Most who argue for limiting state sovereignty in the name of human rights concentrate on showing that when fundamental moral values are at stake *it is permissible* for individual states or organizations of states to engage in intervention if they choose to do so. The approach taken in this volume is more ambitious: I have argued that individuals, working through domestic, regional, and international institutions, are morally *obligated* to act for the protection of basic human rights.

However, it is worth noting that the International Commission on Intervention and State Sovereignty recently concluded that "Where the population is suffering serious harm, as a result of internal war, insurgency, repression or state failure and the state in question is unwilling or unable to halt or avert it, the principle of non-intervention yields to the international responsibility to protect." Although this appeal to responsibility stops short of declaring explicitly that there is an obligation to protect, it comes very close to it, and clearly goes beyond the traditional assumption that at most intervention is permissible.[3] The idea of an international legal order based on obligations to protect human rights may already be becoming less radical.

[3] International Commission on Intervention and State Sovereignty, *The Responsibility to Protect: Report of the International Commission on Intervention and State Sovereignty* (International Development Research Centre, Ottawa, 2001).

Whether a consensus develops in favor of this shift toward obligation will depend in part upon how convincing a case can be made for it. The International Commission does not articulate a clear, principled basis for attributing this responsibility to the international community. In contrast, I have argued explicitly that it is grounded in the Natural Duty of Justice and ultimately in the principle that persons are entitled to equal regard.

To rest content with the statement that it is permissible to limit state sovereignty for the sake of basic human rights is to draw a morally anemic picture of the international legal order and of the stake that responsible agents have in its development. In Chapter 1 I noted that there is a conception of the nature of the state and of the proper role of government according to which the state is nothing more than an association for the mutual benefit of its citizens and the only legitimate function of government is to serve those interests. On that conception, whether the people of a particular state utilize their institutional resources to help develop international legal institutions for the sake of protecting the basic human rights of all persons is up to their discretion, depending upon how they view their own interests.

On the quite different view of the state as a resource for justice— the view I have begun to develop in this volume—supporting a just international legal order is not a matter of discretionary choice; it is morally required. According to this conception of the state, which takes the Natural Duty of Justice seriously, participation in and support for just international legal institutions is not something which the people of a particular state may opt for or not, depending solely upon whether it serves their interests.

This conclusion is reinforced once we see how weak the case is for the thesis that it is permissible for states to pursue the national interest exclusively in their foreign policies. In Chapter 3 I demonstrated the implausibility of the National Interest Thesis.

However, as I argued in Chapter 7, honoring the Natural Duty of Justice does not require supporting every aspect of the existing international legal system and may even mandate fundamental changes in the institutions in which international law is currently embodied. In the next chapter I argue that it may require either major reform of certain aspects of the UN-based system of law or the development of alternative institutions, such as a rule-based regime for humanitarian intervention composed of the more democratic and human rights-respecting states that bypasses the UN Security Council.

The more general point, however, is that once we acknowledge the Natural Duty of Justice, our vision of the nature of the international legal system and our moral relationship to it are transformed. The task of international legal reform is no longer merely a morally permissible option, something to be pursued only so far as it promotes the "national interest"; it is a moral necessity. State leaders are not free to regard the international legal system as something to support or ignore as expediency dictates.[4] Even if their freedom of action is properly constrained by what their fellow citizens democratically authorize, and by their fiduciary duty to give a limited priority to their own citizens, interests, they have a responsibility to exercise leadership in making the case for supporting an international legal system that is a valuable resource for acting on the Natural Duty of Justice.

III. *Linking Justice, Legitimacy, and Self-Determination*

The basic structure of the moral theory of international law I have begun to develop in this volume is provided by a way of understanding the relationships between justice, legitimacy, and self-determination. Justice and legitimacy, as I have emphasized, are distinct concepts. (For one thing, legitimacy does not require perfect or full justice.) But the legitimacy of states, and ultimately of the international legal system itself, must be defined in terms of some threshold approximation to full or perfect justice. My suggestion has been that for the foreseeable future, the concept of basic human rights should serve as that threshold and that it can perform this function without transgressing the proper bounds of tolerance.

Once a justice-based account of state legitimacy is worked out, questions about self-determination become much more tractable.

---

[4] I have not attempted to address the enormously difficult issue of how the responsibility for protecting human rights ought to be distributed; nor the equally difficult issue of how the failure of some states to discharge their obligations affects the character of the obligations others recognize. For a thoughtful discussion of the first question, see Miller, 'Distributing Responsibilities'.

In particular, a justice-based account of state legitimacy supports a Remedial Right Only Theory of the unilateral right to secede, and this latter theory in turn allows us to uncouple the unilateral right to secede from various legitimate interests that groups may have in having their own state or in enjoying intrastate autonomy.

The justice-based, Remedial Right Only Theory of the unilateral right to secede also uncouples self-determination from *nationality*. According to the Remedial Right Only Theory, nations as such do not have a right to secede or even to intrastate autonomy (although in some cases, nations, like other groups, have a right to secede because of the injustices they suffer and in many more cases should be granted intrastate autonomy even if they are not entitled to it as a matter of justice). Thus the justice-based view I have developed provides the most *systematic, principled* refutation available of the Principle of National Self-Determination, whose lack of normative coherence is matched only by the disastrous practical effects of believing it to be true.

I hope to have shown in preceding chapters that a moral theory of self-determination is only plausible if it is grounded on an account of legitimacy, and that to be normatively satisfying an account of legitimacy must ultimately be justice-based. Once the moral implications of judgments conferring legitimacy on states are understood, there is no plausible alternative to a justice-based theory of legitimacy. The only thing that could justify the wielding of political power is the achievement of a minimal threshold of human rights protection. And unless claimants to statehood are at least required to meet this threshold, recognizing them as legitimate makes us accomplices in injustice.

Once a justice-based account of state legitimacy is worked out, we are in a position to make more coherent, morally defensible judgments about which claims of self-determination the international community ought to support and which ones it should reject. Attempts to provide freestanding accounts of the moral right to secede, not grounded in a larger moral theory of the overall institutional system in which claims to self-determination are advanced and opposed by states, are doomed to failure, both theoretically and practically.

In the end, the cogency of the views about legitimacy and self-determination I have advanced in this book depends upon the overall moral appeal and practicality of the theory that connects them with one another. My accounts of legitimacy and self-determination are mutually supporting. An accurate assessment of each requires an appreciation of how they work together with the foundational emphasis on justice to provide the basic architecture of a moral theory of international law. Attempts to criticize the views on self-determination or on legitimacy I have advanced will be inconclusive if they are not grounded in a similarly systematic alternative view.

I am more convinced that a holistic, systematic approach to the urgent issues of international law is necessary than I am of the unique validity of the particular conceptual architecture I have tried to delineate. Nevertheless it seems to me—for now at least—that any plausible moral theory of international law will at least give a very prominent, if not a fundamental place to the concepts of justice, legitimacy, and self-determination and the relationships among them.

IV. *Needed Reforms*

On the basis of this theoretical structure linking justice, legitimacy, and self-determination, I have advanced a number of proposals for reforming several key areas of international law. The most important of these (without repeating the justifications for them) can be listed as follows.

1. *Construction of a normativized practice of conditional, provisional recognition.* New claimants to the status of legitimate statehood must make a credible commitment to achieving a minimal standard of justice, understood primarily as respect for basic human rights at home and abroad, along with minimal democracy. This practice should include: (*a*) legally mandatory recognition of entities that satisfy the threshold justice and minimal democracy requirements, and (*b*) effective sanctions against states that grant recognition to entities that do not satisfy the threshold requirements. Recognition of new entities as states should always be conditional in the sense that it should depend upon satisfaction of the threshold requirements. In the case of new claimants to statehood arising out of secessions, the single most important aspect of the threshold justice requirement is credible guarantees of the basic

human rights of minorities. (Otherwise secession will simply repli-
cate the conflicts it was thought to resolve.) In order to ensure
the effectiveness of these guarantees, the international community
should adapt existing institutional and doctrinal resources for monitoring compliance with human rights norms to the special conditions of "high-risk" secessions. A more ambitious and more distant
goal for reform is to require every existing state to meet the same
normativized criteria that are now appropriate for the recognition
of new states.

Given current realities—for example the inability or unwillingness
of the international community to enforce human rights norms in
powerful countries such as China and Russia—it is unlikely that the
same criteria for legitimacy will be applied to all existing states as those
that should and can be applied to new states. Nevertheless, even if it is
unrealistic to think that recognition could be withdrawn from very
powerful rights-violating states, there are many other forms of pressure, diplomatic and economic, which can be brought to bear, and that
would at least mitigate the international system's complicity in supporting human rights-violating regimes by granting them recognition.

I have emphasized the importance of a normativized practice of
recognition because new entities emerging from self-determination
conflicts typically have incentives to do what is necessary to achieve
recognition. But this is not to say that the only alternatives are
recognition or complete lack of engagement. Moreover, by recognizing a unilateral right to secede on remedial grounds (see 2 below)
international law would in effect be acknowledging that the same
minimal justice standards for recognition of new entities as legitimate states must be met by existing states if they are to preserve
their full rights of territorial integrity.

In some cases new claimants to the status of legitimate statehood
may not be able or willing to satisfy fully the normative criteria for
recognition all at once. Therefore, a normativized international legal
practice of recognition should include the option of "unbundling"
sovereignty and conferring the attributes of legitimate statehood
in stages, as the process of building a rights-respecting state
progresses. If the process falters, it should be possible to withdraw
selected elements of sovereignty until progress resumes. In that
sense, recognition of new states should be not only conditional but
provisional as well.

2. *International legal recognition of a remedial right to unilateral secession.* The international legal right to try to establish an independent state in a portion of the territory of an existing state should be restricted to cases where secession is a remedy of last resort against a persistent pattern of serious injustices, including (*a*) large-scale violations of basic human rights, (*b*) properly documented violations by the state of bona fide autonomy agreements, (*c*) discriminatory redistribution so severe as to constitute violations of the basic human right to the material conditions for a decent human life or egregious discrimination on the basis of race, ethnicity, or nationality, and (*d*) unjust annexations of the territory of legitimate states. By limiting the right to unilateral secession to these cases of serious, persisting, and relatively uncontroversial injustices, the international legal order would unambiguously reject the principle that all nations (or distinct peoples, or ethnic groups) are entitled to their own states and the assumption that any group that has the right of self-determination thereby has the right to opt for secession. Such a remedial international legal right to unilateral secession should not be created, of course, until provisions are made for an appropriate procedure for the impartial adjudication of claims to the right to secede and for enforcing the normative conditions for recognitional legitimacy.

3. *International support for the creation and maintenance of intrastate autonomy regimes.* By uncoupling the legitimate interests that various groups can have in self-determination from the unilateral right to secede, and by uncoupling self-determination from nationality, the international legal order can and should encourage creative departures from the centralized-state, "unbundled" sovereignty paradigm that fuels secession yet virtually never solves the problems that give rise to it. Restriction of the unilateral right to secede to a remedial right would liberate states to consider intrastate autonomy arrangements without embarking on a slippery slope toward their own dissolution. Discontent minorities would be encouraged to opt for intrastate autonomy as an alternative to secession by assuring them of international monitoring of and support for compliance with autonomy agreements in high-risk cases. Dangerously broad references in international legal documents to an international legal right to self-determination should be replaced by clear statements of the unilateral right to secede as a remedial right only and by language

that uncouples the right to secede from legitimate interests in self-determination and uncouples self-determination and nationality. International law should support the legitimate interests of national minorities by strengthening human rights against discrimination and by encouraging states to explore forms of intrastate autonomy, rather than by recognizing a "right of self-determination of peoples" that legitimizes secession by such groups.

4. *International recognition of a unilateral right to intrastate autonomy* in certain special, rather narrow circumstances. First when international law recognizes a group's right to secede, it should also recognize the right of the group to opt for intrastate autonomy if it so chooses. Second, when a group (whether it is a nation or not) qualifies on remedial grounds for a unilateral right to secede but opts instead for intrastate autonomy, the international legal order should recognize its legal right to autonomy and play a constructive role in negotiations to formulate an appropriate intrastate autonomy arrangement and should apply appropriate measures to monitor compliance with it. Third, international law should recognize and support intrastate autonomy for indigenous groups when they are needed to rectify serious injustices suffered by such groups. Fourth and finally, where establishment of an intrastate autonomy regime for a minority is the only way to prevent it from suffering large-scale violations of basic human rights, an instrastate autonomy regime may be imposed upon a state through an appropriate international legal process.

5. *International legal mediation of consensual secessions and consensual intrastate autonomy agreements.* Even in cases where a group does not have a unilateral right to secede, international legal resources should be available to play a mediating, facilitating role in consensual secessions and in the consensual creation of intrastate autonomy regimes. In addition, international legal resources should be employed to monitor compliance with and provide support for the well-functioning of intrastate autonomy regimes in circumstances in which their failure carries a risk of large-scale human rights violations or high-risk unilateral secessions, even when these arrangements are not mandated by the exercise of a *right* to self-determination or to secession.

6. *Integration of the remedial unilateral right to secede with a reformed inter-national legal right of humanitarian intervention.* As

I argue more explicitly in the next section, the international legal community should construct a more morally defensible and practicable international legal practice regarding intervention for the sake of protecting basic human rights, one that does not require Security Council authorization in every instance (under the current arrangement in which each permanent member of the Council has a veto). A new practice of intervention, so far as it applies to secessionist conflicts, should be shaped by and consistent with the remedial right only approach to an international legal right to unilateral secession. Subject to appropriate constraints that apply to justified humanitarian interventions generally (proportional force, protection of noncombatants, etc.), states should be allowed under international law to intervene to support groups that are recognized in international law as having the unilateral right to secede, if other means of redressing the group's grievances have failed or offer little prospect of success in a timely manner. Generally speaking, international law should prohibit states from intervening militarily to support secession by groups that are not recognized under international law as having the unilateral right to secede and should support legitimate states in their efforts to resist illegal secessions. Exceptions to this generalization could include cases where the state has persisted in using unlawful means of war to suppress an illegal secession (for example, indiscriminate and/or disproportionate military force or efforts to suppress the secession that amount to genocide (as is arguably the case in Russia's attacks on Chechnya)).

7. *Building institutional capacity for transnational and international distributive justice.* I argued in Chapter 4 that at present the opportunities for furthering distributive justice through international law are rather limited, due to institutional incapacity broadly defined, which includes but encompasses more than a lack of enforcement capacity. While at the same time pursuing the requirements articulated in the best available ideal theory of global justice indirectly on a number of fronts (liberalized immigration, humane universal labor standards, multilateral aid, trade regimes that give special weight to the interests of the worst off, etc.), the inter-national community should begin to build the needed institutional capacity for playing a more direct role in the pursuit of distributive justice.

8. *Above all, the international community should strengthen the protection of basic human rights that already exist under international*

law, working to safeguard the basic human rights of minorities and especially of indigenous peoples, thereby dampening the fuel for secessionist crises. If the regime of transnational justice becomes more developed and more states meet the threshold requirements of basic human rights protection and minimal democracy, the need of each group to have its own state should diminish and the dominance of the statist paradigm should begin to wane, and with it the attraction of secession.

Perhaps the greatest virtue of the reforms listed above is that together they constitute a *human rights-based* approach to conflicts concerning self-determination and secession, rather than the abandonment of the human rights enterprise in favor of developing a new, practically dangerous and normatively incoherent international legal doctrine and practice that ascribes an expansive right of self-determination to nations, distinct peoples, or cultural groups.

Making progress toward these reforms will require reforms in international law regarding the use of force. In the next and final chapter I explore the morality of paths toward international legal reform, focusing on reforms in the international legal regulation of armed intervention in the name of justice.

CHAPTER 11

The Morality of
International Legal Reform

The preceding chapter summarized the main proposals for reform for which I have argued in this book, briefly restated the moral framework linking justice, legitimacy, and self-determination that grounds them, and noted that implementing the proposed reforms probably would require significant changes in international law regarding armed intervention. The aims of this chapter are (1) to explain more fully why a new legal framework for armed intervention is needed for successful legal reform, (2) to examine the pros and cons of the major types of strategies for achieving the needed reform in the law of armed intervention, from the perspective of both feasibility and morality, and (3) to show that the most promising strategy for reform may be the creation of a treaty-based, rule-governed liberal-democratic regime for armed intervention that bypasses the current UN Charter-based requirement of Security Council authorization and that does *not* depend upon the United States to act as the world's policeman.

In addition, I will argue that although the most promising strategy for reform may require violating existing international law, it is morally justifiable nonetheless. The more general point I will make is that under certain conditions a willingness to violate existing international law for the sake of reforming it can be not only consistent with a sincere commitment to the rule of law, but even required by it.

Exploring the possibility of developing a rule-governed, treaty-based regime for humanitarian armed intervention that bypasses the UN Charter-based law regarding the use of force turns out to be liberating, even if in the end that particular proposal is rejected. It allows us to consider the possibility of a more pluralistic conception of international law, one that makes room for competition among different law-like systems of rules in a dynamic process by which international law becomes a more developed kind of law and a more powerful resource for the pursuit of justice.

Having made this plea for a more expansive conception of the possibilities for international law, I wish to emphasize what I said in the Synopsis that began this volume: Violations of fundamental rules of existing international law, such as the prohibition against preventive war and against any use of force that does not qualify as self-defense and lacks Security Council authorization, are irresponsible, unless they are accompanied by a sincere effort to construct superior international legal structures to replace those they damage or render obsolete.

The morality of international legal reform is a remarkably neglected topic. As I shall show, there has been some discussion of the particular issue of illegal acts directed toward reform, but the waters have been muddied by a failure to distinguish clearly between whether there is a legal justification or legal excuse for violating an existing international legal norm and whether violation is morally justified. Unfortunately, a probing discussion of this issue has been inhibited by the prevalence among international legal scholars of Legal Absolutism, the view that it is virtually never justifiable to violate international law, or at least not the most basic norms of international law, even for the sake of protecting human rights.

Because of the failure to appreciate just how implausible Legal Absolutism is, those favoring major reforms of international law in the name of morality have often yielded to the temptation to stretch the notion of international legality, arguing (unconvincingly) that the law already is what they believe it should be. In contrast I will face head-on the issue of whether, or rather under what conditions, illegal acts directed toward legal reform are morally justifiable.

Before proceeding with an exploration of the morality of efforts to reform the international law of (armed) humanitarian intervention, I wish to emphasize that I believe that most if not all of the work of implementing the reforms summarized in the preceding chapter can be accomplished without recourse to armed intervention. This is especially true of international legal support for intrastate autonomy, but also is likely to be the case regarding the creation of a normativized, conditional practice for recognizing new entities as legitimate states. Especially if the inherent benefits of recognition are augmented by tying recognition to additional economic benefits such as inclusion in trade regimes, recourse to coercion may not be necessary.

I. *The Need for Reform Regarding the Law of Intervention*

The importance of the intervention option: the advantages of coercive diplomacy

Nevertheless, even if armed intervention is never used, it may be needed as an ultimate sanction for the principles I have proposed. An expanded conception of justified intervention creates a correspondingly broadened opportunity for coercive diplomacy—for making credible threats of coercion to make states behave better, both by deterring them from acting badly and by compelling them to act well. For example, if a state knows that armed intervention is a legal option if other sanctions do not succeed in making it stick to the terms of its intrastate autonomy agreement with an oppressed minority group, it may be more willing to honor the agreement. Other things being equal, a threat of intervention will be more credible if intervention is legally permissible.

The question of whether international law regarding (armed[1]) intervention needs overhauling has already arisen, of course, because of the international community's failure to stop the recent genocide in Rwanda and its long delay in responding to ethnic cleansing, crimes against humanity, and war crimes in Bosnia. The focus of the debate has been on *humanitarian* intervention, which may be defined as follows: the use of force across state borders by a state (or group of states) aimed at ending widespread and grave violations of the human rights of persons other than its own citizens, without the permission of the government of the state within whose territory force is applied.

---

[1] For the remainder of this chapter, 'intervention' will refer to armed intervention, unless otherwise specified.

Implementing the reforms summarized in the preceding chapter may require humanitarian intervention thus defined or at least may require an international legal framework that makes the threat of such intervention credible. However, some of the interventions that should be available as a last resort to implement the reforms I have proposed might not qualify as humanitarian interventions in the strict sense just defined.

For example, to make effective a remedial international legal right to unilateral secession, it may prove necessary to construct a legal framework that allows intervention against a state that attempts to prevent a group that has the international legal right to secede from doing so. But this ultimate sanction would not qualify as humanitarian intervention in the sense defined above unless the state, in its attempt to block secession, was engaging in massive violations of human rights. Thus not all interventions for the sake of implementing the justice-based reforms I have proposed are humanitarian interventions strictly speaking, even though the ultimate rationale for them is the same as that for humanitarian interventions, namely, the commitment to protecting basic human rights.

Existing international law regarding the use of armed force is very far from allowing the sorts of interventions that may be needed as an ultimate sanction for the reforms I have proposed. In fact, the existing legal framework poses a formidable barrier to interventions to humanitarian intervention strictly speaking. Interventions to stop horrific, large-scale violations of the most basic human rights are prohibited under international law, unless they qualify as collective self-defense or are authorized by the UN Security Council.

In addition, *preventive* humanitarian intervention—defined as intervention to prevent massive violations of basic human rights that is undertaken before violations are actually occurring or imminent—is also currently legally prohibited.[2] Yet there can be cases—the Rwandan genocide of 1994 may be one of them—when preventive force to protect human rights, or coercive diplomacy using the credible threat of preventive force, would save many lives and do so without unacceptable moral costs.

---

[2] For an argument to show that the use of preventive force for the sake of human rights could be justified under conditions in which the decision to intervene preventively is made within a procedural framework designed to achieve accountability, see Buchanan and Keohane, 'The Preventive Use of Force'.

The deficiency of existing law

The NATO intervention in Kosovo (1999) is only the most recent of a series of illegal interventions for which cogent moral justifications *could* have been given. Others include India's intervention in East Pakistan in response to Pakistan's massive human rights violations there (1971), Vietnam's war against Pol Pot's regime of mass killings in Cambodia (1978), and Tanzania's overthrow of Idi Amin's murderous rule in Uganda (1979). Without commenting on what the dominant motives of the intervenors were, it is accurate to say that in each case military action could have been justified on the grounds that it was needed to stop massive human rights violations.

In all four instances the intervention was, according to the preponderance of international legal opinion, a violation of international law. None was a case of self-defense and none enjoyed UN Security Council authorization.

The charge that the NATO intervention, like those that preceded it, was illegal is based on the most straightforward interpretations of the UN Charter, Articles 2(4) and 2(7).[3] So I will assume what the preponderance of international lawyers seem to hold, namely, that the NATO intervention was illegal; but nothing of substance in this chapter depends upon the truth of that assumption.

The central point is that the UN Charter-based international legal framework for the use of armed force is highly constraining. It allows neither humanitarian intervention strictly speaking nor the sorts of justice-based interventions whose legality likely would be needed to implement the reforms I propose. At present, under the UN Charter-based international legal framework, armed action across borders is only legally permissible in the case of self-defense or in accordance with Security Council authorization under the Council's Chapter VII powers, in response to threats to international peace and security.

The earlier interventions by India, Vietnam, and Tanzania provoked considerable international discussion. However, there is an important difference in the case of the NATO intervention. Much

---

[3] For a thorough account of the reasons for concluding that the NATO intervention was illegal, see Jeffrey Holzgrefe, 'Introduction', in Jeffrey Holzgrefe and Robert O. Keohane (eds.), *Humanitarian Intervention: Ethical, Legal, and Political Dilemmas* (Cambridge University Press, New York, 2003).

more so than with the earlier interventions, NATO's action in Kosovo and the ensuing debate over its justifiability have focused attention on the deficiency of existing international law concerning humanitarian intervention. In the aftermath of Kosovo, there seems to be a broad consensus that there is an unacceptable gap between what international law allows and what morality requires.

However, this way of stating the deficiency is inaccurate because it suggests too stark a separation between the international legal system and moral values. As Kofi Annan emphasized at the time of the NATO intervention in Kosovo, the impossibility of gaining Security Council authorization for the intervention indicated a disturbing tension between *two core values embodied in the international legal system*: respect for state sovereignty and a commitment to peaceful relations among states, on the one hand, and the protection of basic human rights, on the other.[4] The point is not simply that the intervention, though illegal, was morally justifiable; in addition, its best moral justification relied on one of the most important values of the UN and of the UN-based system of international law.

There is a growing consensus, then, that the requirement of Security Council authorization is an obstacle to the protection of basic human rights in internal conflicts. Since the majority of violent conflicts are now within states rather than between them, the time is ripe to consider modifying or abandoning a rule of humanitarian intervention that was created for a quite different world.

In the remainder of this chapter I will focus my exploration of the morality of international legal reform on the problem of how to improve the international law of humanitarian intervention, for two reasons. First, unless a more permissive international law regarding humanitarian intervention is developed—unless it first becomes legally permitted to intervene to stop presently occurring massive violations of basic human rights, as in the cases of genocide and ethnic cleansing, in the absence of Security Council authorization—it is unlikely that it will become legally permissible to intervene to stop a state from crushing a secessionist movement that has the right to secede or to ensure that a state abides by an intrastate autonomy agreement. In other words, liberalizing the international law of

---

[4] Kofi Annan, 'Speech to the General Assembly, September 20, 1999', September 20, 1999; SG/SM/7136 GA/9569: Secretary-G, at 2.

humanitarian intervention is likely to be a necessary condition for achieving the reforms I have proposed.

Second, the basic issues explored in the recent debate about humanitarian intervention are of much wider application, with implications not only for other interventions for the sake of protecting basic human rights, but also for other reforms that do not involve changing the regulation of the use of force. Focusing on the problem of reforming the law of humanitarian intervention will lend concreteness to an examination of the more general topic of how to achieve international legal reform for the sake of justice.

II. *Three Types of Strategies for Legal Reform*

Reform through new custom versus treaty-based reform, within or outside the UN system

As with change in international law generally, the two main options for legal change regarding intervention are the creation of new law by treaty or by the emergence of new customary law. In the case of reforming the law of intervention, change through treaty could come about in two very different ways: either by modifications of the UN Charter-based law of intervention, in particular by amending the Charter to allow intervention without Security Council authorization under certain circumstances; or by the creation of treaties that in effect bypass the UN-based system and attempt to establish an independent international legal regime for intervention. Thus there appear to be three main types of strategies for reforming the international law of intervention: (1) developing new customary law, (2) modifying the UN Charter-based law of intervention, and (3) creating an alternative treaty-based intervention regime outside the UN framework. In the remainder of this section I examine the pros and cons of each of these three types of strategies for legal reform, and conclude that (3) offers the best prospect for morally defensible, effective reform within a reasonable time-span.

Custom

In briefest terms, a new norm of customary law is created as the result of the emergence of a persistent pattern of behavior by states, undertaken in the belief on the part of state actors that the behavior in question is legally required or legally permissible (the *opinio juris* requirement).

The chief advantage of the customary change approach, as Jane Stromseth points out in a thoughtful recent article, is that it is incremental or gradualist, thereby reducing the risks that attend what may turn out to be premature or poorly thought-out attempts to make significant changes all at once, through the drafting of a new treaty.[5] In addition, by the time a new customary rule emerges, the change in attitudes and behavior necessary for its effectiveness will have already largely occurred.

However, several aspects of the process by which new customary law is generated substantially limit the efficacy of this route toward legal reform. First, international law allows states to opt out of the new customary norm's scope by consistently dissenting from it during the process of its "crystallization." Second, how widespread the new pattern of state behavior must be before a new norm can be said to have "crystallized" is not only disputed but also probably not capable of a definitive determination. Third, even if a sufficiently widespread and persisting pattern of behavior is established, the satisfaction of the *opinio juris* requirement may be less clear, more subject to dispute. Pronouncements by state leaders may be ambiguous, in some cases indicating a recognition that the behavior in question is legally required or permissible, in other cases appearing to deny this.

Given these limitations, the efforts of the state or states that first attempt to initiate the process of customary change are fraught with uncertainty. If the new rule they seek to establish addresses a long-standing and widespread pattern of state behavior, and one in which many states profess to be legally entitled to persist, other states may not follow suit. (This is likely to be especially true in the case of behavior that represents an erosion of sovereignty, as is the case with a more permissive rule regarding intervention.) Or, if other states follow suit, they may do so for strictly pragmatic reasons and may attempt to ensure that a new customary rule does not emerge by letting it be known that they do not regard their behavior as

---

[5] Jane Stromseth, 'Humanitarian Intervention: Incremental Change Versus Codification', in Holzgrefe and Keohane (eds.), *Humanitarian Intervention*.

legally required or legally permissible (thus thwarting satisfaction of the *opinio juris* condition).

The point is that new customary norms do not emerge from a single action or even from a persistent pattern of action by one state or a group of states. A new norm is created only when the initial behavior is repeated consistently by a preponderance of states over a considerable period of time and only when there is a shift in the legal consciousness of all or most states as to the legal status of the behavior.

At any stage the process can break down. For example, if one powerful state dissents from an emerging norm, other states may decide it is prudent to register dissent as well or to refrain from pronouncements that would count toward satisfying the *opinio juris* requirement. Thus the initial effort to create a new customary norm is a gamble.

In some areas of law, creating new customary norms is not so difficult and may not require illegal actions. This may be especially true if the new norm fills a legal vacuum, as was the case with laws regarding outer space. But the law of intervention is a different matter. Reforming it by easing the strictures of the UN Charter is a head-on challenge to sovereignty and for that reason the customary route to reform will almost certainly involve illegality, at least in its initial stages.

Moreover, to a certain extent the customary process is a process of approval by the majority of states. Given the hostility of most states toward limitations on sovereignty, this majoritarian aspect of the process makes the creation of a more permissive customary norm of intervention very problematic.

There is another limitation on the strategy of legal reform through change in custom that is troubling from the standpoint of morality. Suppose a state or group of states decides that reform of the law of humanitarian intervention is necessary and seeks to initiate a process that will eventually result in the emergence of a new norm of customary law that allows intervention without Security Council authorization. Suppose, for the sake of the argument, that this was what was intended by the members of NATO in the case of the Kosovo intervention. Suppose also that those attempting to create a new customary norm are aware that to be an improvement—a genuine reform rather than simply a change—the new customary norm must be carefully hedged. It must only authorize intervention without Security Council approval under certain extreme circumstances.

The problem is that there is no assurance that the new customary norm that eventually emerges (if one does) from the process that the reformers initiate will include the proper sort of qualifications and safeguards. For remember, those who try to initiate the process of customary change cannot achieve it on their own; they can merely act in such a way that (they hope) will eventually result in the change they seek, on the assumption that many other agents will act appropriately over a period of time. Any state that has a reasonable appreciation of the dangers of an overly permissive, insufficiently hedged rule of intervention should therefore be quite apprehensive about the moral risks involved in trying to reform the law of intervention by initiating customary change.[6]

To summarize: Although it enjoys the advantages of gradualism, the strategy of reforming international law concerning intervention through the development of new customary law suffers serious liabilities. Significant and timely reform of the law of intervention through the creation of new customary norms is difficult, uncertain, and morally risky.

Reform through treaty within the UN-based system

This might be accomplished by a General Assembly Resolution specifying a new rule of intervention combined with amendments to the UN Charter's Articles 2(4) and 2(7) to make the new rule consistent with those Articles.[7] This route toward reform has two attractions: It would require no illegalities and it would achieve reform by an inclusive, majoritarian process, issuing from a broad base of support in the international community.

---

[6] For a discussion of how NATO could have acted, during *and after* the Kosovo intervention, so as to increase the chances that a reasonably hedged new norm of humanitarian intervention might eventually crystallize, and in particular what NATO could have done (but failed to do) to increase the probability that the *opinio juris* condition would come to be satisfied, see Allen Buchanan, 'Reforming the Law of Humanitarian Intervention', in Holzgrefe and Keohane (eds.), *Humanitarian Intervention*.

[7] Independent International Commission on Kosovo, *The Kosovo Report* (Oxford University Press, New York, 2000).

However, for the foreseeable future this strategy is unlikely to be realized. Given how protective most states are of their sovereignty and given how many states wish to have a free hand to oppress dissenting groups within their borders, it is doubtful that the majority of the members of the UN would vote for such a resolution. Even if the needed two-thirds majority in the General Assembly were mustered, a two-thirds majority of the Security Council that includes all the permanent members is also required for amendment. The same veto power on the part of the permanent members that has resulted in a failure to authorize humanitarian interventions would probably be used to block such a constitutional change.

Reform through treaty outside the UN-based system

If reform through new custom is difficult, uncertain, and morally risky, and if the creation of new law within the UN system offers little prospect for success in the foreseeable future, then proponents of reform should consider the possibility of a treaty-based approach that bypasses the UN system.[8] The most likely and morally defensible version of this alternative would be a coalition of democratic, human rights-respecting states, bound together by a treaty that would specify well-crafted criteria that must be satisfied for intervention to be permissible in the absence of Security Council authorization. The constraining criteria would include familiar elements of just war theory, including necessity, proportional force, and protection of noncombatants, but might also show limited deference to the UN system by requiring General Assembly or Security Council resolutions condemning the human rights violations that provoke the need for intervention.

This strategy for reform might be undertaken either as a result of coming to the conclusion that the UN system is unworkable or in an attempt to spur reform in the UN system by providing a kind of competition for legitimacy regarding intervention. In either case, it would involve illegality, since the actions to be undertaken by the liberal-democratic coalition would violate existing UN-based law on humanitarian intervention. But the hope would be that what was first an intervention treaty among a relatively small number of states

---

[8] I am indebted to Jeff Holzgrefe for urging me to take seriously this strategy.

would eventually gain wider participation and that what was initially illegal would eventually become the law.

Such an approach would unabashedly reject the assumption, which I criticized in Chapter 7, that state majoritarianism is necessary for legitimacy in international law. The crucial point is that it is a mistake to assume that support by a majority of states, either through treaty or in the process of customary change, is a necessary condition for morally justifiable efforts to achieve reform. State majoritarianism, under current conditions in which many states are not democratic and rights respecting, cannot be viewed as having the legitimacy-conferring power of consent by individuals. As I have already argued, at best state majoritarianism has normative weight as a device for constraining abuses by more powerful states.[9]

However, I also argued in Chapter 7 that it is not at all obvious that the only way, or even the best way, to constrain powerful states is by subjecting the process of reforming humanitarian intervention to state majoritarianism. Instead, the needed constraint might be achieved in a treaty-based coalition among the more democratic, human rights-respecting states by a combination of two factors: first, as I have already suggested, specification in the treaty of a rather demanding set of necessary conditions for intervention (including a supermajority of the coalition members, say three-quarters in favor of intervention); second, democratic accountability among and within participating liberal-democratic states under conditions of freedom of expression and political competition through multi-party political systems.[10]

It is worth emphasizing that even if it could be shown that state majoritarianism provides a more effective constraint against great power abuses in the name of humanitarian intervention, reducing that risk of abuse is not an absolute value. One must consider not just the harm, but also the good that a treaty-based, rule-governed

[9] It is exceedingly odd to trumpet the principle of state majoritarianism as a reason for not undertaking efforts to reform the law of intervention by bypassing the UN-based system's requirement of Security Council authorization. For as I have just noted, the major barrier to reform within the UN-based system is an extremely anti-state-majoritarian constraint, namely, the veto power of the permanent members of the Council.

[10] I am grateful to Robert Keohane for making clear to me the importance of this last condition.

liberal-democratic coalition for intervention could do. A properly structured coalition would provide a law-governed regime for intervention that would prove more effective in preventing the most egregious large-scale human rights violations than the current UN system, in which Security Council authorization is mandatory. And the prospects for creating such an intervention regime may be considerably brighter than those for reforming the UN system's approach to intervention.

Let me emphasize that I am not assuming that such a liberal-democratic intervention regime would be dominated by the United States or even that the United States should play an important role in it. On the contrary, there is much to be said for minimizing the U.S. role or even excluding it from participating, both from the standpoint of constraining the world's one superpower and in terms of the perceived legitimacy of the coalition. Given that the United States is widely regarded—and not without reason—as an international scoff-law, the issue of perceived legitimacy ought to be taken seriously.[11]

It might be better to build the coalition on the structure provided by the European Union—which already includes the world's most highly developed human rights regime—with additional members including Canada and Australia and any other country, regardless of its location, that meets these criteria. The chief criterion for admission to the intervention regime would be having a decent record on human rights and having a government that meets the rather minimal criteria for democracy set out in Chapter 6, and this would increasingly encompass some developing countries in both the northern and southern hemispheres.

Surely a coalition all of whose members much more closely approximate the conditions for political legitimacy than the majority of states in the international system has a stronger claim to legitimacy than a state-majoritarian UN entity such as the General Assembly. If the goal is to protect human rights, then who would be better qualified than a coalition of states that have the best records for doing so?

---

[11] Jack Goldsmith, 'International Human Rights Law and the United States Double Standard', *Green Bag* 2d 1 (1998), 365–73.

Of course any attempt to construct a coalition of democratic, human rights-respecting states for humanitarian intervention would require the richer European states to do something they have not done in over fifty years: make a serious investment in military capacity rather than depending upon the United States. Even the best-crafted treaty regime for intervention would be of little value unless it were actually capable of intervening effectively.

It also might be best if the initial interventions undertaken by a coalition whose core was the European Union were restricted to Europe, for two reasons.[12] First, limiting operations to Europe would ease somewhat the coalition's dependence on U.S. military power, since operations within Europe would be less costly. Second, by establishing a good record for intervention within Europe the coalition would do much to enhance its perceived legitimacy. However, unless conflicts involving massive human rights violations arise again in Bosnia or Kosovo or the current conflict in Macedonia escalates, the next occasion for humanitarian intervention is not likely to be in Europe but in sub-Saharan Africa, in some portion of the former Soviet Union, or in the Middle East or South Asia.

At this point it might be objected that unless it could be assured of dominating it, the United States would never permit such a coalition for rule-governed humanitarian intervention to function. I am not convinced, however, that the United States would be able to thwart the creation and operation of such a coalition, if the latter enjoyed the sincere support of most of the other most powerful liberal democracies. For one thing, if the United States did attempt to prevent the formation of such a coalition without proposing any constructive alternative, it would become all too apparent that recent U.S. violations of international law on the use of force are a rejection of the ideal of the rule of law, not a protest against the inadequacy of the current embodiment of that ideal in the institutions of the UN. Such an unambiguous rejection of the ideal of the rule of law in international relations would be a severe cost to the United States, especially if it took the form of coercive diplomacy, under modern conditions of publicity, in which the threat, and its utterly unprincipled motivation, would be apparent to the world.

[12] I am grateful to Rex Martin for suggesting this restriction.

The situation here would be different from the U.S. refusal to participate in the International Criminal Court. It is one thing for the United States to claim, with some credibility, that it will not participate on the grounds that the Rome Statute gives the prosecutor too much discretion in making indictments; it would be quite another to say that it will not permit states with the best human rights records to create a coalition of the willing to discharge responsibilities for protecting basic human rights against genocide that the United States itself has formally recognized.

If my speculation here is too optimistic—if the United States were to try to block the effort to create a liberal-democratic coalition for humanitarian intervention—then the attempt to implement the proposal might still have a beneficial result: It would make it very clear that those who wish to produce a more just international legal order must be willing to do so not only without the support of the United States, but also in the face of its active opposition.

The issue of inclusion

The predictable objection to this proposal for a new, rule-governed regime of humanitarian intervention based on a coalition of democratic, human rights-respecting states is that it would be a retrograde move, from the standpoint of inclusiveness. After all, some would say, one of the signal virtues of the post-1945, UN-based system of international law is that it includes virtually all states—that international law is no longer merely a club (in both senses) of the Great Powers.

This objection is not as telling as it might first appear. It is true that the processes of international law are much more inclusive today than ever before, and it is also true that this inclusiveness is a valuable antidote against both an unwitting cultural parochialism and the calculated abuses of the stronger. However, to a large extent the most valuable sort of inclusiveness has been achieved through the growing empowerment of non-state agencies: transnational nongovernmental human rights organizations, networks for the advocacy of minority rights, indigenous peoples' rights, and so on.

In other words, as emphasized in Chapter 7, it is a mistake to conflate state majoritarianism with greater democratic participation in the processes of international law. A coalition of democratic, human rights-respecting states would be exclusionary of nondemocratic states, but it does not follow that it would be a threat to the sort of inclusiveness that is to be valued.

Furthermore, the transnational organizations that have promoted the most valuable sort of inclusion for the most part have been formed in and protected by democratic, rights-respecting states, not empowered through state majoritarianism. It is therefore wrong to assume that a proposal for a new regime of rule-governed human-itarian intervention centered in a coalition of the sort described would mark a return to a pernicious exclusivity in international law. Such a regime for humanitarian intervention might well be more inclusive, more democratic in the sense of providing better repre-sentation for the perspectives of individuals and substate groups, than a UN-based democracy of states, many of which exclude some or all of their own citizens from meaningful political participation and persistently violate their basic human rights.

Let me emphasize that the proposal under discussion concerns only the reform of the law of humanitarian intervention. It is not a plan for scrapping the entire UN-based system of international law. This is an important distinction, because one should not assume that the only options are a unitary approach to international legal reform in which all progressive change must occur either through the UN-based system or through the development of new agencies for the making of law that bypass the UN system. After all, the cor-pus of international laws is not a seamless web and international legal institutions do not form an integrated, unitary system. Given that there is no global super-state or universal legislature, it is worthwhile to explore the possibility of a more pluralistic concep-tion of the evolution of international law, one in which progress occurs through the development of—and perhaps competition among—different sources of rules and different institutional arrange-ments for implementing them. I have focused on the case of reform in the law of humanitarian intervention because I think it is both morally urgent and probably a prerequisite of the more ambitious reforms I propose, and because I believe that the current UN-based legal regime regarding humanitarian intervention is very recalcitrant to reform from within.

Even in this limited area of reform, I stop short of wholeheartedly endorsing the liberal-democratic coalition strategy at this time.

My purpose is to broaden and deepen the discussion of reform by taking seriously an option that is seldom even mentioned, much less dispassionately evaluated. The pivotal point is that we cannot simply assume unreflectively and without any serious attempt at justification that the path to moral progress in international law lies exclusively within the confines of the UN-based system or that there is only one path. Nor can we assume that at every point in the development of international law, there will be only one system of law. Progress may occur through the development of parallel and sometimes competing law-like systems of rules in distinct but also sometimes overlapping domains of competence.

In the final section of this chapter I take up the issue of illegal acts directed toward legal reform and argue that such acts can be consistent with and may even be mandated by a commitment to the Natural Duty of Justice and to the rule of law as an embodiment of justice. Here I only wish to note that the attempt to reform the law of intervention through treaty outside the system of UN-based law is not the only strategy for reform that requires illegality; reform through the creation of new customary law can as well.

Although change in custom does not always require illegality (recall the case of the creation of new law concerning outer space or other areas where a new customary norm comes to occupy what had been a legal vacuum), it almost certainly would in the case of the development of a new customary norm allowing intervention without Security Council authorization. The first acts that contributed toward such a new customary norm would violate the strictures laid down in the UN Charter. So it seems that from the standpoint of illegality, the customary approach and the strategy of treaty outside the system of UN-based law are on the same footing, when it comes to reforming the law of humanitarian intervention: Both require illegality. But whether this is so or not, illegality does not in itself make an effort directed toward legal reform morally unjustifiable, as I shall argue in the next section of this chapter.

III. *The Morality of Illegal Legal Reform*

I have argued that what may be the most promising strategy for international legal reform concerning intervention will involve illegal acts, namely, violations of the UN-based law of force. But I have also argued that unless a more permissive law of intervention develops it is unlikely that the reforms I have proposed will be achieved. So it is incumbent on me to examine the question of the morality of illegal acts directed toward legal reform. My concern in this section will be to refute the Legal Absolutist, who holds that (in the case of international law or at least its most basic rules or constitutional rules) it is virtually never morally justifiable to violate the law for the purpose of reforming it so as to better serve principles of justice.

Political philosophers, who tend to be familiar with the moral justification of civil disobedience, may be tempted to conclude that the Legal Absolutist is a strawman. They will find it difficult to believe that anyone would actually subscribe to Legal Absolutism for the simple reason that there clearly are some cases in which civil disobedience, which typically involves deliberate violations of the law for the sake of reforming it, is morally justified.

Consider, for example, the case of Dr Martin Luther King, who violated unjust U.S. laws in an effort to have them expunged from the legal system. King's actions were not only morally justifiable; they were morally exemplary, and it is not difficult to give a cogent, principled account of why this is so.

Of course one might argue that King had not only a moral but also a legal justification for breaking the segregation laws: The U.S. Supreme Court decision in *Brown* v. *Board of Education* held that these laws were themselves illegal, in the sense of being unconstitutional, and King began his civil disobedience a year after that decision. Nevertheless, even without the benefit of this constitutional justification for violating the segregation laws, Dr King was surely morally justified in violating them. (Suppose, for example, that his first acts of civil disobedience had taken place two years earlier, before *Brown*, so that no legal justification for them was available.)

Alternatively, consider another case, unencumbered by questions about the constitutionality of the laws violated. Suppose that the citizens of Cambodia had violated the horrific laws promulgated by the Khmer Rouge, in order to prevent the massive human rights violations that compliance entailed.[13] Suppose, also, that the

---

[13] This example is due to Deborah Weiss.

Khmer Rouge regime had succeeded in including such dreadful laws, or the principles from which they were derived, among the most basic laws, the chief elements of the constitution. Can anyone seriously maintain that it would not be morally justifiable to break these laws?

If civil disobedience is ever morally justified in a domestic legal system—which of course it is—then the Legal Absolutist must show us why it is so different in the international legal system. I argue below that attempts to do so fail. My only point at this juncture, is that it is prima facie very implausible to assert that morally motivated violation of the law is never morally justifiable and that this would seem to apply regardless of whether it is in a domestic or international legal system and whether the law in question is basic to the system or not.

Surprising as it may seem to the rest of us, it is fair to say that many if not most international legal scholars are at least implicitly Legal Absolutists. So it is necessary to lay out the Legal Absolutist position and refute it. Although I believe that illegal acts directed toward reform may bear a special burden of justification, at least for those who profess to value the rule of law, I will argue that under certain conditions that burden can be met.

Two Legal Absolutist objections to conscientious law-breaking

Some prominent international legal scholars, including J. S. Watson and Alfred Rubin, roundly condemn acts that violate international law done in the name of morality, including those done for the sake of morally improving the international legal system.[14]

It appears that such condemnation of illegal acts of reform stems from two complaints: One is that those who commit them fail to show proper fidelity to law; the other is that they are guilty of hubris and moral imperialism, being too willing to impose their own views of what is right on others. It will prove helpful, therefore,

---

[14] See Rubin, *Ethics and Authority in International Law*, esp. 70–206; and J. S. Watson, 'A Realistic Jurisprudence of International Law', in *The Yearbook of World Affairs* 34 (Stevens & Sons, London, 1980), 283–5. It appears that Rubin and Watson not only object that attempts to reform international law for the sake of human rights through illegal acts are doomed to failure; they also appear to condemn such attempts as immoral or at least morally unjustifiable and irresponsible.

to distinguish two questions: (1) Does commitment to the rule of law in international relations preclude acts that violate existing international law for the sake of reforming it? And (2) under what conditions, if any, can an agent's judgments about what justice requires count as good reasons for attempting to impose new legal rules on others? In order to answer the first question, we need an account of what the commitment to the rule of law is that will enable us to determine how a would-be reformer should weigh the fact that his proposed action is illegal. In order to answer the second question, we need to determine whether the reformer who is willing to act illegally really is attempting to impose his subjective views and an account of what justifies coercing others to conform to principles of justice.

My strategy will be to construct and evaluate arguments that can be employed to articulate these two complaints, chiefly because I have not yet discovered any published defense of Legal Absolutism that makes the basis of that position clear. Since I have provided what I hope is a thorough critique of Legal Absolutism elsewhere, I will only summarize some of my arguments here, without presenting the full case against this untenable view.[15]

IV. *The Commitment to the Rule of Law*

There are two quite different ways in which the Legal Absolutist may be understanding 'the rule of law' when he charges that the reformer who breaks international law does not act consistently with a commitment to the rule of law. According to the first, 'the rule of law' is shorthand for just institutions. To be committed to the rule of law in international relations in this sense is simply to take seriously the obligation to help create a just international legal order; it is the commitment to achieving justice through international law.

It warrants emphasizing that to be committed to the rule of law in this sense is not to view the legal system simply as an instrument for achieving justice and hence as something that is externally

[15] Allen Buchanan, 'From Nuremburg to Kosovo: The Morality of Illegal International Legal Reform', *Ethics* 111 (2001), 637–704.

related to it. Rather, to be committed to the rule of law in this sense is to acknowledge that a proper legal system partly constitutes justice comprehensively conceived, which includes the realization of the principles that Fuller called the internal morality of law: that the law should address persons capable of taking responsibility for their actions, that consequently the rules they are expected to comply with should be understandable to them and should be publicized in advance so that they can plan their courses of action and coordinate their behavior with others in the light of those rules, that laws should be general and not unduly subject to change, and that all are to be equal before the law. Call this the normatively rich (Fullerian) conception of the commitment to the rule of law.

According to the second interpretation, 'the rule of law' is much less normatively demanding; it is merely a system of coercively backed rules capable of preventing a Hobbesian condition of violent chaos. Call this the Hobbesian conception of the commitment to the rule of law. I will argue that on neither of these two quite different interpretations does the commitment to the rule of law preclude the moral justifiability of illegal acts directed toward legal reform.

The rule of law as the avoidance of violent anarchy

Consider first the commitment to the rule of law on the Hobbesian interpretation. The Legal Absolutist, on this interpretation, asserts that if one is committed to the rule of law in the sense of a system of enforced rules designed to avoid violent anarchy, then it is never justifiable to violate existing international law for the sake of morality.

This is nothing short of an unsupported prediction that any violations undertaken for the sake of morally improving the system pose a significant threat to the minimal order needed to avoid a Hobbesian war of each against all. As a sweeping generalization, the claim that illegal acts of reform run an unconscionable risk of violent anarchy is implausible. It would be more plausible if two assumptions were true: (1) the existence of the international order depends solely upon the efficacy of international law and (2) international law is a seamless web, so that cutting one fiber (violating one rule) will result in an unraveling of the entire fabric.

The first assumption is dubious. It almost certainly overestimates the role of law by underestimating the contributions of political and economic relations and the various institutions of transnational civil society to peace and stability in international relations. But even if the first assumption were justified, the second, "seamless web" assumption is far-fetched. History refutes it. As I have argued elsewhere, there have been illegal acts that were directed toward and that actually contributed to significant reforms in the past—some aspects of the Nuremburg prosecutions and the British Navy's interdiction of the transatlantic slave trade come to mind— yet they did not result in a collapse of the international legal system.[16] And these illegalities were violations of the rules concerning sovereignty which, according to the Legal Absolutist, are basic or constitutional elements of the international legal system. So on the Hobbesian interpretation of the 'rule of law' argument, even what might be called Moderate Legal Absolutism, the thesis that it is never morally justifiable to violate basic or constitutional rules of international law, looks dubious.

Moreover, as I have already observed, change through the creation of new customary norms often includes illegalities in the initial stages, yet this has not resulted in the destruction of the international legal system and a descent into Hobbesian violent chaos. So if the commitment to the rule of law means the commitment to avoiding Hobbesian chaos, this is not incompatible with being willing to violate existing international law, even basic international law. I now turn to the other interpretation of the commitment to the rule of law to see whether it precludes illegal acts of reform.

The commitment to the rule of law as the commitment to achieving justice through law

On this normatively rich interpretation, the commitment to the rule of law is not the commitment to having some set of enforceable rules or other so long as they achieve sufficient order to avoid the Hobbesian predicament. Instead, it is the commitment to achieving justice that is primary, with a recognition that the right sort of legal system can do much to further this goal and partly constitutes

---

[16] Allen Buchanan, 'From Nuremburg to Kosovo: The Morality of Illegal International Legal Reform', *Ethics* 111 (2001), 637–704.

the goal comprehensively understood. But if this is what is meant by the commitment to the rule of law, then it is clear that honoring this commitment is consistent with—and indeed may even require—violating some laws in a legal system that is very imperfect from the standpoint of justice, if this is necessary to make the system more just.

Progress toward justice is especially likely to require illegal acts if the system's imperfections include serious barriers to expeditious, legally permissible reform. And as I argued earlier in this chapter, that is precisely the case regarding the existing international legal system's capacity for reforming the law of intervention. The UN Charter-based law of intervention is recalcitrant to legally permissible reform because the same obstacles to securing Security Council authorization for morally justifiable interventions make it unlikely that the Charter will be amended to relax the requirement of Security Council authorization. Being willing to act illegally to make a very unjust system more just need not be inconsistent with a commitment to justice through law; it may indeed be required by it.

To make this point clearer, consider again the proposal for a treaty-based, rule-governed intervention regime whose members would be restricted to the most democratic, human rights-respecting states. To the extent that it authorizes humanitarian interventions in the absence of Security Council authorization, such a regime would violate existing international law. But it would embody, rather than repudiate, a commitment to the rule of law in the normatively rich sense.

The proposal is *not* for a single state or even a collection of states to intervene lawlessly. Instead, the idea is to create a new system of rules—new principles, processes, and institutions—that embody the normatively rich conception of the rule of law. The point is that an action may violate the law and yet be *lawful*—that is, mindful of the importance of law understood in the normatively rich way—and hence may be consistent with, and even be an expression of, the commitment to the rule of law thus understood.

In a well-reasoned and insightful recent paper, the French international legal scholar Brigitte Stern argues persuasively that "the deficiencies of international law are no excuse for its violation."[17]

---

[17] Brigitte Stern, 'How to Regulate Globalization?', in Michael Byers (ed.), *The Role of Law in International Politics* (Oxford University Press, New York, 2000), 261.

I agree entirely, if this means that the mere fact that some rule of international law is defective does not justify violating it.

However, if the members of the European Union undertook to form the core of a well-crafted, rule-governed intervention regime of the sort I have described, and did so for the sake of better protection of basic human rights, their justification for acting illegally would *not* simply be that the existing law of intervention is defective. Identifying a defect in existing law is only the first step toward developing a justification for illegal acts directed toward reform. Whether illegality is justified will depend upon a number of factors, including the reasonable judgment that reform through actions in conformity with existing law is not feasible and that the new rule-governed regime would be both effective and not subject to unacceptable risks of abuse or error.

The sort of illegal act that Stern rightly condemns is one undertaken unilaterally by a single state. Her example is the adoption by the United States of the Helms–Burton and D'Amato acts, which she believes illegally extended the extra-territorial jurisdiction of the United States. (These two laws authorize legal actions and sanctions against foreign nationals and corporations in ways that Stern believes exceed the international legal powers that constitute U.S. sovereignty.) She notes that such legislation disregards the fact that international law is made by states, not by the unilateral action of one state. My point is that the proposed treaty-based regime for humanitarian intervention would embody new norms that are made, not by a state, but by a group of states that includes the most legally developed members of the international community, just as the UN system of law itself was created in 1945 by a group of states, not by all states.

Stern's otherwise excellent discussion may not distinguish with sufficient clarity between the question of whether illegal acts are justified and the question of whether they have a legal justification.[18] Her article poses the question: How should globalization be regulated? She argues that a unilateral attempt to forge new law by a single state is not the way to regulate globalization. If she is asking which ways of creating new law are morally justified, then pointing out that unilateralist efforts such as that of the United States in

---

[18] Ibid.

the case of the Helms–Burton and D'Amato laws are not *legally* justified because international law is made by states, not unilaterally by a single state, does not answer the question.

I am persuaded by her reasoning that the United States did act illegally—that is, contrary to existing international legal rules—and without any legal justification or legal excuse for doing so. I also happen to believe that the particular illegalities involved in the Helms–Burton and D'Amato laws are not *morally* justifiable all things considered.

Yet none of this shows that an action that violates international law cannot be morally justified. My contention is that an illegal act that is part of a responsible, well-crafted effort to reform existing law can be morally justified even if there is no legal justification or legal excuse for it. Again, the case of acts of civil disobedience, such as those undertaken by Dr King or Mohandas Gandhi, shows that illegal acts directed toward legal reform, if undertaken in a responsible manner, can be morally justified, even when there is no legal justification or legal excuse for them. The same would be true of a responsible effort to develop a rule-governed humanitarian intervention regime by a suitable treaty among the most democratic, human rights-respecting states.

The Legal Absolutist might at this point protest that any attempt to reform the law through illegal acts nevertheless betrays a failure to honor the full commitment to the rule of law. The normatively rich conception of the rule of law, he would argue, includes not just the Fullerian principles of the internal morality of law noted above, but also the idea that *change must come about through lawful means*. After all, one of the great virtues of law as an institution is that it preserves order in the process of change, by reliance upon the authoritative processes which it establishes.

To this I would reply that in the assertion that morally justified change in the legal system must be lawful the term 'lawful' is ambiguous. If it means simply "mindful of the value of law" then those who undertake to develop a liberal-democratic regime for intervention could say that their efforts are "mindful of the value of law"— that is why they are careful to include procedural safeguards, to insist that interventions must be justified by appeals to publicly known principles, must be applied consistently not retroactively, and so on. In contrast, if 'lawful' means "allowing change only through legal means," that is, only in ways that are consistent with existing law, then the Legal Absolutist begs the question when he asserts that to be morally justified an act directed toward reform must be lawful.

It may be true that the normatively rich ideal of the rule of law includes a *presumption* that changes in the legal system are to be brought about by actions that are compatible with existing legal rules; but this cannot be an absolute requirement. If illegal acts are necessary to bring about important substantive improvements in the system whose rules for legal change are serious impediments to progress, and if these acts are undertaken in a responsible way, with appropriate precautions to reduce the risks of error and abuse, and with a proper regard for the dangers of undermining confidence in the law, then this presumption in favor of change through legal means can be overridden. To fail to see this is arbitrarily to privilege what is at best one element of the normatively rich conception of the commitment to the rule of law—the presumption in favor of changing the law through legal means—at the expense of other elements and substantive justice. A group of states willing to act illegally to bring about reform in the law of intervention can honor the presumption that change in the law is to be brought about by legal means—by proceeding to act illegally only after they have made a responsible determination that reform through legal means is not feasible due to the current system's deficiency, in this case, the morally arbitrary and overly constraining concentration of power in the hands of the permanent members of the Security Council.

I can now summarize the results of my critique of the first Legal Absolutist argument against illegal acts directed toward legal reform, the assertion that a commitment to the rule of law precludes illegality even in the name of legal reform. First, it is not cogent to argue that illegal acts of reform always constitute an unacceptable threat to peace and stability, because the international legal system is not a fragile, seamless web and because international order depends on many factors in addition to law. So the commitment to the rule of law, understood as the commitment to a system of enforced rules capable of avoiding Hobbesian violent chaos, is not incompatible with illegality for the sake of legal reform.

Second, a commitment to the rule of law, understood as the commitment to institutions that embody the normatively rich ideal of the rule of law, is not only consistent with illegal acts of reform; it may in some cases make such acts obligatory. Illegal acts of reform can be a part of a reasonable strategy for reform that is mindful of the value of law and that honors the presumption that reform of the law is to be achieved by legal means. So if illegal acts directed toward reform are to be categorically rejected, as the Legal Absolutist contends, it is not because they are inconsistent with a sincere commitment to the rule of law. I now turn, therefore, to the second prong of the Legal Absolutist attack.

V. *Moral Authority*

The charge of subjectivism

The second prong of the Legal Absolutist rejection of illegal acts directed toward legal reform contends that those who would violate international law to improve it are guilty of a kind of moral hubris. Opponents of illegal reform such as Rubin heap scathing criticism on those who would impose their own personal or subjective views of morality or justice on others. The suggestion is that those who endorse violations of international law, and especially those who disregard the requirement of state consent, are intolerant ideologues who would deny to others the right to do what they seek to do. It is a mistake, however, to assume as these critics apparently do that the only alternatives are subjectivism or strict adherence to legality.

Internalist moral criticism of the system

An agent who seeks to breach international law in order to initiate a process of bringing about a moral improvement in the system need not be appealing to a subjective or merely personal view about morality. Instead, he or she may be relying upon widely held moral values that are already clearly expressed in the system. Recall that some who were sympathetic to NATO's intervention in Kosovo, including UN Secretary General Kofi Annan, believed that this intervention was supported by one of the most morally defensible fundamental principles of the international legal system, respect for human rights, even though it was inconsistent with another principle of the system, the norm of sovereignty understood as prohibiting intervention in the domestic affairs of the former

Yugoslav Republic.[19] In brief, it is wildly inaccurate to characterize those who supported the intervention by appealing to basic human rights principles internal to the international legal system as ideologues trying to impose their personal or subjective moral views on others.

The fact that there are cases of justified domestic civil disobedience makes even clearer the implausibility of assuming that anyone who violates the law is a kind of moral narcissist. When Martin Luther King violated segregation laws, he did so out of the reasoned conviction that those laws contradicted not only the most progressive principles of U.S. Constitutional law but also the most basic principles of morality. To say that by violating the law he showed an unseemly propensity to impose his own moral views on others is absurd.

Finally, there is a great difference between one state violating existing law for the sake of justice and a coalition of the most democratic, rights-respecting states, bound together by an explicit treaty that embodies the commitment to the normatively rich ideal of the rule of law, doing so. No member of such a coalition could be justly accused of being willing to impose its own view on others; instead, each member could truthfully say that it is relying upon the collective judgment of the group as to whether to intervene in any particular case and upon safeguards that have been developed through the exercise of the group's collective judgment. The fact that each member of such a group enjoys a well-functioning domestic regime for the protection of basic rights, as well as a free press and institutionalized political competition, is a basis for some degree of confidence in the group's collective judgments, both about what sorts of safeguards are needed and about the appropriateness of intervening or not in any particular case. So it is quite wrong to assume, as Legal Absolutists seem to do, that illegal acts of reform are bound to be based on the unaided "subjective" judgment of a single state.

To summarize: Legal Absolutism is an untenable view; there is no good reason to rule out categorically illegal acts directed toward international legal reform, even acts that violate the most basic or constitutional norms. Whether such acts are morally justified will depend upon other factors than their illegality. Moreover, given the limited resources for legal reform that the current UN-based legal

[19] Annan, 'Speech to the General Assembly'.

regime for humanitarian intervention possesses, illegal acts may well be needed for significant and timely reform. Instead of precluding a reasoned discussion of the morality of illegal international legal reform by assuming the truth of Legal Absolutism, theorists of international law should embrace the task of developing an account of the morality of international legal reform in all its complexity, recognizing that in some instances illegal actions may be not only permissible but required.

When faced with the prospect that significant reform seems to require violating existing law, some international legal scholars yield to the temptation to evade the issue of whether illegal acts of reform can be morally justifiable. They do this by stretching the concept of legality—arguing that the needed reform is not really illegal. Such evasion ought to be vigorously resisted, both because it leads to an overly malleable conception of the law and to a confusion between claims about what the law is and what it ought to be, and because it concedes too much to the Legal Absolutist, by proceeding as if it is necessary to show that an act directed toward reform is legally permissible in order to establish that it is justifiable.

Armed intervention, the risk of violent death, and the "excessive cost" limitations on the natural duty of justice

Since I first explained the idea of the Natural Duty of Justice in Chapter 2, I have stressed that it is a principle of limited obligation: We are only obligated to work with others, utilizing our shared institutional resources and augmenting them when necessary, to help ensure that all persons have access to institutions that protect their basic rights, so long as we can do so without excessive costs to ourselves. But the question arises: Won't armed intervention virtually always result in excessive costs for some, namely, the military personnel who risk violent death in the collective effort to protect basic human rights?[20]

What prompts this question is the notion that violent death—particularly if it comes as a result of the deliberate hostile actions of

---

[20] I thank (and blame) David Luban for gently pressuring me to take up this daunting issue.

other human beings, with all the ego-threatening implications that this implies—is a harm that human beings especially fear, a cost of a different order of magnitude than other costs.[21] But even without the assumption that human beings generally have a great fear of violent death, the finality of death and the fact that it terminates all our strivings, enjoyments, and attachments makes it an extremely high cost, if not the highest cost.

This question raises perplexing issues that I can only treat here in the most gestural fashion. However, before embarking on what no doubt will be a very unsatisfactory attempt to frame the most basic of these, let me reemphasize that most of the reforms I have proposed would not involve armed intervention. Even if the Natural Duty does not require us to risk our lives for the sake of protecting basic human rights, it certainly requires those of us who have the good fortune to live in wealthy, influential countries to do more than what is currently being done to promote justice through international legal institutions.

Nevertheless, let us assume *arguendo* that the risk of violent death through participation in armed humanitarian intervention is a peculiarly awful cost, and one that is in some sense incommensurate with or at least much more severe than other costs. It seems to me that what makes this risk problematic from the standpoint of the "excessive costs" proviso is a *lack of reciprocity*. It is true that a commitment to justice requires us to bear some significant costs for the sake of protecting the basic human rights of others who are not in a position to help protect our basic human rights, or whose help we will never need because our basic human rights are secure. That much follows, as I have argued in Chapter 2, from the profound moral priority of the fundamental shared human interests that are secured when basic human rights are respected. But being obligated to bear the "cost" of a risk of violent death seems to be a different matter. Here the lack of reciprocity of risk seems to count.

Consider in contrast the case where there *is* reciprocity of risk of violent death. Suppose that you and I and a number of others find ourselves thrown together in a condition of radical insecurity—the hypothetical state of nature Hobbes describes, which unfortunately

[21] I am indebted to Lance Stell for suggesting this way of formulating the nature of the "cost" of the risk of violent death.

exists today in parts of the world where there is no functioning state and the rule of law has collapsed. Suppose we unite to protect ourselves, pledging that each will incur the risk of violent death in collective self-defense, on condition that all others will do the same. Under these circumstances, it is unproblematic to say that we all ought to be willing to risk violent death for our mutual protection. None of us can argue that it is somehow unfair to us or too demanding to ask that we be willing to risk our lives.[22] But it is arguably quite different in the case of humanitarian intervention. The citizens of the countries that are able to undertake effective intervention are generally the least vulnerable to violations of their basic human rights and those whose basic human rights they would protect through intervention are in no position to help protect the rights of the intervenors. The reciprocity condition that makes the obligation to risk violent death plausible does not obtain.

I am *not* suggesting that our duties to aid others generally depend upon reciprocity. As I have argued all along, the Natural Duty of Justice requires us to help ensure that all persons have access to institutions that protect their basic rights, simply because they are persons, not because we are connected to them by cooperative relationships or any other conditions of reciprocity. The point, rather, is that a risk of violent death seems to be an "excessive cost" if anything is; and if this is so, then appeal to the Natural Duty of Justice would seem to justify only the permissibility of humanitarian intervention, not its obligatoriness, except perhaps where there is reciprocity of risk.

A look at the domestic case of support for the protection of rights may provide the key to bridging the gap between the permissibility of humanitarian intervention and the obligatoriness of supporting it. In virtually any real-world society, as opposed to the hypothetical state of nature or the case of radical insecurity in conditions of state breakdown, the reciprocity condition does not hold among all citizens. If I am physically weak or disabled or old or mentally impaired, I will never be called upon to risk my life to protect you; yet in an emergency, you might be called upon to risk your life for me, as when our country is invaded by ruthless aggressors and all

----

[22] Whether it would be in one's rational self-interest to attempt to not comply with such an agreement is another question, of course.

able-bodied citizens are called upon to take up arms. And even in nonemergency situations, in the normal functioning of society, it is only some persons—police, firefighters, etc.—who are expected to risk their lives to protect the basic human rights of their fellow citizens. So long as these roles are filled voluntarily, our institutions can function and through them we can fulfill our obligations to help ensure that the basic rights of all our fellow citizens are protected, without anyone having to acknowledge an obligation to risk death simply as a result of the fact that we are all subject to the Natural Duty of Justice.

Similarly, if the forces used in humanitarian interventions are voluntary, then the moral justification for supporting armed humanitarian intervention need not depend upon the problematic assumption that risking our lives does not count as an excessive cost.[23] So, even if it is true that the Natural Duty of Justice does not require us to risk violent death for the sake of protecting other persons' basic human rights, it still obligates us to support institutions for armed humanitarian intervention, even when there is no reciprocity regarding the risk of violent death, so long as these institutions only entail a risk of violent death for those who accept it voluntarily.

Of course, this solution to the problem of showing how we can be obligated to support humanitarian intervention when reciprocity of vulnerability to violent death is absent works only if those who risk violent death and thereby help us to discharge our Natural Duty of Justice really do so voluntarily. And needless to say, in many countries the incentive of economic need calls into question the voluntariness of the decision to join the military. But this only shows that our duties to promote justice must be considered holistically. It may be necessary to do more to promote distributive justice at home before we can be in a position to promote the protection of basic human rights abroad through armed humanitarian intervention.

VI. *Conclusions*

With this chapter I conclude this volume's attempt to develop a moral theory of international law by beginning to explore a neglected but

[23] Teson, 'A Kantian Theory of Humanitarian Intervention', in Holzgrefe and Keohane (eds.), *Humanitarian Intervention*.

important topic: the morality of international legal reform. I first argued that achieving the reforms proposed in this book and summarized in Chapter 10 will likely require significant changes in the law of intervention, not because they will necessitate frequent interventions, but because the ability to make a credible threat to intervene may be necessary to implement the proposed reforms.

Next, I articulated and evaluated three main types of strategies for achieving the needed changes in the law of intervention: change through the creation of a new customary norm, treaty-based change within the UN Charter-based system of law, and change through the creation of a treaty-based, rule-governed intervention regime composed of the more democratic, human rights-respecting states that would operate outside the strictures of the UN Charter-based intervention regime. I then argued that the third alternative may be the most promising route to reform.

Finally, I acknowledged that achieving meaningful and timely reform of the law of intervention may require illegal actions, but then showed that, contrary to the Legal Absolutist, illegality for the sake of justice may be not only morally justified but morally obligatory.

VII. *The Future of International Law at the Beginning of the Twenty-First Century*

Ending this volume with a chapter on the morality of legal reform seems appropriate to me for two reasons. First, as I emphasized at the beginning of this chapter, liberalizing the international law of humanitarian intervention is likely to be a necessary condition for making progress on the reforms my theorizing has led me to propose. Second, it may help to remind those whom I hope to stimulate to develop a more cogent moral theory of international law than I have been able to construct, that a moral theory is only an intellectual exercise for those who have the luxury of indulging their curiosity, unless it helps us to move from where we are to a better place.

However, some may protest that talk about reforming international law is at present naively optimistic. They would say that a candid appraisal of recent events indicates that international law has suffered blows from which it may not recover. The NATO intervention in Kosovo, which occurred without UN Security Council authorization and was not a case of self-defense, was seen by some as a signal that international law is becoming even less relevant than it has been to the solution of major international problems. This intervention, it could be argued, not only violated UN-based law, but also demonstrated that the UN is both impotent and unnecessary, at least so far as humanitarian intervention is concerned. Similarly, the recent invasion of Iraq by the United States is seen by many as another indication of the decline of international law.

These events should cause anxiety, but they do not warrant such profound pessimism. There *is* a palpable danger that the attempt to ignore the existing illegal prohibition against preventive war in launching an attack on Iraq, or, in the case of the NATO intervention, to use a regional defense alliance not just to bypass but to replace the UN, will not be steps toward the reform of international law, but causes of its ruin. However, the thrust of my argument in this chapter is that we are not faced with a choice of either preserving existing international law with all its doctrinal and institutional deficiencies or acting lawlessly. The third—and the only morally defensible—option is to work for genuine international legal reform by refusing to rest content with the most serious defects of the existing system while at the same time rejecting any attempt to replace it with a lawless vigilantism perpetrated by the world's one superpower.

Given the risks that the rhetoric of humanitarian intervention can be a disguise for great power or hegemon opportunism, NATO's illegal intervention in Kosovo should not be greeted as a sign of moral progress—unless it is followed by a sincere attempt to develop a new legal regime for the controlled authorization of humanitarian intervention that is superior to the UN Charter-based system for regulating the use of force that it may well have irrevocably damaged. Likewise, relaxing the prohibition against preventive war, in the absence of a well-designed procedure for authorizing responsible preventive action, is not a reform of international law regarding the use of force in the light of the new dangers of rapid deployable weapons of mass destruction, but rather a cynical rejection of the idea that the use of force must be constrained by the rule of law.

It is too early to tell whether these recent efforts to use force in the name of protecting human rights will turn out to be harbingers of progress or the first steps toward abandoning the enterprise of international law. For as I have argued, to turn away from some elements of UN Charter-based law is not necessarily to turn one's back on international law. Whether international law will deteriorate or flourish will depend upon whether the idea of the rule of law comes to be embodied in new, more responsive institutional structures, within which new, more sensitive principles will be appropriately applied. However, this much is clear: In the absence of a vigorous dialogue about the moral foundations of international law and an open-minded, critical exploration of the morality of international legal reform, the path of least resistance is likely to be destruction without reconstruction, the abandonment of existing legal constraints on the exercise of power without the development of new legal structures to take their place.

BIBLIOGRAPHY

Anaya, S. James, *Indigenous Peoples in International Law* (Oxford University Press, New York, 1996).

Annan, Kofi, 'Speech to the General Assembly, September 20, 1999', September 20, 1999; SG/SM7136 GA/9569: Secretary-G, at 2.

Barry, Brian, 'International Society from a Cosmopolitan Perspective', in David Mapel and Terry Nardin (eds.), *International Society: Diverse Ethical Perspectives* (Princeton University Press, Princeton, 1998).

——*Culture & Equality: An Egalitarian Critique of Multiculturalism* (Harvard University Press, Cambridge, MA, 2001).

Beigbeder, Yves, *International Monitoring of Plebiscites, Referenda and National Elections: Self-Determination and Transition to Democracy* (M. Nijhoff, Dordrecht, 1994).

Beitz, Charles, *Political Theory and International Relations* (Princeton University Press, Princeton, 1979).

——'International Liberalism and Distributive Justice: A Survey of Recent Thought', *World Politics* 51 (1999), 269–98.

——'Rawls's Law of Peoples', *Ethics* 110/4 (2000), 669–98.

Beran, Harry, 'A Liberal Theory of Secession', *Political Studies* 32 (1984), 21–31.

——*The Consent Theory of Obligation* (Croom Helm, New York, 1987).

——'A Democratic Theory of Political Self-Determination for a New World Order', in Percy Lehning (ed.), *Theories of Secession* (Routledge, New York, 1998), 32–59.

Bhattacharjea, Ajit, *Kashmir: The Wounded Valley* (UBS Publishers Distributors, New Delhi, 1994), 20.

Bose, Sumantra, *The Challenge of Kashmir: Democracy, Self-Determination and a Just Peace* (Sage Publications, New Delhi, 1997).

Brighouse, Harry, 'Against Nationalism', in Jocelyne Couture, Kai Nielsen, and Michel Seymour (eds.), *Rethinking Nationalism* (University of Calgary Press, Calgary, 1998).

Brilmayer, Lea, 'Secession and Self-Determination: A Territorialist Interpretation', *Yale Journal of International Law* 16 (1991), 177–202.

Brody, Baruch, *The Ethics of Biomedical Research: An International Perspective* (Oxford University Press, New York, 1998).

Buchanan, Allen, 'Deriving Welfare Rights from Libertarian Rights', in Peter Brown, Conrad Johnson, and Paul Vernier (eds.), *Income Support: Conceptual and Policy Issues* (Rowman & Littlefield, Totowa, NJ, 1981).

Buchanan, Allen, *Marx and Justice: The Radical Critique of Liberalism* (Rowman & Allanheld, Totowa, NJ, 1982).

—— 'Justice and Charity', *Ethics* 97 (1987), 558–75.

—— 'What's so Special about Rights?', *Social Philosophy and Policy* 12/1 (1987), 61–83.

—— 'Assessing the Communitarian Critique of Liberalism', *Ethics* 99 (1989), 852–82.

—— 'Justice as Reciprocity Versus Subject-Centered Justice', *Philosophy and Public Affairs* 19 (1990), 227–52.

—— *Secession: The Morality of Political Divorce from Fort Sumter to Lithuania and Quebec* (Westview Press, Boulder, CO, 1991).

—— 'The Right to Self-Determination: Analytical and Moral Foundations', *Arizona Journal of International and Comparative Law* 8/2 (1991), 41–50.

—— 'Liberalism and Group Rights', in Jules Coleman and Allen Buchanan (eds.), *In Harm's Way* (Cambridge University Press, New York, 1994).

—— 'Federalism, Secession, and the Morality of Inclusion', *Arizona Law Review* 37/1 (1995), 53–63.

—— 'Self-Determination, Secession, and the Rule of Law', in Robert McKim and Jeff McMahan (eds.), *The Morality of Nationalism* (Oxford University Press, New York, 1997).

—— 'Theories of Secession', *Philosophy and Public Affairs* 261 (1997), 31–61.

—— 'The Quebec Secession Issue: Democracy, Minority Rights, and the Rule of Law', a paper commissioned by the Privy Council, Government of Canada (1998), repr. in Stephen Macedo and Allen Buchanan (eds.), *Self-Determination and Secession, Nomos* XLV (New York University Press, New York, forthcoming).

—— 'Democracy and Secession', in Margaret Moore (ed.), *National Self-Determination and Secession* (Oxford University Press, New York, 1998).

—— 'What's So Special about Nations?', in Jocelyne Couture, Kai Nielsen, and Michel Seymour (eds.), *Rethinking Nationalism* (University of Calgary Press, Calgary, 1998).

—— 'Recognitional Legitimacy and the State System', *Philosophy and Public Affairs* 28 (1999), 46–78.

—— 'Rule-Governed Institutions Versus Act-Consequentialism: A Rejoinder to Naticchia', *Philosophy and Public Affairs* 28 (1999), 258–70.

—— 'The Internal Legitimacy of Humanitarian Intervention', *Journal of Political Philosophy* 7 (1999), 71–87.

——'Justice, Legitimacy, and Human Rights', in Victoria Davion and Clark Wolf (eds.), *The Idea of Political Liberalism* (Rowman & Littlefield, Lanham, MD, 2000).

——'Rawls's Law of Peoples: Rules for a Vanished Westphalian World', *Ethics* 110/4 (2000), 697–721.

——'From Nuremberg to Kosovo', *Ethics* 111 (2001), 673–704.

——'Political Legitimacy and Democracy', *Ethics* 112/4 (2002), 689–719.

——'Reforming the Law of Humanitarian Intervention', in Jeffrey Holzgrefe and Robert O. Keohane (eds.), *Humanitarian Intervention: Ethical, Legal and Political Dilemmas* (Cambridge University Press, New York, 2003).

——'Secession, State Break-Down, and Intervention', in Deen Chatterjee and Donald Scheid (eds.), *The Ethics of Intervention* (Cambridge University Press, Cambridge, forthcoming).

——'Beyond the National Interest', in Martha Nussbaum and Chad Flanders (eds.), *Global Inequalities*, a special issue of *Philosophical Topics* (forthcoming).

——and David Golove, 'Philosophy of International Law', in Jules Coleman, Scott Shapiro, and Kenneth Himma (eds.), *The Oxford Handbook of Jurisprudence and Philosophy of Law* (Oxford University Press, New York, 2002).

——and Robert Keohane, 'The Preventive Use of Force: A Cosmopolitan Institutional Perspective' (unpublished paper).

——Dan Brock, Norman Daniels, and Daniel Wikler, *From Chance to Choice: Genetics and Justice* (Cambridge University Press, Cambridge, 2000).

Bull, Hedley, *The Anarchical Society: A Study of Order in World Politics* (Columbia University Press, New York, 1977).

Byers, Michael, *Custom, Power and the Power of Rules* (Cambridge University Press, Cambridge, 1999).

Byock, Jesse, *Viking Age Iceland* (Penguin Books, New York, 2001).

Carens, Joseph, *Migration, Membership, and Morality: The Ethics of Immigration in Contemporary Liberal Democracy* (forthcoming).

Carter, Barry, and Phillip Trimble, *International Law*, 2nd edn. (Little, Brown & Company, Boston, 1995).

——*International Law: Selected Documents* (Little, Brown & Company, Boston, 1995).

Casesse, Antonio, *Self-Determination of Peoples: A Legal Reappraisal* (Cambridge University Press, Cambridge, 1995).

Christiano, Thomas, 'Democracy and Distributive Justice', *Arizona Law Review* 37 (1995), 65–72.

——*The Rule of the Many* (Westview Press, Boulder, CO, 1996).

Christiano, Thomas, 'Justice and Disagreement at the Foundations of Political Authority', review of Christopher Morris, *An Essay on the Modern State, Ethics* 110 (2000), 165–87.

Compa, Lance, and Stephen Diamond (eds.), *Human Rights, Labor Rights, and International Trade* (University of Pennsylvania Press, Philadelphia, 1996).

Conroy, John, *Unspeakable Acts, Ordinary People: The Dynamics of Torture* (Alfred A. Knopf, New York, 2000).

Copp, David, 'Do Nations Have the Right of Self-Determination?', in Stanley French (ed.), *Philosophers Look at Canadian Confederation* (Canadian Philosophical Association, Montreal, 1979).

Couture, Jocelyne, Kai Nielsen, and Michel Seymour (eds.), *Rethinking Nationalism* (University of Calgary Press, Calgary, 1998).

Cranston, Maurice, *What Are Human Rights?* (Taplinger Publishing Co., New York, 1973).

Dahbour, Omar, 'Self-Determination in Political Philosophy and International Law,' *History of European Ideas* 16 (1993), 879–84.

D'Amato, Anthony, *The Concept of Custom in International Law* (Cornell University Press, Ithaca, NY, 1971).

Doyle, Michael, 'Kant, Liberal Legacies, and Foreign Affairs, Parts 1 and 2', *Philosophy and Public Affairs* 12 (1983), 205–35, 323–53.

Dworkin, Ronald, *Taking Rights Seriously* (Harvard University Press, Cambridge, MA, 1978).

Ellickson, Robert, *Order without Law: How Neighbors Settle Disputes* (Harvard University Press, Cambridge, MA, 1991).

Enloe, Cynthia, *Bananas, Beaches, and Bases: Making Feminist Sense of International Politics* (University of California Press, Berkeley and Los Angeles, 1990).

——*The Morning After: Sexual Politics at the End of the Cold War* (University of California Press, Berkeley and Los Angeles, 1993).

Forsberg, Randall, 'Creating a Cooperative Security System', *Boston Review* 17/6 (1992), 7–10.

Franck, Thomas, 'The Emerging Right to Democratic Governance', *American Journal of International Law* 86 (1992), 46–91.

——*Fairness in International Law and Institutions* (Clarendon Press, Oxford, 1995).

Frank, Andre Gunder, *Latin America: Underdevelopment or Revolution. Essays on the Development of Underdevelopment and the Immediate Enemy* (Monthly Review Press, New York, 1970).

Frank, Robert H., *Passions within Reason: The Strategic Role of the Emotions* (Norton, New York, 1988).

Glenny, Misha, *The Fall of Yugoslavia: The Third Balkan War* (Penguin Books, New York, 1994).

Goldsmith, Jack, 'International Human Rights Law and the United States Double Standard', *Green Bag* 2d 1 (1998), 365–73.

Gow, James, *Legitimacy and the Military: The Yugoslav Crisis* (St Martin's Press, New York, 1992).

—— *Triumph of the Lack of Will: International Diplomacy and the Yugoslav War* (Hurst, London, 1997).

Grand Council of the Crees of Quebec, *Sovereign Injustice* (The Grand Council of the Crees, Nemaska, Quebec, 1995).

Gunn, Geoffrey, *East Timor and the United Nations: The Case for Intervention* (Red Sea Press, Lawrenceville, NJ, 1997).

Gurr, Ted, *Minorities at Risk: A Global View of Ethnopolitical Conflict* (United States Institute of Peace Press, Washington, DC, 1993).

Halperin, Morton, David Sheffer, and Patricia Small, *Self-Determination in the New World Order* (Carnegie Endowment for International Peace, Washington, DC, 1992).

Hampshire, Stuart, *Innocence and Experience* (Harvard University Press, Cambridge, MA, 1989).

Hancock, Graham, *Lords of Poverty: The Power, Prestige, and Corruption of the International Aid Business* (Atlantic Monthly Press, New York, 1989).

Hannum, Hurst, 'Rethinking Self-Determination', *Virginia Journal of International Law* 34 (1993), 1–69.

—— *Autonomy, Sovereignty, and Self-Determination: The Accommodation of Conflicting Rights* (University of Pennsylvania Press, Philadelphia, 1996).

Hart, H. L. A., *The Concept of Law* (Clarendon Press, Oxford, 1961).

Henkin, Louis, 'International Law: Politics, Values and Functions', *Collected Courses of the Hague Academy of International Law 1989* (Martinus Nijhoff Publishers, Dordrecht, 1990), iv. 214–15.

Hessler, Kristen, 'A Theory of Interpretation for Human Rights', Ph.D. dissertation (University of Arizona, 2001).

—— and Allen Buchanan, 'Specifying the Content of the Human Right to Health Care', in Rosamond Rhodes, Margaret Battin, and Anita Silvers (eds.), *Medicine and Social Justice: Essays on the Distribution of Health Care* (Oxford University Press, New York, 2002).

Hohfeld, W. N., *Fundamental Legal Conceptions as Applied in Judicial Reasoning*, ed. Walter Wheeler Cook (Yale University Press, New Haven, 1923).

Holder, Cindy, 'Group Rights and Special Obligations: Towards an Ethics of Group Membership', Ph.D. dissertation (University of Arizona, 2001).

Holder, Cindy, 'Cultural Rights in the U.N. Draft Declaration on the Rights of Indigenous Peoples', unpublished manuscript (University of Victoria, British Columbia).

Holmes, Stephen, and Cass Sunstein, *The Cost of Rights: Why Liberty Depends on Taxes* (W. W. Norton, New York, 1999).

Holzgrefe, Jeffrey, 'Introduction', in Jeffrey Holzgrefe and Robert O. Keohane (eds.), *Humanitarian Intervention: Ethical, Legal and Political Dilemmas* (Cambridge University Press, New York, 2003).

Horowitz, Donald, *Ethnic Groups in Conflict* (University of California Press, Berkeley and Los Angeles, 1985).

—— 'Self-Determination: Politics, Philosophy, and Law', in Ian Shapiro and Will Kymlicka (eds.), *Ethnicity and Group Rights, Nomos* XXXIX (New York University Press, New York, 1997).

—— 'A Right to Secede', in Stephen Macedo and Allen Buchanan (eds.), *Self-Determination and Secession, Nomos* XLV (New York University Press, New York, forthcoming).

Human Rights Watch (1999), 'Behind the Kashmir Conflict: Abuses by Indian Security Forces and Militant Groups Continue' [Internet, http://www.hrw.org/reports/1999/kashmir/].

Hurrell, Andrew, and Ngaire Woods, 'Globalisation and Inequality', *Millennium: Journal of International Studies* 24/3 (1995), 447–70.

Independent International Commission on Kosovo, *The Kosovo Report* (Oxford University Press, New York, 2000).

International Commission on Intervention and State Sovereignty, *The Responsibility to Protect: Report of the International Commission on Intervention and State Sovereignty* (International Development Research Centre, Ottawa, 2001).

Joint Centre for Bioethics, University of Toronto (2002), *Top 10 Biotechnologies for Improving Health in Developing Countries* [Internet, http://www.utoronto.ca/jcb/].

Kant, Immanuel, *Perpetual Peace*, trans. and ed. Lewis White Beck (Bobbs-Merril Educational Publishing, Indianapolis, 1957).

Kennan, George F., *American Diplomacy, 1900–1951* (University of Chicago Press, Chicago, 1951).

Keohane, Robert, 'Political Authority after Intervention: Gradations in Sovereignty', in Jeffrey Holzgrefe and Robert Keohane (eds.), *Humanitarian Intervention: Ethical, Legal, and Political Dilemmas* (Cambridge University Press, Cambridge, 2003).

—— and Joseph Nye, *Power and Interdependence*, 3rd edn. (Addison Wesley Longman, Boston, 2001).

Kingsbury, Benedict, 'Sovereignty and Inequality', *European Journal of International Law* 9 (1998), 599–625.

Kolers, Avery, 'A Theory of Territory', Ph.D. dissertation (University of Arizona, 2000).

Kronman, Anthony, 'Contract Law and the State of Nature' *Journal of Law, Economics, and Organization* 1 (1985), 5–32.

Kukathas, Chandran, 'Are There Any Cultural Rights?', *Political Theory* 20 (1992), 105–40.

Kymlicka, Will, *Liberalism, Community, and Culture* (Oxford University Press, New York, 1989).

——(ed.), *The Rights of Minority Cultures* (Oxford University Press, New York, 1995).

——*Multicultural Citizenship* (Oxford University Press, New York, 1995).

Lapidoth, Ruth, *Autonomy: Flexible Solutions to Ethnic Conflicts* (United States Institute of Peace Press, Washington, DC, 1996).

Lehning, Percy, (ed.), *Theories of Secession* (Routledge, New York, 1998).

Levy, Jacob, *The Multiculturalism of Fear* (Oxford University Press, New York, 2000).

Lewis, David, *Convention: A Philosophical Study* (Harvard University Press, Cambridge, MA, 1969).

Lipjhart, Arend, *Democracy in Plural Societies: A Comparative Exploration* (Yale University Press, New Haven, 1977).

Locke, John, *The Second Treatise on Civil Government* (Prometheus Books, Buffalo, NY, 1986).

Luban, David, 'Just War and Human Rights', *Philosophy and Public Affairs* 9 (1980), 160–81.

——'Intervention and Civilization: Some Unhappy Lessons of the Kosovo War', in Pablo de Greiff and Ciaran Cronin (eds.), *Global Justice and Transnational Politics: Essays on the Moral and Political Challenges of Globalization* (MIT Press, Cambridge, MA, 2002).

McBride, Jeremy, 'Reservations and the Capacity to Implement Human Rights Treaties', in J. P. Gardner (ed.), *Human Rights as General Norms and a State's Right to Opt Out: Reservations and Objections to Human Rights Conventions* (The British Institute of International and Comparative Law, London, 1997).

Macdonald, Laura, 'Globalising Civil Society: Interpreting International NGOs in Central America', *Millennium: Journal of International Studies* 23/2 (1994), 267–85.

Macedo, Stephen, and Allen Buchanan (eds.), *Self-Determination and Secession, Nomos* XLV (New York University Press, New York, forthcoming).

MacIntyre, Alasdair, *After Virtue: A Study in Moral Theory* (University of Notre Dame Press, Notre Dame, IN, 1984).

McKim, Robert, and Jeff McMahan (eds.), *The Morality of Nationalism* (Oxford University Press, New York, 1997).

Mansbridge, Jane (ed.), *Beyond Self-Interest* (University of Chicago Press, Chicago, 1990).

Margalit, Avashai, and Joseph Raz, 'National Self-Determination', *Journal of Philosophy* 87 (1990), 439–61.

Mill, John Stuart, *Utilitarianism, Liberty, and Representative Government* (E. P. Dutton & Co., Inc., New York, 1951).

Miller, David, *On Nationality* (Clarendon Press, New York, 1995).

—— 'Distributing Responsibilities', *Journal of Political Philosophy* 9/4 (2001), 453–71.

Moellendorf, Darrel, 'Constructing the Law of Peoples', *Pacific Philosophical Quarterly* 772 (1996), 132–54.

—— *Cosmopolitan Justice* (Westview Press, Boulder, CO, 2002).

Moore, John, *A Digest of International Law* (8 vols.) (U.S. Government Printing Office, Washington, DC, 1906).

Moore, Margaret, 'Introduction', in Margaret Moore (ed.), *National Self-Determination and Secession* (Oxford University Press, New York, 1998).

—— *The Ethics of Nationalism* (Oxford University Press, New York, 2001).

—— (ed.), *National Self-Determination and Secession* (Oxford University Press, New York, 1998).

—— 'The Right of Indigenous Peoples to Collective Self-Determination', in Stephen Macedo and Allen Buchanan (eds.), *Self-Determination and Secession, Nomos* XLV (New York University Press, New York, forthcoming).

Moravcsik, Andrew, 'Taking Preferences Seriously: A Liberal Theory of International Politics', *International Organization* 51 (1997), 513–54.

Morgenthau, Hans J., *Politics among Nations: The Struggle for Power and Peace*, 6th edn., rev. Kenneth W. Thompson (Alfred A. Knopf, New York, 1985).

Morris, Christopher, *An Essay on the Modern State* (Cambridge University Press, New York, 1998).

Murphy, Liam, 'Institutions and the Demands of Justice', *Philosophy and Public Affairs* 274 (1998), 251–91.

—— *Moral Demands in Nonideal Theory* (Oxford University Press, New York, 2000).

Nardin, Terry, *Law, Morality, and the Relations of States* (Princeton University Press, Princeton, 1983).

Naticchia, Chris, 'Recognition and Legitimacy: A Reply to Buchanan', *Philosophy and Public Affairs* 28/3 (1999), 242–57.

Nickel, James, *Making Sense of Human Rights* (University of California Press, Berkeley and Los Angeles, 1987).

Norman, Wayne, 'The Ethics of Secession as the Regulation of Secessionist Politics', in Margaret Moore (ed.), *National Self-Determination and Secession* (Oxford University Press, New York, 1998).

Nussbaum, Martha, *Women and Human Development* (Cambridge University Press, Cambridge, 2000).

Philpott, Daniel, 'In Defense of Self-Determination', *Ethics* 105/2 (1995), 352–85.

Pogge, Thomas, *Realizing Rawls* (Cornell University Press, Ithaca, NY, 1989).

—— 'An Egalitarian Law of Peoples', *Philosophy and Public Affairs* 23 (1994), 195–224.

Power, Jonathan, *Like Water on Stone: The Story of Amnesty International* (Northeastern University Press, Boston, 2001).

Rawls, John, *A Theory of Justice* (The Belknap Press of Harvard University Press, Cambridge, MA, 1971).

—— *Political Liberalism* (Columbia University Press, New York, 1993).

—— *The Law of Peoples* (Harvard University Press, Cambridge, MA, 1999).

Raz, Joseph, *The Morality of Freedom* (Clarendon Press, Oxford, 1986).

Rice, Condoleeza, 'Campaign 2000: Promoting the National Interest', *Foreign Affairs* 79 (2000), 45–62.

Richardson, Henry S., *Democratic Autonomy: Public Reasoning about the Ends of Policy* (Oxford University Press, New York, 2002).

Ripstein, Arthur, 'Context, Continuity, and Fairness', in Robert McKim and Jeff McMahan (eds.), *The Morality of Nationalism* (Oxford University Press, New York, 1997).

Risse, Thomas, Stephen Ropp, and Kathryn Sikkink (eds.), *The Power of Human Rights: International Norms and Domestic Change* (Cambridge University Press, New York, 1999).

Rothert, Mark, 'U.N. Intervention in East Timor', *Columbia Journal of Transnational Law* 39 (2000), 257–82.

Rubin, Alfred, *Ethics and Authority in International Law* (Cambridge University Press, Cambridge, 1997).

Russett, Bruce, *Grasping the Democratic Peace: Principles for a Post-Cold War World* (Princeton University Press, Princeton, 1993).

Sanders, Douglas, 'The Re-emergence of Indigenous Questions in International Law', *Canadian Human Rights Yearbook* 3 (1983), 12–30.

Scanlon, Thomas, 'Human Rights as a Neutral Concern', in Peter Brown and Douglas MacLean (eds.), *Human Rights and U.S. Foreign Policy* (Lexington Books, Lexington, MA, 1979).

Scanlon, Thomas, *What We Owe to Each Other* (The Belknap Press of Harvard University Press, Cambridge, MA, 1998).

Scheffler, Samuel, 'Conceptions of Cosmopolitanism', *Utilitas* 11 (1999), 255–76.

Sen, Amartya, 'Equality of What?', in *The Tanner Lectures on Human Values*, I (Cambridge University Press, Cambridge, 1980).

—— *Poverty and Famines: An Essay on Entitlement and Deprivation* (Oxford University Press, New York, 1981).

Shue, Henry, *Basic Rights: Subsistence, Affluence, and U.S. Foreign Policy*, 2nd edn. (Princeton University Press, Princeton, 1996).

Simmons, A. John, *Moral Principles and Political Obligations* (Princeton University Press, Princeton, 1979).

Sisk, Timothy, *Power Sharing and International Mediation in Ethnic Conflicts* (United States Institute of Peace Press, Washington, DC, 1996).

Slaughter, Anne-Marie, 'International Law and International Relations Theory: A Dual Agenda', *American Journal of International Law* 87 (1993), 205–39.

—— 'International Law in a World of Liberal States', *European Journal of International Law* 6 (1995), 503–38.

—— 'The Liberal Agenda for Peace: International Relations Theory and the Future of the United Nations', *Transnational and Contemporary Problems* 4 (1995), 377–420.

Steiner, Henry, 'Ideals and Counter-Ideals in the Struggle over Autonomy Regimes for Minorities', *Notre Dame Law Review* 66 (1991), 1539–60.

—— and Philip Alston (eds.), *International Human Rights in Context: Law, Politics, Morals. Text and Materials* (Oxford University Press, Oxford, 2000).

Stern, Brigitte, 'How to Regulate Globalization?', in Michael Byers (ed.), *The Role of Law in International Politics* (Oxford University Press, New York, 2000).

Stromseth, Jane, 'Humanitarian Intervention: Incremental Change Versus Codification', in Jeffrey Holzgrefe and Robert O. Keohane (eds.), *Humanitarian Intervention: Ethical, Legal and Political Dilemmas* (Cambridge University Press, New York, 2003).

Tamir, Yael, *Liberal Nationalism* (Princeton University Press, Princeton, 1993).

Teson, Fernando, *A Philosophy of International Law* (Westview, Boulder, CO, 1998).

—— 'The Liberal Case for Humanitarian Intervention', in Jeffrey Holzgrefe and Robert O. Keohane (eds.), *Humanitarian Intervention: Ethical, Legal, and Political Dilemmas* (Cambridge University Press, New York, 2003).

Thucydides, *Complete Writings: The Peloponnesian War*, the unabridged Crawley translation, introd. John H. Finley, Jr. (Modern Library, New York, 1951).

Tomuschat, Christian, 'Self-Determination in a Post-Colonial World', in Christian Tomuschat (ed.), *Modern Law of Self-Determination* (M. Nijhoff Publishers, Dordrecht, 1993).

Von Glahn, Gerhard, *Law among Nations: An Introduction to Public International Law*, 7th edn. (Allyn & Bacon, Boston, 1996).

Waldron, Jeremy, 'Superseding Historic Injustice', *Ethics* 103 (1992), 4–28.

—— 'Special Ties and Natural Duties', *Philosophy and Public Affairs* 22 (1993), 3–30.

Wallace-Bruce, Nii Lante, *Claims to Statehood in International Law* (Carlton Press, New York, 1994).

Waltz, Kenneth, *Man, the State, and War: A Theoretical Analysis* (Columbia University Press, New York, 1959).

—— *Theory of International Politics* (Addison-Wesley, Reading, MA, 1979).

Walzer, Michael, *Just and Unjust Wars: A Moral Argument with Historical Illustrations* (Basic Books, New York, 1977).

Watson, J. S., 'A Realistic Jurisprudence of International Law,' in *The Yearbook of World Affairs* 34 (Stevens & Sons, London, 1980).

Wellman, Christopher, 'A Defense of Secession and Political Self-Determination', *Philosophy and Public Affairs* 24 (1995), 357–72.

—— 'Liberalism, Samaritanism, and Political Legitimacy', *Philosophy and Public Affairs* 25 (1996), 211–37.

Wendt, Alexander, and Daniel Friedheim, 'Hierarchy under Anarchy: Informal Empire and the East German State,' *International Organization* 49/4 (1995), 689–721.

Wood, Robert, *From Marshall Plan to Debt Crisis: Foreign Aid and Development Choices in the World Economy* (University of California Press, Berkeley and Los Angeles, 1986).

Woodward, Susan, *Balkan Tragedy: Chaos and Dissolution after the Cold War* (Brookings Institution, Washington DC, 1995).

Legal Materials

Alvarez v. Machain, 266 F.3d 1045 (9th Cir. 1991).

Conference for Security and Co-operation in Europe, 'Document of the Copenhagen Meeting of the Conference on the Human Dimension of the Conference for Security and Co-operation in Europe', *International Legal Materials* 29 (1990), 1306.

Conference on Yugoslavian Arbitration Commission (The Badinter Commission), 'Opinions on Questions Arising from the Dissolution of Yugoslavia', *International Legal Materials* 31 (1992), 1488–530.

Filartiga v. *Pena-Irala*, 630 F.2d 876, 880 (2nd Cir. 1980).

Independent International Commission on Kosovo, *The Kosovo Report* (Oxford University Press, New York, 2000).

Kellogg–Briand Treaty [Internet, http://www.Yale.edu/lawweb/avalon/imt/rbpact.htm].

Lubicon Lake Band v. *Canada*, Communication No. 167/1984 (1990), UN Doc. Supp. No. 40 (A/45/40) at 1.

Reference re Secession of Quebec, 1998. 2 SCR.

Seventh International Conference of American States (1933), 'The Inter-American Convention on the Rights and Duties of States (The Montevideo Convention of 1933)', repr. in Weston Burns, Richard Falk, and Anthony D'Amato (eds.), *Basic Documents in International Law and World Order*, 2nd edn. (West Publishing, St Paul, MN, 1990), 12.

The Paquete Habana, 175 U.S. 677, 700, 44 L. Ed. 320, 20 S. Ct. 290 (1900).

United Nations (1945), 'Statute of the International Court of Justice', repr. in Barry E. Carter and Philip Trimble (eds.), *International Law: Selected Documents* (Little, Brown & Company, Boston, 1995), 29–43.

——(1948), 'Universal Declaration of Human Rights', repr. in Barry E. Carter and Phillip Trimble (eds.), *International Law: Selected Documents* (Little, Brown & Company, Boston, 1995), 381–6.

——(1966), 'International Covenant on Civil and Political Rights', repr. in Barry E. Carter and Phillip Trimble (eds.), *International Law: Selected Documents* (Little, Brown & Company, Boston, 1995), 387–403.

——(1966), 'International Covenant on Economic, Social and Cultural Rights', repr. in Barry E. Carter and Philip Trimble (eds.), *International Law: Selected Documents* (Little, Brown & Company, Boston, 1995), 410–18.

——(1969), 'Vienna Convention on the Law of Treaties', repr. in Barry E. Carter and Phillip Trimble (eds.), *International Law: Selected Documents* (Little, Brown & Company, Boston, 1995), 55–80.

United Nations General Assembly (1948), 'Convention on the Prevention and Punishment of the Crime of Genocide', repr. in Barry E. Carter and Phillip Trimble (eds.), *International Law: Selected Documents* (Little, Brown & Company, Boston, 1995), 419–21.

——(1960), 'Declaration on the Granting of Independence to Colonial Countries and Peoples' [Internet, http://www.unhchr.ch/html/menu3/b/c_coloni.htm].

United States v. *Smith*, 18 U.S. 153, 160–1, 5 L. Ed. 57 (1820).

Working Group Established in Accordance with United Nations Commission on Human Rights Resolution 1995/32 (1998), 'Report of the Working Group', UN Doc. E/CN.4/1999/82 at 40.

INDEX

Note: **Bold** page numbers indicate chapters.

Abkhazia 10
Abscriptivist (Nationalist) theories of
	secession 352–3, 371, 379, 394
	accommodating nationalist interests with
		state 384–7
	critics of 382
	infeasibility objection 382
Absolutism, Legal 298, 308
absolutist objection to conscientious
	law-breaking 458–9, 464
abstract moral rights, *see* human rights
access to institutions of justice, obligation
	to ensure, *see* commitment to justice
accountability, government 146, 279
act-consequentialism 287
Afghanistan 169
Africa 165
	OAS 340
	recognitional legitimacy 264, 282
	reform, international legal 443, 444, 454
	Rwanda genocide 14, 442, 443
	secession 337, 338, 357, 368
African-Americans 121, 418
agency-justification 240, 292
aggression, *see* force; violence; war
aid to burdened societies 193, 194,
	205, 215
Al Qaeda 114
Albanians, Kosovar 280, 358, 365, 403
alliances, *see* treaties
Alston, Philip 304 n.
Alvarez v. *Machain* 186 n.
ambiguity of "right to secede" 333–4
Amin, Idi 444
anarchy 241
	rule of law as avoidance of 460–1
Anaya, S. James 332 n., 352n.
Annan, Kofi 445, 466
annexation, *see* territory
Antarctica 52, 206
Anticipation, Principle of 30
anti-redistributive theories of distributive
	justice 222–3

application indeterminacy of human rights
	180, 185
arbiter, primary 219–20
armed conflict, *see* war
armed intervention as deterrence 442
	regime needed, *see* reform
	as ultimate sanction 442, 443
	violent death and "excessive cost"
		limitations 442, 468–9
arrest and imprisonment, arbitrary, rights
	against 139, 157
Ascriptive Right Theory 373
Asia 353, 435
	commitment to justice 80, 111
	international legal system 318, 319
	reform, international legal 443, 444, 452
assault, freedom from 196
assembly, *see* association
association/assembly
	freedom/right of 136, 146, 196, 268, 279
	see also discretionary association
associative group theories of secession, *see*
	Plebiscitary
asymmetry
	between domestic and international
		orders 222
	of power 250
Australia 452
authority, moral, legal reform and 440–1,
	448, 466
	international criticism 466–7
	subjectivism 466
authority, political, *see* political authority
authorization, democratic, *see* consent
autonomy:
	as criterion for recognitional legitimacy
		264
	Autonomy of States 304
	consensual 439
	and distributive justice, *see* Societal
		Distributive Autonomy
	interstate agreements 394
	of persons (Kantian interpretation) 132

autonomy (*cont.*)
  respect for 242
  violation as reason for secession 351,
    357–8, 364
  see also intrastate autonomy; secession;
    self-determination

Badinter Commission 272
Baltic Republics 339, 353, 355
Bangladesh 353
Barry, Brian 87, 381, 382
Basques 390
Battin, Margaret 126 n.
Beigbeder, Yves 279n.
Beitz, Charles 18 n., 30 n., 35 n., 195,
    202 n., 304
Belgium 391
Beran, Harry 19 n., 376 n.
Bhattacharjea, Ajit 475
bicameral representation 320
bill of rights 146
    International, *see* Covenants; Universal
      Declaration
borders, intact 340–1
Bosnia-Hercegovina 339, 442, 453
breach of international law, not breached
    264, 267
Bretons 390
Brighouse, Harry 388 n.
Brilmayer, Lea 19 n., 337 n.
Britain 62, 297, 381, 461
  and United States 32, 112, 396
Brock, Dan 122 n.
Brody, Baruch 39 n.
Brown, Peter 66 n., 198 n.
Brown v. *Board of Education* 457–8
Buchanan, Allen (other works by):
  genetic engineering 122 n.
  human rights 151 n., 168 n., 409 n.; and
    liberalism 158 n., 198 n., 413 n.
  illegal legal reform 460–1
  international legal system 315 n.
  justice 265 n.; commitment to 106 n.,
    112 n.; distributive 195 n., 197 n.,
    199 n., 407 n.
  Legal Absolutism 459 n.
  legitimacy; aggressive war 272 n.;
    democracy 233 n., 234 n., 239 n.,
    249 n., 258 n.; humanitarian
    intervention 98 n., 449 n.;

  recognitional 28 n., 261 n.,
    285 n., 337 n.
  preventive intervention 443 n.
  Rawl's *Laws of Peoples* 17 n., 160 n.,
    209 n., 216 n.
  realism and national interest 36 n.
  secession 19 n., 351 n.; and democracy
    315 n., 378 n.; nation states 388 n.,
    390 n.
  self-determination 344 n., 417 n.; state
    breakdown and intervention 340 n.,
    366 n.; theories of 63 n., 337 n., 349
    n., 354 n., 373 n., 376 n.
Bull, Hedley 214 n.
burdened societies, *see* aid
Bush, George W. 29–30
Byers, Michael 462 n.
Byock, Jesse 46 n.

Cambodia 444, 457
Canada 33, 153, 452
  see also Quebec
capabilities, central human 137–8
Carens, Joseph 69 n.
Carter, Barry 48 n., 50 n., 68–9 n., 156 n.,
    303 n.
case-by-case recognition, argument against
    285–6
Casesse, Antonio 333 n.
caste systems, *see* hereditary classes
challenging assumptions of international
    system 45–6
Charity, Not Justice Argument 195
Charter of United Nations 58–9, 303, 410
  reform, morality of international legal
    440–1, 456, 461, 472–3
Chatterjee, Deen 340 n.
Chechnya/Chechens, Russia and 9, 24, 26,
    319, 340, 341, 357, 438
China 79, 111, 319, 320, 435
"choice system", legal system as 277
Chou En Lai 392
Christianity:
  "Christian Businessmen" 182
  and religious imperialism 136, 141, 172
Christiano, Thomas:
  distributive justice 202 n., 218
  human rights 143 n., 145, 166, 173
  legitimacy 241, 252 n.
  political participation 323 n.

Churchill, Sir Winston 114
citizenship, full, *see* nationality
civil disobedience 457–8, 464, 465
claim-rights 123, 333–4
    see also human rights; secession
class, *see* hereditary classes
Clinton, Bill 341
clitoridectomy 171
coalitions:
    liberal-democratic 455–6
    see also cooperation; treaties
coercion/coercive:
    credible threats of 442
    diplomacy, advantages of 442–3
    power 241, 270; of prisons and mental
        hospitals 236 n.; of state 237; *see
        also* force
    rule of law as 460
cognitivism 151, 152, 153
Cohen, Joshua 62 n.
cold war 111
Coleman, Jules 315 n., 413 n.
collectivities:
    collective action, *see* cooperation rights
        of 427
colonialism, *see* decolonization; imperialism
commitment to justice 73–117, 403
    strategy 73–4
    see also National Interest Thesis; Natural
        Duty of Justice; primary moral goal
common good 162
    conception of justice 161–2, 164, 170
    welfarist interpretation of human rights
        132–3
commonality, moral, lack of 109–10
commons, global, conventions on 193, 194,
        205, 209
communitarian relativists 152–3
community:
    ethical 383
    and human rights 155–7
    moral 253
    political 252–3
Compa, Lance 206 n.
compensatory financing, multinational 206
compliance 51, 244
    with distributive justice 224, 228
    with political legitimacy 252, 254
    reasons for 238–9, 241
Congo 368

congruence, moral 63
Conroy, John 134 n.
conscientious law-breaking, absolutist
        objection to 458–9, 464–5
"conscientious secession" 364–5
consensus/consensual
    autonomy 438
    constitutional secession 338–40, 363, 437
    lack, *see* Institutional Incapacity View
    on principles, lack of 340–1 and will
        220–1
consent (democratic authorization) 104,
        241, 254
    demanded as denial of politics 243
    inertia not 244
    and legitimacy 234
    limit of 257–8
    non-consensual conditions for 244–5
    open-ended 245–6
    particularity problem 255
    and political authority 242, 246
    and political power 242
    promising different 245
    rejected 234
    tacit 244
    theory of international legal system
        301–2
conservatism, inevitable 53–4
conservative progressivity 63
constitutions/constitutional 320–1
    breakdown and secession 366
    Constitutional Positivist Argument
        305–6
    democracy 146
    essentials of state 281
    secession 337–8, 362, 436
    state consent as option 312–13
    of USA 104, 145, 182, 277
constitutive self-determination 332
constraints of institutions 125–6
"consultation hierarchy" 169
"contract of government" 243
control questioned by egalitarians
        250–1, 254
Conventions:
    on Elimination of All Forms of
        Discrimination against Women 119
    on International Civil and Political
        Rights 154
    see also Covenants

cooperation/cooperative 162–3
  fair terms of 162
  interactions 83, 93–4
Copp, David 19 n.
correlative obligations 123
cosmopolitanism 88
  "Moderate Cosmopolitanism" 103, 184
costs of moral action 93 n.
Couture, Jocelyne 19 n., 388 n.
Covenants on Human Rights 50, 51,
    109, 129
  Civil and Political 156 n., 160
  Economic, Social and Cultural 156 n., 159
  see also Conventions
Cranston, Maurice 195 n.
credible threats of coercion 442
Cree Indians 153
criminal justice system 89
  claims ultimate arbiter rights 198
  goals 74, 77, 78
Croatia 272, 339
Cronin, Ciaran 104 n.
culture/cultural:
  ceremonies (cultural integrity):
    jettisoning 406; rights against
    interference with 409, 412
  Covenant 156 n., 159
  ethical relativism and human rights 147–8;
    descriptive 154–5; meta-ethical 151–2
  groups 379–80
  imperialism 120, 121, 154–5
  integrity as limitation on human rights
    176–8
custom/customary:
  change strategy for legal reform
    446–8, 456
  law 47–8, 420

Dahbour, Omar 344 n., 388 n.
D'Amato Act (US) 463–4
D'Amato, Anthony 264 n.
Daniels, Norman 122 n.
Davion, Victoria 162 n.
Dayton Accords 303
de Greiff, Pablo 104 n.
"decent and worthwhile life" 215, 224
decision-making, see majoritarianism
decolonization 16 n., 109, 339–40
  as justification for secession 332, 333,
    339, 341

"saltwater" 410, 417
  see also imperialism
Deep Disagreement on human rights 428
Deep Distributive Pluralism 201, 203, 219,
    223, 225, 230
  extent and permanence 204–5
  fairness in existing international law
    205–6
  and secession 396
democracy/democratic 6, 15
  as human right 130–9, 182
  as necessary condition in international
    legal system 303–13
  authorization, see consent
  constitutional 136
  "democratic deficit" 304, 313
  Democratic (Internal) Peace
    Hypothesis 69
  justification for 131–9, 368
  majoritarianism 136, 241, 269, 305–11
  minimum 135–40, 286
  peace 69, 134–5
  and political legitimacy 239–60; as element
    of justice 256; authorization, limit of
    227–8; mere salience versus 258–9;
    mutual obligations 252–7; only
    legitimate government 235;
    particularity problem 254–7; see also
    participation and recognitional
    legitimacy
  and secession 387–90; and distributive
    justice 378, 387–90; multinational,
    premature pessimism about 390–4
  transformation into 323–5
  variant of discretionary association for
    mutual advantage 99–100
Democratic (Internal) Peace Hypothesis 79
descriptive cultural ethical relativism 154–7
deterrence 75, 442
Diamond, Stephen 206 n.
Difference Principle 199, 224, 227
disabled and human rights 139–41
discretionary association for mutual
    advantage view of state 98–109
  democratic variant 99–103
  rejected 102–3
discrimination:
  redistributional 396–7
  rights against 129, 268, 274
  see also racism; women

disintegrated state, *see* Yugoslavia
dissent from emerging norm 448
distributive justice 96, **191–230**, 375
  and democracy 378, 388–90
  goals 192–5
  and human rights 191, 193, 223, 230
  in international law 194–201
  and intrastate autonomy 406
  positive rights of 182–4
  and principled proposals for
    reform 438
  rejecting prominent role in international
    justice, *see* Deep Distributive
    Pluralism; Institutional Capacity
    View; Societal Distributive
    Autonomy and secession 378, 386,
    387–8, 396–7
  transnational and international justice
    distinct 191–3
"Do No Harm" version of interactionist
    view of commitment to justice 94–7
Doyle, Michael 33 n.
due process (legal rights) 129, 141, 144,
    157, 187, 267
duress, consent under 303–4
Dworkin, Ronald 17 n., 123

East Pakistan 353, 444
economy/economic development:
  democracy sometimes incompatible
    with 168
  global 203–6
  opportunities, rights to 194
  rights, *see* distributive justice
  self-sufficiency 209
  trade relations, equitable 193, 195
Edmundson, Bill 147 n., 207 n.
education, right to 197
effectivity/effectiveness:
  abandoning 6
  Effectiveness of Rights Argument 198
  Legal Nihilism 51–3
  "principle of" 264
  recognitional legitimacy 272–3
egalitarianism 249, 251–2, 255
Ellickson, Robert 294 n.
emigration right 160
empire, *see* decolonization
employment, *see* labor standards
enforcer, primary 219–21

enforcment capacity, lack of 219–20
Enloe, Cynthia 214 n.
entitlement 207
  see also human rights
enviromental, regulation 193–4
epistemic benefit of participation in human
    rights 121–3
epistemic justification for abandoning
    National Interest Thesis 112–16
Equal Moral Consideration/Regard
    Principle, *see* Moral Equality/Equity
equality 87
  before law (legal rights) 129, 144, 157,
    187, 267
  equal say notion 145, 378; *see also*
    democracy:
  equitable sharing, *see* fairness
  freedom 102
  individuals 102, 142, 317
  and international legal system 318–20
  and liberty 242–3
  and political power 241–2, 249–52
  of states 312, 318–20
  see also inequalities; Moral
    Equality/Equity
Eritrea 357
Estonia, *see* Baltic Republics
ethical community 384
ethical imperialism (moral) 111, 155–6,
    158–9, 458
ethical relativism and human rights 148–56
Ethiopia 338
ethnicity:
  conflict 126; ethno-national 382–3; *see*
    also Kosovo
  ethnic cleansing, *see* genocide
  rights against discrimination 268
  see also racism
Europe, Western (and EU) 32, 214, 272
  and international legal system 295, 315,
    318, 324
  reform, international legal 451, 454, 462
  secession 337, 392, 396, 399 n.
  see also Britain
"excessive cost" limitations 468–71
exit costs, high 244

failed states and secession 339, 341, 357,
    358, 365–70
  see also Yugoslavia

fairness:
  in existing international law 205–8
  terms of cooperation 163
  see also distributive justice
Falk, Richard 264 n.
fallibilism 179
famines as political phenomena 143
feasibility 61, 345
  see also Infeasibility Objection
Fiduciary Realism 35–8, 107–9
Filartiga v. *Pena-Irala* 186 n.
financing, multinational compensatory 206
Flanders, Chad 36 n., 106 n.
food, right to sufficient 197
forbidden (if not forbidden then
       permissible) 338–9
force:
  acceptable and non-acceptable 163–5
  excessive, as reason for secession 355, 357
  occupying 147
  preventing secession 341
  primary enforcer 219–20
  private enforcement of rules 294
  treaty made void by 303–4
  see also coercion; violence; war
formal equality of states 312
Forsberg, Randall 179 n.
France 297, 412
Franck, Thomas 142 n., 194 n., 201 n.,
       205–8, 265 n., 399
Frank, Andre Gunder 213 n.
freedom/liberty 123
  from assault and theft 196
  of association/assembly 129, 146, 268,
       279
  equality 102
  from persecution 129–31, 136, 141, 160
  right to 141
  of speech 146, 279
  see also human rights
French, Stanley 19 n.
Friedheim, Daniel 214 n.
Fuller, Melville 460, 464
functional capabilities 137–9
future of international law 472–3

Gandhi, Mohandas 464
Gardner, J. P. 196 n.
Garrisonians 364
gender discrimination, *see* women

generality of human rights 121–2
  intervention and 177–9
  Rwanda 14, 442, 443
  secession and 351, 388
Georgia (former USSR) 9, 341
Germany 273, 297, 410
global/globalization:
  basic structure 83–4, 96, 212, 213
  commons, conventions on 193, 205
  economy 205–6
  problem 463
  see also international; transnational
goals of international law 76–7
God, will of 92
Goldsmith, Jack 452 n.
Golove, David 46 n., 49 n., 96 n., 191 n.,
       315 n., 354 n., 373 n., 409 n.
good:
  government not enough 215
  social 123
  see also common good
Gorbachev, Mikhail 15
government:
  accountability 145
  compliance owed to 238–9
  "contract of" 243
  defined 281
  democracy as only legitimate 235
  functioning, as criterion for recognitional
       legitimacy 264
  good not enough 215
  obligations of 122
  only legitimate 235
  right to be obeyed, preoccupation with
       240–6; *see also* consent
  secession 353–55
  and state distinct 99–101, 241, 292–3
  see also democracy; political;
       self-government
Gow, James 14 n.
group rights and interests 19, 69–70, 156–7,
       159, 409–13
  theories of secession, *see* Plebiscitary
  see also indigenous peoples; intrastate
       autonomy
Gunn, Geoffrey 279 n.
Gurr, Ted 332 n.

Halperin, Morton 343 n., 344 n.
Hampshire, Stuart 109, 150 n.

Hancock, Graham 213 n.
Hannum, Hurst 19 n., 344 n., 406 n., 407 n.
happiness 139
harm, moral obligation to avert 85, 110, 248 n.
Hart, H. L. A. 46, 48, 49, 306
health care, right to 197, 226
Helms–Burton Act (US) 463–4
Helsinki Accords 119, 186
Henkin, Louis 58
hereditary classes and caste systems 141, 160, 210
Hessler, Kristen
  human rights 125 n., 126 n., 187
  legitimacy of international legal system 294–6
  moral theory of international law 40 n., 66 n.
Himma, Kenneth 315 n.
Hinduism 141
Hitler, Adolf 114
Hobbes, Thomas
  enforcement 46
  realism 29, 31, 34, 36, 52; commitment to justice 81, 106, 107, 115
  reform 257–60, 465
Hohfeld, W. N. 123 n., 338
Holder, Cindy 66 n., 409 n., 418 n.
holism 28
Holmes, Stephen 184 n., 196 n.
Holzgrefe, Jeffrey 281 n., 305 n., 444 n., 447 n., 449 n., 450 n.
Horowitz, Donald 22 n., 273, 377, 404, 407 n.
human rights, basic 4, 114, **118–89**
  abstract moral 118–21
  commitment to justice 73, 77, 80, 89–91, 110
  critiques of 147–58
  cultural ethical relativism 147–56
  cultural integrity as limitation 176–9
  democracy as 142–7
  distributive justice 191, 192, 224, 229
  generality of 122–3
  idea of 118–26
  indigenous peoples 193, 229, 342, 408–14; preventing violations 418–19
  individualism, excessive 156–7, 159
  ineliminable indeterminacy of 180–92
  international covenants, *see* Covenants

international legal system 294–7, 309, 323, 325
intrastate autonomy 404–6; limits on 421–2; violations 403, 406
'lean' list of, *see* human rights
moral equality 131–7, 137, 143
moral theory of international law 40, 43, 51, 59
national interest abandoned 70, 106, 107
obligations 90–1
political legitimacy 247, 250
and principled proposals for reform 439
protection 86–90, 404–5
  as peace 77–9
recognitional legitimacy 261–4, 268, 272–3, 278–81, 284–5
secession 343–7, 378, 393–6; ambiguity of 334–5
treaties/conventions *see* Covenants
universality of 121
violation: and reform, international legal 443, 457; Remedial Right theory 351, 355, 360, 363, 367
see also abstract moral rights; freedom; negative rights;
positive rights; self-determination; toleration *and* assertions *under* justification
humanistic reasons for existence of human rights 129–31
humanitarian intervention 28, 287
  defined 442
  and human rights 176–9
  and international legal system 304, 326
  and reform, international legal 448, 463, 467; justification 464, 467; not allowed 444; now rule-governed 454, 472; permissible and obligatory 470; preventive 443; *see also* NATO and Kosovo
  reformed legal right 437–8
Hungarians in Slovak Republic 178
Hurrell, Andrew 214 n.
hyper-institutionalist concept of justice, *see* commitment to justice

Iceland 178
ideal market and self-interest 108
ideal (moral) theory 59, 193, 216–17
  and non-ideal theory 54–5

illegal acts
  and humanitarian intervention *see* NATO
    and Kosovo
  legal at time of performance 277
illegal legal reform 456–60, 461, 463–64
illegitimate states 282
IMF (International Monetary Fund) 214
immigration:
  limited to prevent secession 378
  rights 193, 194, 206
imperfect system, pursuit of justice in
    322–74
imperialism:
  cultural 121, 154–6
  moral/ethical 111, 155–6, 158–9, 458
  religious, Christianity and 136, 141, 172
  see also decolonization
incentives
  for innovation 193
  for just behaviour 271
  and institutions 76
  secession 348–9, 360
inclusion/inclusiveness and international
    legal reform 455–6
inconsistency:
  objection 80
  of recognitional legitimacy 273, 275–7
independence, *see* secession
independent action 93, 93 n.
Indeterminacy Argument 199
  indeterminancy of human rights,
    ineliminable 180–90, 222
India 444
indigenous peoples 19, 153
  in Americas 153, 391
  rights 192, 230, 342, 407–13, 417–18
  see also remedial justification;
    self-government
individual
  autonomy of 132–3
  equal consideration for 142, 318
  equal freedom of 101
  indigenous peoples' rights not for 408–9
  nature of 83, 92
  security, right to 129, 141, 267
individualism:
  excessive, human rights and 156–7, 159
  justificatory 156–8, 175–81, 413–14
ineliminable indeterminacy 180–90, 222
inequalities:
  indefensible 165
  and international legal system 318–22

justified 210–11
  see also equality; human rights
inertia not consent 244
Infeasibility Objection to secession
    382, 391–2
"inherent dignity" concept 224
injustice not required for secession, *see*
    Primary Right
innovation, incentives for 193
insecurity, radical 469
Institutional Incapacity View 202–3,
    216–30, 397
  compliance, institutional capacity for
    monitoring 225, 228
  nature and consequences 218
  range of disagreement about distributive
    justice 222–4
  sources of 221
  state-building 227–9
  will and consensus 220–1
institutions/institutional 66
  defined 1–3
  democratic 145
  human rights 121, 124–6
  hyper-institutionalist concept of justice,
    see commitment to justice
  implications of assertions 124–7
  incapacity, *see* Institutional Incapacity
  and incentives 76
  justice, obligation to ensure access to, *see*
    commitment to justice
  lack of focus on 18–21
  moral reasoning 21–28
  multilateral lending 206
  Remedial Right Only theory 359–60
  and secession 23–9, 343–7, 359–60
  see also moral reasoning; transnational
    organizations
instrumentalism 146
  and human rights, democracy as 142
  Instrumentalist Justification for abandoning
    National Interest Thesis 107–12
  Predation Prevention (Instrumental)
    Argument 310–12
interactionist approach 83, 85, 93–8
interests:
  and human rights 137–40
  morally important, protection of 124
  self-interested reciprocity 97–8
  see also group rights and interests;
    National Interest Thesis
interference, lack of, *see* non-interference

internal morality of law 460
International Bill of Human Rights, *see* Covenants; Universal Declaration
International Commission on Intervention and State Sovereignty 430
International Court of Justice 48 n.
International Covenants, *see* Covenants
International Criminal Court 454
international justice and transnational justice distinct 191–2
international legal system, legitimacy of **289–327**
  consent theory of 301–14
  democracy as necessary condition 314–22
  and human rights, basic 294–8, 309, 324, 326
  justice-based conception of 299–301
  Moral Minimalist View 308–11
  Natural Duty of Justice and 291–9, 324
  need for 293–99
  pursuit of justice in imperfect system 322–7
  see also majoritarianism; moral theory of international law
international organizations, *see* transnational
international political legitimacy, *see* recognitional legitimacy
intervention 430
  regime needed, *see* reform
  see also armed intervention; humanitarian intervention
intrastate autonomy 57, **404–423**
  human rights 403–7, 421–2; indigenous peoples 408–15; international recognition of 435–7
  international support for 422–4, 436–8
  and secession 404
  and transnational justice 401–9; aspirations not valid claims of justice 402; distinguishing from right to secede 404; forms of 407; human rights protected 404–6; isolate and proliferate strategy 401–3
  see also secession; state *and under* human rights
Iraq 12, 357, 473
Ireland (IRA) 298
"isolate and proliferate" strategy 358–62 *passim*, 373, 395, 401–3
Italy 51
  Northern League 397, 399 n.

Johnson, Conrad 198 n.
judiciary, independence of 146
justice 4
  as primary moral goal 76–82
  -based conception of international legal system 299–301
  legitimacy and self-determination 432–3; *see also* moral theory of international law
  Not Charity Argument 199
  not perfect 300–2
  perfect, political legitimacy not conflated with 237
  and Self-Interested Reciprocity 97–8
  see also commitment to justice; criminal justice; distributive justice; human rights
justice-based approach 427–30, 444
justice-based moral theory of international law 118
  see also human rights
justice-based theory of recognitional legitimacy, requirements for 261–3, 266–81
  double standard 276–7
  internal and external 266, 267, 269–75
  non-usurpation condition 266, 267, 275, 286
  partial recognition 280
  secondary, to make recognition effective 272–4
  see also minimal requirements
justice-based theory of secession 345–7
justification/justificatory
  agency 239, 292
  assertions about existence of human rights 127–31; adequate 127; basic 127–30 humanistic reasons, requirement of 128–31; *see also* plurality of converging
  democracy 142–7, 378
  humanitarian intervention 464, 468
  individualism 156–7, 177–80, 412–13
  Instrumentalist 108–12
  legal 462
  moral, as legitimacy 187
  National Interest Thesis abandonment 107–16
  remedial 404, 416–22
  responsibility 136, 175, 181
  secession 332, 334, 339, 341
  unequal treatment required 211–13

Kant, Immanuel 17
  equality 87
  human rights 131–4, 175
  justice 218–20
  peace 79
  tyranny, risk of 56
Kennan, George F. 29 n.
Keohane, Robert 12, 305 n.
  moral theory of international law 30 n., 31
  recognitional legitimacy 272 n., 281
  reform 443 n., 447 n., 449 n., 451 n.
Khmer Rouge 457
King, Martin Luther 457–8, 464, 467
Kingsbury, Benedict 64, 312, 342 n.
Kolers, Avery 64
Kosovo 280, 357–8, 453
  intervention in, *see* NATO
  and sovereignty 55
  and United States 10, 101, 104
Kronman, Anthony 47 n.
Kukathas, Chandran 19 n.
Kurds 357
Kymlicka, Will 19, 22 n.

labor standards, international 194,
    206, 226
land claims settlements 419
Lapidoth, Ruth 342, 344 n., 405 n.
Latin America 178
Latvia, *see* Baltic Republics
Law of Intervention, need for reform of
    442–6
  coercive diplomacy, advantages of 442–3
  deficiency of existing law 444–5
Law of Sea Convention 208
law-breaking, conscientious, absolutist
    objection to 458–9, 464–5
lawlessness, *see* anarchy
Leaf-Blower Theorizing 28
League of Nations 409
Legal Absolutism and international legal
    system 8–9, 298–308
  reform of 448, 456–65 *passim*, 472
Legal Nihilism 20, 45–52
  challenging assumptions of international
    system 45–60
  effectiveness 51–2
  sovereignty, misunderstanding 50–2
  unduly restrictive assumptions about
    law 46–8

legal system:
  as "choice system" 277
legal rights (due process and equality before
    law) 129, 141, 144, 157, 187, 267
  see also criminal justice; international
    legal system
legitimacy 5, 69
  government, democracy as only 235
  and international legal system 305, 314
  justice and self-determination linked
    432–3
  moral justification as 187
  and principled proposals for reform
    432–3
  right to 335
  of state system, *see* moral legitimacy
    statehood, right to 335
  see also international legal system; moral
    legitimacy; political legitimacy;
    recognitional legitimacy
Lehning, Percy 19 n., 376 n.
lending institutions, multilateral 206
Levy, Jacob 380, 416 n., 420 n.
Lewis, David 294 n.
liberal-democratic
  coalition 454
  regime for armed intervention needed,
    see reform, morality of theories
    99, 222–3
liberty, *see* freedom
life, right to 129
limitation on human rights, cultural
    integrity as 176–9
Lincoln, Abraham 15, 341
Lipjhart, Arend 405 n., 407 n.
Lithuania, *see* Baltic Republics
Locke, John:
  compliance 244
  justice 218–20
  legal system 81, 292–9
  state 98–9
Luban, David 60 n., 84 n., 95 n., 104,
    325 n., 468 n.
Lubicon Lake case (*Lubicon Lake Band
    v.Canada*) 153, 154 n.

McBride, Jeremy 196 n.
Macdonald, Laura 214 n.
Macedo, Stephen 274 n., 351 n., 417 n.
Macedonia 453

MacIntyre, Alasdair 152–3, 204
McKim, Robert 19 n., 377 n.
MacLean, Douglas 66 n.
McMahan, Jeff 19 n., 377 n.
majoritarianism 146, 251, 279, 315–20
Mansbridge, Jane 33 n.
Mapel, David 88 n.
Margalit, Avashai 19 n., 176 n.,
        380, 386, 393
Martin, Rex 453 n.
Marx, Karl/Marxism 151 n., 390
Mazzini, Giuseppi 379
meta-ethical cultural ethical relativism 151–4
    see also Deep Distributive pluralism
Middle East 114, 453
military coup, unjust, reclaiming
        land after 333–4
Mill, John Stuart 388, 390–1
Miller, David 94 n., 432 n.
    distributive justice 192, 194, 227 n.
    self determination 380, 384–5
Milošović, Slobodan 15, 358, 364
minimal requirements of justice and
    recognitional legitimacy 266–8, 275,
        282, 286
    democracy 265, 278–80
    and human rights, basic 262–3, 267,
        271–3, 278, 280, 284–5
    Moral Minimalist View 38–44, 308–10
minimum, democratic 296
    problem and secession 360–3, 393
    see also intrastate autonomy
"Moderate Cosmopolitanism" 103, 184
Moderate Legal Absolutism 461
Moellendorf, Darrel 18 n., 195, 216 n., 346 n.
mononationality 391–3
Montenegro 263, 364
Montevideo Convention (1933) 264
Moore, John 76 n.
Moore, Margaret 19 n., 372 n., 378 n., 381
moral accessibility and secession 349, 370
moral action, costs of 93 n.
moral agents of international law 290
    see also international legal system
moral commonality, lack of 109
moral community, political association
        as 252
moral congruence 63
moral convergence and secession 349 n.,
        369–71

Moral Equality/Equity Principle 324
    and commitment to justice 86–92, 94
    and human rights 131–5, 137, 142
    and political legitimacy 247 n., 256, 258
    see also equality
moral goal of international law *see* primary
        moral goal
moral imperialism 111, 155–6, 158–9, 458
moral justification as legitimacy 187
moral legitimacy of state system 53–9
    conservatism, inevitable 53–4
    international legal system as obstacle to
        progress 57
    sovereignty, unbundling as subversive
        strategy 55–8
    state paradigm, possibility of
        transcending 55–7
Moral Minimalist View of international
        legal system 38–44, 308–10
moral obligations, *see* obligations
moral progressivity 63
moral reasoning 148
    abstract moral rights specified through
        118–21
    goals in 74–6
    justifying rights statements 25–7
    secession as institutional concept 23–5,
        345–7
    systematic philosophy of international
        law, idea of 28–9
moral reform, *see* reform, morality of
moral revulsion and secession 364
moral rights 144
    abstract, *see* human rights
moral theory of international law 3–5, 14–70
    curious neglect of 17–23
    institutional moral reasoning 22–9
    justice, *see* commitment to justice;
        criminal justice; distributive justice;
        human rights
    legitimacy, *see* international legal system;
        moral legitimacy; political
        legitimacy; recognitional legitimacy
    Moral Minimalist challenge 38–45,
        308–10
    need for 14; moral legitimacy
    self-determination, *see* intrastate
        autonomy; principled proposals for
        reform; secession
    see also Legal Nihilism; Realism; reform

moral theory of recognition 266, 283–4
morally imperative primary goal, justice as
    73, 83
  see also Natural Duty of Justice
morally important interests, protection
    of 124
Moravcsik, Andrew 18 n.
Morgenthau, Hans J. 36, 108–11
Morris, Christopher 47 n., 166 n.
motivational individualism 158
Murphy, Liam 18 n., 64 n., 86
mutual advantage, *see* discretionary
    association

NAFTA 214
Nardin, Terry 38 n., 45, 88 n.
Naticchia, Chris 20 n., 284–5
nation:
  defined 379
  not cultural group 379–80
  and state 114, 384–5, 387
National Interest Thesis 8, 9, 432
  abandoning 106–33; epistemic
    justification for 112–13;
    instrumental justification for 107–18
  and survival 113
nationalism 372, 388–9
  see also Abscriptivist; Primary Right
nationality 388
  mononationality 391–5
  uncoupling 343
nation-states, need for 387–8
NATO and Kosovo intervention 10, 12, 62,
    104, 303, 365, 403
  and reform, international legal 443,
    449 n., 465, 472
"natural" act of consent non-existent 244
Natural Duty of Justice 27, 74, 85–97, 106
  and discretionary association view of
    state 99, 100, 102
  and distributive justice 216–18, 229
  and international legal system 290–9,
    323
  plurality of ways of acting on 105
  and political legitimacy 254, 257
  and principled proposals for reform 430
  and reform, morality of international
    legal 456, 468–72
Naturalism 21
negative duties 91–2, 95

negative rights (rights against) 129, 134–5,
    156, 159
  and distributive justice 192–200
  and recognitional legitimacy 267, 272–3,
    282
  see also persecution, religious; torture
negotiated secession 337
new customary norms needed 446–9, 456
new states recognized, *see* recognitional
    legitimacy; secession; Yugoslavia as
    disintegrated state
Ngorno-Karabhak 339
Nickel, James 119 n.
Nielsen, Kai 19 n.
Nihilism, *see* Legal Nihilism
NIT, *see* National Interest Thesis
noncognitivism 151
nonconsequentialist argument for
    recognitional legitimacy 267, 268–70
non-expansionist society 161
non-governmental organizations 119
non-ideal moral theory, *see* minimal
    requirements
non-interference:
  in internal affairs, state's right to 263
  obligation 333
  right 160, 162
  self-determination 178
Nonusurpation Requirement (for
    recognitional legitimacy) 264, 265,
    267, 275, 286
Norman, Wayne 19 n.
norms:
  legality of 313
  new customary 446–9, 456
  operationalization of 119
  recognition 433–35
  super-norm of state consent 301–10
North American Free Trade Association
    214
Northern Ireland 381
Norway 182, 297, 338
Nuremburg trials 461
Nussbaum, Martha 36 n., 106 n.
  human rights 126, 135–9, 155 n., 169
Nye, Joseph 30 n., 31

obedience and political legitimacy 236–7
Obligation Not to Support Injustice
    Argument 270, 270–1

obligations 122
  correlative 122
  and distributive justice 195
  and human rights 89–90
  legal, recognition as 272
  non-interference 334
  not mere permissibility 430–2
  primary goal, *see* morally imperative
    primary goal
  to avert harm 85, 110, 248 n.
  to ensure access to institutions of justice,
    see commitment to justice
  to obey 237; *see also* political authority
  weighty, owed to right-holders 123
obstacle to progress 57–61
occupying force and political legitimacy
    236
oceans, seabeds and continental shelves
    206, 208
ongoing self-determination 332
ontological individualism 157
open-ended consent 245–6
operationalization of norms 119
opinio juris 49, 447, 448
Organization of African Unity 340–1

Paquette Habana 186 n.
partial recognition 280
partiality and international legal
    system 294
participation, democratic 145, 250–2
  in human rights 119–21, 124, 159, 197
particularity problem 254–5
past injustices, *see* remedial justification
paternalism 150
peace 60
  democratic 79, 142–4
  human rights protection as 77–9, 112
  as primary moral goal 76–82
  as proper goal 279
  sovereignty and 445
perfect justice, political legitimacy not
    conflated with 237
permanent minority problem and secession
    360–3
permanent population as criterion for
    recognitional legitimacy 264
permissibility, obligation not
    mere 430–2
permission 123

persecution, religious, right to freedom
    from 129–31, 136, 147, 160, 184
person, *see* individual
philosophy of international law 28, 408
Philpott, Daniel 19 n.
physical security 129, 141, 267
Plato 168
pleasure 139
Plebiscitary Theories of secession 352–3,
    371, 373–8, 394, 398
pluralism 55
  see also Deep Distributive Pluralism
plurality of converging justifications for
    human rights 131–40
  capabilities, central human 137–9
  Moral Equity Principle 131–6, 137
  religious justification 141
  utilitarian argument 139–40
Pogge, Thomas 18 n., 85, 94–5, 97, 195
Pol Pot 444
political authority and political legitimacy
    234, 237, 238–9
  absent 240–1, 246–51
  and consent 242, 245
  distinct 241
  political community 252–9
  reasons for seeming importance 241
political conception of justice, *see* Rawls
"political decision", recognition as 272
political inequality and international legal
    system 320–2
political legitimacy **233–59**
  defined 233
  and international legal system 322
  and morality of political power 234–8
  theory of, towards 246
  see also consent; government;
    international legal system; political
    authority; political power;
    recognitional legitimacy *and under*
    democracy
political participation, *see* participation,
    democratic
political power:
  and consent 242
  and equality 241–2, 249–52
  and international legal system 289–90
  morality and political legitimacy 234–8
  and recognitional legitimacy 270, 279–80,
    285

political will, lack of, *see* Institutional Incapacity View
popular sovereignty 102, 374
positive duties 91, 92
positive rights (rights to) 126, 129, 134, 140, 157–62
  and distributive justice 192–201, 207, 216
  ineliminable indeterminancy of 183–5
  legal 130, 142, 144, 156, 187, 267
  mistaken rejection of 195–200
  and recognitional legitimacy 262, 267
  see also subsistence
Positivism 20, 305
  legal, *see* Legal Absolutism
Power, Jonathan 52 n.
power 30
  asymmetry of 250
  coercive 236 n., 242, 270
  see also political power
predation risk 64
  Predation Prevention (Instrumental) Argument 310–12
preferences:
  satisfaction of (utilitarianism) 139–40, 183
  state 31–3
presidency, limited term 126
presumption of legality 465
prevention:
  of human rights violations 418
  of intervention 443
  of predation 9, 310–12
  of secession 341, 378
  of war 11–12
primary moral goal of international law, justice as 73, 74–98
  global basic structure 83–4
  institutional moral reasoning 74–6
  peace or justice 76–83
  see also morally imperative primary goal
Primary Right theory of unilateral right to secede 350, 352–3, 372–87, 394
  and Remedial Right 394, 400
  see also Abscriptivist; Plebiscitary
primary subject of justice, global basic structure as 95
primitive legal system 49
Principle of National Self-Determination 433
principled proposals for reform **427–39**

justice, legitimacy and self-determination linked 432–3
justice-based approach 427–9
  obligation not mere permissibility 430–2
  reforms needed 434–9
"prioritist" view of distributive justice 224, 227
proceduralist response to human rights 186–9
progressive conservatism and secession 348
progressivity 63
Proper Realism 34–8
protection
  of human rights 77–8, 86–9, 112, 114, 363–405
  of interests 124
  against predation 310–12
provisional recognition, normativized construction of 434–5
Putin, Vladimir 9

Quebec and secession question 153, 338, 362–3, 366, 392, 393

racism and rights against 121, 170–1, 211, 268, 273, 283
  apartheid in South Africa 165, 282, 389
  see also ethnicity; genocide
Rawls, John 17
  consensus 350
  "decent societies" 41
  distributive justice; Difference Principle 199, 223, 226; Societal Distributive Autonomy 201–2, 209–15
  global basic structure, importance of 212, 260
  human rights 41–4, 63; to aid not defined 215; tolerance, bounds of 17, 159–76, 180, 210
  ideal/non-ideal theory 55–6
  international incapacity 217
  justice 84–7 *passim*, 100, 192, 194, 308, 432
  legitimacy 282, 283
  moral minimalism 40–4
  women, discrimination against 161, 168, 169–71
Raz, Joseph 19 n., 176 n., 411 n.
  secession 379, 384, 393

Realism 20, 29–38, 52
  critique of 31–5
  Fiduciary 9, 35–6, 107
  Proper 35–7
  see also Hobbes
reasonableness 210
reasoning, *see* moral reasoning
reciprocity 97
  lack of 469
recognitional legitimacy 3, **261–87**
  concept of 261–7
  desirable 265
  human rights 262, 267, 273, 278–80,
    284–5
  moral theory of 266, 282–3
  and political power 270, 278–81, 285
  provisional, normativized construction of
    434–6
  and secession 263, 273, 280, 334–5, 393–6
  of states versus governments 281–7;
    conceptual priority 281–4; rule-governed
    practice, recognition as 284–6
  see also justice-based theory; minimal
requirements
rectificatory justice, *see* remedial
    justification
redistribution:
  and nationalism 389
  theories of distributive justice 222
redistribution, discriminatory 396–7
Reducibility Thesis 302, 306
reform, morality of international legal 4,
    440–74
  future of international law 472–3
  moral authority, *see* authority
  rule of law 459–65
  strategies for 440, 446–56
  see also Law of Intervention; principled
    proposals
relativism:
  cultural ethical, human rights and 147–56
  ethical 147–56
  meta-ethical communitarian 151–4
religion 172
  discrimination, rights against 267, 273
  disturbances 380–2
  Hinduism 141
  justification for human rights 141
  see also Christianity; persecution,
    religious

remedial justification 402, 405, 416–21
  see also self-government
Remedial Right Only theory of (and
    reasons for) secession 331, 337, 343,
    350–73, 401, 433, 436
  autonomy, violation of 351, 357–8, 364
  "conscientious secession" 364–5
  failed states 366–8
  force, excessive 356, 357
  genocide 351
  government and 354–5
  human rights (basic) violation 351, 355,
    361, 364, 367
  incentives 360
  institutionalizing 359
  irrelevance objection 372–3
  minority problem 360–3, 392
  moral accessibility and convergence
    370–1
  moral revulsion 364
  and Primary Right compared 376, 382,
    384, 386, 394–9
  resources and 368
  sauve qui peut separation 366–9
  statist bias objection 371
  strength of approach 369
  territory annexed unjustly 355–6,
    364, 370
  see also "isolate and proliferate"
remedial right to unilateral secession 451
representation 283
  bicameral 320
  majoritarianism 146, 251, 279, 315–20
requirements for recognitional legitimacy,
    see justice-based theory
resources:
  availability and human rights 126
  and secession 368
  see also subsistence
responsibility:
  justificatory 136, 174, 180
  and voluntariness 95–6
restraint, burden of 198–200
restrictive assumptions about law 46–8
Rhodes, Rosamond 126 n.
Rhodesia 265
Rice, Condoleeza 112–3
Richardson, Henry S. 250 n., 323 n.
right-holder 123
  see also human rights

"rights-based" argument for recognitional
    legitimacy 267, 268–70
Ripstein, Arthur 390 n.
Risse, Thomas 18 n., 32 n., 52 n., 110 n.
rival, lack of 236
Ropp, Stephen 18 n., 32 n., 52 n., 110 n.
Rothert, Mark 279 n.
Rousseau, Jean-Jacques 56
Rubin, Alfred 312 n., 458, 466
rule/rules 16
    -governed practice, recognition as 284–7
    -governed regime for armed intervention
        needed, *see* reform
    just, state's right to make 263
    of law, commitment to 459–65
    new 462; *see also* reform
    private enforcement of 294
    see also international legal system
ruling classes 142, 161, 210
Russett, Bruce 33 n.
Russia/Soviet Union 9, 15, 319, 435
    and Baltic Republics 339, 353, 355
    preventing secession 378
    and reform, international legal 454
    see also Chechnya
Rwanda genocide 14, 442, 443

sacrifice not required 89
Sandel, Michael 152
Sanders, Douglas 342 n.
satisfaction of preferences *see* utilitarianism
sauve qui peut separation and secession
    366–9
Scanlon, Thomas 66, 128 n., 245
Scheffler, Samuel 103, 184
Scheid, Donald 340 n.
Scottish Nationalism 381
"seamless web" assumption 461
secession 1, 4, 19, **331–400**, 434
    ambiguity of "right to secede" 334–5
    constitutional 338–40, 362, 437
    and democracy 378, 388–93
    and distributive justice 378, 386–90,
        396–9
    existing law, flaws of 339–41
    failed states 331, 341, 358, 359, 366–70
    institutions 23–5, 345–8, 359
    intrastate autonomy-status in
        international law 342, 404
    justice-based theory of 344–7
    justification 333, 334, 339, 340

and nationalism 388–9
nation-states, need for 386–8
prevention 340, 378
and recognition 262, 273, 280, 334–5,
    394–6
rights, *see* human rights
status in international law 333–4
territorial claims 337, 355–7, 364, 370
theories of unilateral right to secede
    347–93;
    criteria for evaluating rival theories
        348–50; *see also* Abscriptivist;
        Plebiscitary; Primary Right; Remedial
        Right
unilateral versus
    consensual/constitutional 337–9, 437
violent 10–11
see also intrastate autonomy
Second World War 78, 114, 409
Security Council, UN 2, 12, 110
    and international legal system 304, 310
    and principled proposals for reform 433,
        438
    and reform, international legal 440, 443,
        444, 444–74; rule of law,
        commitment to 461–5; strategies
        446–9, 456
security of person, right to 129, 140, 267
self-defeating view of recognitional
    legitimacy not valid, *see* minimal
    requirements
self-defense and secession 366–8
self-determination 5, 69–70, 157
    extreme form, *see* secession
    justice and legitimacy linked 432–3
    moral theory of international law 15, 18,
        69–70
    need for comprehensive theory of 332
    and non-intervention 177
    see also autonomy; intrastate autonomy;
        principled proposals; secession;
        self-government
self-government for indigenous peoples 412
    alternative to incorporation of customary
        law 420
    land claims settlements 419
    nonpaternalistic mechanisms for
        preventing human rights violations
        418
    restoration for indigenous peoples 415–17
self-interested reciprocity 97

self-sufficiency, economic 209
Self-Sufficiency Plus Toleration View 192
Sen, Amartya 33 n., 137, 138, 143, 210, 399
"separatism" 366
  see also secession
Serbia/Serbs 10
  and recognitional legitimacy 262, 263,
    281
  and secession 339, 359, 363–8
sexism, *see* women
Seymour, Michel 19 n., 388 n.
Shafer-Landau, Russell 366 n.
Shapiro, Ian 22 n.
Shapiro, Scott 191 n., 315 n.
sharing, *see* distributive justice; fairness
Sheffer, David 343 n., 344 n.
Shue, Henry 18 n., 195
Sikkink, Kathryn 18 n., 32 n., 52 n., 110 n.
Silvers, Anita 126 n.
Simmons, A. John 239 n., 244, 246
Simple Positivist Argument 307
Sisk, Timothy 405 n., 407 n.
Slaughter, Anne-Marie 18 n., 32 n.
slavery 62, 164, 277, 461
  abolition 141, 364
  rights against 129, 159, 267
  and secession in USA 341, 364
Slovak Republic 178
Slovenia 320
Small, Patricia 343 n., 344 n.
social contract 99, 243
social good, maximization of 123
social rights, *see* distributive justice
Societal Distributive Autonomy 201–2,
    209–16, 219, 223
  aid to burdened societies 215–16
  global basic structure 212, 213, 260
  good government not enough 215
  rejected by Rawls 202, 209–15
  tolerance not ruling out transnational
    distributive justice 210–12
Somalia 14
South Africa 165, 282, 389
sovereignty 110, 187
  disputable, secession and 355–7
  erosion of 447
  and human rights 445
  juridical characteristics defining 263
  and Kosovo 57
  misunderstanding 50–3
  and peace 444

popular 102, 374
  "unbundled" 7, 56–7, 280
Soviet Union, former, *see* Russia/
    Soviet Union
space, outer 206
speech, freedom of 129, 197
state 73, 98–105
  as coercive institution 237
  building and Institutional Incapacity
    View 227–30
  consent 6, 234, 301–14
  constitutional essentials of 281
  defined 283
  disintegrated *see* Yugoslavia
  equality and international legal system
    312, 319–21
  and government distinct 99–101,
    241, 292
  and international legal system *see*
    majoritarianism
  legitimacy, *see* moral legitimacy
  and nation 114, 384–7, 387–90
  paradigm, possibility of transcending 55–6
  preferences 32–4
  repudiating control of, right to 336
  secession and nationalism 383–7
  statist bias objection to secession 371
  see also discretionary association;
      recognitional legitimacy
  "stateless" people 386
Steiner, Henry 304 n., 343 n.
Stell, Lance 469 n.
Stern, Brigitte 462
Stromseth, Jane 447
subjectivism 466
subjects of international law, compliance
    of 290
  see also international legal system
subsidies 206
subsistence resources, right to 129, 134,
    141, 143, 160, 224, 267
subversive strategy, sovereignty unbundling
    as 56–7
Sudan 357
Sunstein, Cass 184 n., 196 n.
super-norm of state consent 301–10
supremacy as lack of rival 235–6
survival, national interest as 113
Sweden 338
system legitimacy, *see* international legal
    system

Taliban 169
Tamir, Yael 19 n., 380
Tanzania 444
teleological arguments 75, 269, 279
　see also justice-based theory
　　territory/territorial 380
　　annexation claim and secession 337, 348,
　　　394; unjust reason for 355–7, 364, 371
　　integrity, state's right to 263
　　and recognitional legitimacy, criterion
　　　for 264
"terrorism" 9–12, 14, 113
Teson, Fernando 17 n., 21, 305 n., 471 n.
theft, freedom from 196
Thompson, Kenneth W. 36 n.
Thucydides 29 n.
toleration/tolerance, bounds of 42, 136,
　　158–80
　　moral imperialism alleged 158–9
　　not ruling out transnational distributive
　　　justice 210–12
　　Rawls' views on 17, 159–76, 180, 210
　　Walzer on cultural integrity as limitation
　　　on human rights 176–9
Tomuschat, Christian 344 n.
torture, rights against 124, 129, 133–4, 137,
　　140, 157, 195, 268
　　ineliminable indeterminancy 182
trade, *see* economy
transitional status for secessional states 281
transnational justice 294
　　and autonomy, *see* intrastate autonomy
　　and international justice distinct 191–2
　　see also international legal system;
　　　intrastate autonomy
transnational organizations 110, 120, 216,
　　454
　　see also institutions; United Nations
treaties, alliances and coalitions 49, 467
　　for legal reform 446, 449–51
　　made void by force 303
　　state's right to make 263
　　treaty-based regime for armed
　　　intervention needed *see* reform
　　Vienna Convention on 49, 303
　　see also Covenants
Trimble, Phillip 48 n., 50 n., 50 n., 156 n.,
　　303 n.
Tudjman, Franjo 15
tyranny, world, risk of 56

Uganda 444
unilateral illegal act 463
unilateral right to secede *see* Primary Right
　　theory; secession
unilateral versus constitutional secession
　　337–9, 436
unitary state paradigm rejected 7–8
United Kingdom *see* Britain
United Nations 2, 12
　　General Assembly 265, 273, 319, 449,
　　　452
　　Committee of Twenty-Four 359
　　High Commissioner on National
　　　Minorities 423
　　and human rights 186 n., 423
　　Indigenous Peoples, Draft Declaration
　　　on 409
　　International Court 48 n.
　　low opinions of 57
　　and reform, international legal 440–56,
　　　460–6, 471–3
　　Resolutions 16
　　and United States 58
　　Vienna Convention 49
　　Working Group on Rights of Indigenous
　　　Peoples 423
　　see also Charter; Security Council
United States 282
　　and Britain 32, 114, 397
　　'Christian Businessmen' 182
　　civil rights legislation 407
　　Cold War 111
　　Constitution 105, 121, 182, 277
　　distributive justice 229
　　expenditure on foreign aid 94 n.
　　human rights 186 n.
　　indigenous people 153, 229, 404, 412
　　and Kosovo 10, 101, 104
　　non-compliance with laws 51
　　reform, international legal 440, 452,
　　　456–8, 462–6, 472
　　and secession 331, 341
　　Second World War 114
　　Supreme Court 147, 186 n.
　　and United Nations 58
　　Vietnam War 111
　　"war against terrorism" 9–11, 114
　　and Yugoslavia's dissolution 14–15
Universal Declaration of Human Rights 50,
　　156, 159, 309

universality of human rights 121
uti possidetis 15, 340–1
utilitarianism 37, 139–40, 183
utopianism 324
   not valid, *see* minimal requirements

Valls, Andrew 355 n.
Vanishing Subject Matter Problem 53
Vernier, Paul 198 n.
Vienna Convention on Treaties 49, 303–8
Vietnam War 111, 444
violation
   of autonomy 402, 405
     as reason for secession 351, 358–9, 363
   human rights, prevention of 418
violence 30
   against women 123, 170
   anarchy, rule of law as avoidance of
     460–1
   human rights 4, 9–15
   secession 10
   violent death and "excessive cost"
     limitations 468–71
   within states 77–81
   see also force; war
voluntariness and responsibility 95
voluntarist theory of secession *see*
     Plebiscitary
Von Glahn, Gerhard 264 n.
voting *see* majoritarianism

Waldron, Jeremy 258
Wallace-Bruce, Nii Lante 264 n.
Waltz, Kenneth 29 n.
Walzer, Michael
   distributive justice 192, 194, 200, 203,
     216, 227 n.
   human rights 150, 159, 176–9
   see also Deep Distributive Pluralism
war 77
   "against terrorism" (US) 9–11, 114
   aggressive, prohibited 50, 271–2,
     357, 441
   civil, intervention in 178 n.
   credible threats 272 n.
   crimes, *see* genocide

international legal system 297
just, state's right to make 263
mitigation of miseries as goal 76
paradigm rejected 7–8
preventive 12
prohibited 110
right to go to 77
Second World 78, 114
see also violence
Watson, J. S. 458
Webster, Daniel 76
Weiss, Deborah 457 n.
welfarist interpretation of human
   rights 132–3
well-being *see* good
Wellman, Christopher 19 n., 244, 246,
   248 n., 346 n.
Wendt, Alexander 214 n.
West
   cultural imperialism 121, 154–5
   and human rights 152, 157
   see also Europe; United States
Wheeler Cook, Walter 123 n.
White Beck, Lewis 56 n.
Wikler, Daniel 122 n.
will, lack of *see* Institutional Incapacity
     View
Wolf, Clark 162 n.
women, discrimination against 123, 127
   by Rawls 160, 167, 169–72
   and rights 134–5, 192, 267
   violence 123, 177, 211
Wood, Robert 213 n.
Woods, Ngaire 214 n.
World Bank 95, 214
World Trade Center (September 11th) 9
World Trade Organization 315

Yemen 9
Yugoslavia as disintegrated state 14–15
   and international legal system 304, 318
   and recognitional legitimacy 262, 272,
     280
   and secession 339, 341, 357, 359, 364–6,
     369
   see also Kosovo; Montenegro